DEAD
INSIDE ™

SCRIPT **JOHN ARCUDI** ART **TONI FEJZULA**

COLORS **ANDRÉ MAY** LETTERS **JOE SABINO**

COVER ART AND CHAPTERS TWO TO FIVE TITLE PAGE ART **DAVE JOHNSON**

CHAPTER ONE TITLE PAGE ART **FAITH ERIN HICKS**

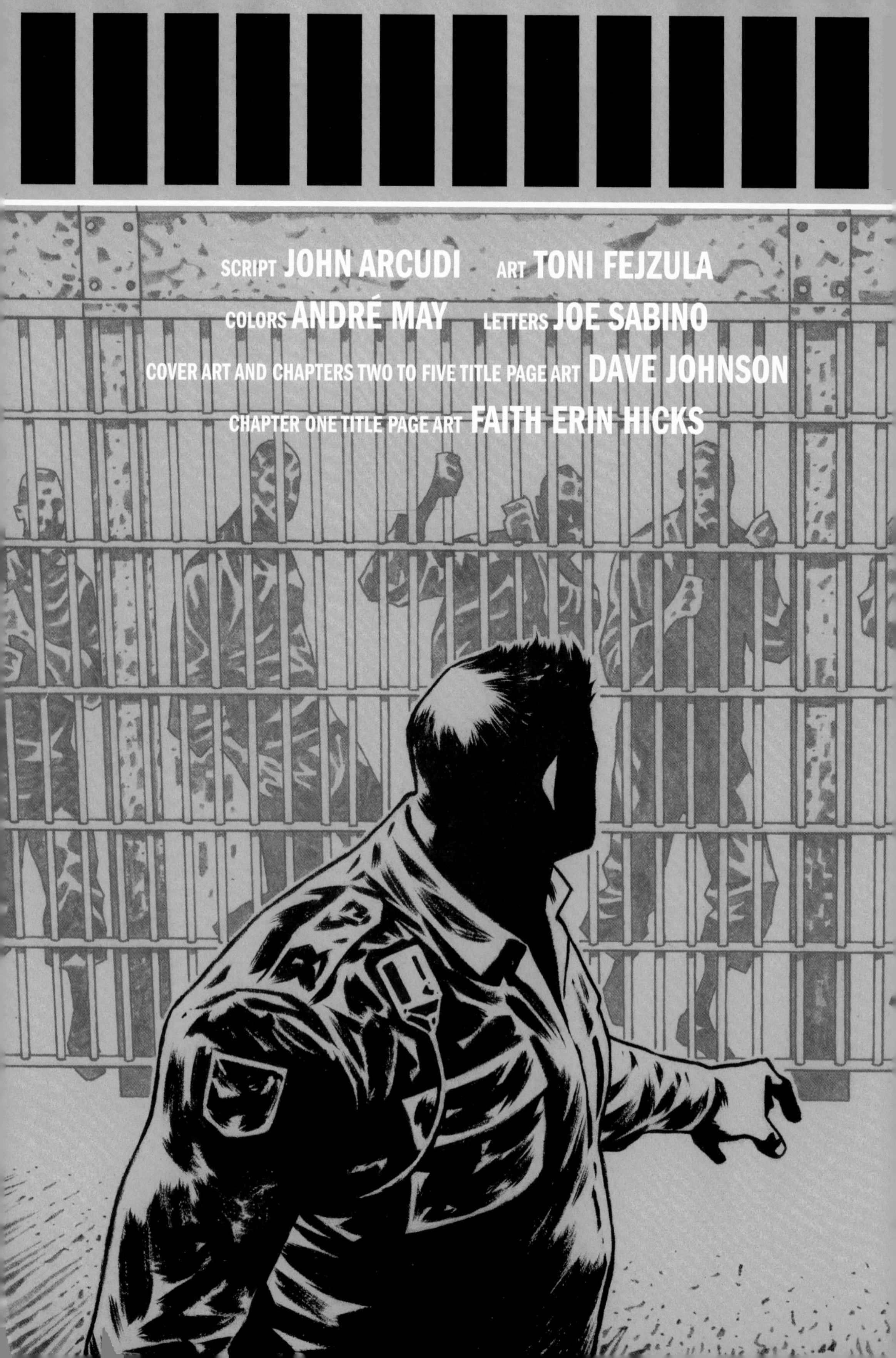

DEAD INSIDE™

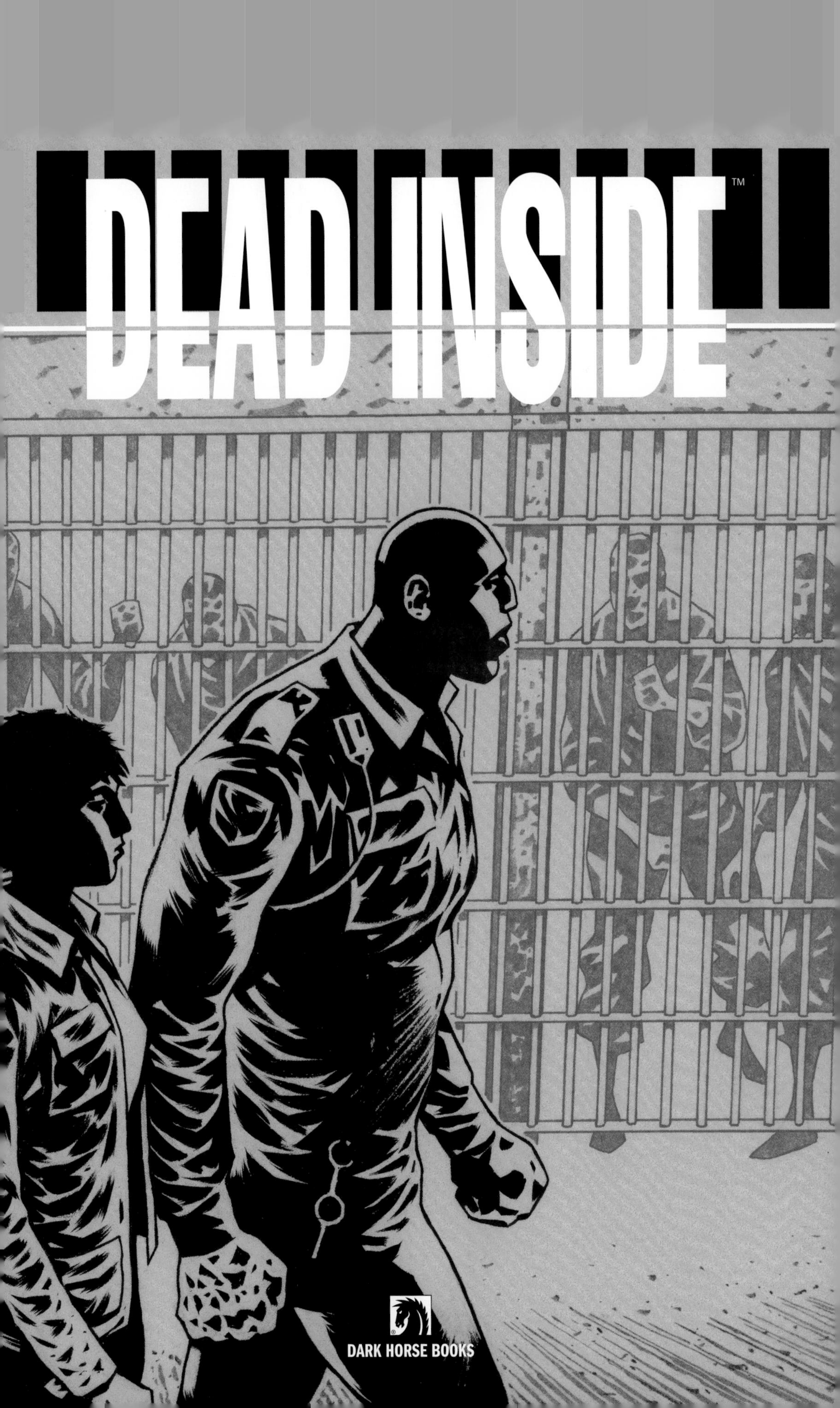

DARK HORSE BOOKS

PRESIDENT & PUBLISHER **MIKE RICHARDSON**

EDITOR **DANIEL CHABON**

ASSOCIATE EDITOR **CARDNER CLARK**

DESIGNERS **ETHAN KIMBERLING** AND **CINDY CACEREZ-SPRAGUE**

DIGITAL ART TECHNICIAN **CHRISTINA McKENZIE**

This volume collects issues #1–#5 of the Dark Horse Comics series *Dead Inside*.

Library of Congress Cataloging-in-Publication Data

Names: Arcudi, John, author. | Fejzula, Toni, artist. | May, Andre, colourist. | Sabino, Joe, letterer. | Johnson, Dave, 1966- artist.
Title: Dead Inside / script by John Arcudi ; art by Toni Fejzula ; colors by Andre May ; letters by Joe Sabino ; cover art and chapter breaks by Dave Johnson.
Description: First edition. | Milwaukie, OR : Dark Horse Books, 2017. | "This volume collects issues #1-#5 of the Dark Horse Comics series Dead Inside"
Identifiers: LCCN 2017005038 | ISBN 9781506702223 (paperback)
Subjects: LCSH: Comic books, strips, etc. | BISAC: COMICS & GRAPHIC NOVELS / Crime & Mystery. | COMICS & GRAPHIC NOVELS / General.
Classification: LCC PN6728.D3538 A73 2017 | DDC 741.5/973--dc23
LC record available at https://lccn.loc.gov/2017005038

Published by
Dark Horse Books
A division of Dark Horse Comics, Inc.
10956 SE Main Street
Milwaukie, OR 97222

DarkHorse.com

To find a comics shop in your area, call the Comic Shop Locator Service toll-free at 1-888-266-4226.
International Licensing: (503) 905-2377

First edition: August 2017
ISBN 978-1-50670-222-3

1 3 5 7 9 10 8 6 4 2
Printed in China

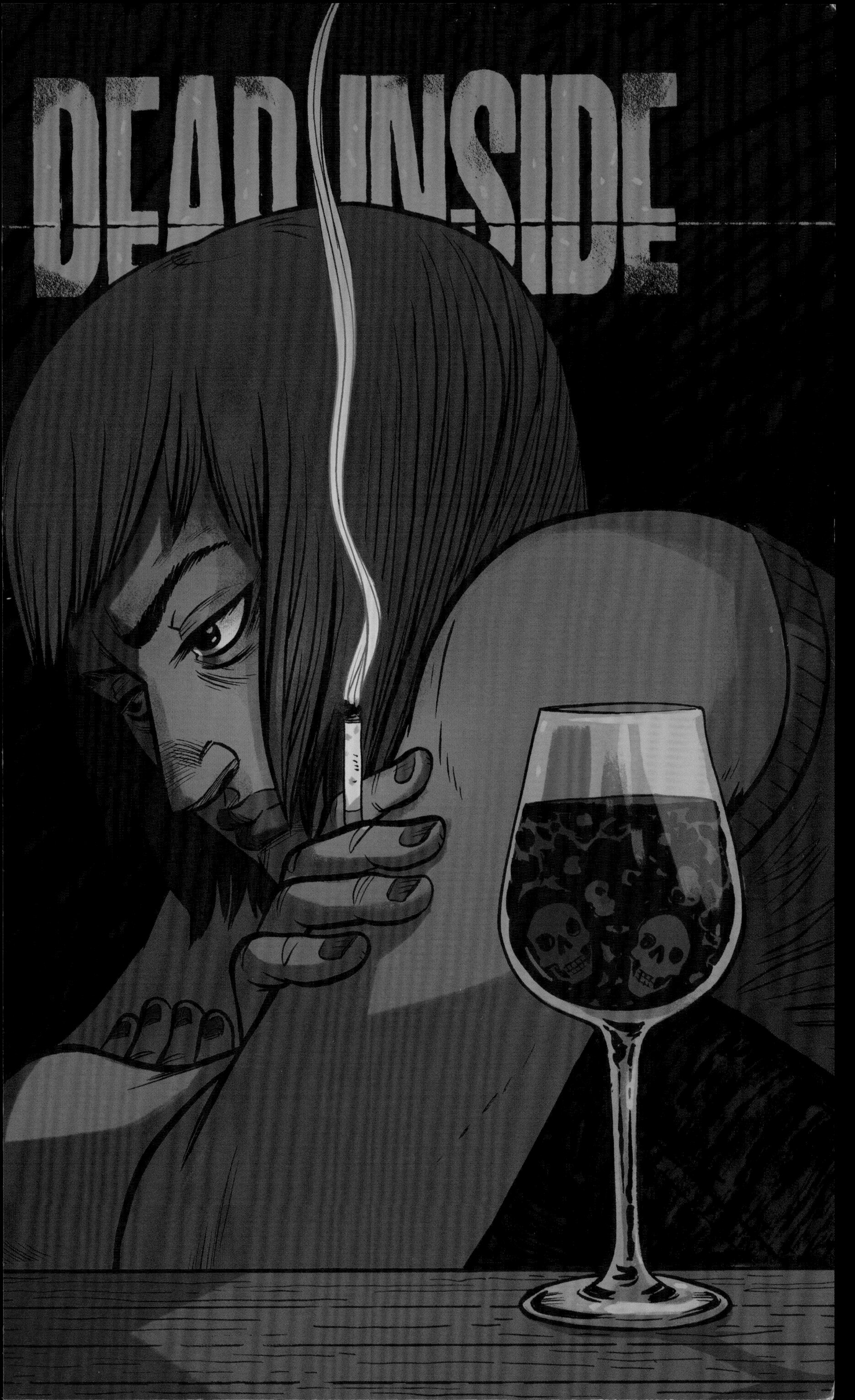
DEAD INSIDE

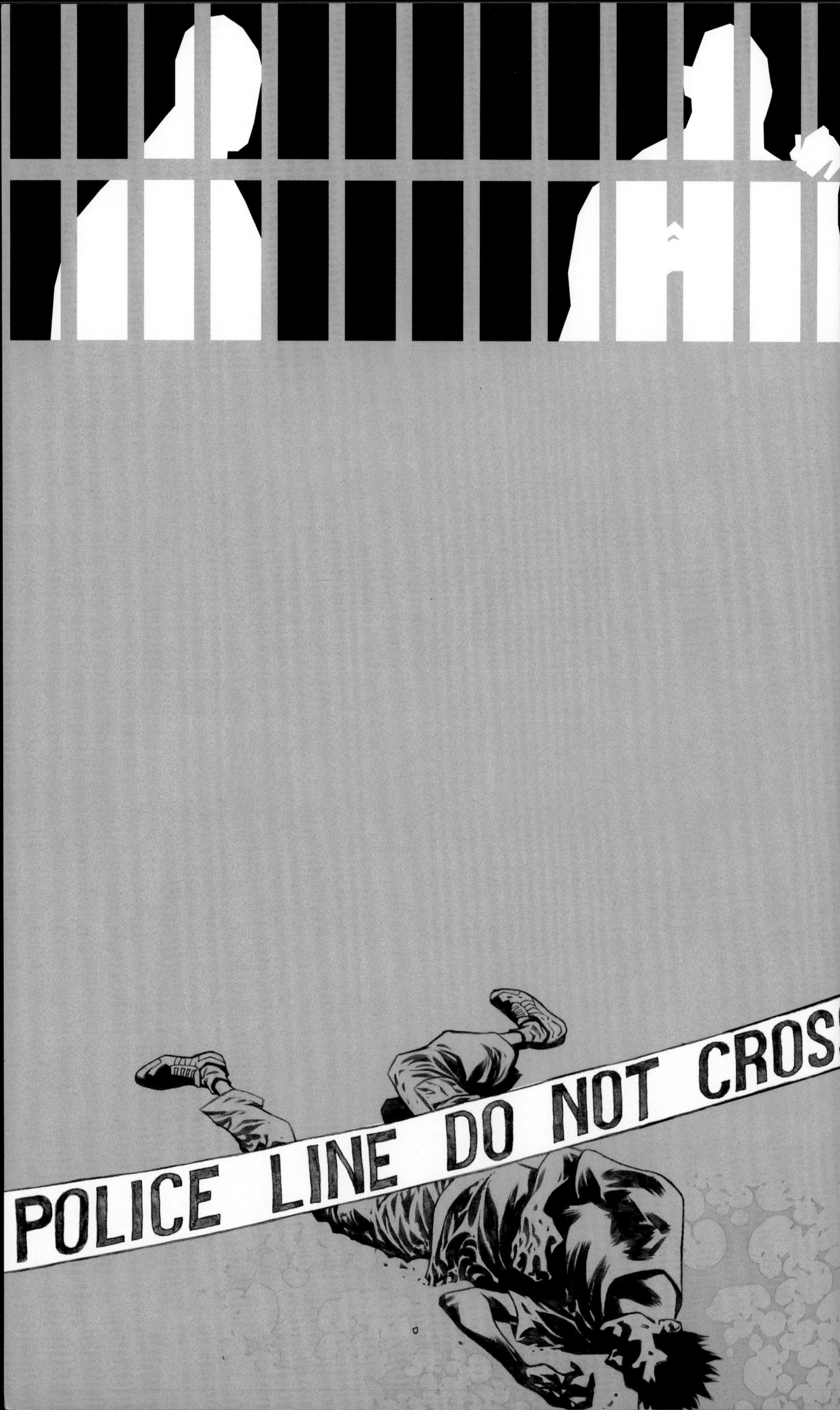
POLICE LINE DO NOT CROS

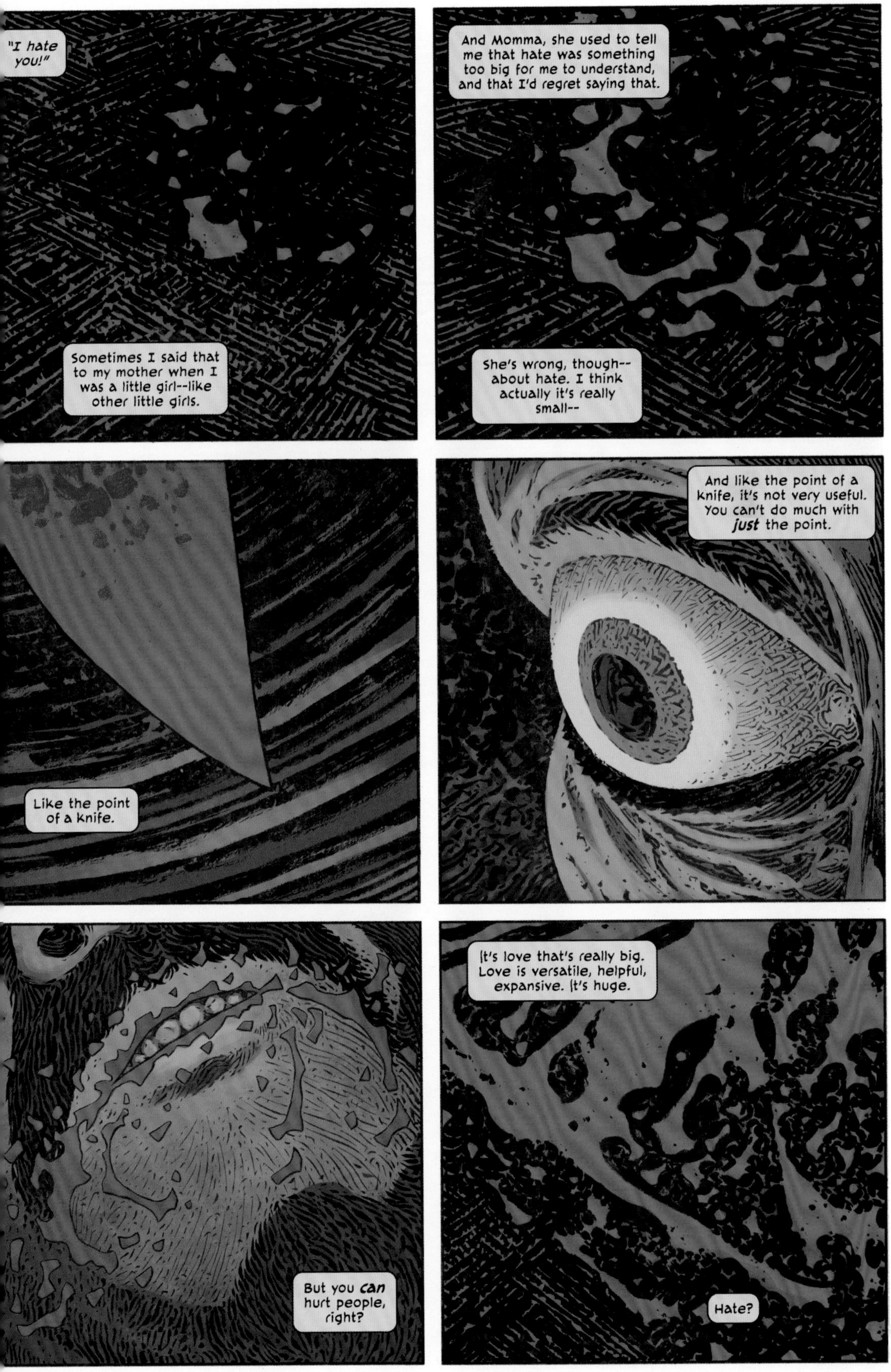
"I hate you!"
Sometimes I said that to my mother when I was a little girl--like other little girls.
And Momma, she used to tell me that hate was something too big for me to understand, and that I'd regret saying that.
She's wrong, though--about hate. I think actually it's really small--
Like the point of a knife.
And like the point of a knife, it's not very useful. You can't do much with *just* the point.
But you *can* hurt people, right?
It's love that's really big. Love is versatile, helpful, expansive. It's huge.
Hate?

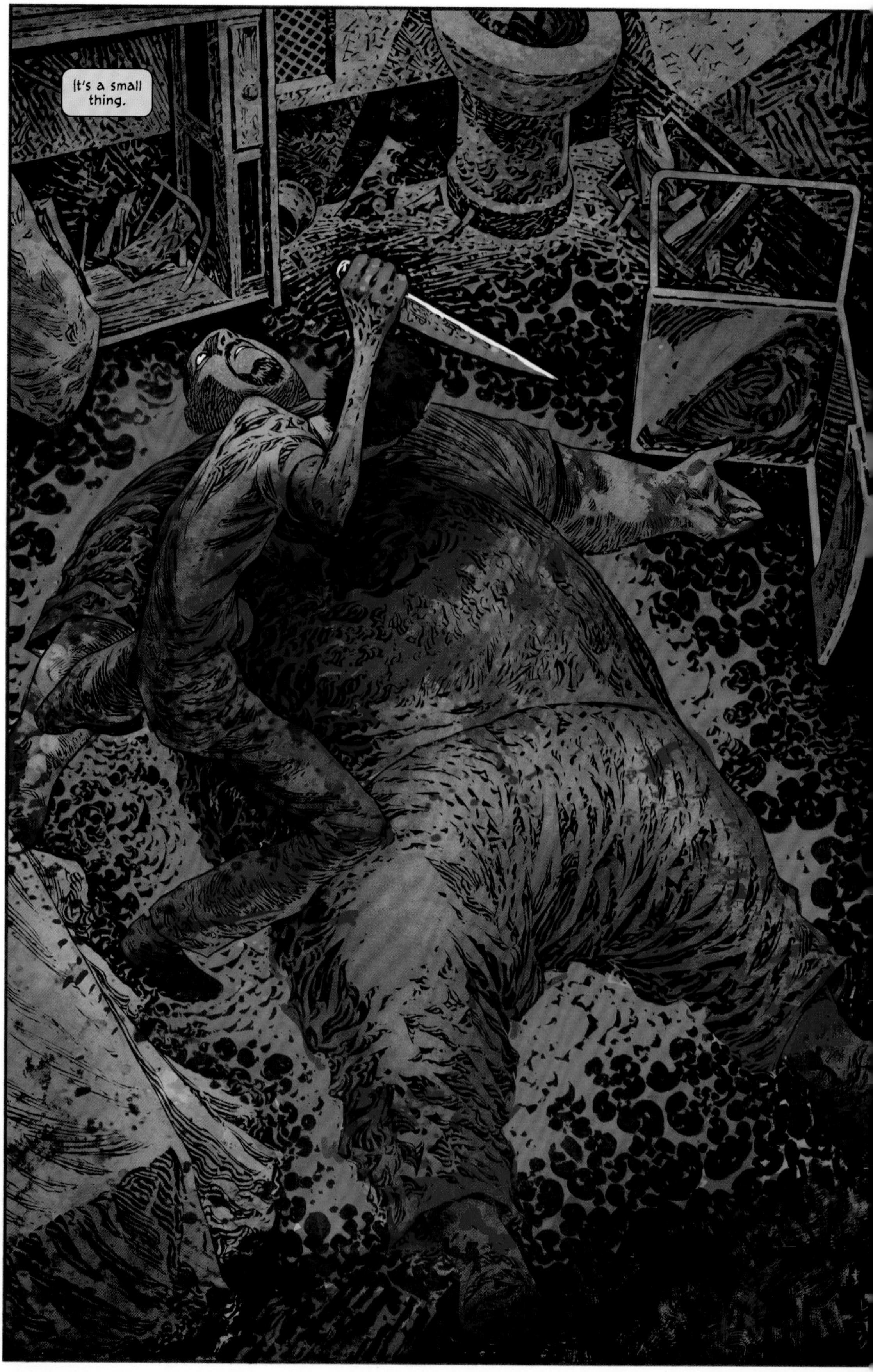
It's a small thing.

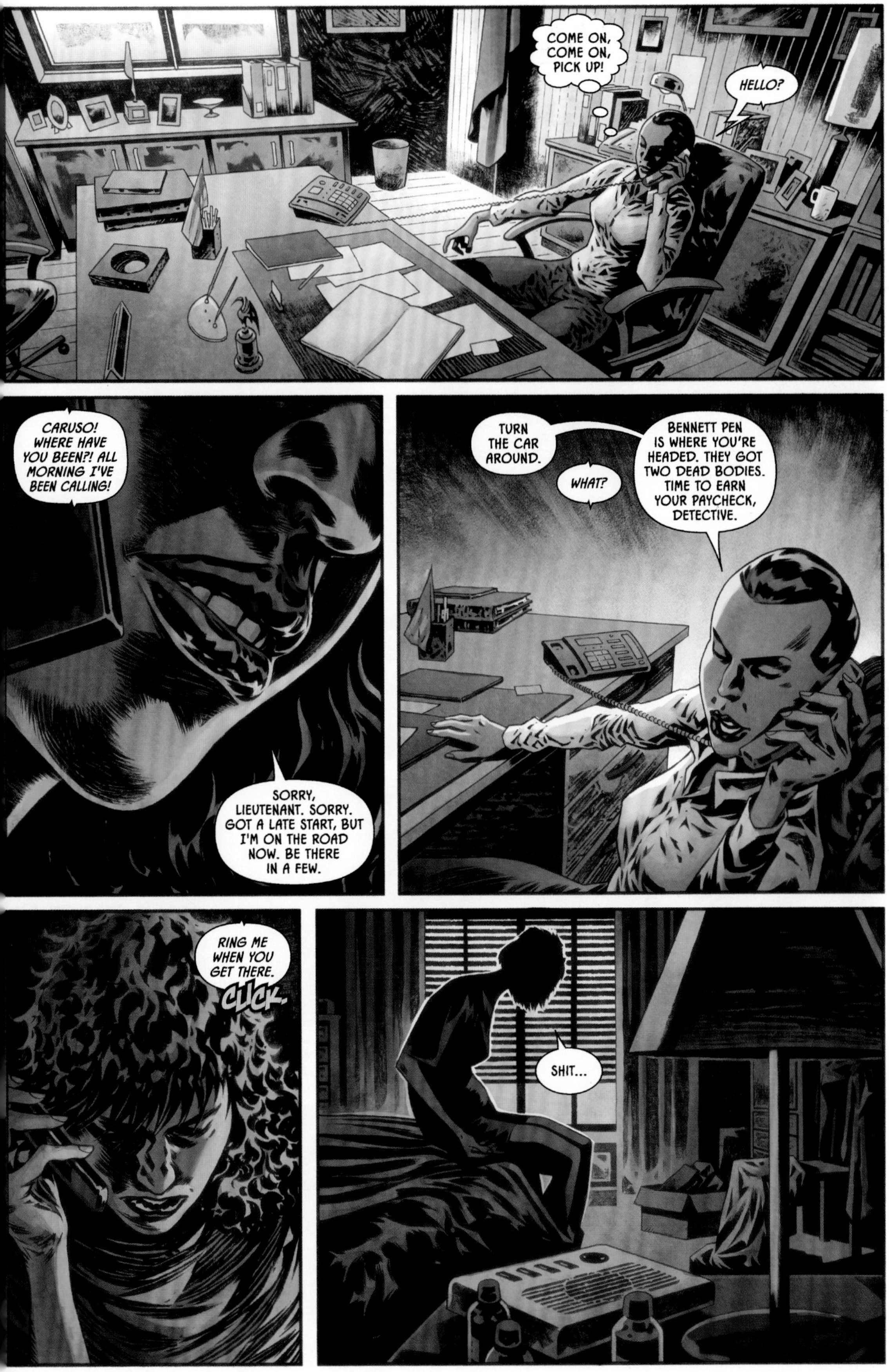
COME ON, COME ON, PICK UP!
HELLO?
CARUSO! WHERE HAVE YOU BEEN?! ALL MORNING I'VE BEEN CALLING!
SORRY, LIEUTENANT. SORRY. GOT A LATE START, BUT I'M ON THE ROAD NOW. BE THERE IN A FEW.
TURN THE CAR AROUND.
WHAT?
BENNETT PEN IS WHERE YOU'RE HEADED. THEY GOT TWO DEAD BODIES. TIME TO EARN YOUR PAYCHECK, DETECTIVE.
RING ME WHEN YOU GET THERE.
CLICK
SHIT...

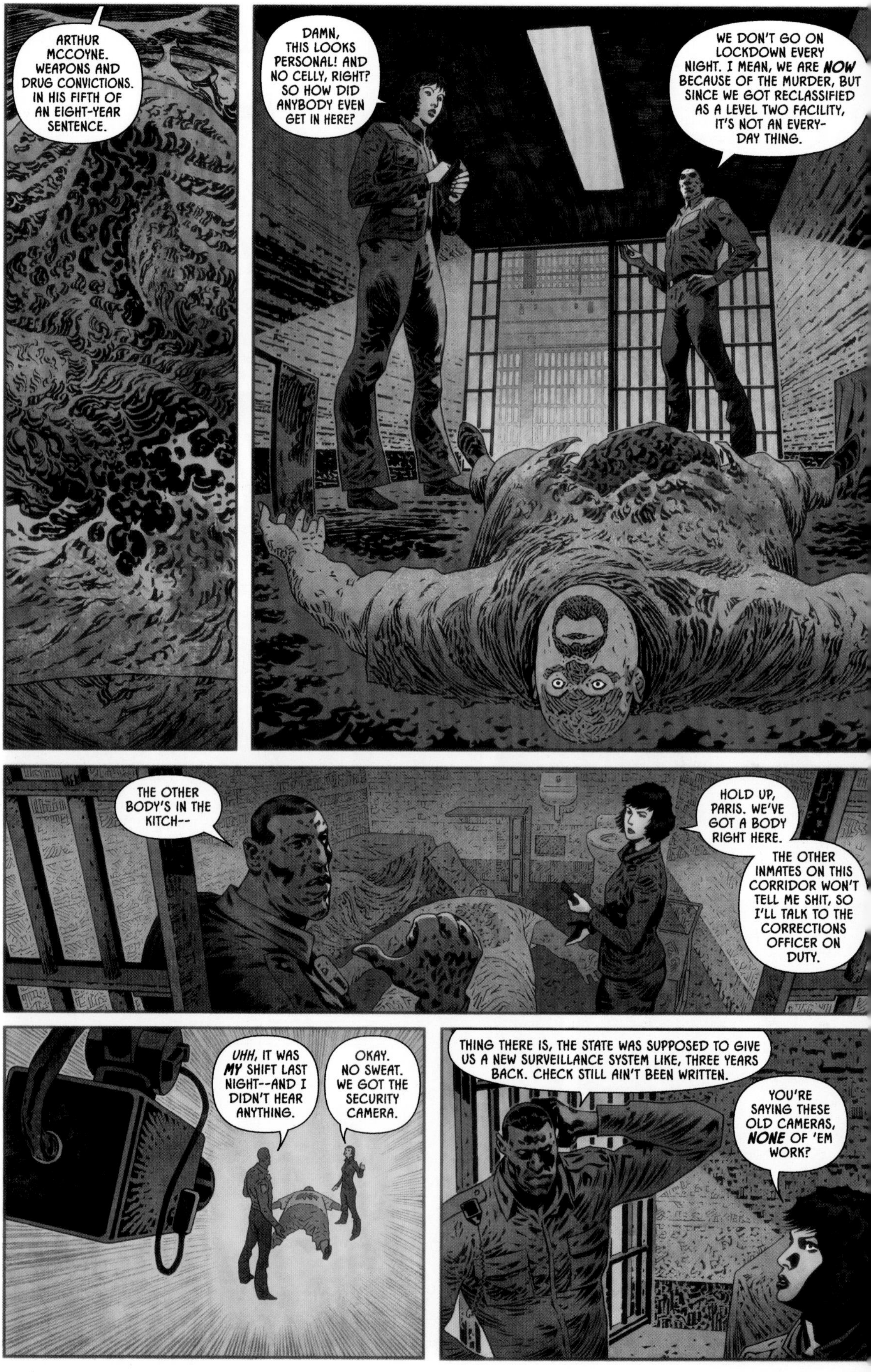
ARTHUR MCCOYNE. WEAPONS AND DRUG CONVICTIONS. IN HIS FIFTH OF AN EIGHT-YEAR SENTENCE.
DAMN, THIS LOOKS PERSONAL! AND NO CELLY, RIGHT? SO HOW DID ANYBODY EVEN GET IN HERE?
WE DON'T GO ON LOCKDOWN EVERY NIGHT. I MEAN, WE ARE NOW BECAUSE OF THE MURDER, BUT SINCE WE GOT RECLASSIFIED AS A LEVEL TWO FACILITY, IT'S NOT AN EVERY-DAY THING.
THE OTHER BODY'S IN THE KITCH--
HOLD UP, PARIS. WE'VE GOT A BODY RIGHT HERE.
THE OTHER INMATES ON THIS CORRIDOR WON'T TELL ME SHIT, SO I'LL TALK TO THE CORRECTIONS OFFICER ON DUTY.
UHH, IT WAS MY SHIFT LAST NIGHT--AND I DIDN'T HEAR ANYTHING.
OKAY. NO SWEAT. WE GOT THE SECURITY CAMERA.
THING THERE IS, THE STATE WAS SUPPOSED TO GIVE US A NEW SURVEILLANCE SYSTEM LIKE, THREE YEARS BACK. CHECK STILL AIN'T BEEN WRITTEN.
YOU'RE SAYING THESE OLD CAMERAS, NONE OF 'EM WORK?

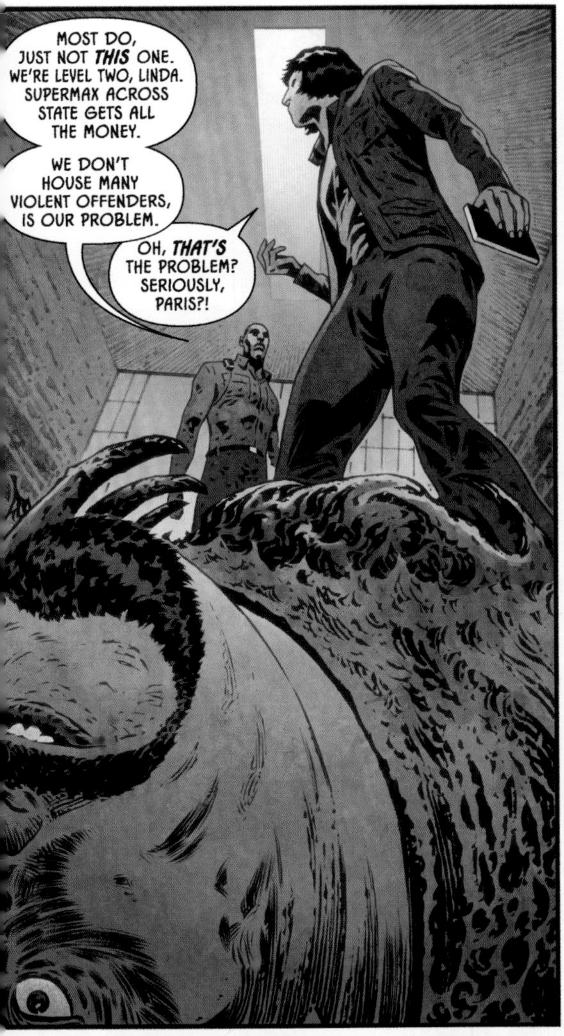
MOST DO, JUST NOT THIS ONE. WE'RE LEVEL TWO, LINDA. SUPERMAX ACROSS STATE GETS ALL THE MONEY.
WE DON'T HOUSE MANY VIOLENT OFFENDERS, IS OUR PROBLEM.
OH, THAT'S THE PROBLEM? SERIOUSLY, PARIS?!

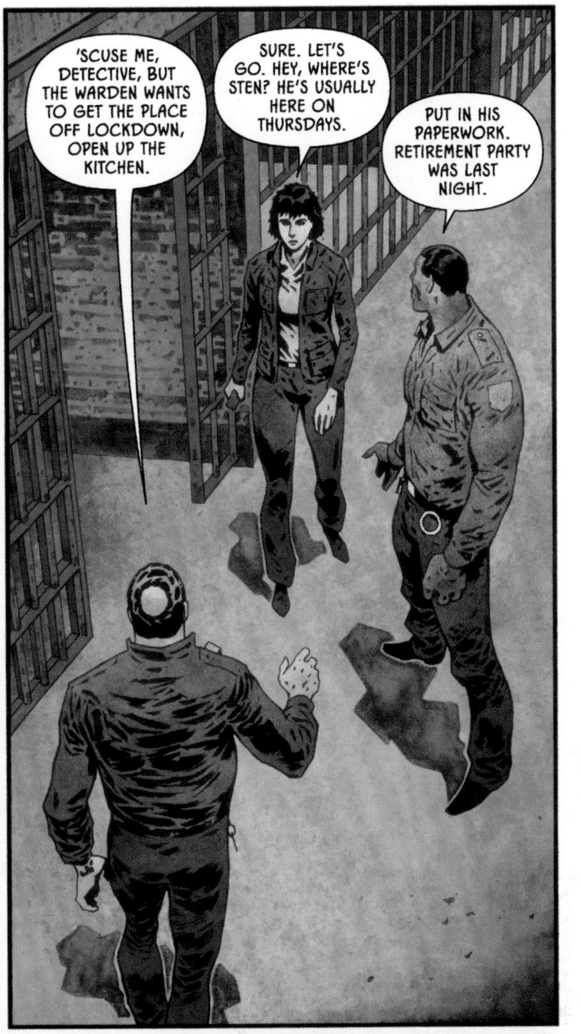
'SCUSE ME, DETECTIVE, BUT THE WARDEN WANTS TO GET THE PLACE OFF LOCKDOWN, OPEN UP THE KITCHEN.
SURE. LET'S GO. HEY, WHERE'S STEN? HE'S USUALLY HERE ON THURSDAYS.
PUT IN HIS PAPERWORK. RETIREMENT PARTY WAS LAST NIGHT.

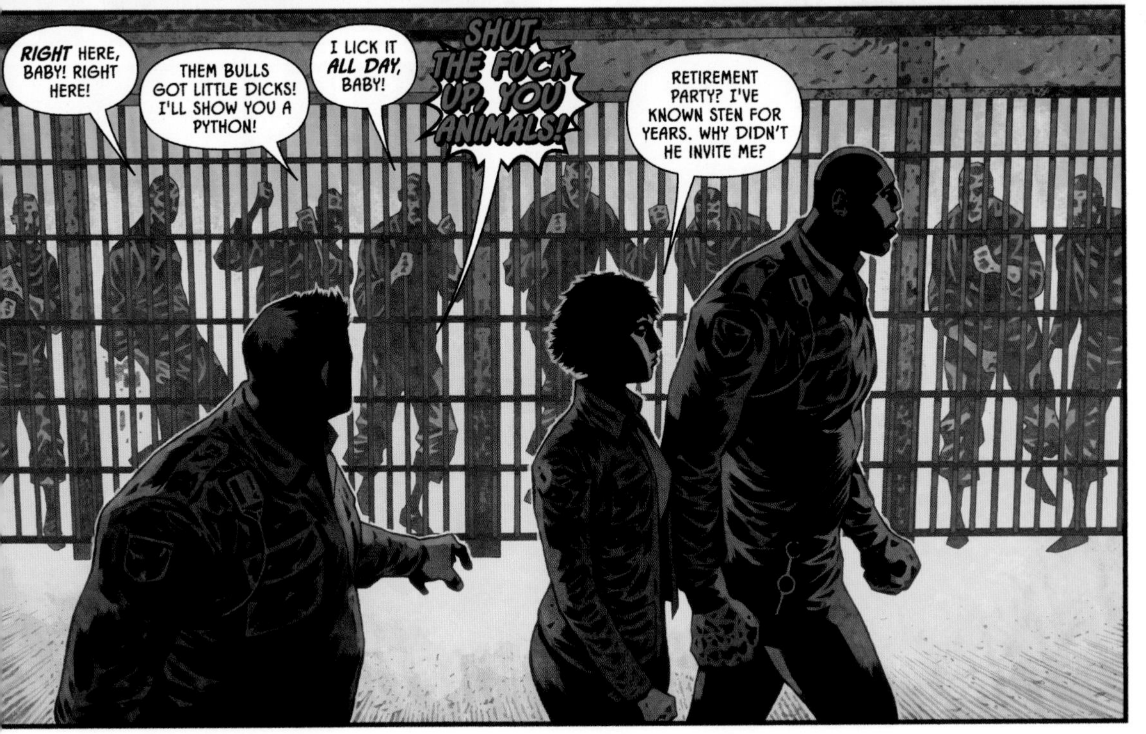
RIGHT HERE, BABY! RIGHT HERE!
THEM BULLS GOT LITTLE DICKS! I'LL SHOW YOU A PYTHON!
I LICK IT ALL DAY, BABY!
SHUT THE FUCK UP, YOU ANIMALS!
RETIREMENT PARTY? I'VE KNOWN STEN FOR YEARS. WHY DIDN'T HE INVITE ME?

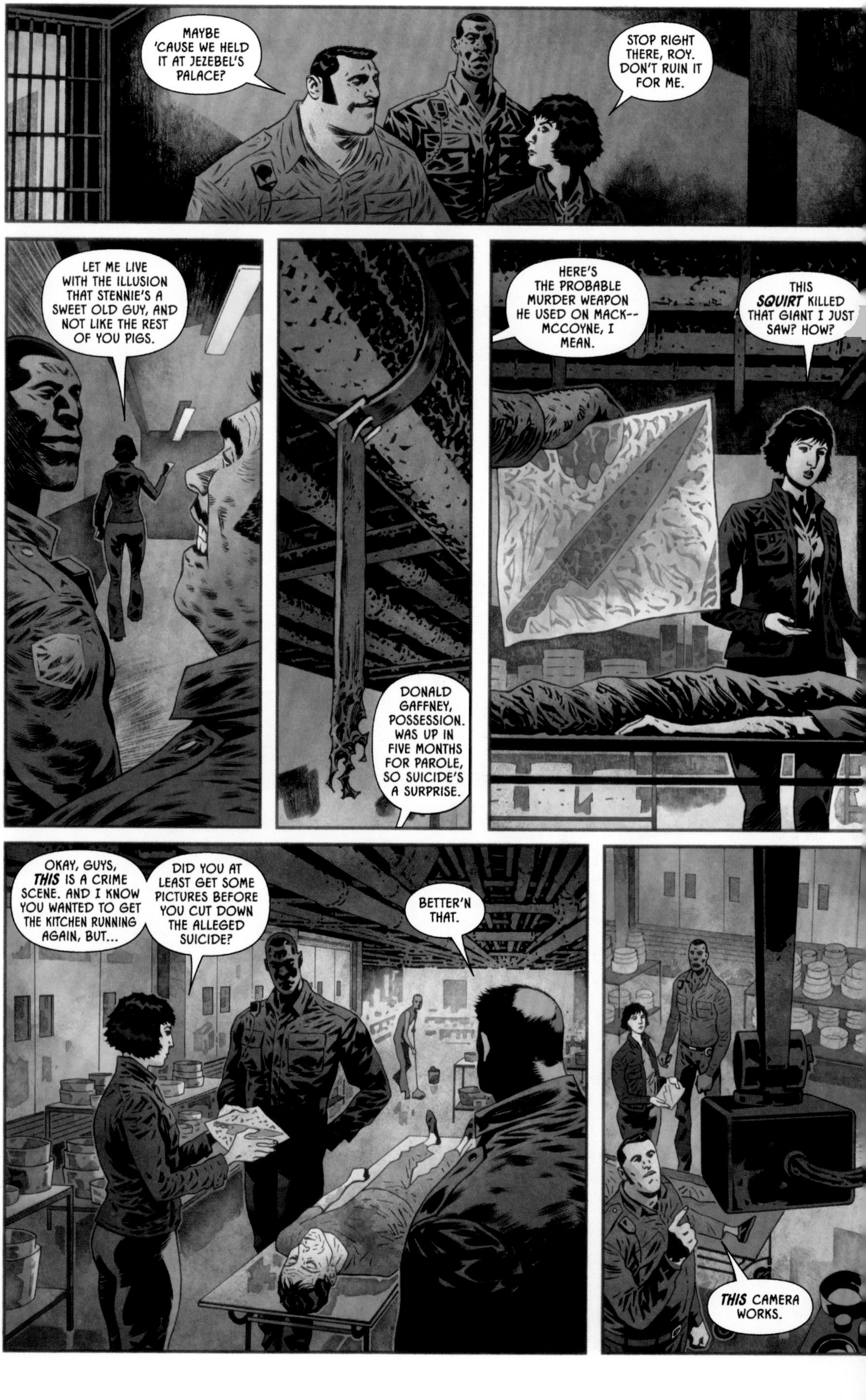
MAYBE 'CAUSE WE HELD IT AT JEZEBEL'S PALACE?
STOP RIGHT THERE, ROY. DON'T RUIN IT FOR ME.
LET ME LIVE WITH THE ILLUSION THAT STENNIE'S A SWEET OLD GUY, AND NOT LIKE THE REST OF YOU PIGS.
DONALD GAFFNEY, POSSESSION. WAS UP IN FIVE MONTHS FOR PAROLE, SO SUICIDE'S A SURPRISE.
HERE'S THE PROBABLE MURDER WEAPON HE USED ON MACK--MCCOYNE, I MEAN.
THIS SQUIRT KILLED THAT GIANT I JUST SAW? HOW?
OKAY, GUYS, THIS IS A CRIME SCENE. AND I KNOW YOU WANTED TO GET THE KITCHEN RUNNING AGAIN, BUT...
DID YOU AT LEAST GET SOME PICTURES BEFORE YOU CUT DOWN THE ALLEGED SUICIDE?
BETTER'N THAT.
THIS CAMERA WORKS.

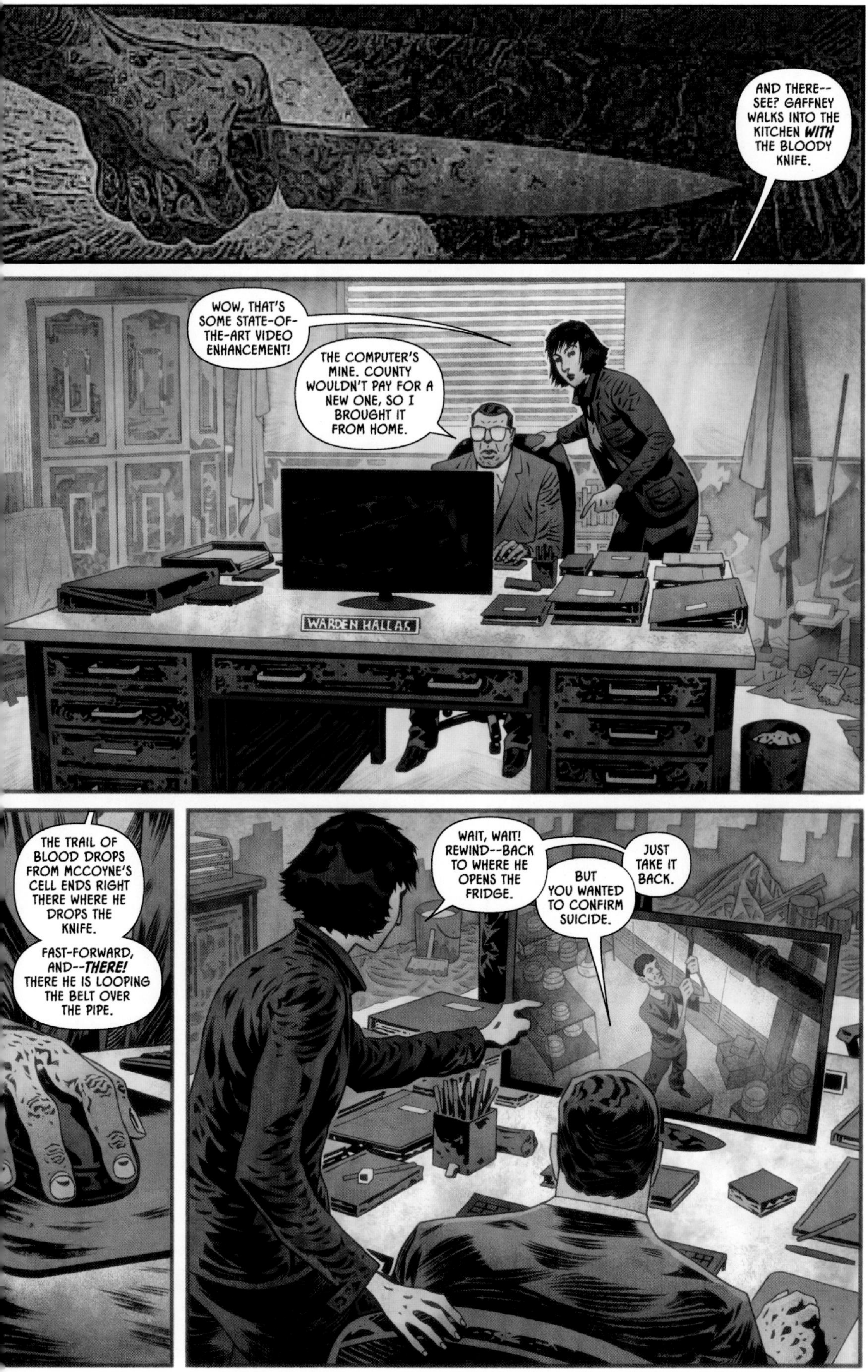
AND THERE--SEE? GAFFNEY WALKS INTO THE KITCHEN *WITH* THE BLOODY KNIFE.
WOW, THAT'S SOME STATE-OF-THE-ART VIDEO ENHANCEMENT!
THE COMPUTER'S MINE. COUNTY WOULDN'T PAY FOR A NEW ONE, SO I BROUGHT IT FROM HOME.
WARDEN HALLAS
THE TRAIL OF BLOOD DROPS FROM MCCOYNE'S CELL ENDS RIGHT THERE WHERE HE DROPS THE KNIFE.
FAST-FORWARD, AND--*THERE!* THERE HE IS LOOPING THE BELT OVER THE PIPE.
WAIT, WAIT! REWIND--BACK TO WHERE HE OPENS THE FRIDGE.
BUT YOU WANTED TO CONFIRM SUICIDE.
JUST TAKE IT BACK.

DAMN, LOOK AT HIM GO! DID HE DOWN THE WHOLE THING?

I SAW AN INMATE MOPPING UP IN THE KITCHEN. YOU CAN'T DO THAT, WARDEN! IT'S A *CRIME* SCENE.

THE CRIME OF STEALING MILK? WE HAVE THE C.O.D.* FOR YOU HERE ON VIDEO!

*CAUSE OF DEATH

OH, COME ON. MCCOYNE'S GOT A HUNDRED AND FIFTY POUNDS ON GAFFNEY. HOW'S HE GONNA TAKE DOWN THAT MOOSE UNLESS HE'S TWEAKING?

"TWEAKING"? DETECTIVE, WE HAVE NO CONTRABAND IN MY FACILITY. *PERIOD*.

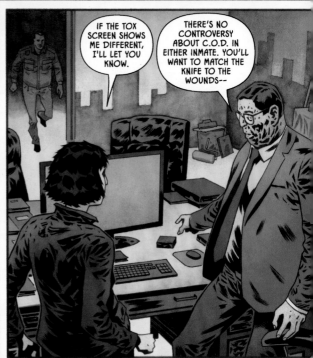

IF THE TOX SCREEN SHOWS ME DIFFERENT, I'LL LET YOU KNOW.

THERE'S NO CONTROVERSY ABOUT C.O.D. IN EITHER INMATE. YOU'LL WANT TO MATCH THE KNIFE TO THE WOUNDS--

--BUT A TOX SCREEN'S NOT CALLED FOR.

WARDEN... YOUR OFFICERS HAVE BEEN RUSHING ME THROUGH THE PRISON, CRIME SCENES HAVE BEEN TAMPERED WITH, BUT AUTOPSIES ARE *MY* TERRITORY!

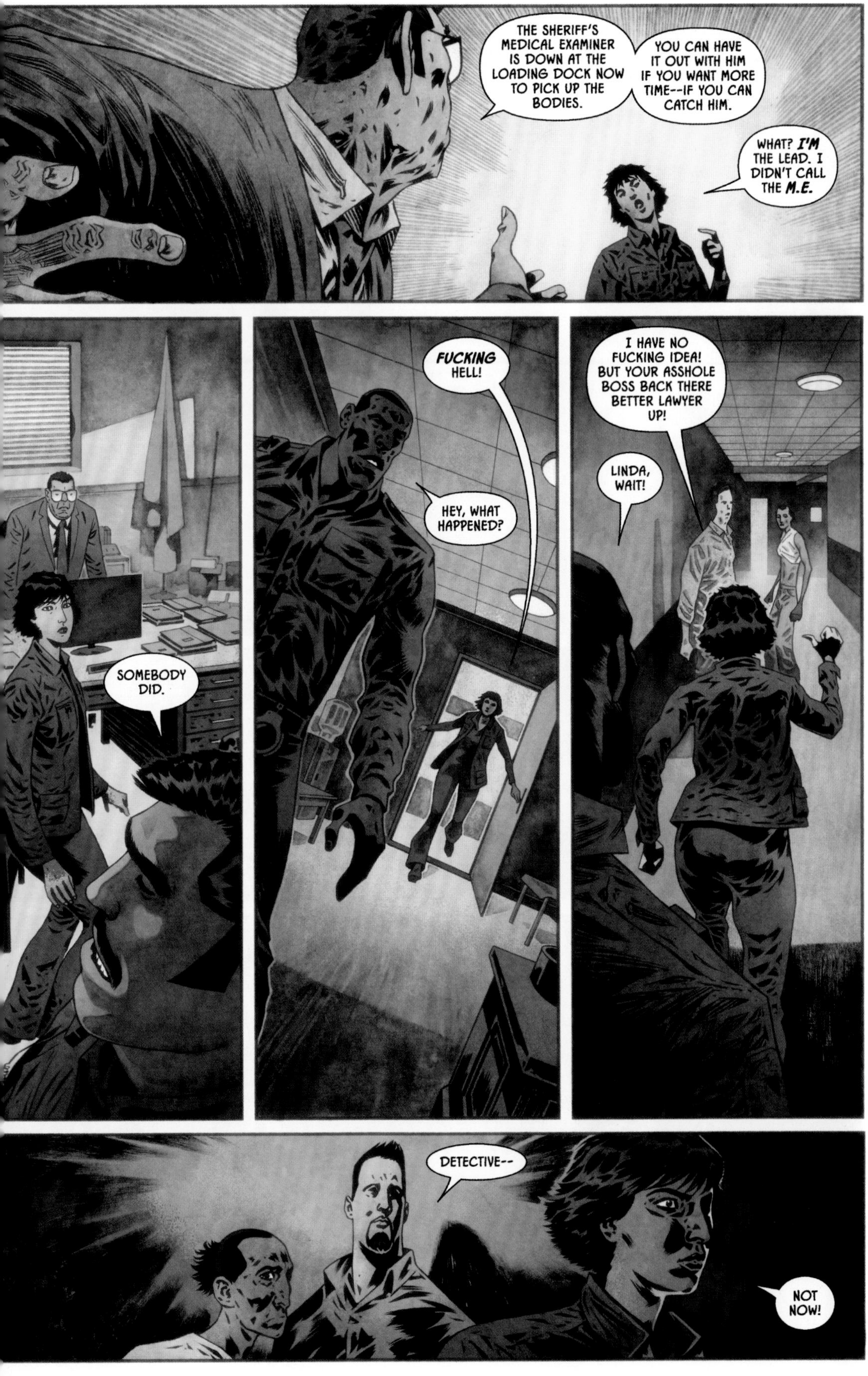
THE SHERIFF'S MEDICAL EXAMINER IS DOWN AT THE LOADING DOCK NOW TO PICK UP THE BODIES.
YOU CAN HAVE IT OUT WITH HIM IF YOU WANT MORE TIME--IF YOU CAN CATCH HIM.
WHAT? I'M THE LEAD. I DIDN'T CALL THE M.E.
SOMEBODY DID.
FUCKING HELL!
HEY, WHAT HAPPENED?
I HAVE NO FUCKING IDEA! BUT YOUR ASSHOLE BOSS BACK THERE BETTER LAWYER UP!
LINDA, WAIT!
DETECTIVE--
NOT NOW!

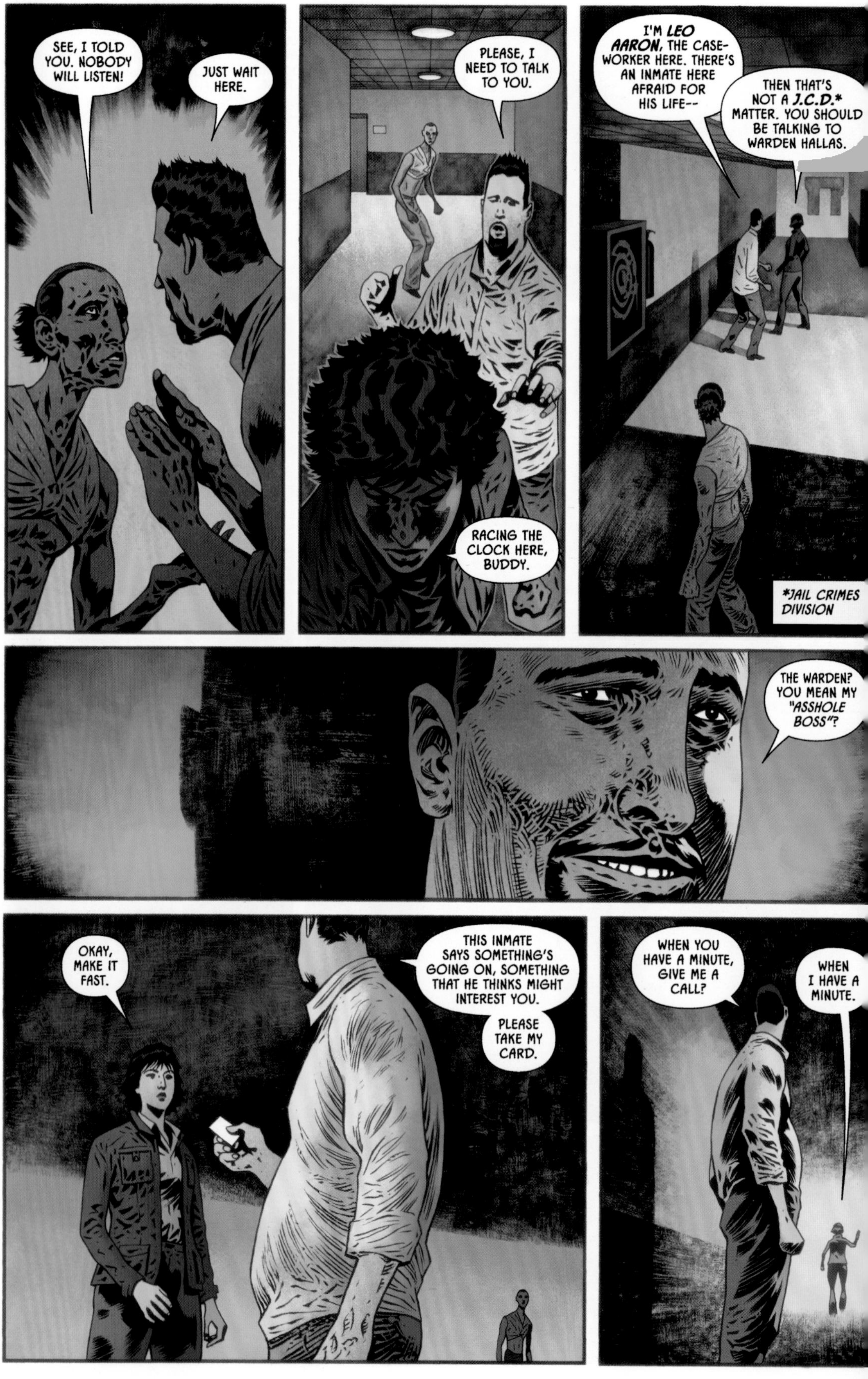
SEE, I TOLD YOU. NOBODY WILL LISTEN!
JUST WAIT HERE.
PLEASE, I NEED TO TALK TO YOU.
RACING THE CLOCK HERE, BUDDY.
I'M *LEO AARON*, THE CASE-WORKER HERE. THERE'S AN INMATE HERE AFRAID FOR HIS LIFE--
THEN THAT'S NOT A *J.C.D.** MATTER. YOU SHOULD BE TALKING TO WARDEN HALLAS.
*JAIL CRIMES DIVISION
THE WARDEN? YOU MEAN MY "ASSHOLE BOSS"?
OKAY, MAKE IT FAST.
THIS INMATE SAYS SOMETHING'S GOING ON, SOMETHING THAT HE THINKS MIGHT INTEREST YOU.
PLEASE TAKE MY CARD.
WHEN YOU HAVE A MINUTE, GIVE ME A CALL?
WHEN I HAVE A MINUTE.

IT'S NOT NECESSARY.

LT. ELEANOR PAYTON

NO AUTOPSY? ON A *MURDER?!*

WE'LL RUN TESTS ON THE KNIFE AND INMATE MCCOYNE'S WOUNDS, OF COURSE.

OKAY, GREAT. BUT GAFFNEY WAS UP FOR PAROLE IN FIVE MONTHS, AND HE SUDDENLY GOES MURDER-SUICIDE? MAKES ME THINK SPEED-- OR *SOMETHING!*

IT'S NOT UNDER THE AUTHORITY OF THE JAIL CRIMES DIVISION TO INVESTIGATE DRUG TRAFFICKING UNTIL AND UNLESS PRISON OFFICIALS FIND ACTUAL CONTRABAND.

THIS IS HOW WE'LL FIND IT!

DETECTIVE, A TRACE OF CRANK IN AN INMATE'S BLOODSTREAM WON'T RISE TO THE STANDARD.

WORSE YET, THE TOX SCREEN COMES UP NEGATIVE. THEN THE COMPTROLLER ASKS US WHY WE BOTHERED AT ALL--WHAT WITH OBVIOUS C.O.D. IN BOTH CASES.

AND THEN MAYBE HE STARTS AUDITING *ALL* OF OUR AUTOPSIES. IT'S NOT WORTH IT.

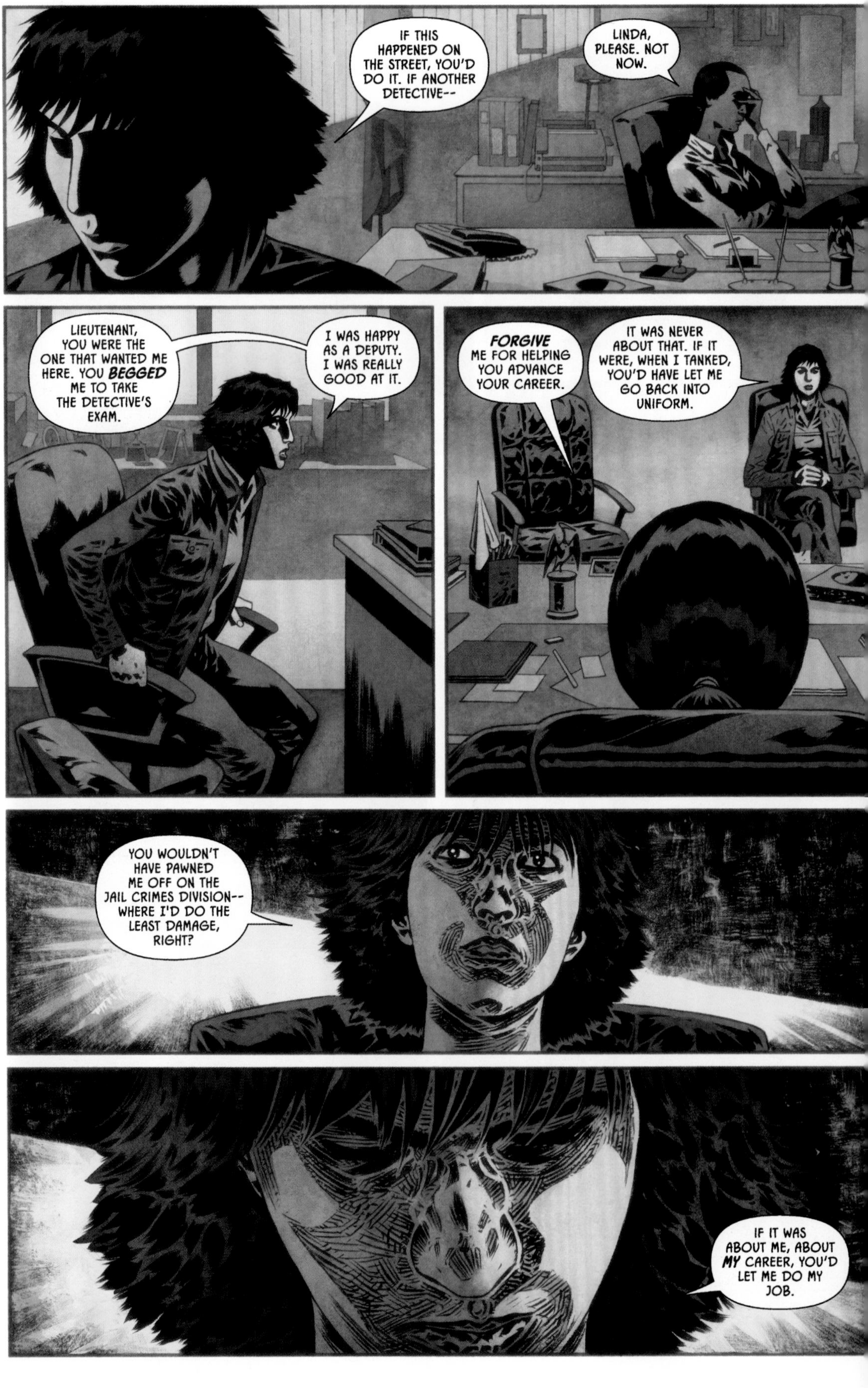
IF THIS HAPPENED ON THE STREET, YOU'D DO IT. IF ANOTHER DETECTIVE--
LINDA, PLEASE. NOT NOW.
LIEUTENANT, YOU WERE THE ONE THAT WANTED ME HERE. YOU **BEGGED** ME TO TAKE THE DETECTIVE'S EXAM.
I WAS HAPPY AS A DEPUTY. I WAS REALLY GOOD AT IT.
FORGIVE ME FOR HELPING YOU ADVANCE YOUR CAREER.
IT WAS NEVER ABOUT THAT. IF IT WERE, WHEN I TANKED, YOU'D HAVE LET ME GO BACK INTO UNIFORM.
YOU WOULDN'T HAVE PAWNED ME OFF ON THE JAIL CRIMES DIVISION-- WHERE I'D DO THE LEAST DAMAGE, RIGHT?
IF IT WAS ABOUT ME, ABOUT **MY** CAREER, YOU'D LET ME DO MY JOB.

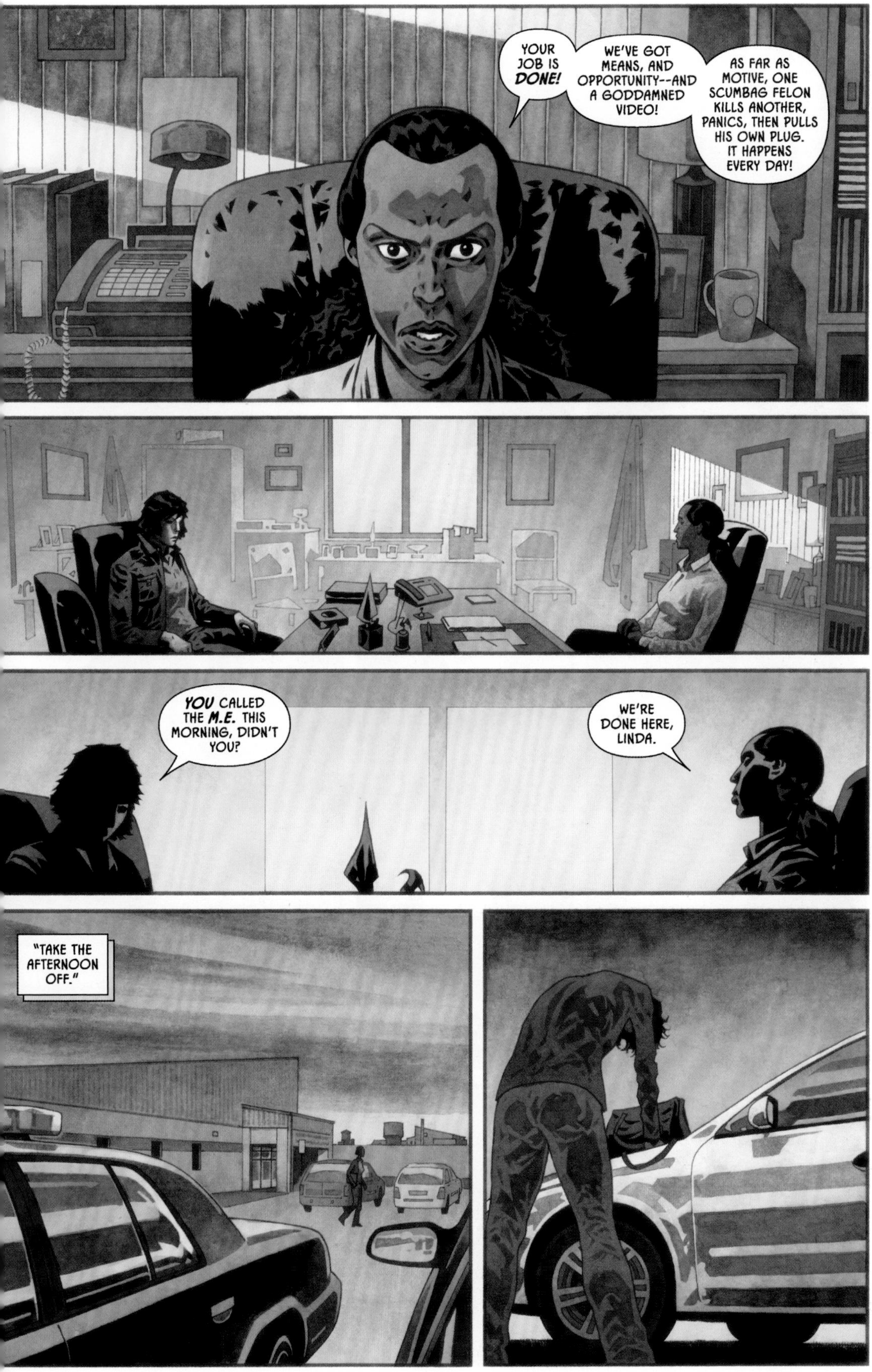
YOUR JOB IS DONE!
WE'VE GOT MEANS, AND OPPORTUNITY--AND A GODDAMNED VIDEO!
AS FAR AS MOTIVE, ONE SCUMBAG FELON KILLS ANOTHER, PANICS, THEN PULLS HIS OWN PLUG. IT HAPPENS EVERY DAY!
YOU CALLED THE M.E. THIS MORNING, DIDN'T YOU?
WE'RE DONE HERE, LINDA.
"TAKE THE AFTERNOON OFF."

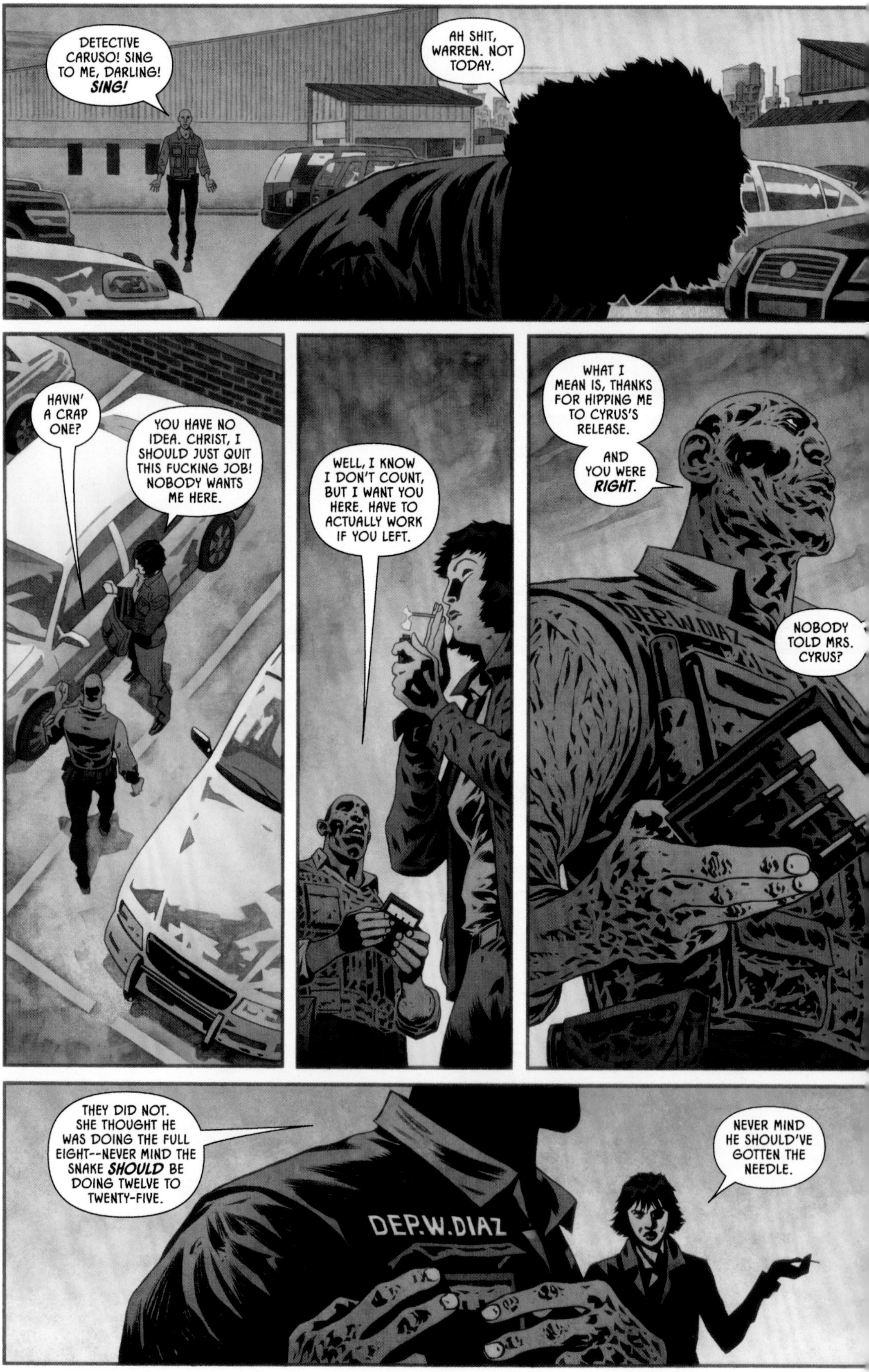
DETECTIVE CARUSO! SING TO ME, DARLING! SING!
AH SHIT, WARREN. NOT TODAY.
HAVIN' A CRAP ONE?
YOU HAVE NO IDEA. CHRIST, I SHOULD JUST QUIT THIS FUCKING JOB! NOBODY WANTS ME HERE.
WELL, I KNOW I DON'T COUNT, BUT I WANT YOU HERE. HAVE TO ACTUALLY WORK IF YOU LEFT.
WHAT I MEAN IS, THANKS FOR HIPPING ME TO CYRUS'S RELEASE.
AND YOU WERE RIGHT.
DEP. W. DIAZ
NOBODY TOLD MRS. CYRUS?
THEY DID NOT. SHE THOUGHT HE WAS DOING THE FULL EIGHT--NEVER MIND THE SNAKE SHOULD BE DOING TWELVE TO TWENTY-FIVE.
NEVER MIND HE SHOULD'VE GOTTEN THE NEEDLE.
DEP. W. DIAZ

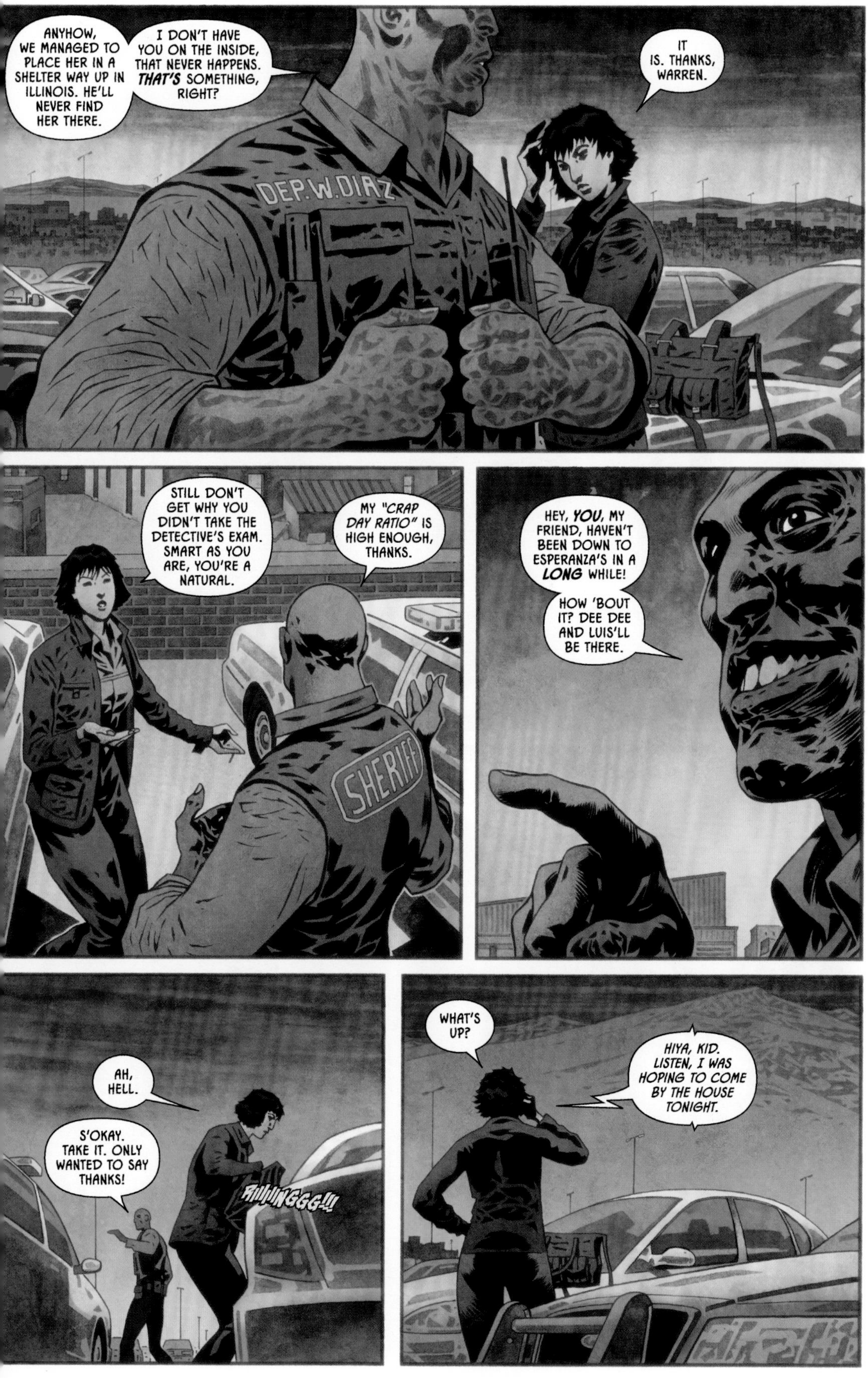

ANYHOW, WE MANAGED TO PLACE HER IN A SHELTER WAY UP IN ILLINOIS. HE'LL NEVER FIND HER THERE.
I DON'T HAVE YOU ON THE INSIDE, THAT NEVER HAPPENS. THAT'S SOMETHING, RIGHT?
IT IS. THANKS, WARREN.
DEP. W. DIAZ
STILL DON'T GET WHY YOU DIDN'T TAKE THE DETECTIVE'S EXAM. SMART AS YOU ARE, YOU'RE A NATURAL.
MY "CRAP DAY RATIO" IS HIGH ENOUGH, THANKS.
SHERIFF
HEY, YOU, MY FRIEND, HAVEN'T BEEN DOWN TO ESPERANZA'S IN A LONG WHILE!
HOW 'BOUT IT? DEE DEE AND LUIS'LL BE THERE.
AH, HELL.
S'OKAY. TAKE IT. ONLY WANTED TO SAY THANKS!
RIIIINGGG!!!
WHAT'S UP?
HIYA, KID. LISTEN, I WAS HOPING TO COME BY THE HOUSE TONIGHT.

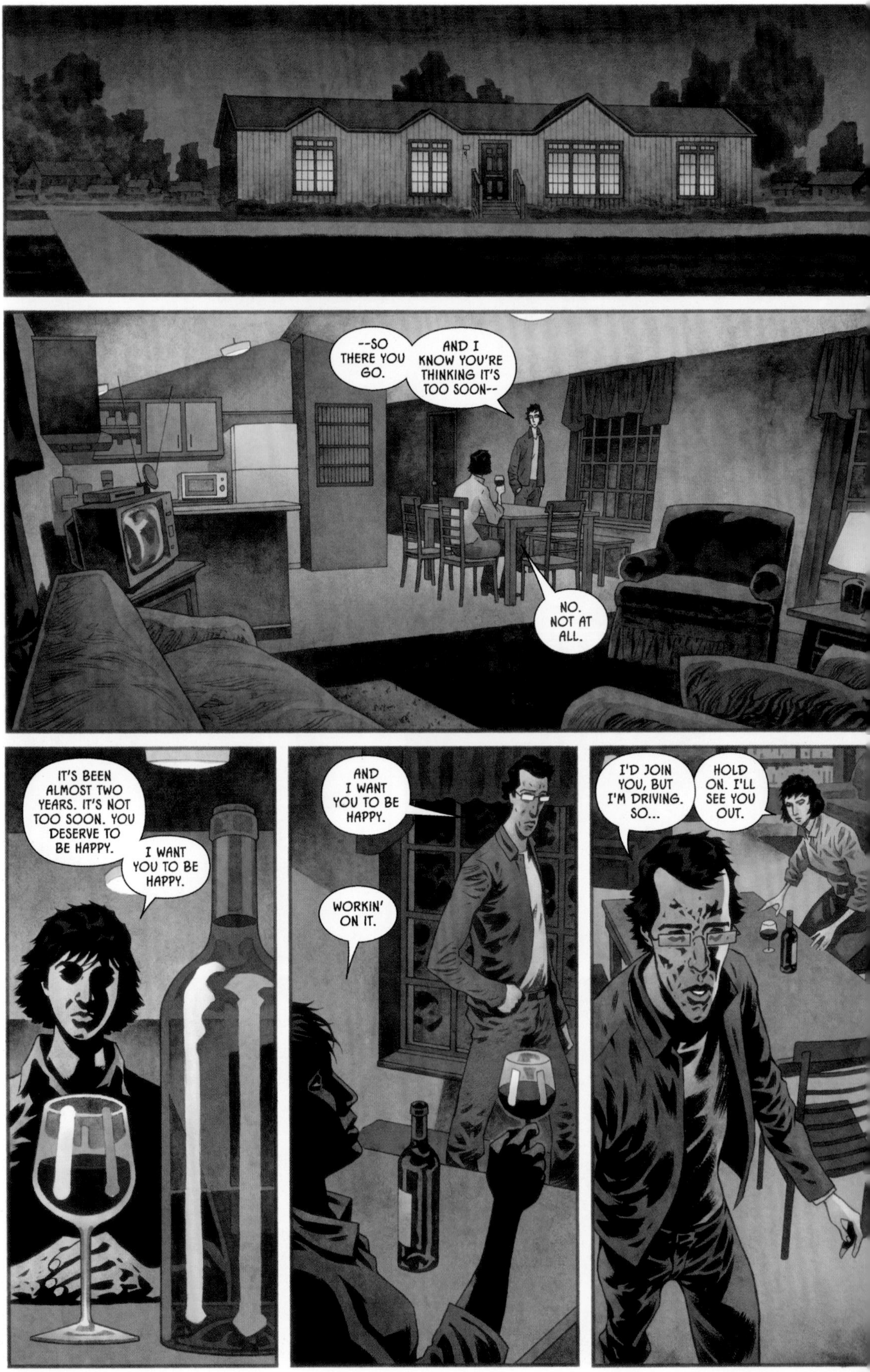

--SO THERE YOU GO.
AND I KNOW YOU'RE THINKING IT'S TOO SOON--
NO. NOT AT ALL.
IT'S BEEN ALMOST TWO YEARS. IT'S NOT TOO SOON. YOU DESERVE TO BE HAPPY.
I WANT YOU TO BE HAPPY.
AND I WANT YOU TO BE HAPPY.
WORKIN' ON IT.
I'D JOIN YOU, BUT I'M DRIVING. SO...
HOLD ON. I'LL SEE YOU OUT.

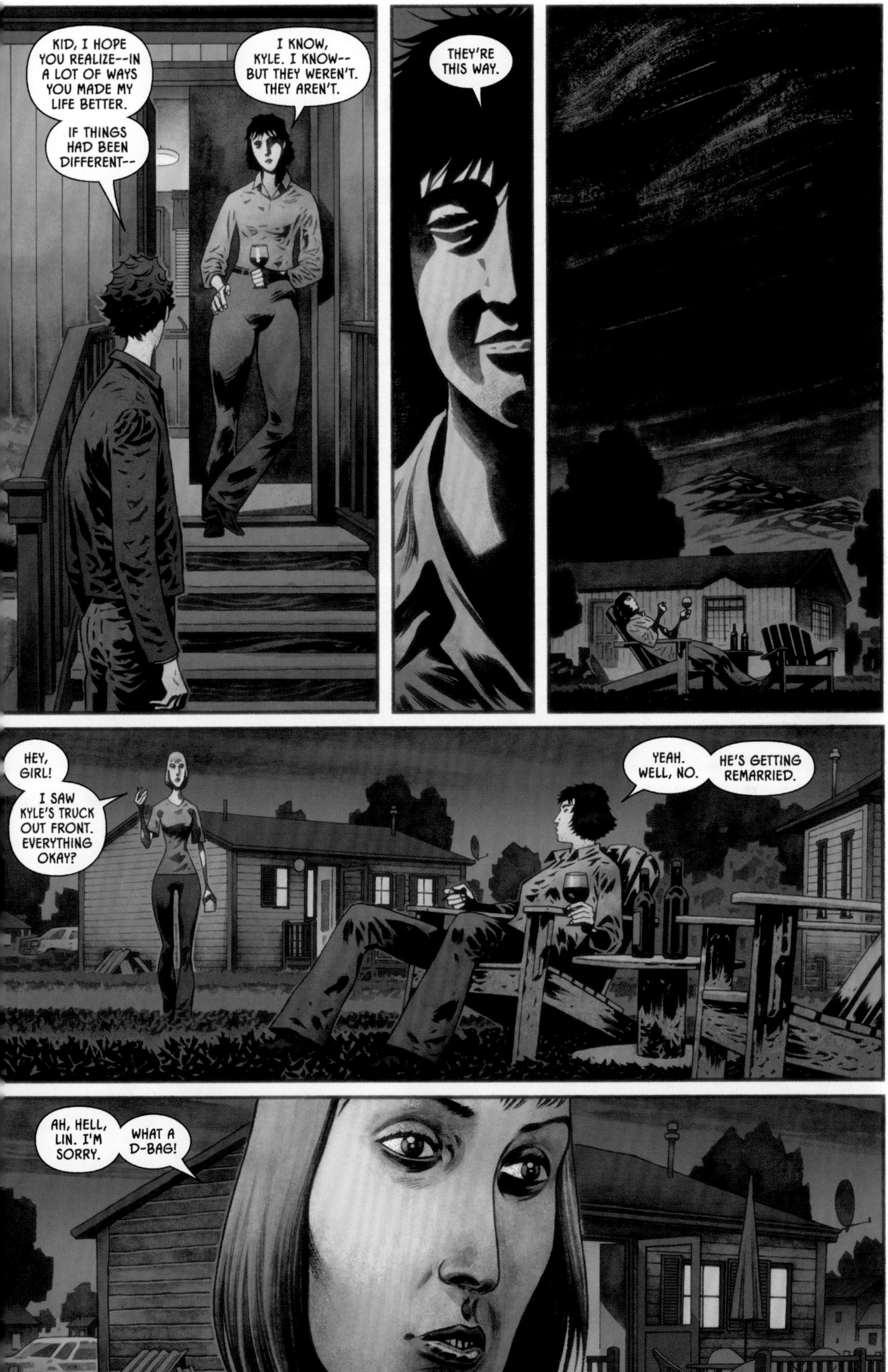
KID, I HOPE YOU REALIZE--IN A LOT OF WAYS YOU MADE MY LIFE BETTER.
IF THINGS HAD BEEN DIFFERENT--
I KNOW, KYLE. I KNOW-- BUT THEY WEREN'T. THEY AREN'T.
THEY'RE THIS WAY.
HEY, GIRL!
I SAW KYLE'S TRUCK OUT FRONT. EVERYTHING OKAY?
YEAH. WELL, NO.
HE'S GETTING REMARRIED.
AH, HELL, LIN. I'M SORRY.
WHAT A D-BAG!

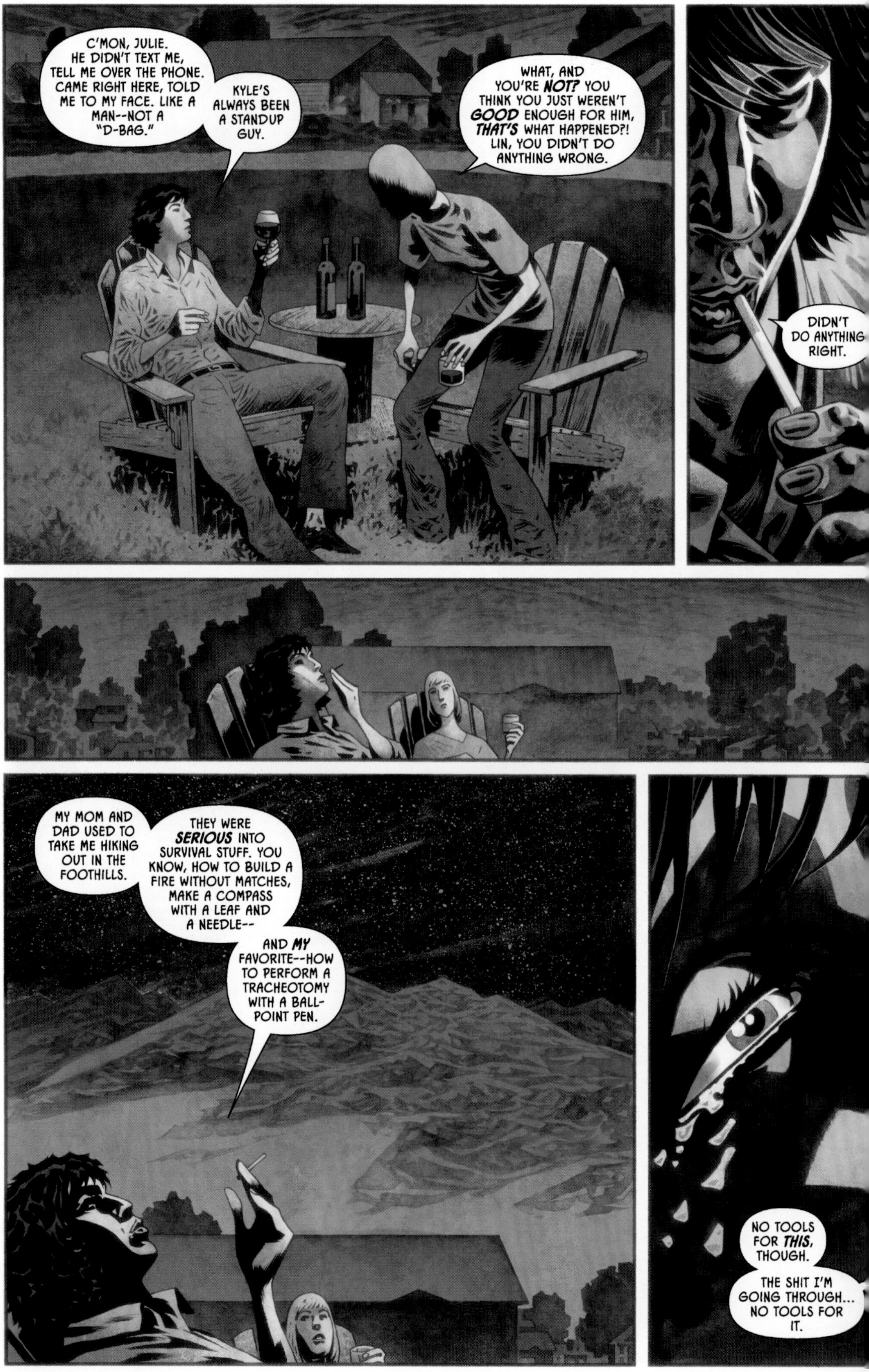
C'MON, JULIE. HE DIDN'T TEXT ME, TELL ME OVER THE PHONE. CAME RIGHT HERE, TOLD ME TO MY FACE. LIKE A MAN--NOT A "D-BAG."
KYLE'S ALWAYS BEEN A STANDUP GUY.
WHAT, AND YOU'RE NOT? YOU THINK YOU JUST WEREN'T GOOD ENOUGH FOR HIM, THAT'S WHAT HAPPENED?! LIN, YOU DIDN'T DO ANYTHING WRONG.
DIDN'T DO ANYTHING RIGHT.
MY MOM AND DAD USED TO TAKE ME HIKING OUT IN THE FOOTHILLS.
THEY WERE SERIOUS INTO SURVIVAL STUFF. YOU KNOW, HOW TO BUILD A FIRE WITHOUT MATCHES, MAKE A COMPASS WITH A LEAF AND A NEEDLE--
AND MY FAVORITE--HOW TO PERFORM A TRACHEOTOMY WITH A BALL-POINT PEN.
NO TOOLS FOR THIS, THOUGH.
THE SHIT I'M GOING THROUGH... NO TOOLS FOR IT.

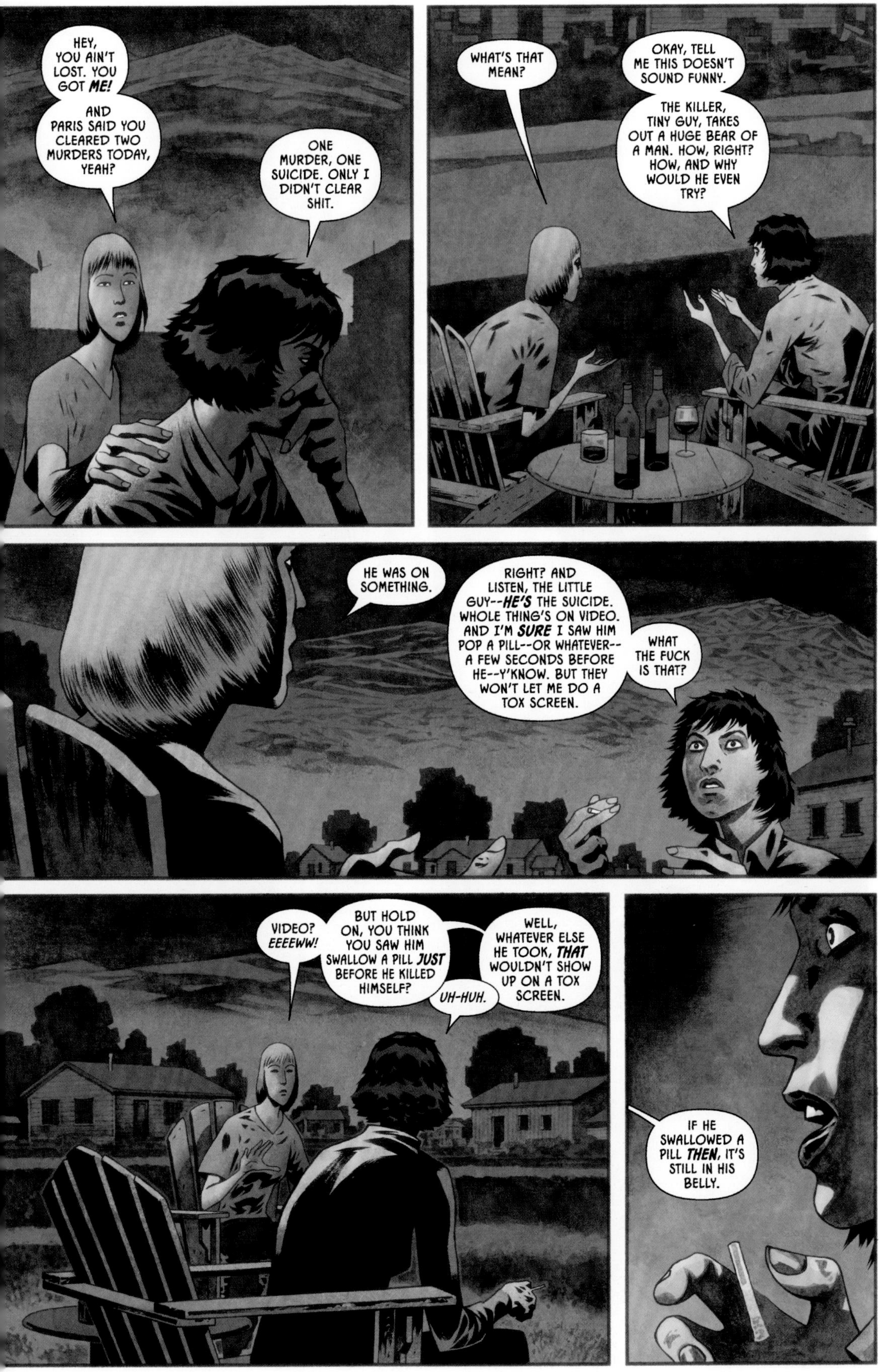
HEY, YOU AIN'T LOST. YOU GOT ME!
AND PARIS SAID YOU CLEARED TWO MURDERS TODAY, YEAH?
ONE MURDER, ONE SUICIDE. ONLY I DIDN'T CLEAR SHIT.
WHAT'S THAT MEAN?
OKAY, TELL ME THIS DOESN'T SOUND FUNNY.
THE KILLER, TINY GUY, TAKES OUT A HUGE BEAR OF A MAN. HOW, RIGHT? HOW, AND WHY WOULD HE EVEN TRY?
HE WAS ON SOMETHING.
RIGHT? AND LISTEN, THE LITTLE GUY--HE'S THE SUICIDE. WHOLE THING'S ON VIDEO. AND I'M SURE I SAW HIM POP A PILL--OR WHATEVER--A FEW SECONDS BEFORE HE--Y'KNOW. BUT THEY WON'T LET ME DO A TOX SCREEN.
WHAT THE FUCK IS THAT?
VIDEO? EEEEWW!
BUT HOLD ON, YOU THINK YOU SAW HIM SWALLOW A PILL JUST BEFORE HE KILLED HIMSELF?
UH-HUH.
WELL, WHATEVER ELSE HE TOOK, THAT WOULDN'T SHOW UP ON A TOX SCREEN.
IF HE SWALLOWED A PILL THEN, IT'S STILL IN HIS BELLY.

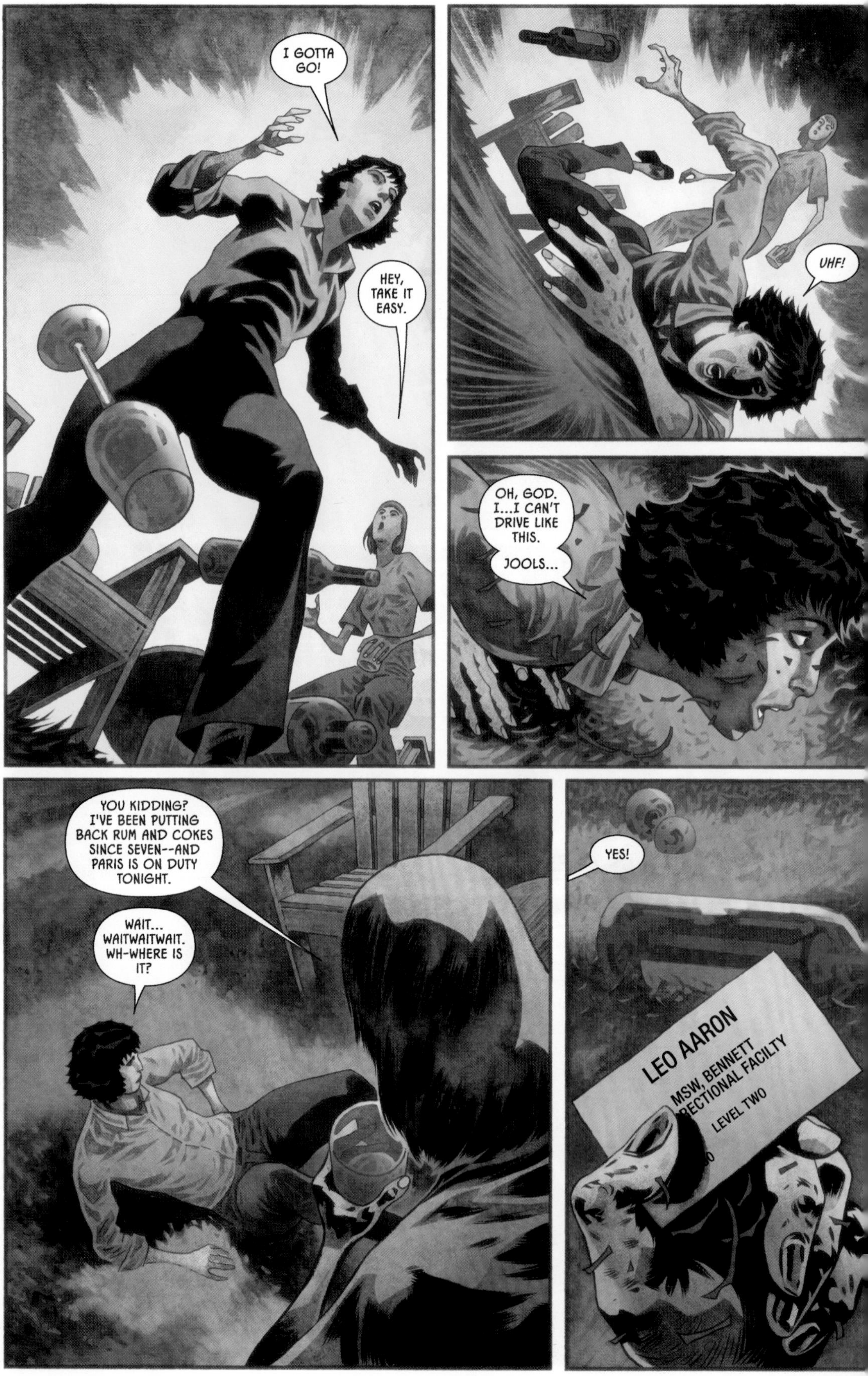
I GOTTA GO!
HEY, TAKE IT EASY.
UHF!
OH, GOD. I...I CAN'T DRIVE LIKE THIS.
JOOLS...
YOU KIDDING? I'VE BEEN PUTTING BACK RUM AND COKES SINCE SEVEN--AND PARIS IS ON DUTY TONIGHT.
WAIT... WAITWAITWAIT. WH-WHERE IS IT?
YES!
LEO AARON
MSW, BENNETT
RECTIONAL FACILTY
LEVEL TWO

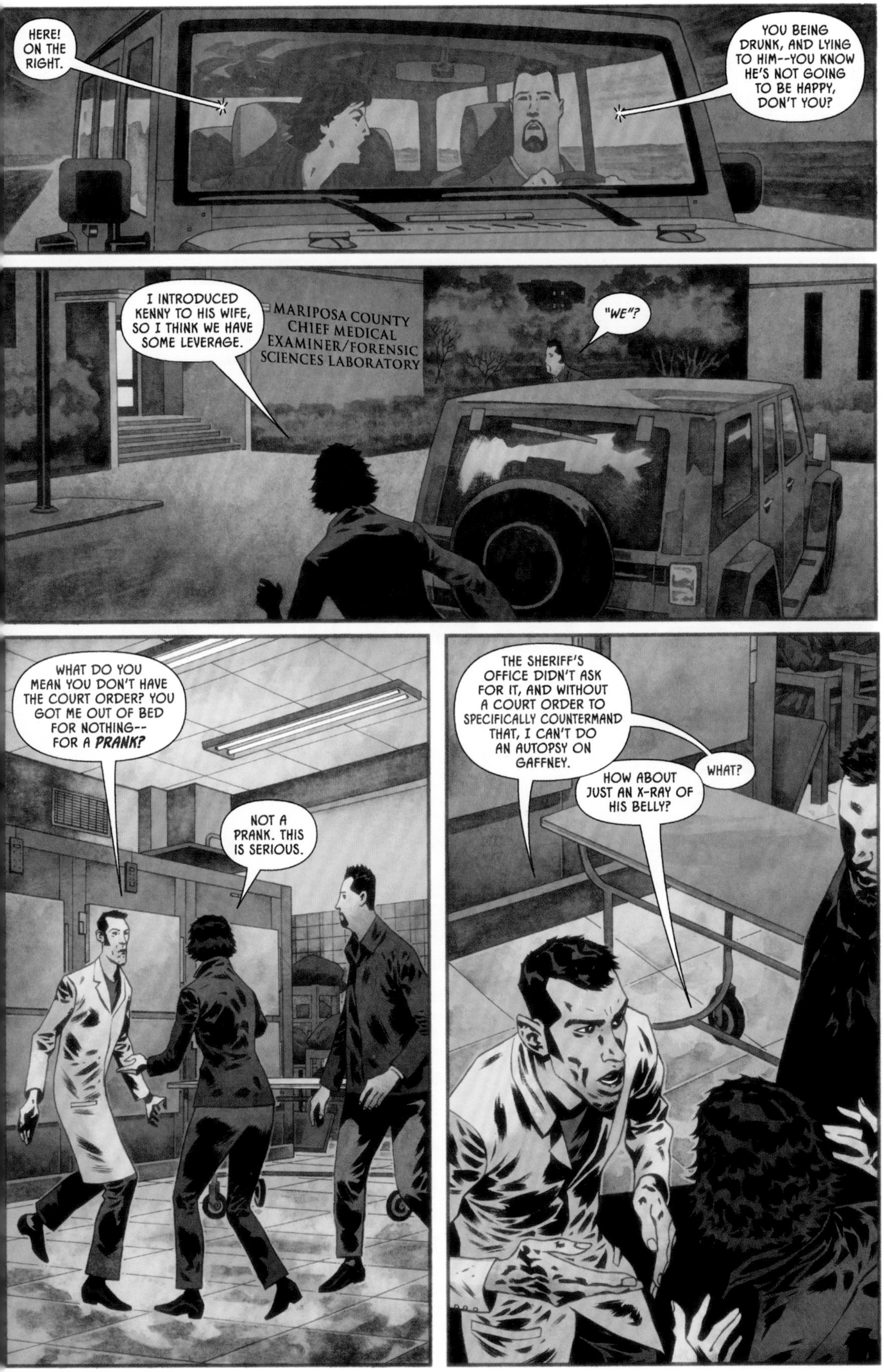
HERE! ON THE RIGHT.
YOU BEING DRUNK, AND LYING TO HIM--YOU KNOW HE'S NOT GOING TO BE HAPPY, DON'T YOU?
I INTRODUCED KENNY TO HIS WIFE, SO I THINK WE HAVE SOME LEVERAGE.
MARIPOSA COUNTY CHIEF MEDICAL EXAMINER/FORENSIC SCIENCES LABORATORY
"WE"?
WHAT DO YOU MEAN YOU DON'T HAVE THE COURT ORDER? YOU GOT ME OUT OF BED FOR NOTHING-- FOR A PRANK?
NOT A PRANK. THIS IS SERIOUS.
THE SHERIFF'S OFFICE DIDN'T ASK FOR IT, AND WITHOUT A COURT ORDER TO SPECIFICALLY COUNTERMAND THAT, I CAN'T DO AN AUTOPSY ON GAFFNEY.
HOW ABOUT JUST AN X-RAY OF HIS BELLY?
WHAT?

GAFFNEY SWALLOWED SOMETHING-- PRETTY SURE--RIGHT BEFORE HE HANGED HIMSELF. MEANS IT'S UNDIGESTED, RIGHT?

A TABLET, A CAPSULE, *MIGHT* SHOW UP ON FILM.

"MIGHT"? "PRETTY SURE"? FORGET IT!

KENNY, HOW'RE MARIE AND THE BOYS DOING? LUCKY TO HAVE MET HER, WEREN'T YOU?

AH, C'MON, LINDA! REALLY?

I LIKED YOU A LOT BETTER WHEN YOU WERE STILL A DEPUTY.

ME TOO, SWEETHEART.

SO HOW LONG DOES AN X-RAY TAKE? BECAUSE I'D LIKE TO GET *SOME* SLEEP TONIGHT.

I FORGOT TO SAY THANK YOU, DIDN'T I? SORRY, LEO. I OWE YOU.

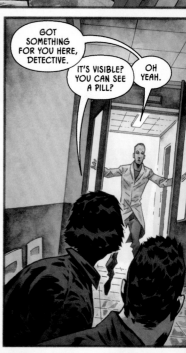

GOT SOMETHING FOR YOU HERE, DETECTIVE.

IT'S VISIBLE? YOU CAN SEE A PILL?

OH YEAH.

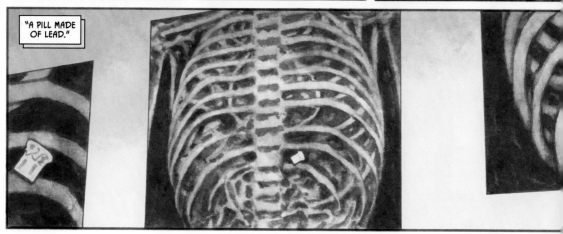

"A PILL MADE OF LEAD."

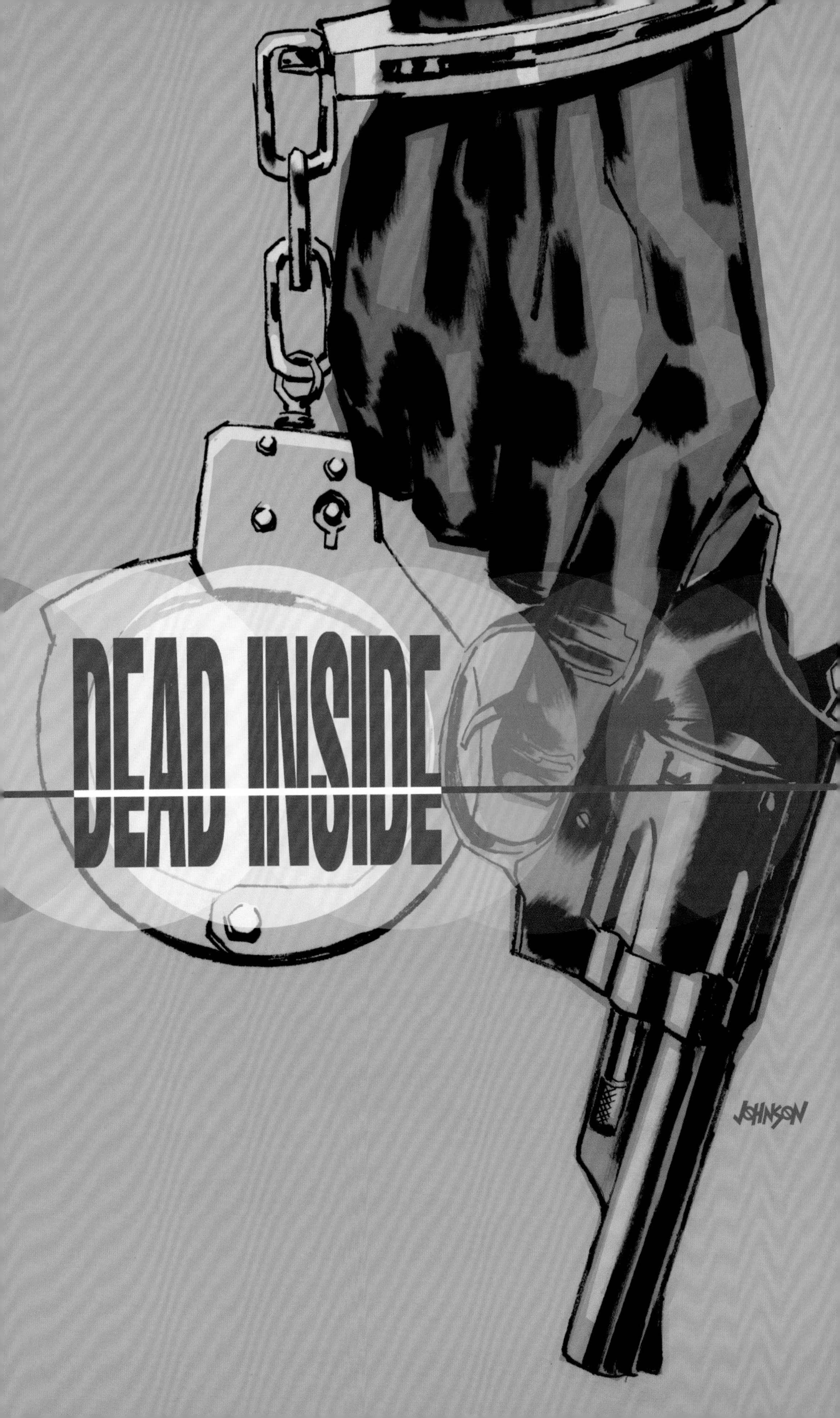
DEAD INSIDE
JOHNSON

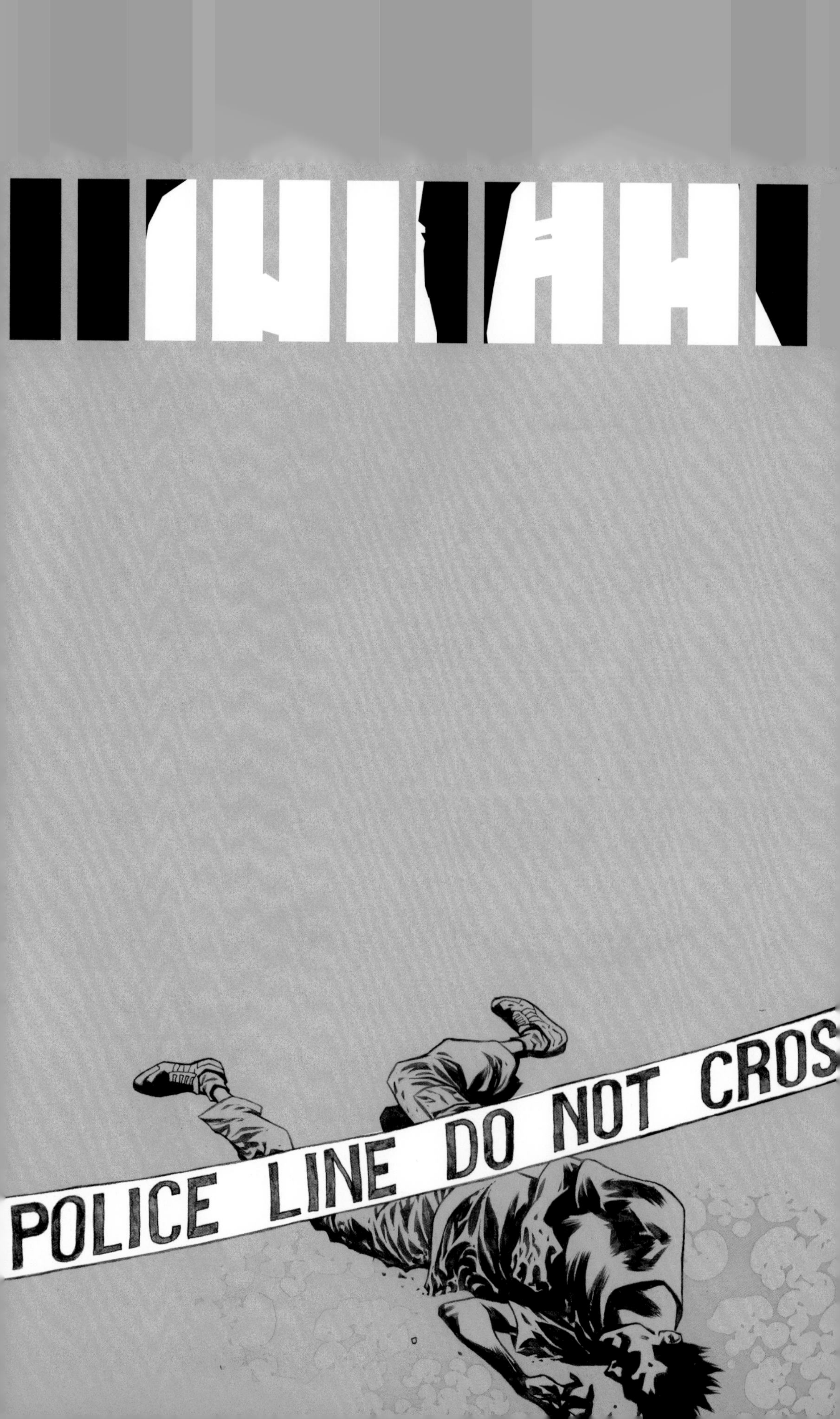
POLICE LINE DO NOT CROS

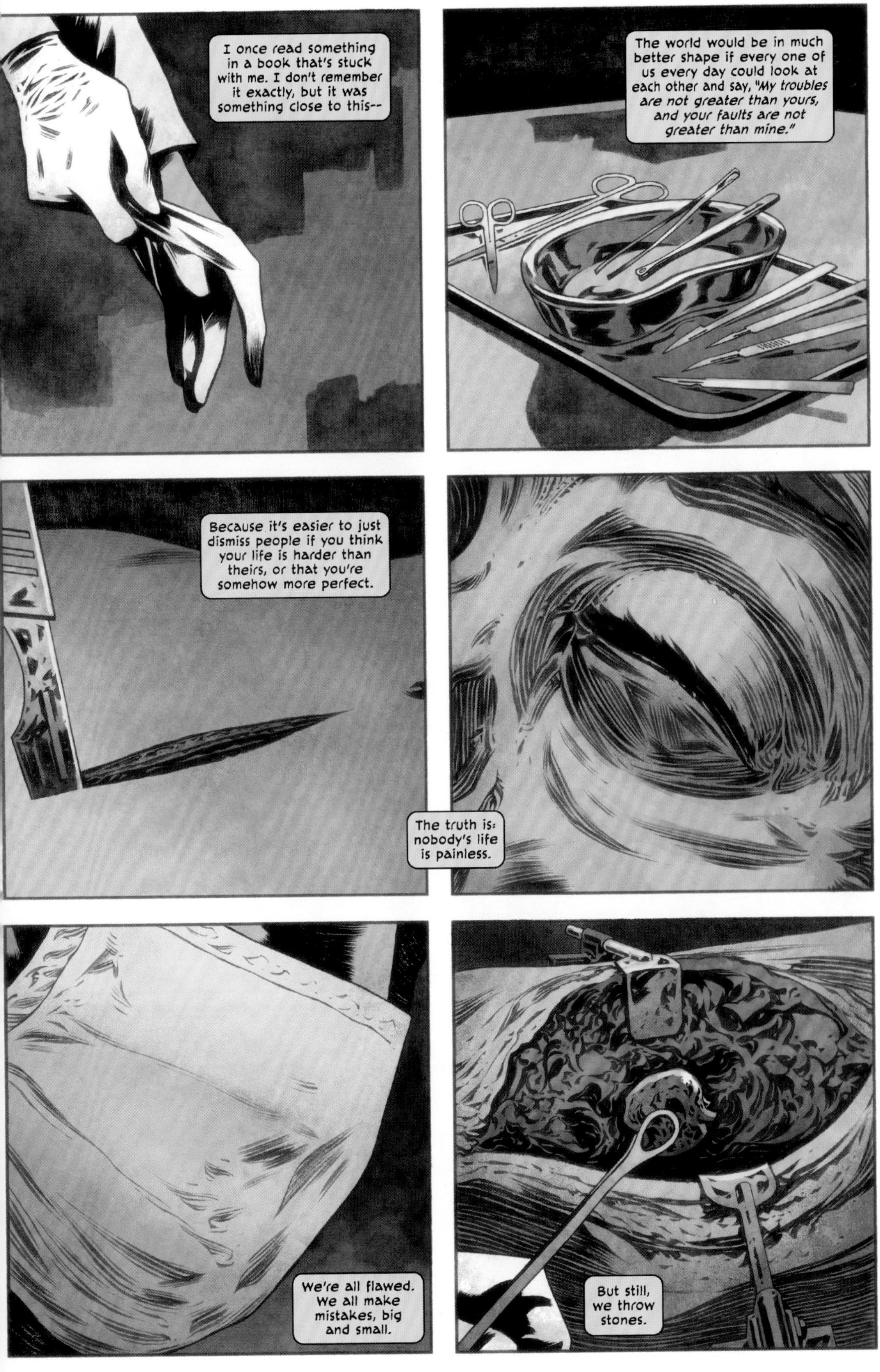
I once read something in a book that's stuck with me. I don't remember it exactly, but it was something close to this--
The world would be in much better shape if every one of us every day could look at each other and say, "My troubles are not greater than yours, and your faults are not greater than mine."
Because it's easier to just dismiss people if you think your life is harder than theirs, or that you're somehow more perfect.
The truth is: nobody's life is painless.
We're all flawed. We all make mistakes, big and small.
But still, we throw stones.

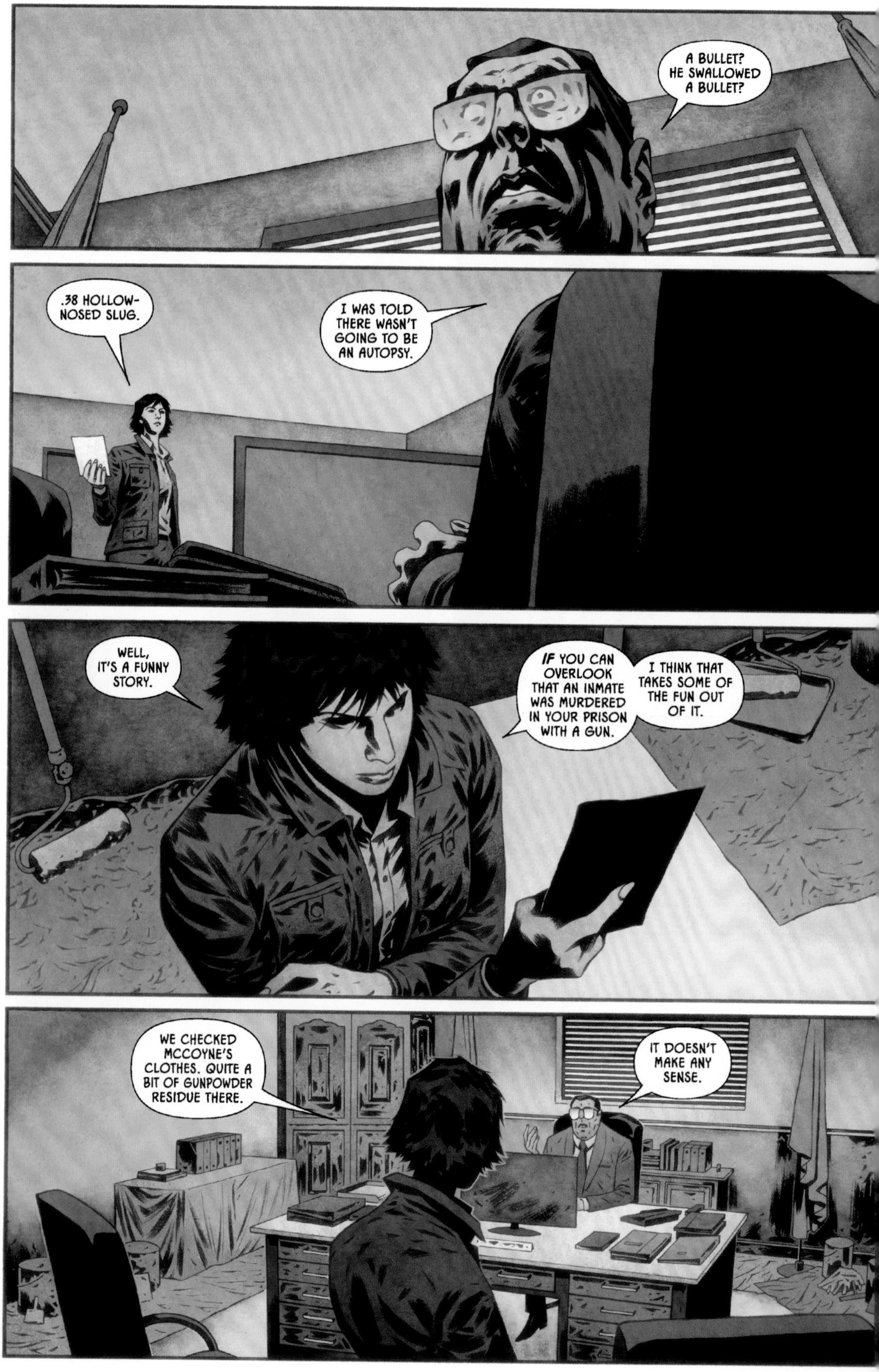
A BULLET? HE SWALLOWED A BULLET?
.38 HOLLOW-NOSED SLUG.
I WAS TOLD THERE WASN'T GOING TO BE AN AUTOPSY.
WELL, IT'S A FUNNY STORY.
IF YOU CAN OVERLOOK THAT AN INMATE WAS MURDERED IN YOUR PRISON WITH A GUN.
I THINK THAT TAKES SOME OF THE FUN OUT OF IT.
WE CHECKED MCCOYNE'S CLOTHES. QUITE A BIT OF GUNPOWDER RESIDUE THERE.
IT DOESN'T MAKE ANY SENSE.

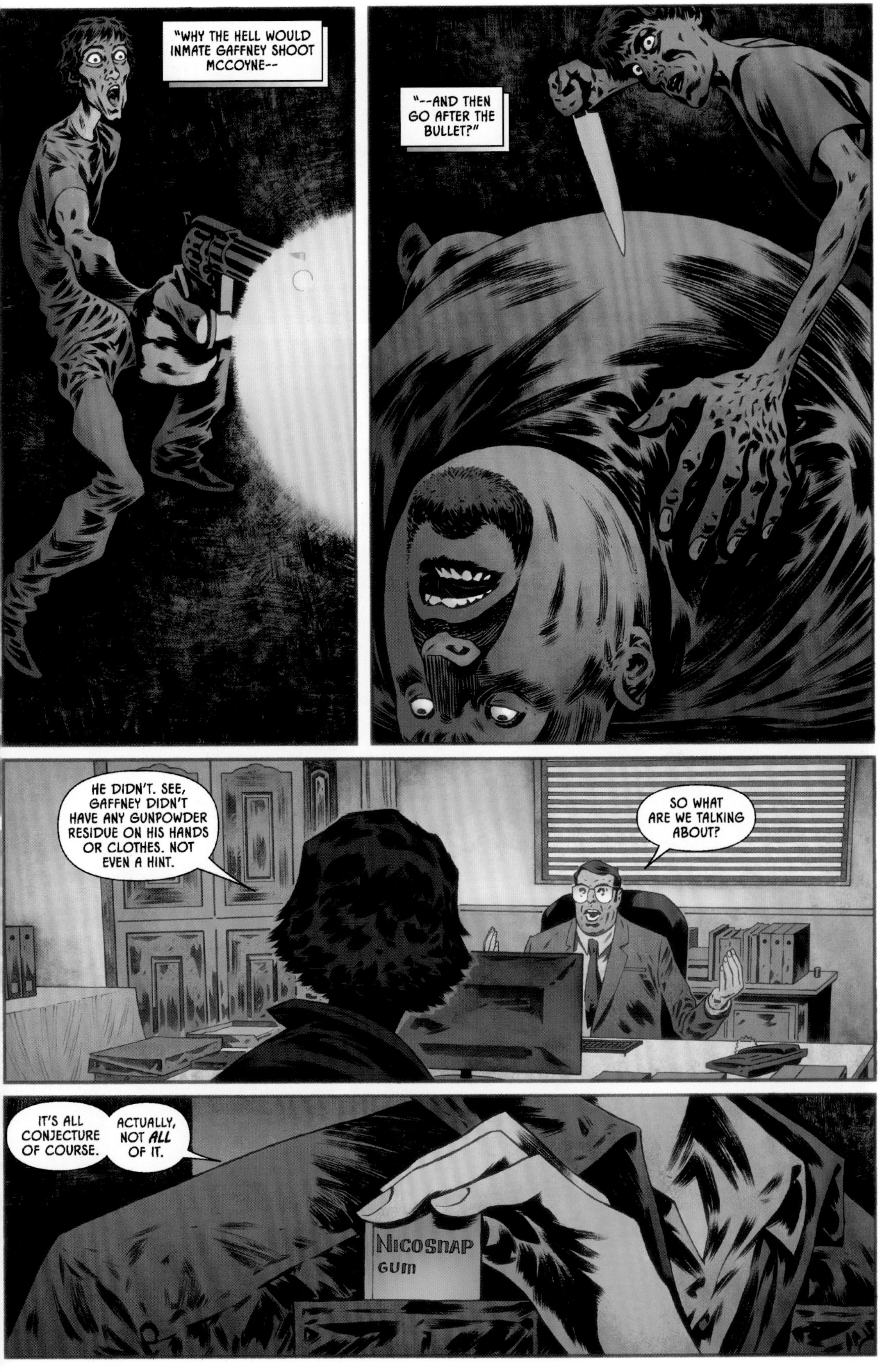
"WHY THE HELL WOULD INMATE GAFFNEY SHOOT MCCOYNE--
"--AND THEN GO AFTER THE BULLET?"
HE DIDN'T. SEE, GAFFNEY DIDN'T HAVE ANY GUNPOWDER RESIDUE ON HIS HANDS OR CLOTHES. NOT EVEN A HINT.
SO WHAT ARE WE TALKING ABOUT?
IT'S ALL CONJECTURE OF COURSE.
ACTUALLY, NOT ALL OF IT.
NicoSnap
GUM

"BECAUSE OBVIOUSLY, SOMEBODY *ELSE* SHOT MCCOYNE.

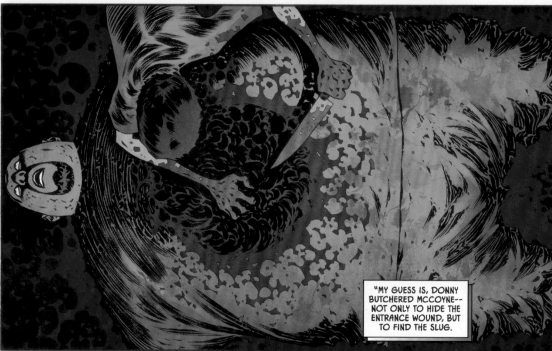

"MY GUESS IS, DONNY BUTCHERED MCCOYNE-- NOT ONLY TO HIDE THE ENTRANCE WOUND, BUT TO FIND THE SLUG.

"BECAUSE WHOEVER *DID* SHOOT MACK DIDN'T WANT ANYBODY TO KNOW A GUN HAD BEEN USED AT ALL."

AND DOWN THE BULLET WENT.

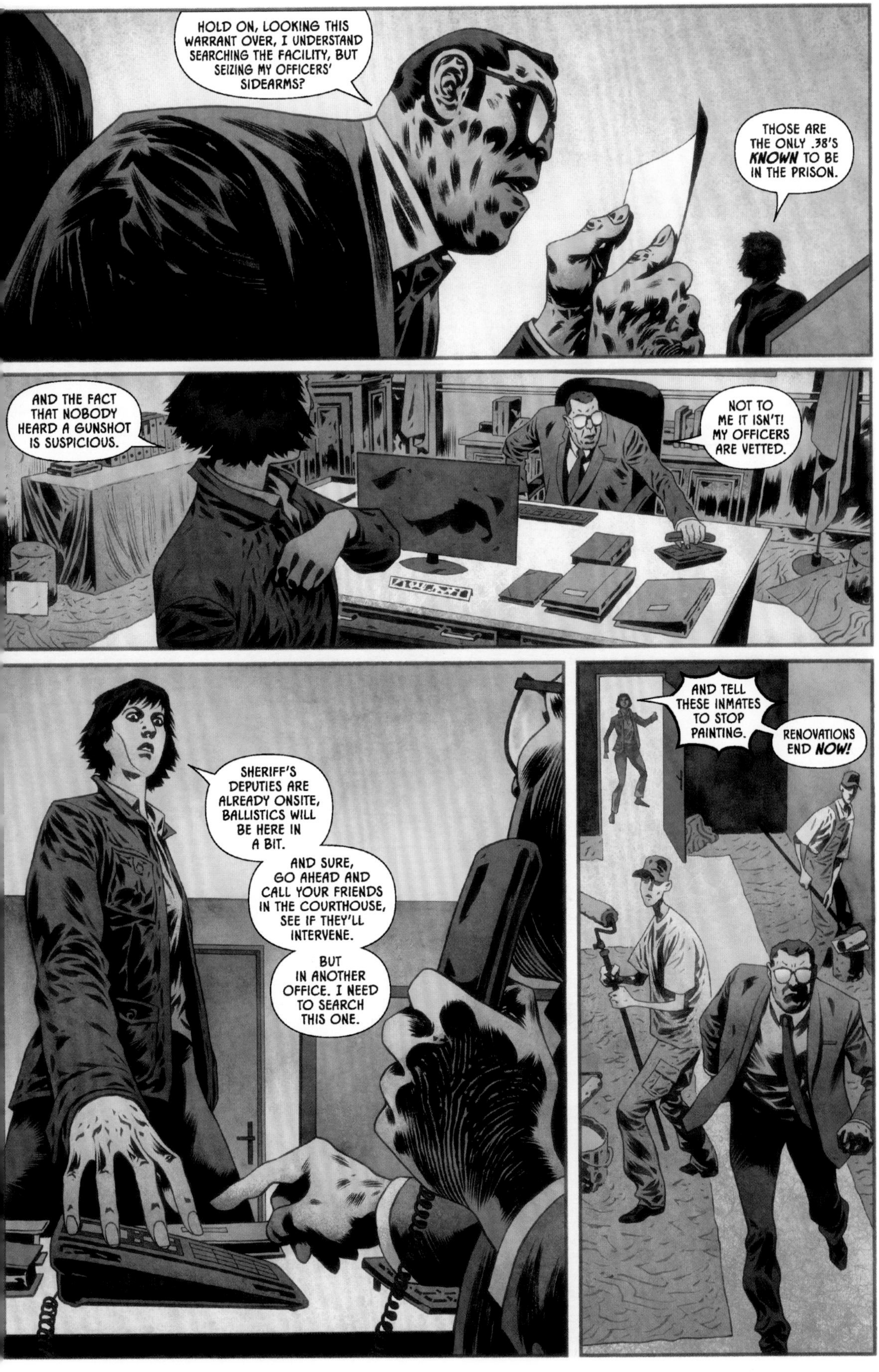
HOLD ON, LOOKING THIS WARRANT OVER, I UNDERSTAND SEARCHING THE FACILITY, BUT SEIZING MY OFFICERS' SIDEARMS?
THOSE ARE THE ONLY .38'S ***KNOWN*** TO BE IN THE PRISON.
AND THE FACT THAT NOBODY HEARD A GUNSHOT IS SUSPICIOUS.
NOT TO ME IT ISN'T! MY OFFICERS ARE VETTED.
SHERIFF'S DEPUTIES ARE ALREADY ONSITE, BALLISTICS WILL BE HERE IN A BIT.
AND SURE, GO AHEAD AND CALL YOUR FRIENDS IN THE COURTHOUSE, SEE IF THEY'LL INTERVENE.
BUT IN ANOTHER OFFICE. I NEED TO SEARCH THIS ONE.
AND TELL THESE INMATES TO STOP PAINTING.
RENOVATIONS END ***NOW!***

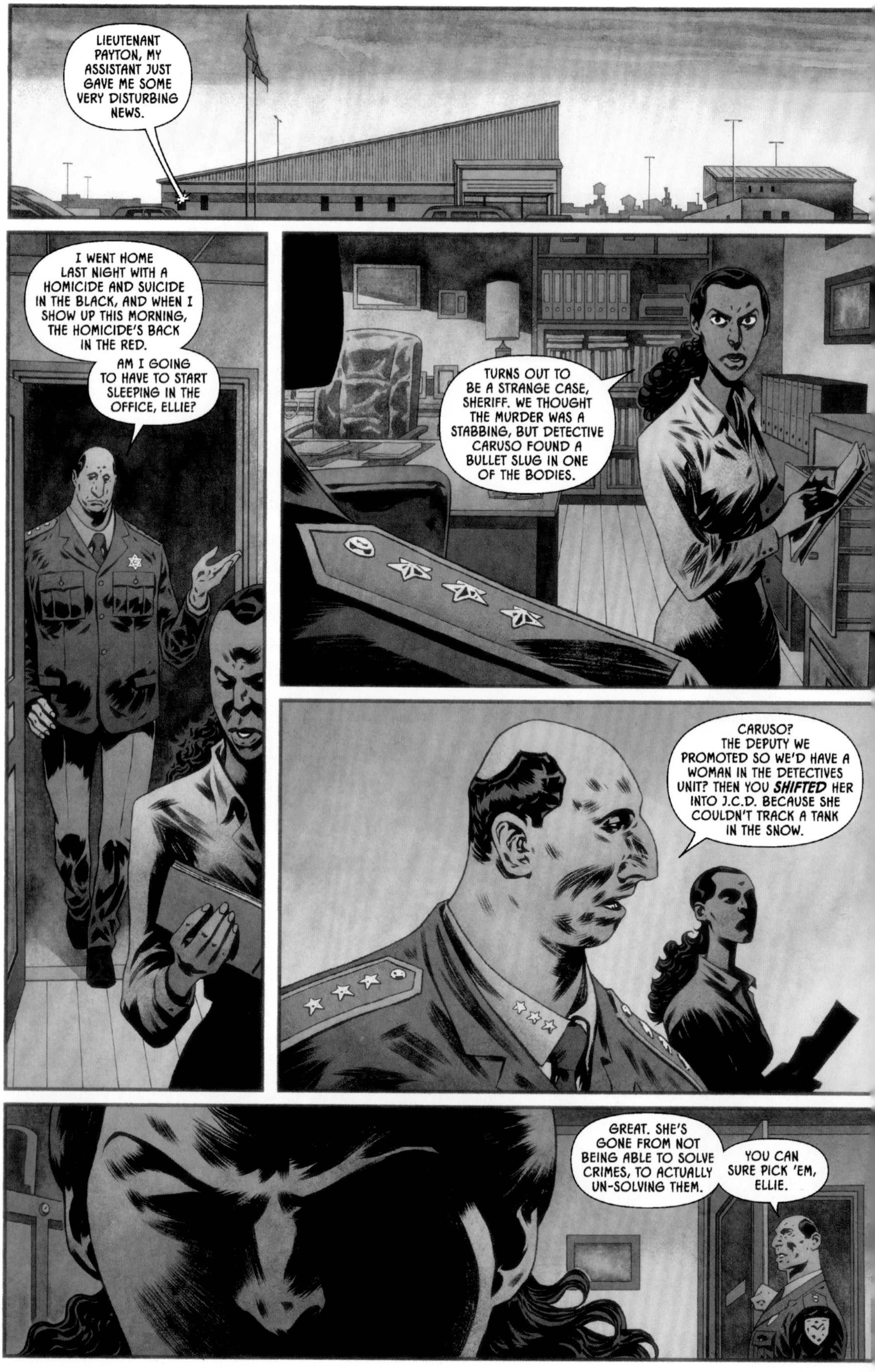
LIEUTENANT PAYTON, MY ASSISTANT JUST GAVE ME SOME VERY DISTURBING NEWS.
I WENT HOME LAST NIGHT WITH A HOMICIDE AND SUICIDE IN THE BLACK, AND WHEN I SHOW UP THIS MORNING, THE HOMICIDE'S BACK IN THE RED.
AM I GOING TO HAVE TO START SLEEPING IN THE OFFICE, ELLIE?
TURNS OUT TO BE A STRANGE CASE, SHERIFF. WE THOUGHT THE MURDER WAS A STABBING, BUT DETECTIVE CARUSO FOUND A BULLET SLUG IN ONE OF THE BODIES.
CARUSO? THE DEPUTY WE PROMOTED SO WE'D HAVE A WOMAN IN THE DETECTIVES UNIT? THEN YOU ***SHIFTED*** HER INTO J.C.D. BECAUSE SHE COULDN'T TRACK A TANK IN THE SNOW.
GREAT. SHE'S GONE FROM NOT BEING ABLE TO SOLVE CRIMES, TO ACTUALLY UN-SOLVING THEM.
YOU CAN SURE PICK 'EM, ELLIE.

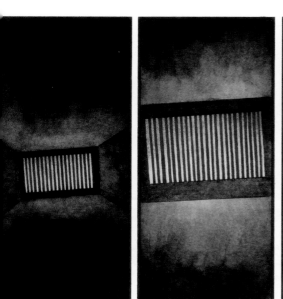

WHEW! THIS IS WORSE THAN WHEN WE SERVED ON THAT HOUSE FULL OF CHICKENS.

HOW THE HELL DO THE INMATES EAT IN HERE WITH ALL THESE PAINT FUMES?

'CAUSE THEY AIN'T A BUNCH OF PUSSIES--LIKE SOME DEPUTIES I KNOW.

SPEAK UP, KEILOR. TELL US HOW YOU REALLY FEEL.

UHH, I DIDN'T KNOW YOU WERE HERE, DETECTIVE. SORRY.

SORRY FOR WHAT? DIAZ? BECAUSE HE *IS* A PUSSY.

OH, *REAL* NICE, CARUSO!

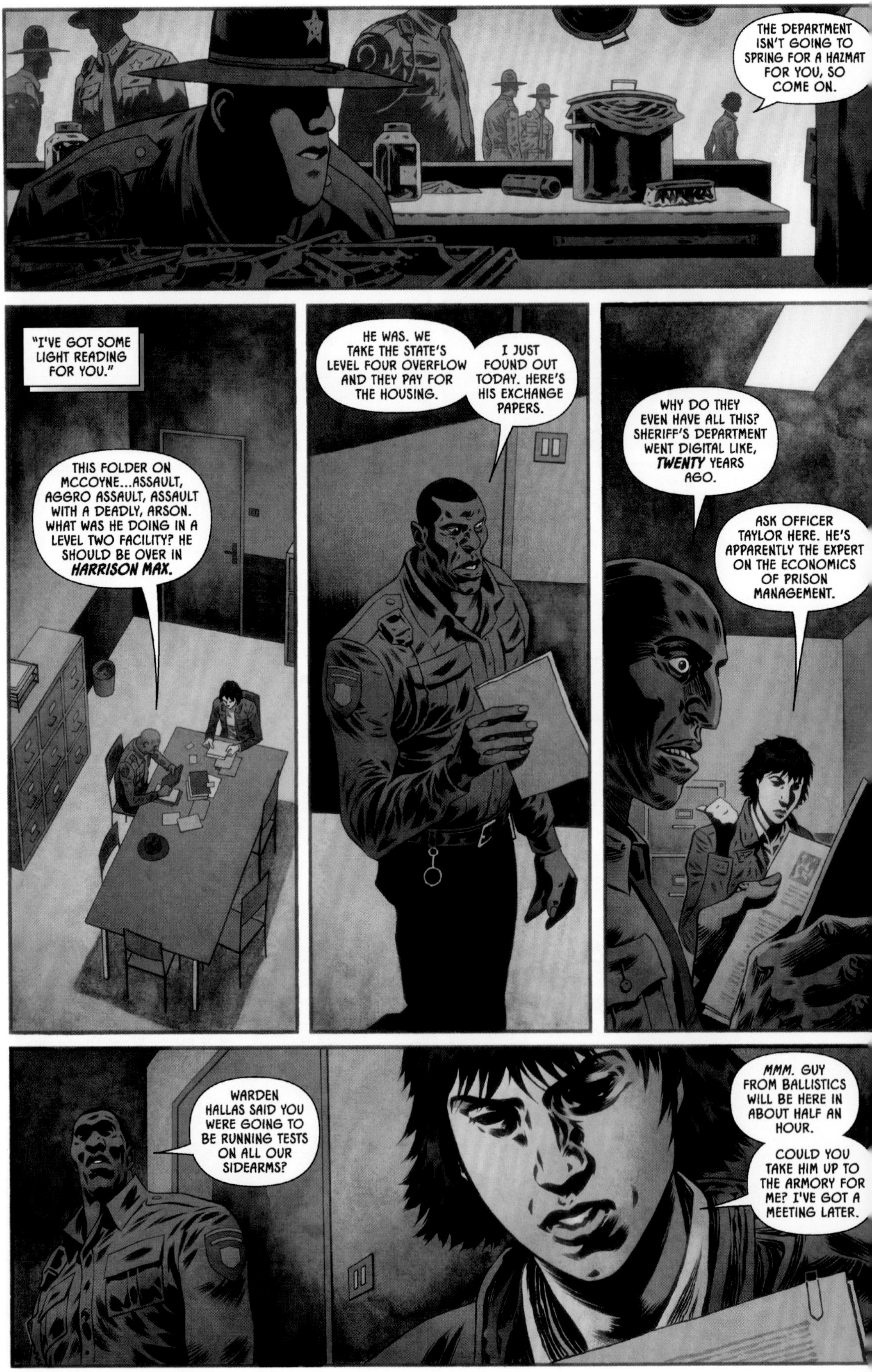
THE DEPARTMENT ISN'T GOING TO SPRING FOR A HAZMAT FOR YOU, SO COME ON.
"I'VE GOT SOME LIGHT READING FOR YOU."
THIS FOLDER ON MCCOYNE...ASSAULT, AGGRO ASSAULT, ASSAULT WITH A DEADLY, ARSON. WHAT WAS HE DOING IN A LEVEL TWO FACILITY? HE SHOULD BE OVER IN *HARRISON MAX.*
HE WAS. WE TAKE THE STATE'S LEVEL FOUR OVERFLOW AND THEY PAY FOR THE HOUSING.
I JUST FOUND OUT TODAY. HERE'S HIS EXCHANGE PAPERS.
WHY DO THEY EVEN HAVE ALL THIS? SHERIFF'S DEPARTMENT WENT DIGITAL LIKE, *TWENTY* YEARS AGO.
ASK OFFICER TAYLOR HERE. HE'S APPARENTLY THE EXPERT ON THE ECONOMICS OF PRISON MANAGEMENT.
WARDEN HALLAS SAID YOU WERE GOING TO BE RUNNING TESTS ON ALL OUR SIDEARMS?
MMM. GUY FROM BALLISTICS WILL BE HERE IN ABOUT HALF AN HOUR.
COULD YOU TAKE HIM UP TO THE ARMORY FOR ME? I'VE GOT A MEETING LATER.

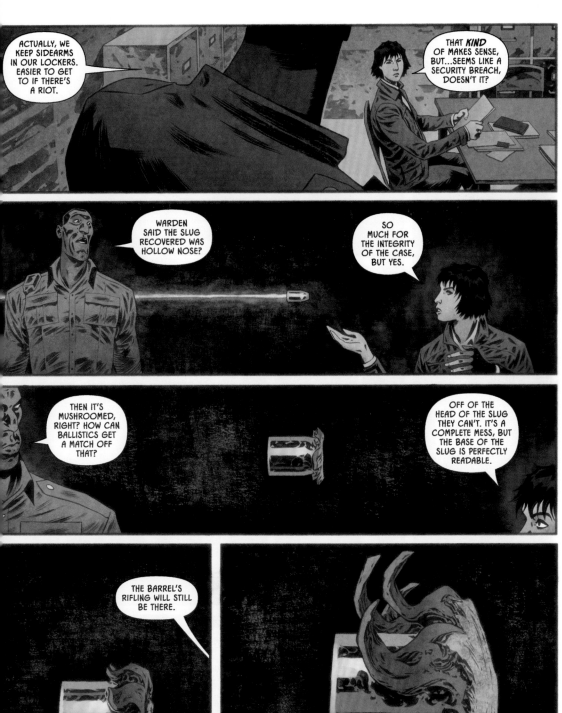

ACTUALLY, WE KEEP SIDEARMS IN OUR LOCKERS. EASIER TO GET TO IF THERE'S A RIOT.

THAT *KIND* OF MAKES SENSE, BUT...SEEMS LIKE A SECURITY BREACH, DOESN'T IT?

WARDEN SAID THE SLUG RECOVERED WAS HOLLOW NOSE?

SO MUCH FOR THE INTEGRITY OF THE CASE, BUT YES.

THEN IT'S MUSHROOMED, RIGHT? HOW CAN BALLISTICS GET A MATCH OFF THAT?

OFF OF THE HEAD OF THE SLUG THEY CAN'T. IT'S A COMPLETE MESS, BUT THE BASE OF THE SLUG IS PERFECTLY READABLE.

THE BARREL'S RIFLING WILL STILL BE THERE.

OUR GUY SAYS MAKING A MATCH WON'T BE HARD AT ALL.

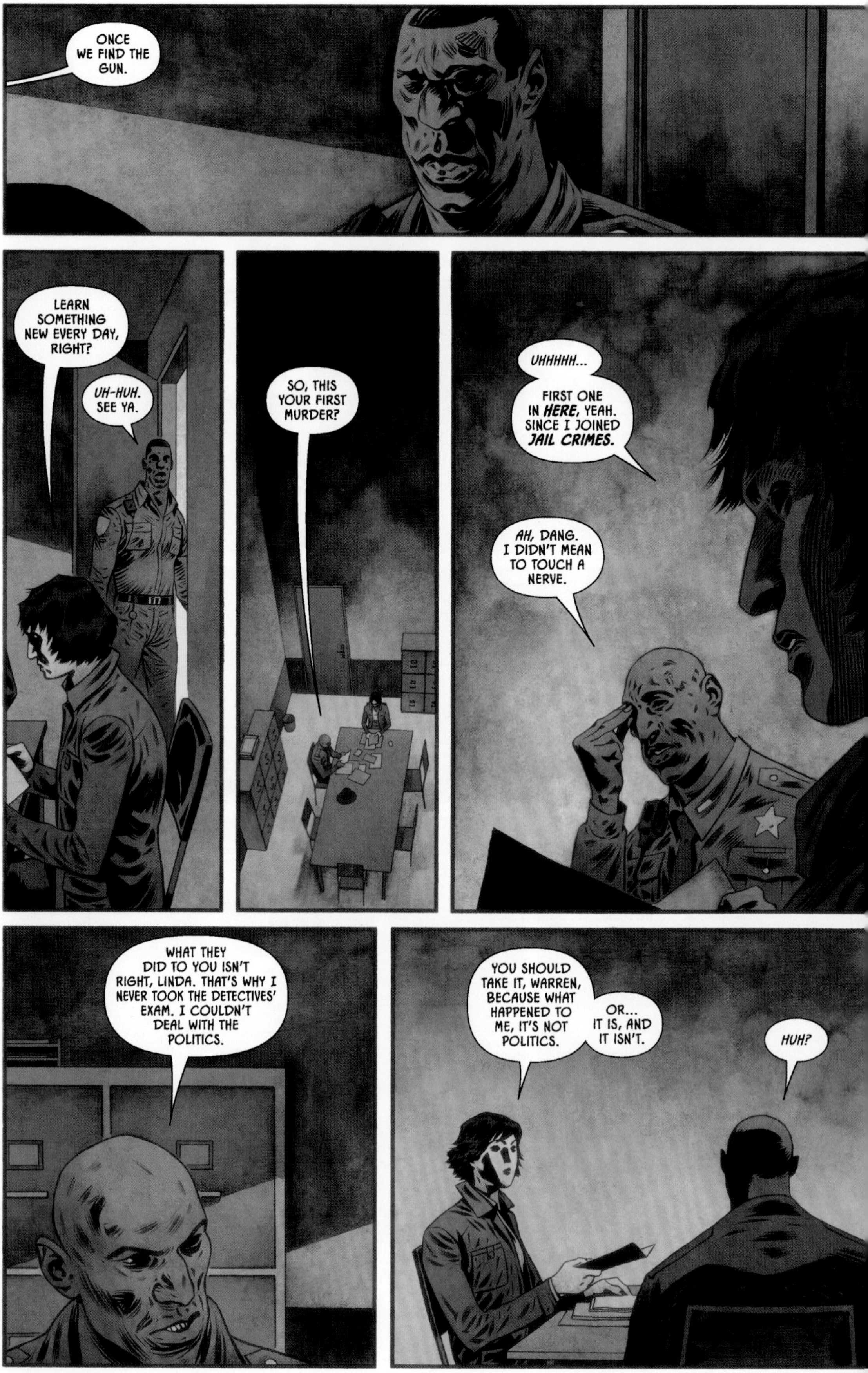
ONCE WE FIND THE GUN.
LEARN SOMETHING NEW EVERY DAY, RIGHT?
UH-HUH. SEE YA.
SO, THIS YOUR FIRST MURDER?
UHHHHH...
FIRST ONE IN HERE, YEAH. SINCE I JOINED JAIL CRIMES.
AH, DANG. I DIDN'T MEAN TO TOUCH A NERVE.
WHAT THEY DID TO YOU ISN'T RIGHT, LINDA. THAT'S WHY I NEVER TOOK THE DETECTIVES' EXAM. I COULDN'T DEAL WITH THE POLITICS.
YOU SHOULD TAKE IT, WARREN, BECAUSE WHAT HAPPENED TO ME, IT'S NOT POLITICS.
OR... IT IS, AND IT ISN'T.
HUH?

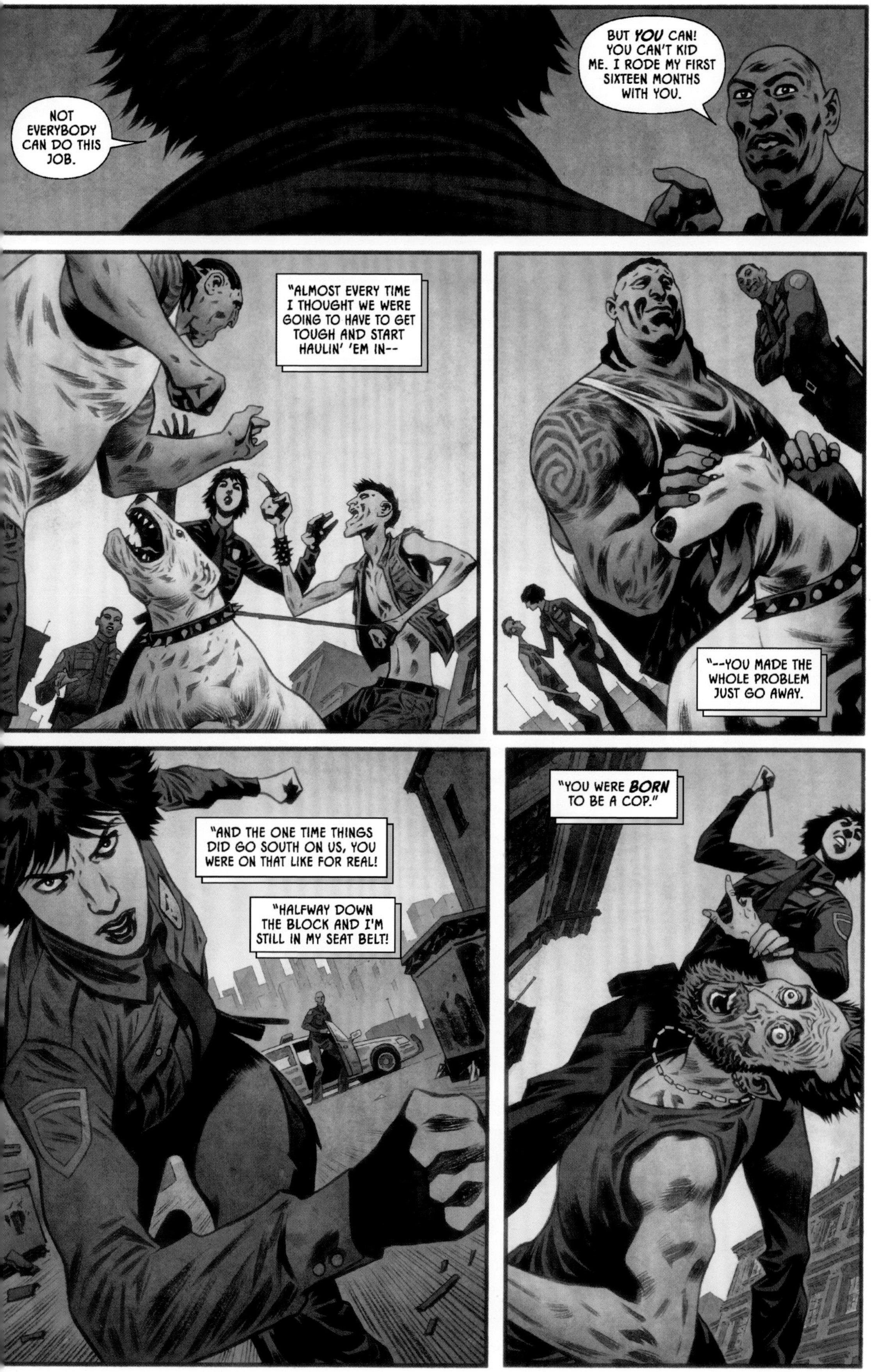
NOT EVERYBODY CAN DO THIS JOB.
BUT YOU CAN! YOU CAN'T KID ME. I RODE MY FIRST SIXTEEN MONTHS WITH YOU.
"ALMOST EVERY TIME I THOUGHT WE WERE GOING TO HAVE TO GET TOUGH AND START HAULIN' 'EM IN--
"--YOU MADE THE WHOLE PROBLEM JUST GO AWAY.
"AND THE ONE TIME THINGS DID GO SOUTH ON US, YOU WERE ON THAT LIKE FOR REAL!
"HALFWAY DOWN THE BLOCK AND I'M STILL IN MY SEAT BELT!
"YOU WERE BORN TO BE A COP."

LOOK, THINK ABOUT EVERYTHING YOU JUST SAID. SURE, I DEFUSED SOME TENSE SITUATIONS.

I LIKE PEOPLE. TALKING TO THEM IS EASY FOR ME. STOPPING CRIMES FROM HAPPENING IS WHAT DEPUTIES DO.

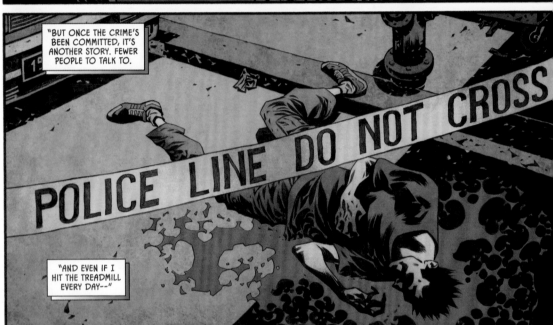

"BUT ONCE THE CRIME'S BEEN COMMITTED, IT'S ANOTHER STORY. FEWER PEOPLE TO TALK TO."

POLICE LINE DO NOT CROSS

"AND EVEN IF I HIT THE TREADMILL EVERY DAY--"

NOBODY CAN RUN FAST ENOUGH TO CHANGE THE PAST.

THEN THERE'S SO MUCH MORE TO BEING A DETECTIVE THAT'S...ANTIHUMAN, Y'KNOW?

LIKE THE "PAPER TRAIL." HOURS OF GOING THROUGH DATES, ADDRESSES, BANK ACCOUNTS. CHRIST, I HATED THAT.

HOLD ON... PAPER...?

THAT WHY YOU BROUGHT ME IN HERE?

SEE? YOU'LL MAKE IT TO DETECTIVE YET, WARREN.

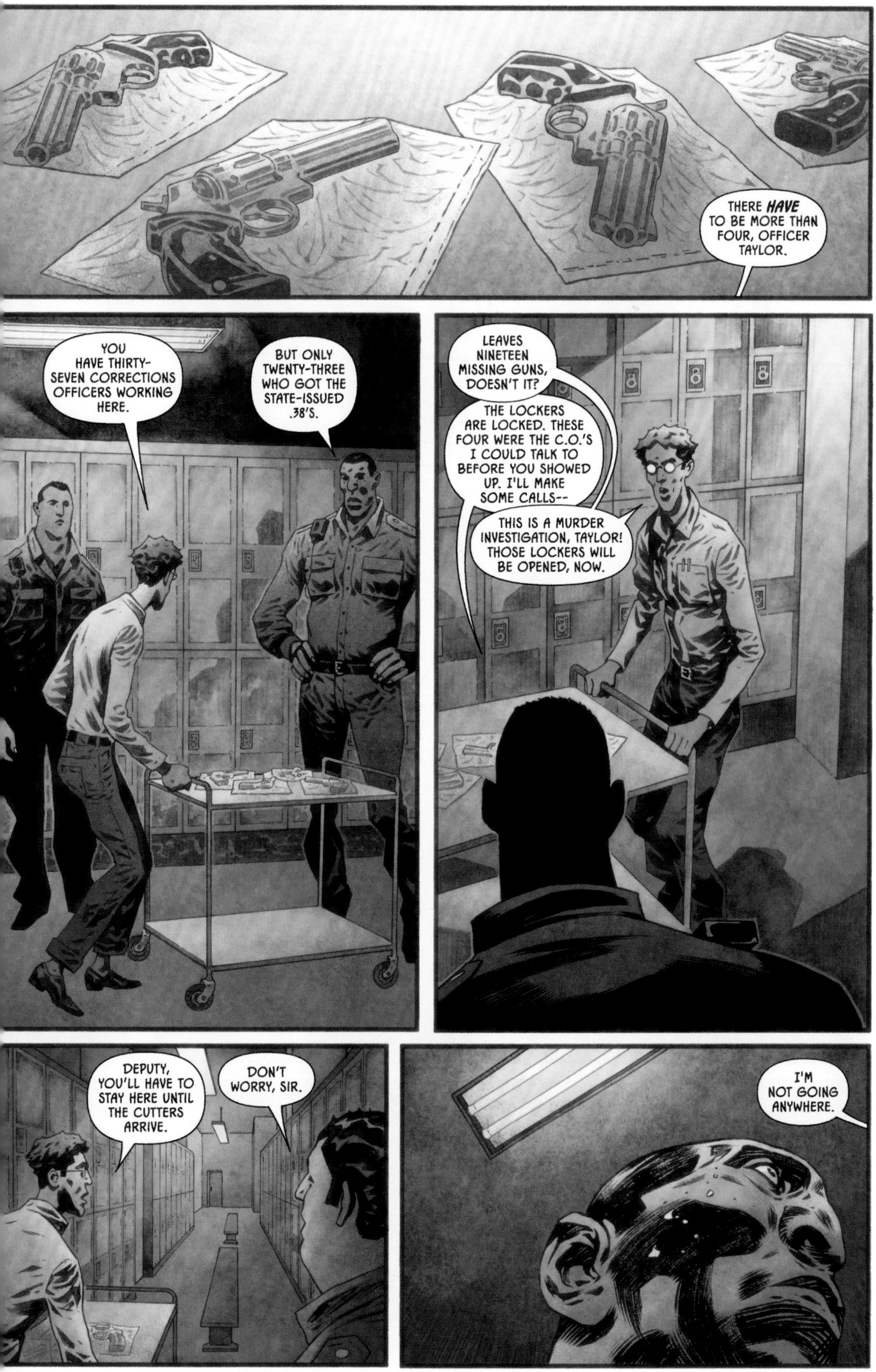
THERE HAVE TO BE MORE THAN FOUR, OFFICER TAYLOR.
YOU HAVE THIRTY-SEVEN CORRECTIONS OFFICERS WORKING HERE.
BUT ONLY TWENTY-THREE WHO GOT THE STATE-ISSUED .38'S.
LEAVES NINETEEN MISSING GUNS, DOESN'T IT?
THE LOCKERS ARE LOCKED. THESE FOUR WERE THE C.O.'S I COULD TALK TO BEFORE YOU SHOWED UP. I'LL MAKE SOME CALLS--
THIS IS A MURDER INVESTIGATION, TAYLOR! THOSE LOCKERS WILL BE OPENED, NOW.
DEPUTY, YOU'LL HAVE TO STAY HERE UNTIL THE CUTTERS ARRIVE.
DON'T WORRY, SIR.
I'M NOT GOING ANYWHERE.

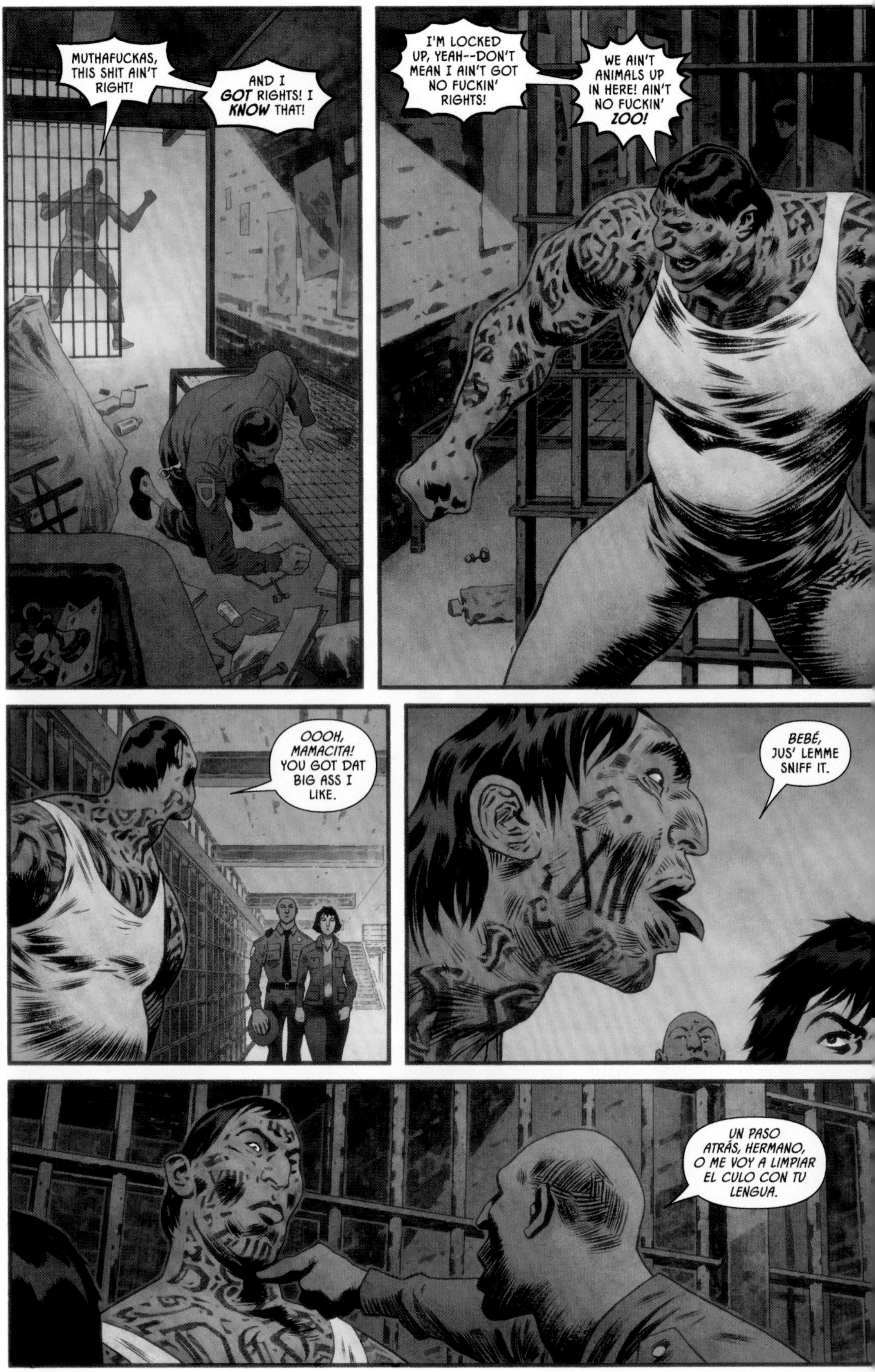
MUTHAFUCKAS, THIS SHIT AIN'T RIGHT!
AND I GOT RIGHTS! I KNOW THAT!
I'M LOCKED UP, YEAH--DON'T MEAN I AIN'T GOT NO FUCKIN' RIGHTS!
WE AIN'T ANIMALS UP IN HERE! AIN'T NO FUCKIN' ZOO!
OOOH, MAMACITA! YOU GOT DAT BIG ASS I LIKE.
BEBÉ, JUS' LEMME SNIFF IT.
UN PASO ATRÁS, HERMANO, O ME VOY A LIMPIAR EL CULO CON TU LENGUA.

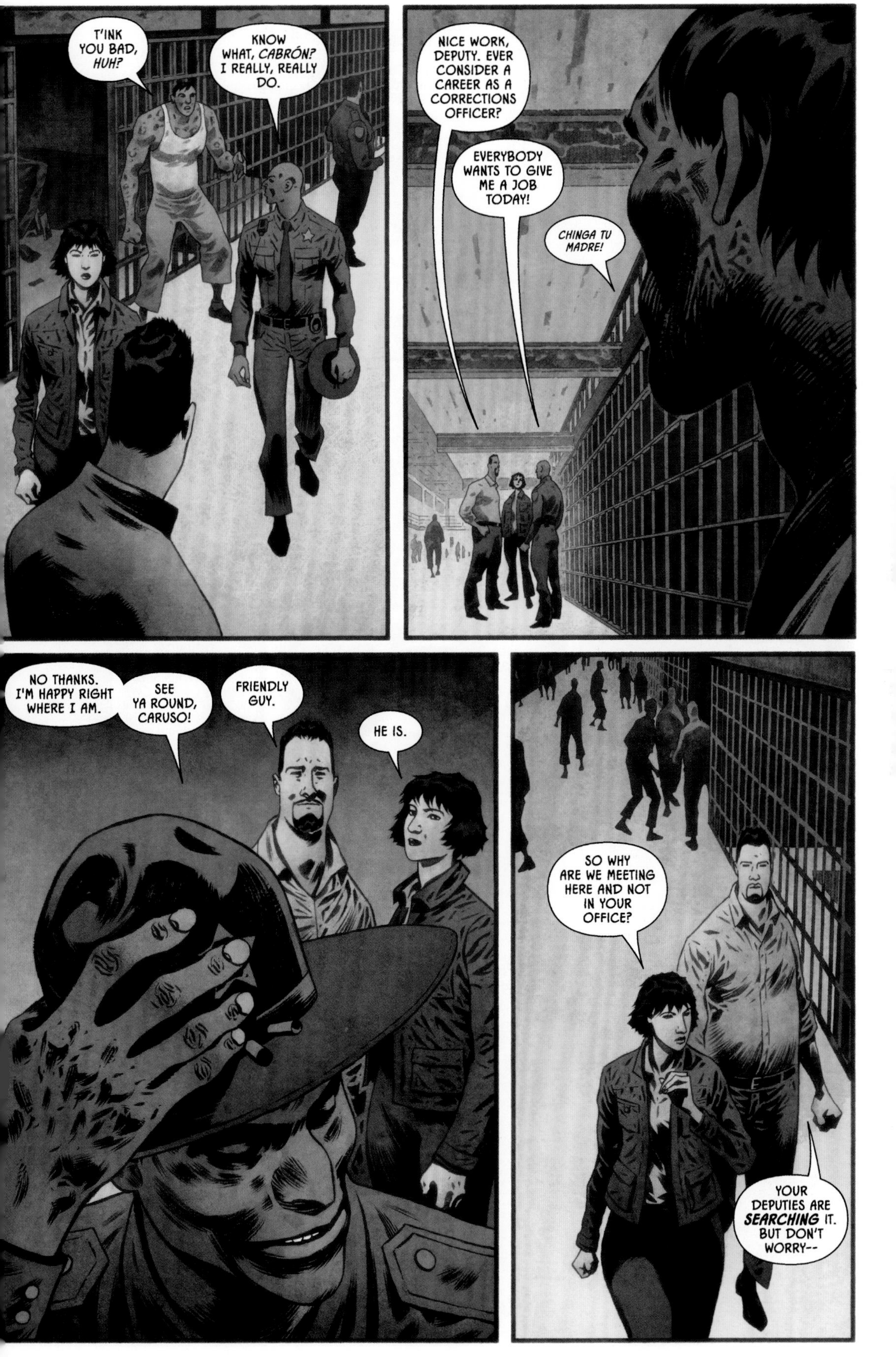
T'INK YOU BAD, *HUH?*
KNOW WHAT, *CABRÓN?* I REALLY, REALLY DO.
NICE WORK, DEPUTY. EVER CONSIDER A CAREER AS A CORRECTIONS OFFICER?
EVERYBODY WANTS TO GIVE ME A JOB TODAY!
CHINGA TU MADRE!
NO THANKS. I'M HAPPY RIGHT WHERE I AM.
SEE YA ROUND, CARUSO!
FRIENDLY GUY.
HE IS.
SO WHY ARE WE MEETING HERE AND NOT IN YOUR OFFICE?
YOUR DEPUTIES ARE ***SEARCHING*** IT. BUT DON'T WORRY--

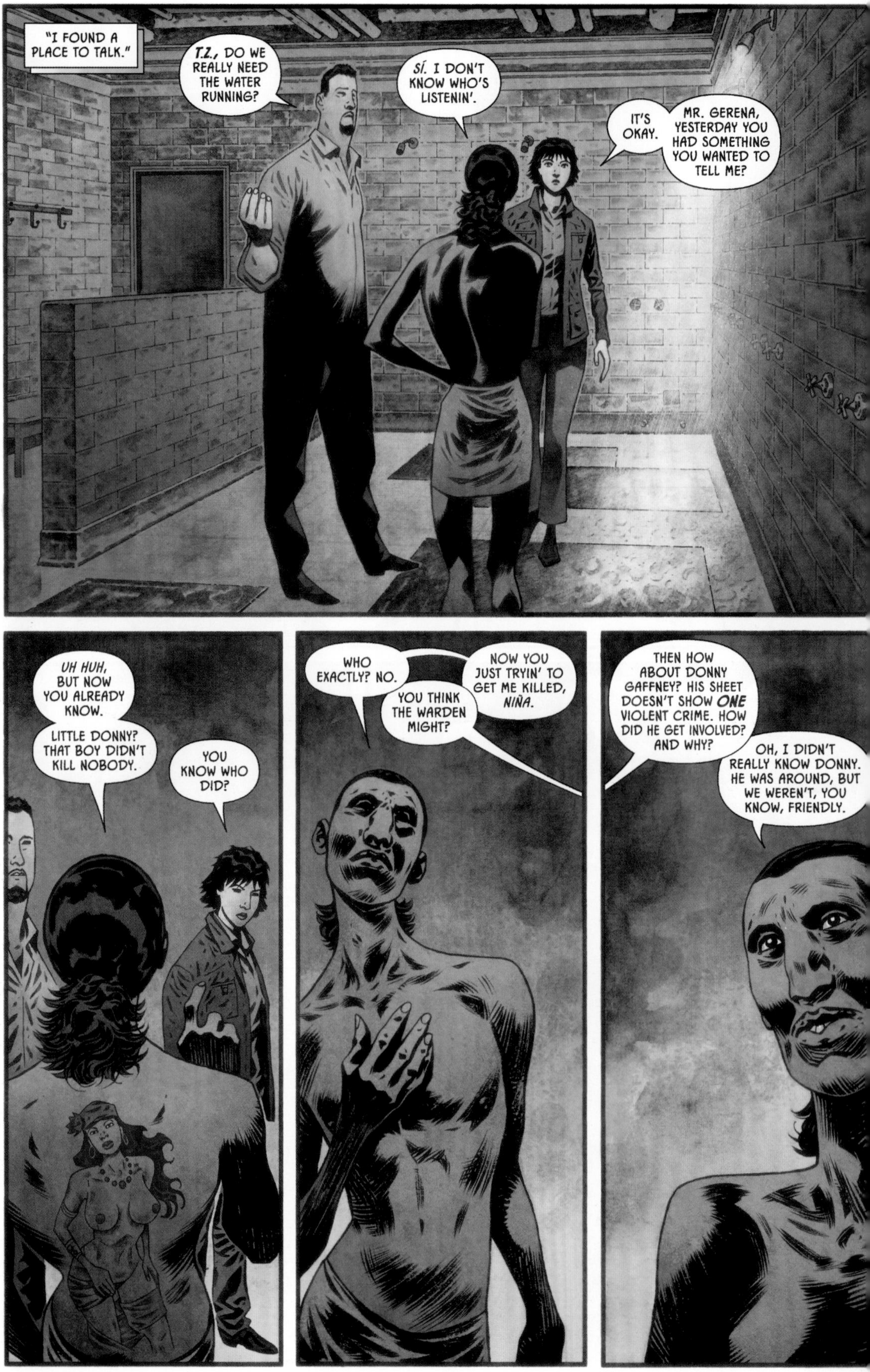
"I FOUND A PLACE TO TALK."
T.Z., DO WE REALLY NEED THE WATER RUNNING?
SÍ. I DON'T KNOW WHO'S LISTENIN'.
IT'S OKAY.
MR. GERENA, YESTERDAY YOU HAD SOMETHING YOU WANTED TO TELL ME?
UH HUH, BUT NOW YOU ALREADY KNOW.
LITTLE DONNY? THAT BOY DIDN'T KILL NOBODY.
YOU KNOW WHO DID?
WHO EXACTLY? NO.
NOW YOU JUST TRYIN' TO GET ME KILLED, NIÑA.
YOU THINK THE WARDEN MIGHT?
THEN HOW ABOUT DONNY GAFFNEY? HIS SHEET DOESN'T SHOW ONE VIOLENT CRIME. HOW DID HE GET INVOLVED? AND WHY?
OH, I DIDN'T REALLY KNOW DONNY. HE WAS AROUND, BUT WE WEREN'T, YOU KNOW, FRIENDLY.

DOESN'T SEEM LIKE *ANYBODY* KNEW HIM.

I COULDN'T EVEN FIND NEXT OF KIN IN HIS FILE.

WHAT? OH, I DON'T THINK THAT'S RIGHT.

BIG MACK, I KNEW. *EVERYBODY* KNEW GORDO.

"SOON AS HE ROLL IN, HE TAKE ALL THAT *CHIVA* AND *MUJER* HUSTLE.

"AND GIRL, I DON'T MEAN JUST PAPERS, UNNERSTAN'? *PAPI* MOVE WEIGHT!

"RUN THIS WHOLE PRISON.

"SEE, HE DIDN'T NEED TO HIRE OUT FOR HIS MUSCLE.

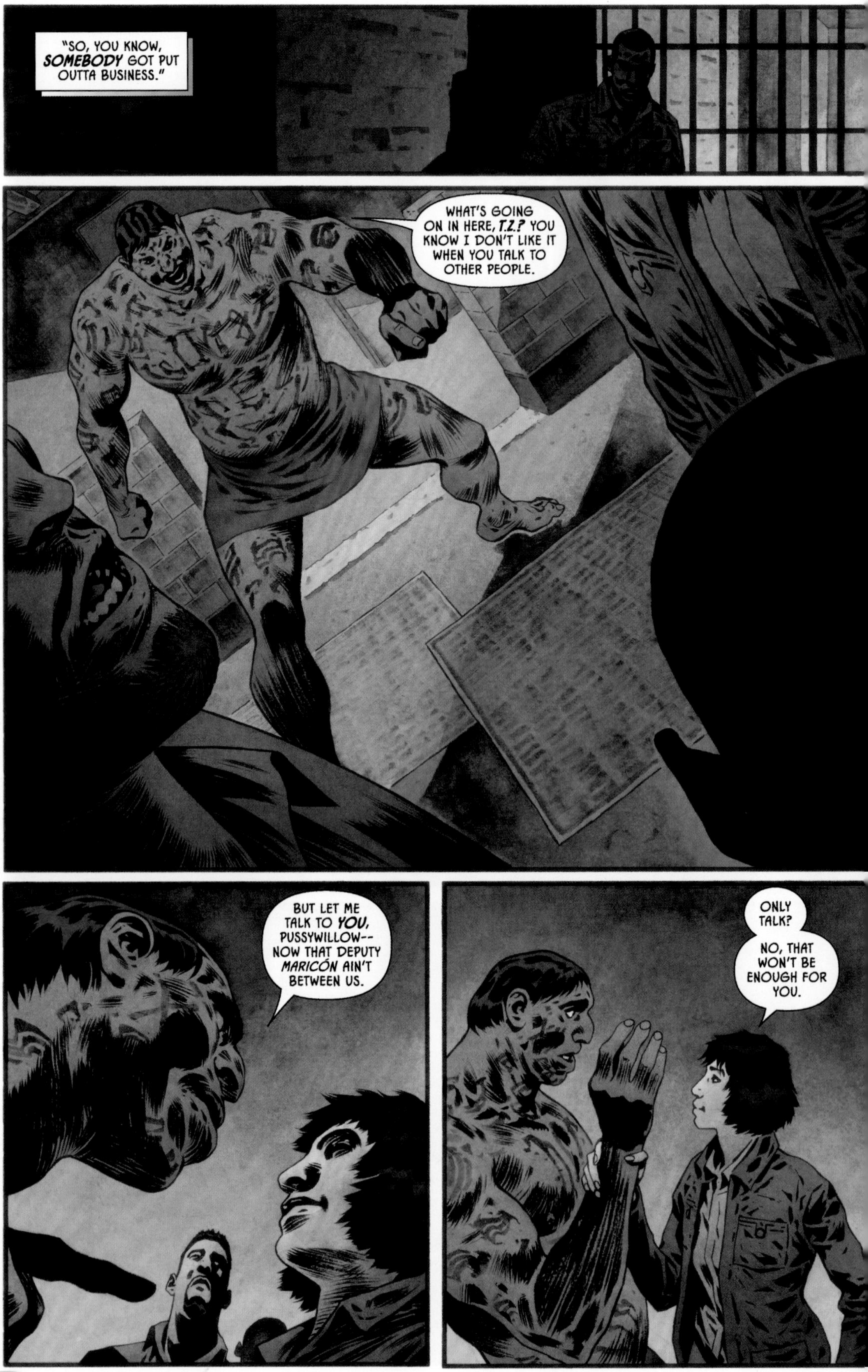
"SO, YOU KNOW, SOMEBODY GOT PUT OUTTA BUSINESS."
WHAT'S GOING ON IN HERE, T.Z.? YOU KNOW I DON'T LIKE IT WHEN YOU TALK TO OTHER PEOPLE.
BUT LET ME TALK TO YOU, PUSSYWILLOW-- NOW THAT DEPUTY MARICÓN AIN'T BETWEEN US.
ONLY TALK?
NO, THAT WON'T BE ENOUGH FOR YOU.

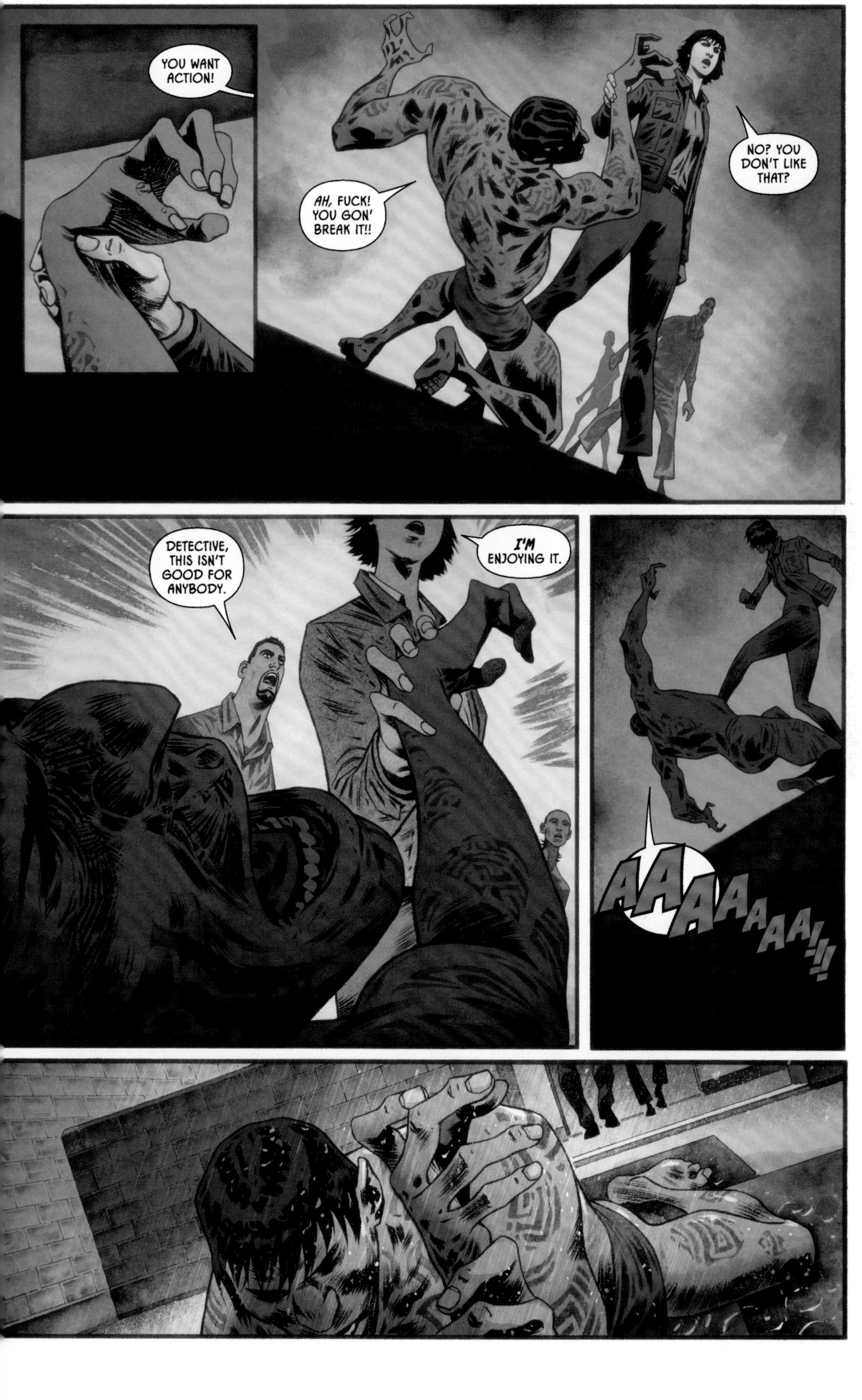
YOU WANT ACTION!
AH, FUCK! YOU GON' BREAK IT!!
NO? YOU DON'T LIKE THAT?
DETECTIVE, THIS ISN'T GOOD FOR ANYBODY.
I'M ENJOYING IT.
AAAAAAAI-!!!

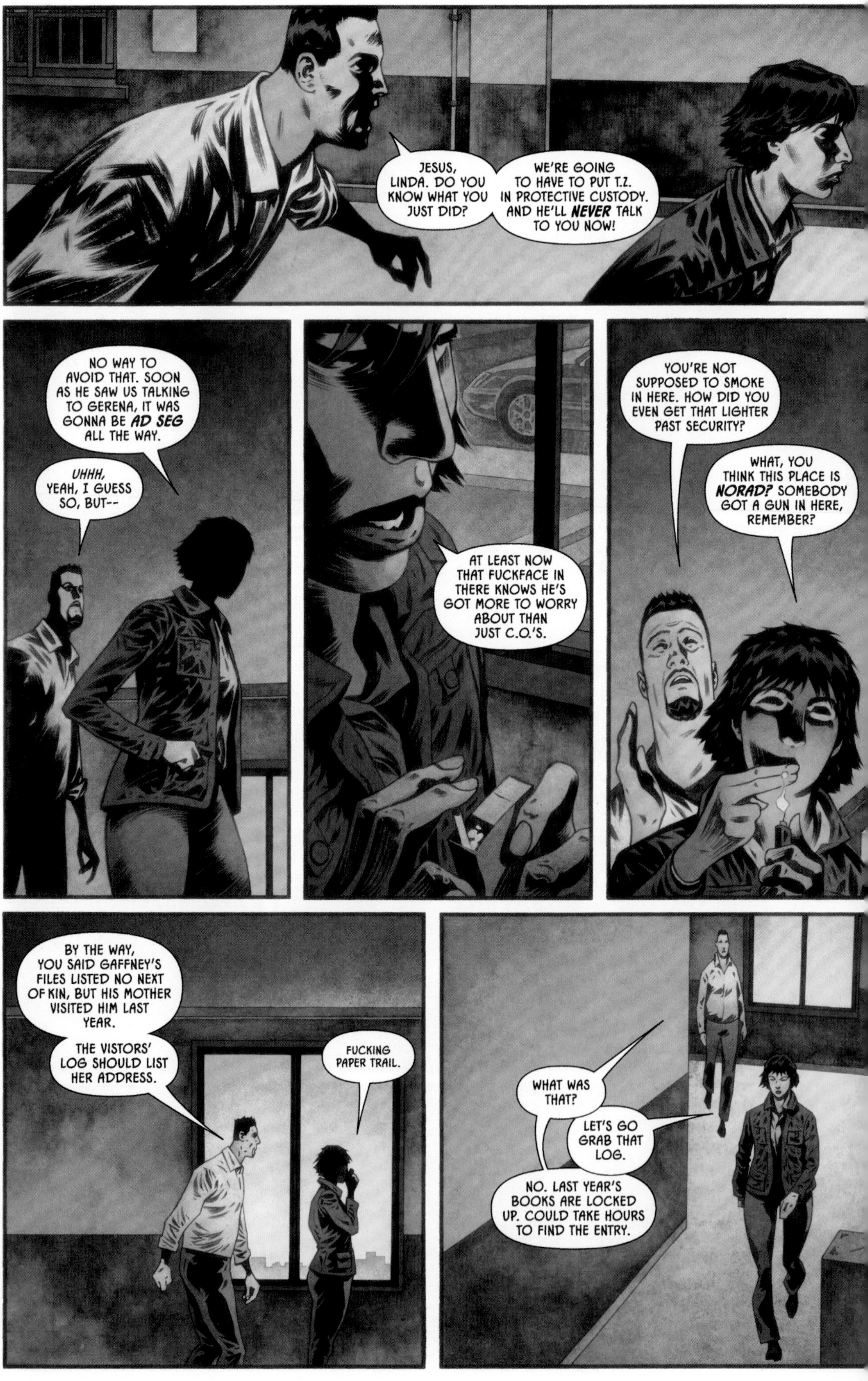

JESUS, LINDA. DO YOU KNOW WHAT YOU JUST DID?
WE'RE GOING TO HAVE TO PUT T.Z. IN PROTECTIVE CUSTODY. AND HE'LL *NEVER* TALK TO YOU NOW!
NO WAY TO AVOID THAT. SOON AS HE SAW US TALKING TO GERENA, IT WAS GONNA BE *AD SEG* ALL THE WAY.
UHHH, YEAH, I GUESS SO, BUT--
AT LEAST NOW THAT FUCKFACE IN THERE KNOWS HE'S GOT MORE TO WORRY ABOUT THAN JUST C.O.'S.
YOU'RE NOT SUPPOSED TO SMOKE IN HERE. HOW DID YOU EVEN GET THAT LIGHTER PAST SECURITY?
WHAT, YOU THINK THIS PLACE IS *NORAD?* SOMEBODY GOT A GUN IN HERE, REMEMBER?
BY THE WAY, YOU SAID GAFFNEY'S FILES LISTED NO NEXT OF KIN, BUT HIS MOTHER VISITED HIM LAST YEAR.
THE VISTORS' LOG SHOULD LIST HER ADDRESS.
FUCKING PAPER TRAIL.
WHAT WAS THAT?
LET'S GO GRAB THAT LOG.
NO. LAST YEAR'S BOOKS ARE LOCKED UP. COULD TAKE HOURS TO FIND THE ENTRY.

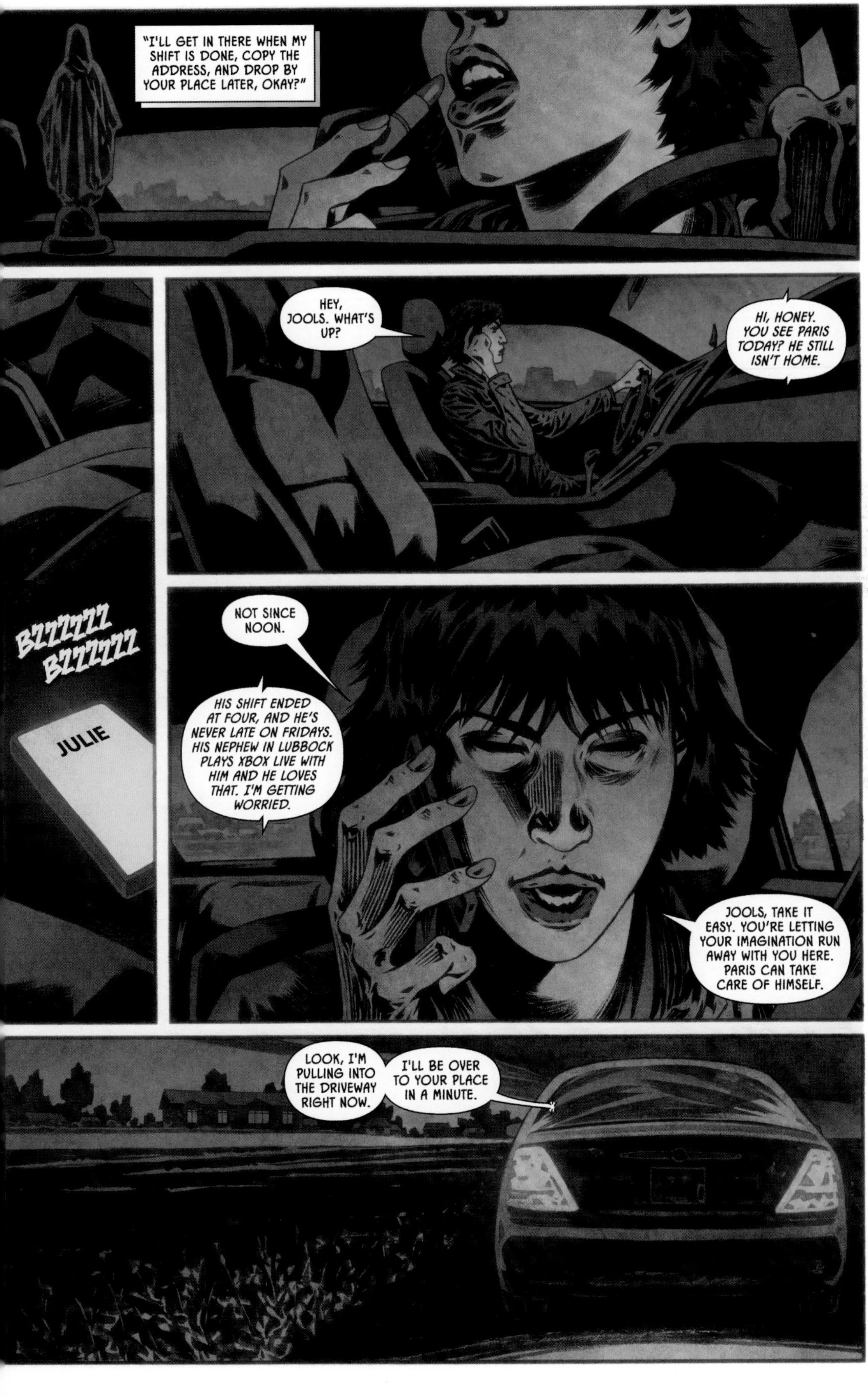
"I'LL GET IN THERE WHEN MY SHIFT IS DONE, COPY THE ADDRESS, AND DROP BY YOUR PLACE LATER, OKAY?"
HEY, JOOLS. WHAT'S UP?
HI, HONEY. YOU SEE PARIS TODAY? HE STILL ISN'T HOME.
BZZZZZZ BZZZZZZ
JULIE
NOT SINCE NOON.
HIS SHIFT ENDED AT FOUR, AND HE'S NEVER LATE ON FRIDAYS. HIS NEPHEW IN LUBBOCK PLAYS XBOX LIVE WITH HIM AND HE LOVES THAT. I'M GETTING WORRIED.
JOOLS, TAKE IT EASY. YOU'RE LETTING YOUR IMAGINATION RUN AWAY WITH YOU HERE. PARIS CAN TAKE CARE OF HIMSELF.
LOOK, I'M PULLING INTO THE DRIVEWAY RIGHT NOW.
I'LL BE OVER TO YOUR PLACE IN A MINUTE.

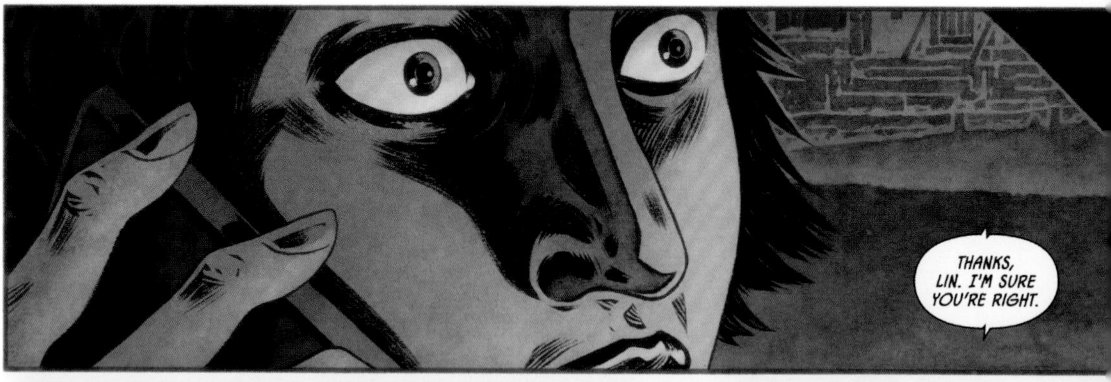
THANKS, LIN. I'M SURE YOU'RE RIGHT.

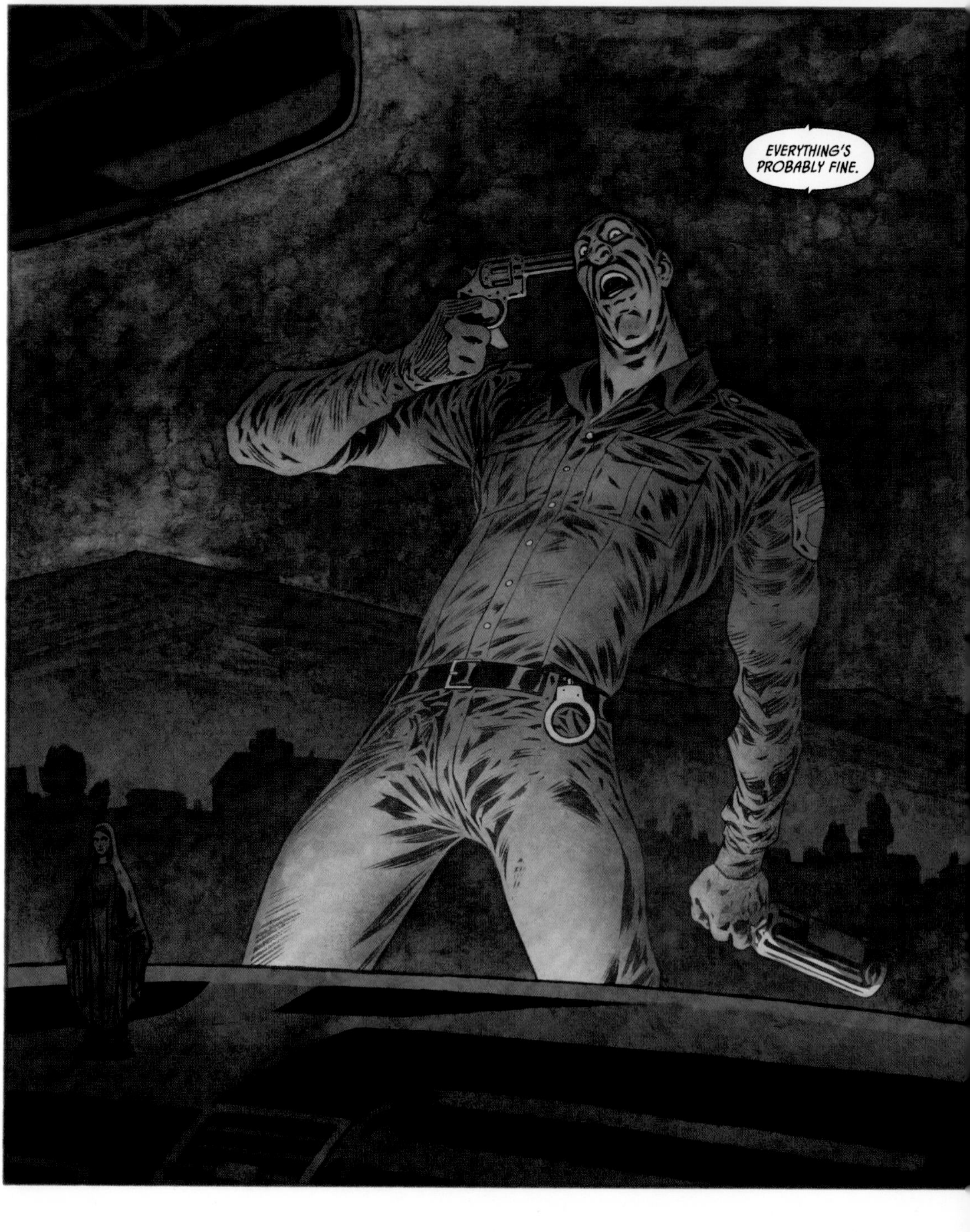
EVERYTHING'S PROBABLY FINE.

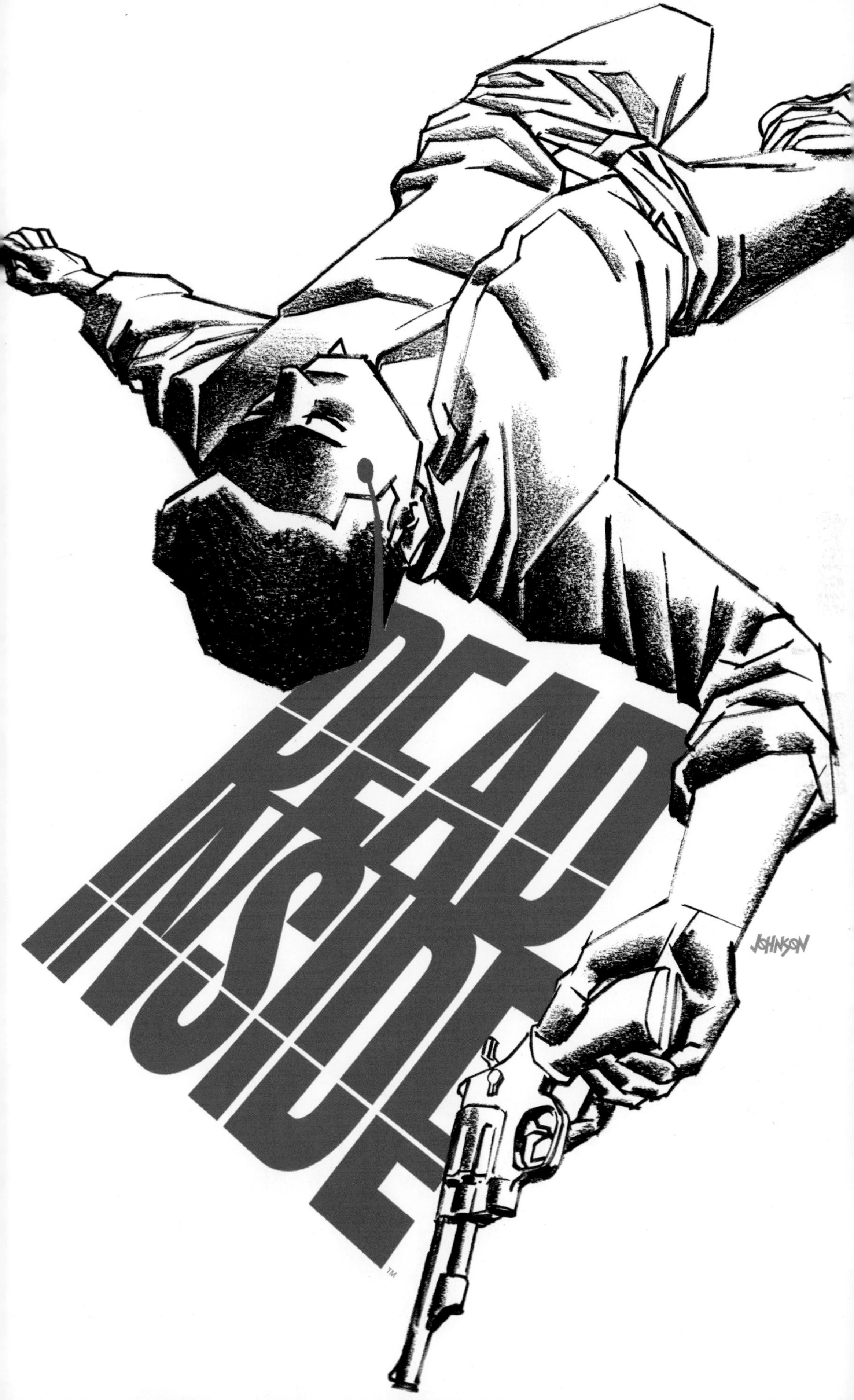

DEAD INSIDE
™
JOHNSON

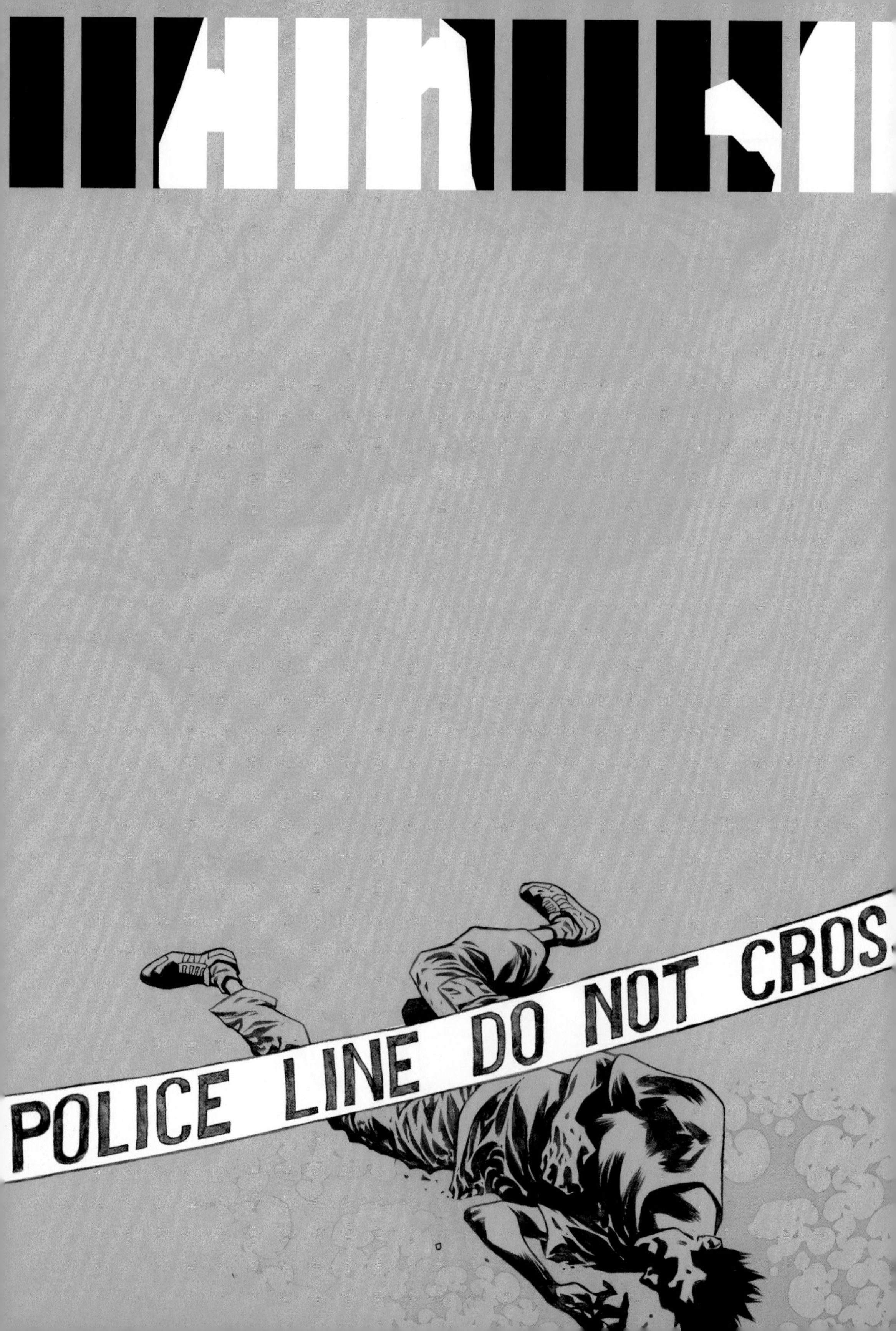
POLICE LINE DO NOT CROS

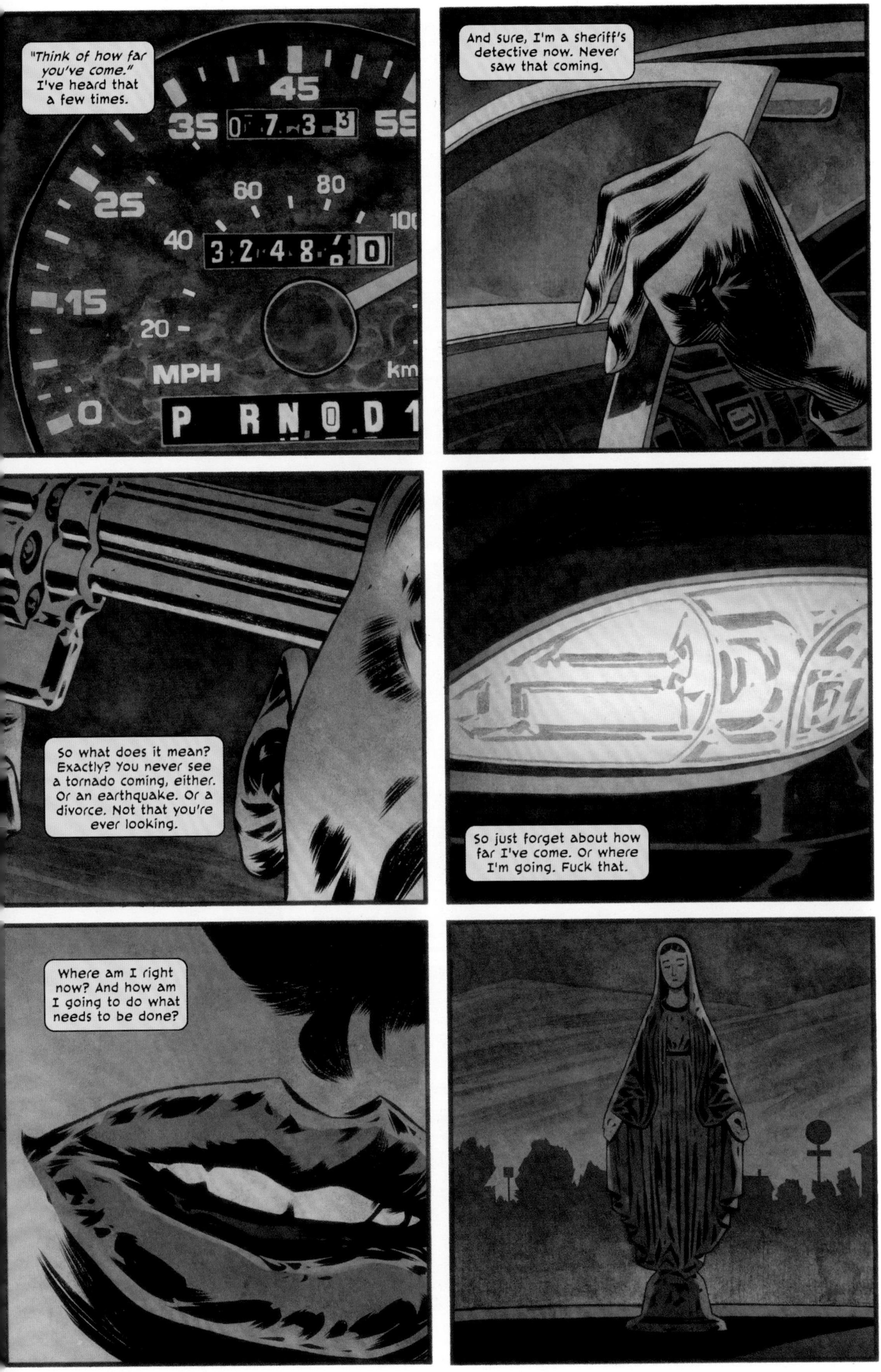
"Think of how far you've come." I've heard that a few times.
And sure, I'm a sheriff's detective now. Never saw that coming.
So what does it mean? Exactly? You never see a tornado coming, either. Or an earthquake. Or a divorce. Not that you're ever looking.
So just forget about how far I've come. Or where I'm going. Fuck that.
Where am I right now? And how am I going to do what needs to be done?

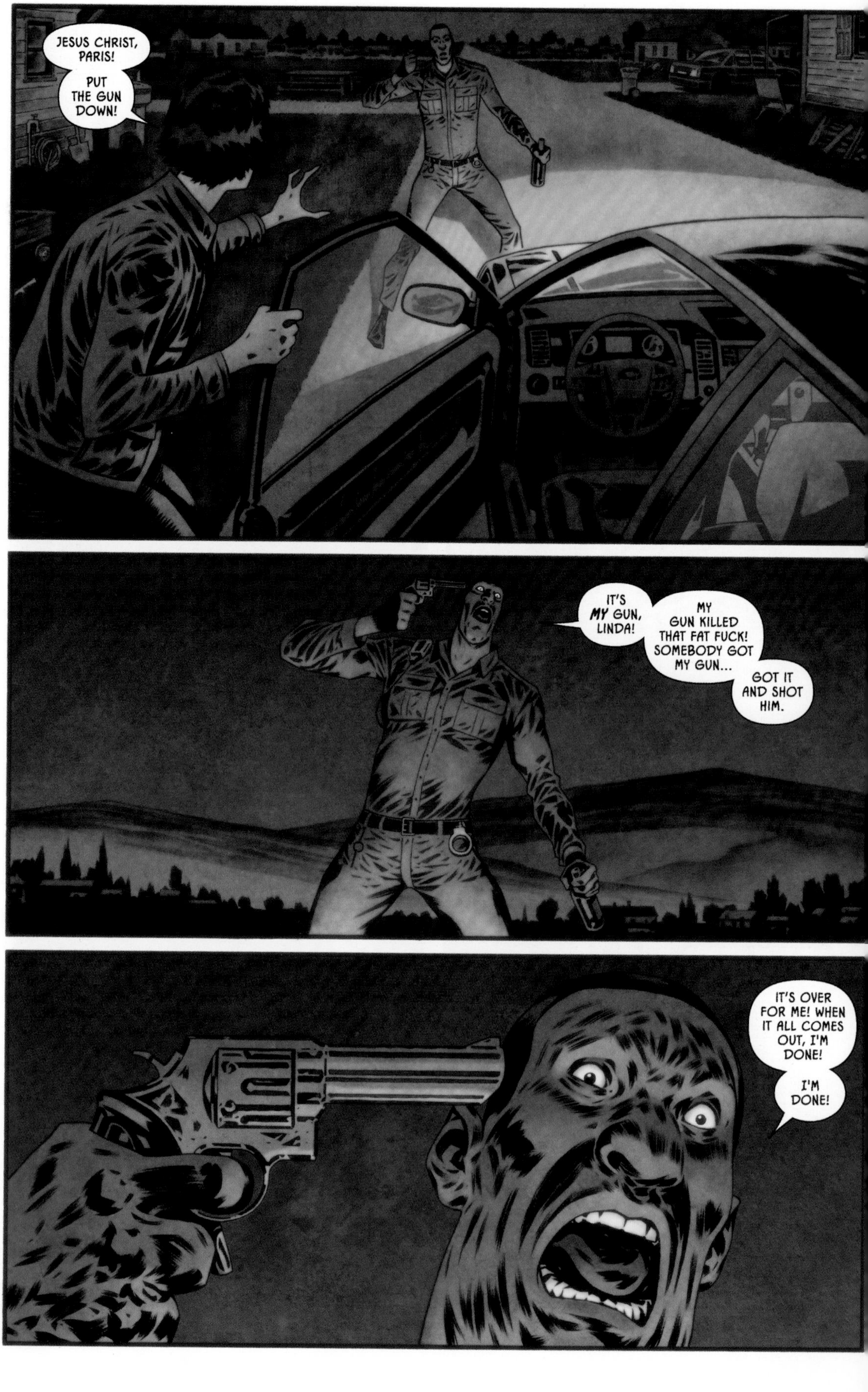

JESUS CHRIST, PARIS!
PUT THE GUN DOWN!
IT'S *MY* GUN, LINDA!
MY GUN KILLED THAT FAT FUCK! SOMEBODY GOT MY GUN...
GOT IT AND SHOT HIM.
IT'S OVER FOR ME! WHEN IT ALL COMES OUT, I'M DONE!
I'M DONE!

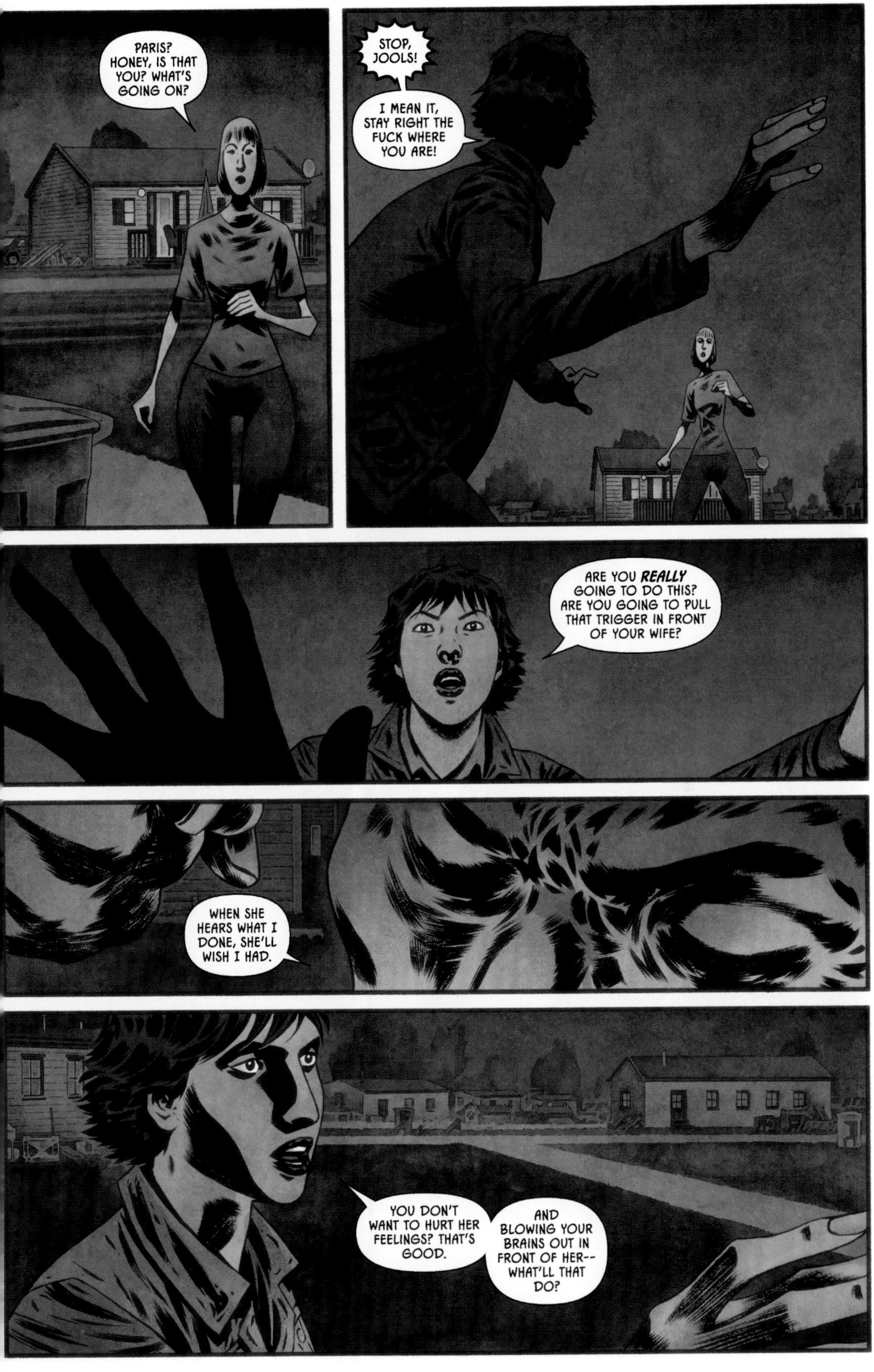
PARIS? HONEY, IS THAT YOU? WHAT'S GOING ON?
STOP, JOOLS!
I MEAN IT, STAY RIGHT THE FUCK WHERE YOU ARE!
ARE YOU REALLY GOING TO DO THIS? ARE YOU GOING TO PULL THAT TRIGGER IN FRONT OF YOUR WIFE?
WHEN SHE HEARS WHAT I DONE, SHE'LL WISH I HAD.
YOU DON'T WANT TO HURT HER FEELINGS? THAT'S GOOD.
AND BLOWING YOUR BRAINS OUT IN FRONT OF HER-- WHAT'LL THAT DO?

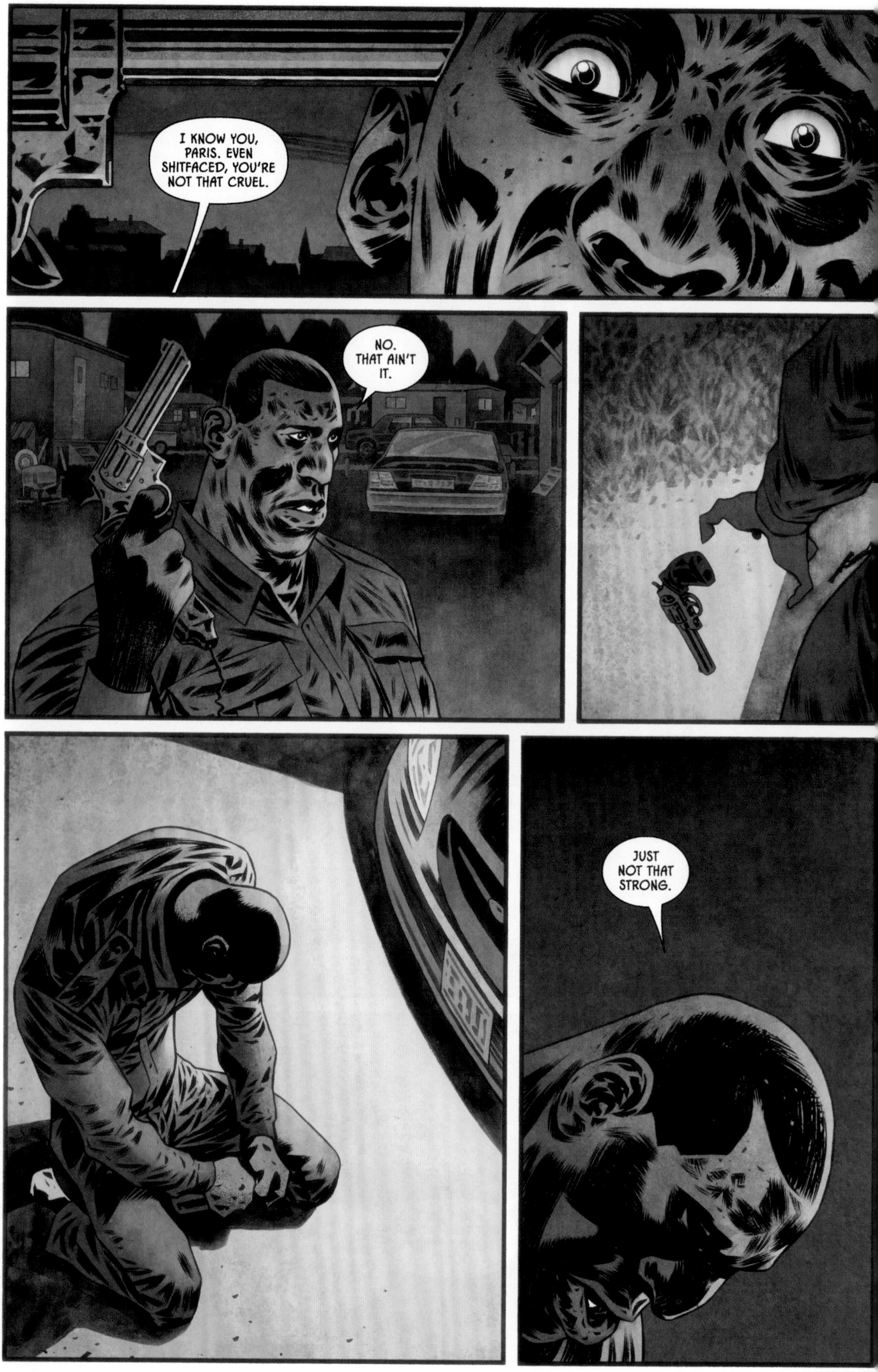
I KNOW YOU, PARIS. EVEN SHITFACED, YOU'RE NOT THAT CRUEL.
NO. THAT AIN'T IT.
JUST NOT THAT STRONG.

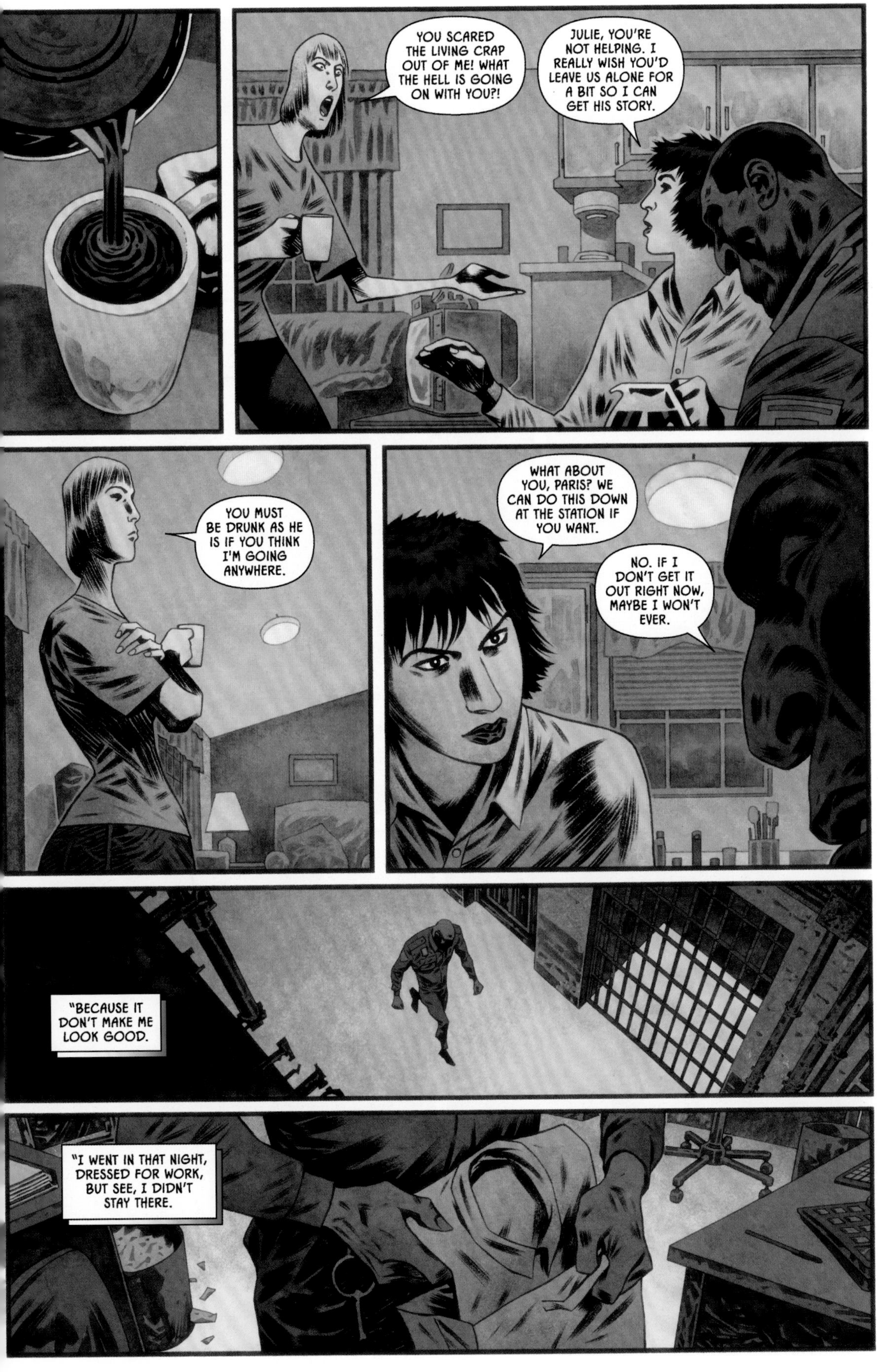
YOU SCARED THE LIVING CRAP OUT OF ME! WHAT THE HELL IS GOING ON WITH YOU?!
JULIE, YOU'RE NOT HELPING. I REALLY WISH YOU'D LEAVE US ALONE FOR A BIT SO I CAN GET HIS STORY.
YOU MUST BE DRUNK AS HE IS IF YOU THINK I'M GOING ANYWHERE.
WHAT ABOUT YOU, PARIS? WE CAN DO THIS DOWN AT THE STATION IF YOU WANT.
NO. IF I DON'T GET IT OUT RIGHT NOW, MAYBE I WON'T EVER.
"BECAUSE IT DON'T MAKE ME LOOK GOOD.
"I WENT IN THAT NIGHT, DRESSED FOR WORK, BUT SEE, I DIDN'T STAY THERE.

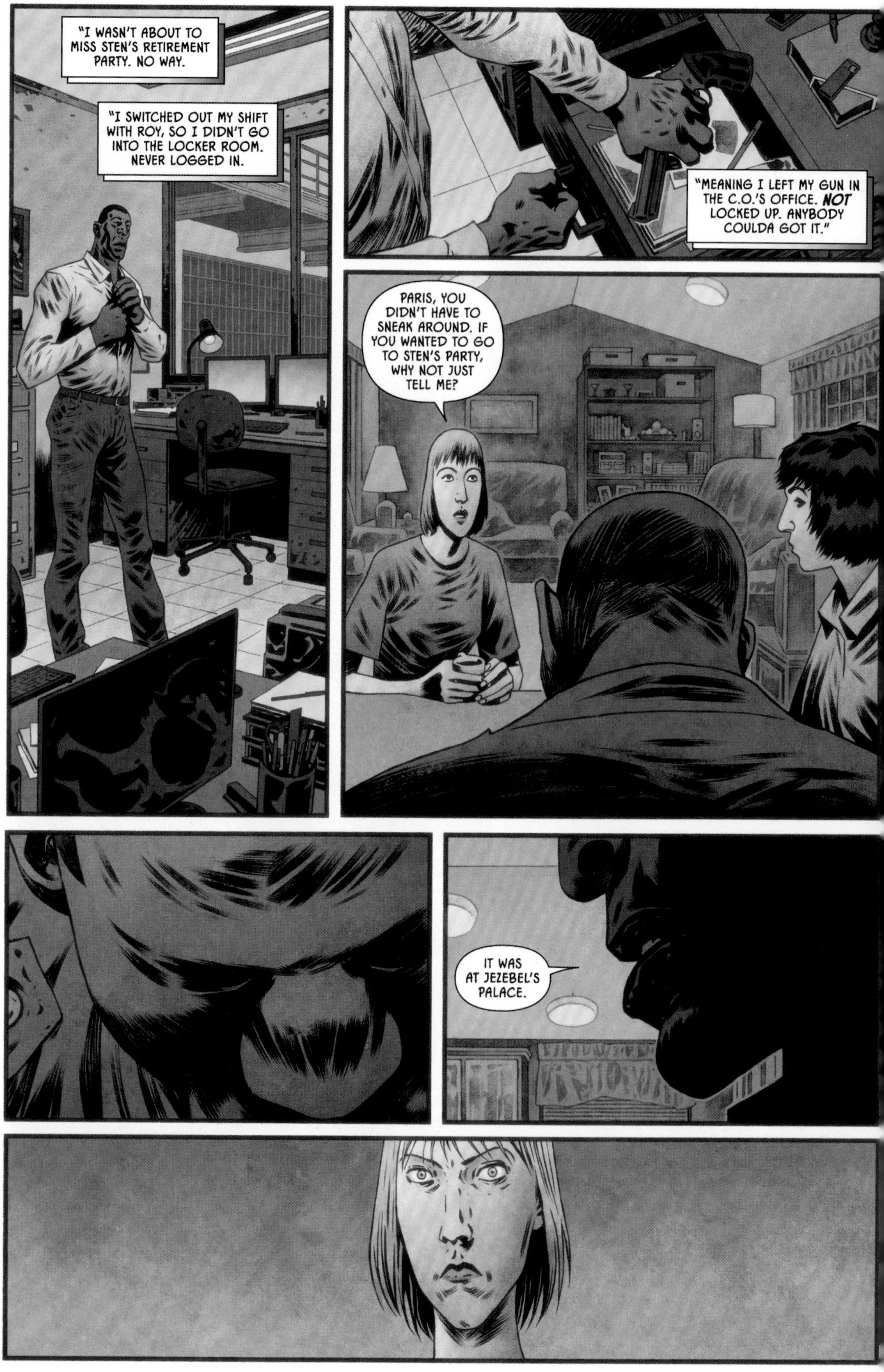
"I WASN'T ABOUT TO MISS STEN'S RETIREMENT PARTY. NO WAY.
"I SWITCHED OUT MY SHIFT WITH ROY, SO I DIDN'T GO INTO THE LOCKER ROOM. NEVER LOGGED IN.
"MEANING I LEFT MY GUN IN THE C.O.'S OFFICE. NOT LOCKED UP. ANYBODY COULDA GOT IT."
PARIS, YOU DIDN'T HAVE TO SNEAK AROUND. IF YOU WANTED TO GO TO STEN'S PARTY, WHY NOT JUST TELL ME?
IT WAS AT JEZEBEL'S PALACE.

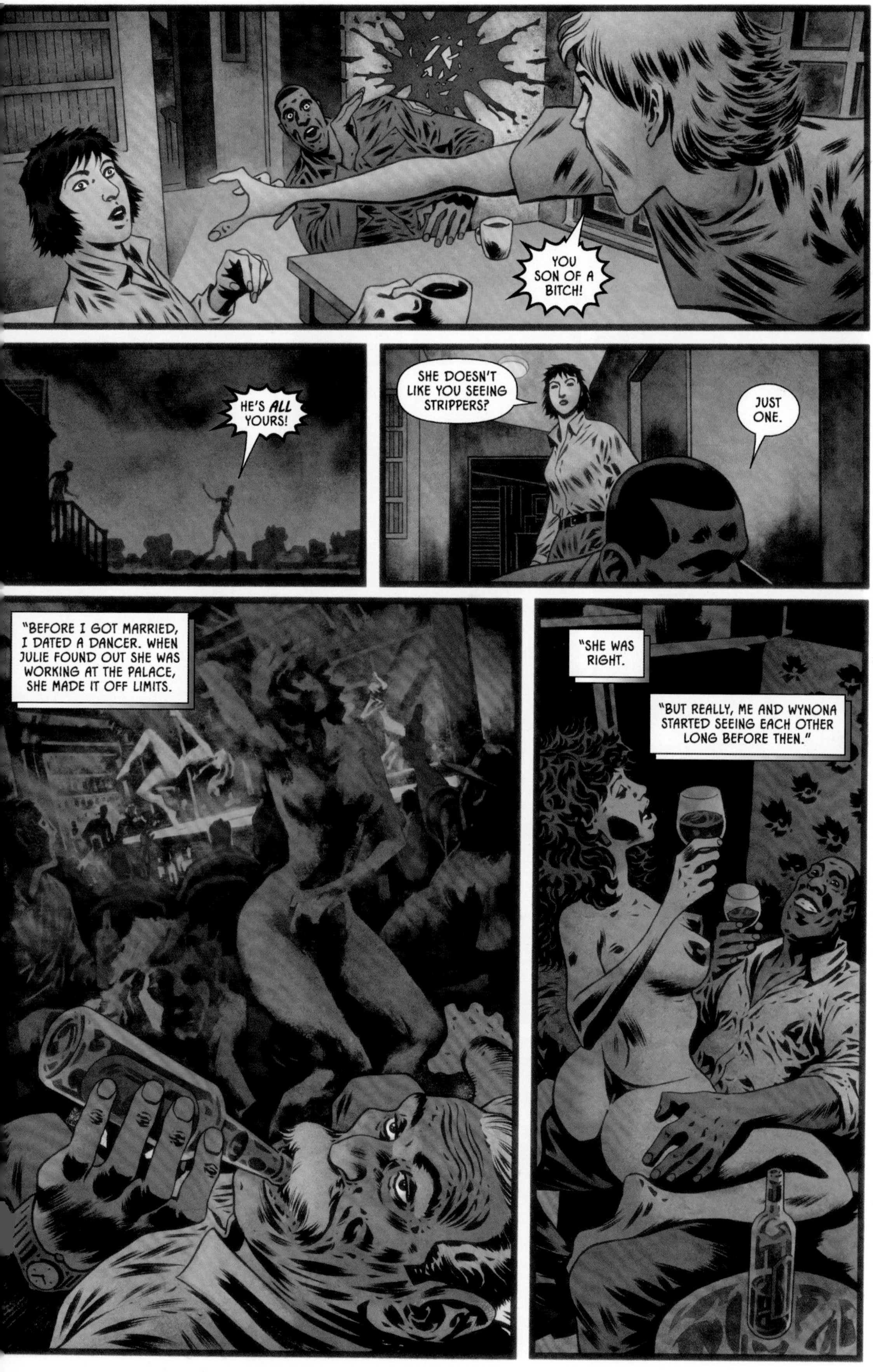
YOU SON OF A BITCH!
HE'S ALL YOURS!
SHE DOESN'T LIKE YOU SEEING STRIPPERS?
JUST ONE.
"BEFORE I GOT MARRIED, I DATED A DANCER. WHEN JULIE FOUND OUT SHE WAS WORKING AT THE PALACE, SHE MADE IT OFF LIMITS.
"SHE WAS RIGHT.
"BUT REALLY, ME AND WYNONA STARTED SEEING EACH OTHER LONG BEFORE THEN."

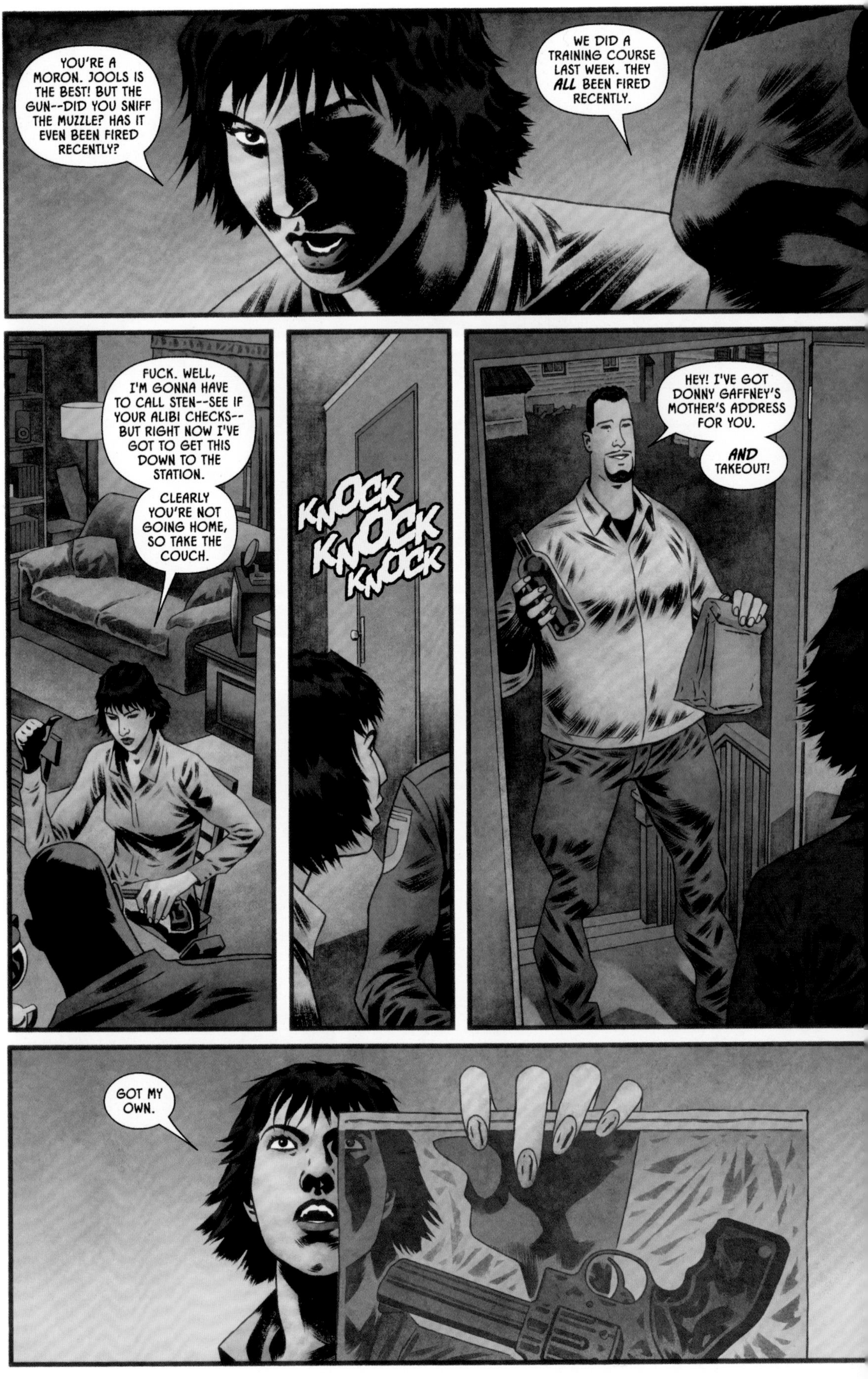
YOU'RE A MORON. JOOLS IS THE BEST! BUT THE GUN--DID YOU SNIFF THE MUZZLE? HAS IT EVEN BEEN FIRED RECENTLY?
WE DID A TRAINING COURSE LAST WEEK. THEY ALL BEEN FIRED RECENTLY.
FUCK. WELL, I'M GONNA HAVE TO CALL STEN--SEE IF YOUR ALIBI CHECKS--BUT RIGHT NOW I'VE GOT TO GET THIS DOWN TO THE STATION.
CLEARLY YOU'RE NOT GOING HOME, SO TAKE THE COUCH.
KNOCK KNOCK KNOCK
HEY! I'VE GOT DONNY GAFFNEY'S MOTHER'S ADDRESS FOR YOU.
AND TAKEOUT!
GOT MY OWN.

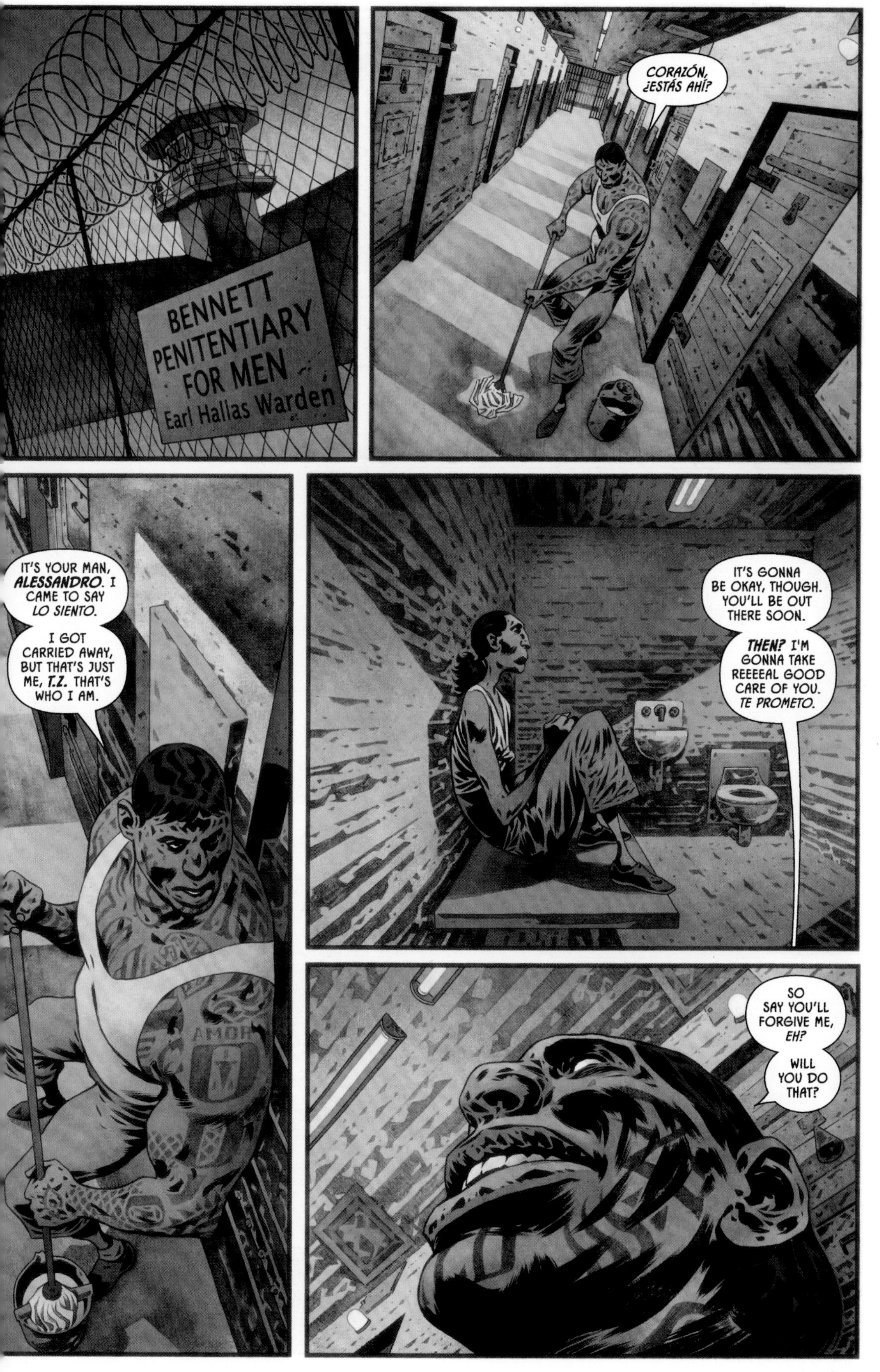
BENNETT PENITENTIARY FOR MEN
Earl Hallas Warden
CORAZÓN, ¿ESTÁS AHÍ?
IT'S YOUR MAN, ALESSANDRO. I CAME TO SAY LO SIENTO.
I GOT CARRIED AWAY, BUT THAT'S JUST ME, T.Z. THAT'S WHO I AM.
AMOR
IT'S GONNA BE OKAY, THOUGH. YOU'LL BE OUT THERE SOON.
THEN? I'M GONNA TAKE REEEEAL GOOD CARE OF YOU. TE PROMETO.
SO SAY YOU'LL FORGIVE ME, EH?
WILL YOU DO THAT?

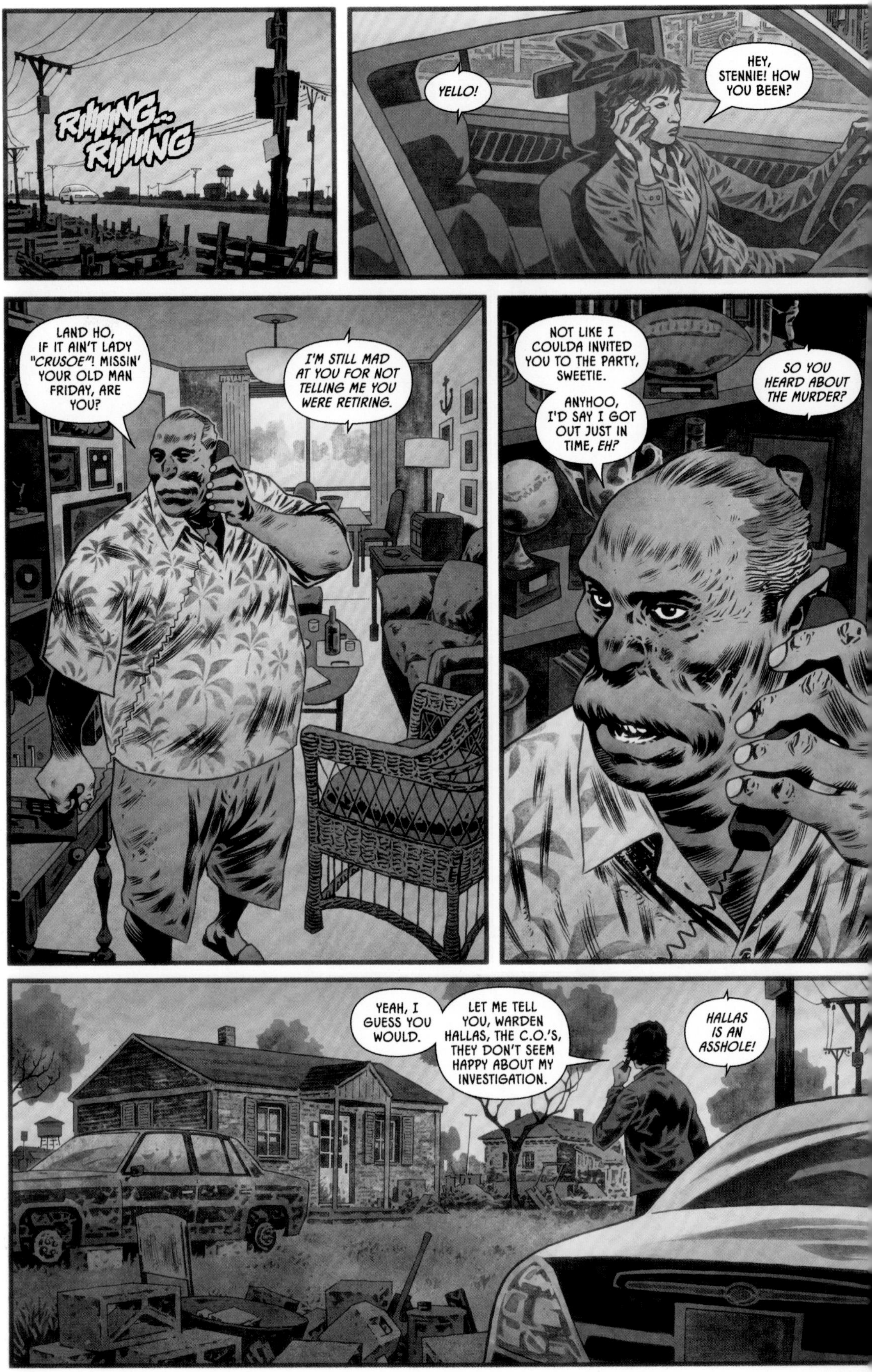
RIIIING~ RIIIING
YELLO!
HEY, STENNIE! HOW YOU BEEN?
LAND HO, IF IT AIN'T LADY "CRUSOE"! MISSIN' YOUR OLD MAN FRIDAY, ARE YOU?
I'M STILL MAD AT YOU FOR NOT TELLING ME YOU WERE RETIRING.
NOT LIKE I COULDA INVITED YOU TO THE PARTY, SWEETIE.
ANYHOO, I'D SAY I GOT OUT JUST IN TIME, EH?
SO YOU HEARD ABOUT THE MURDER?
YEAH, I GUESS YOU WOULD.
LET ME TELL YOU, WARDEN HALLAS, THE C.O.'S, THEY DON'T SEEM HAPPY ABOUT MY INVESTIGATION.
HALLAS IS AN ASSHOLE!

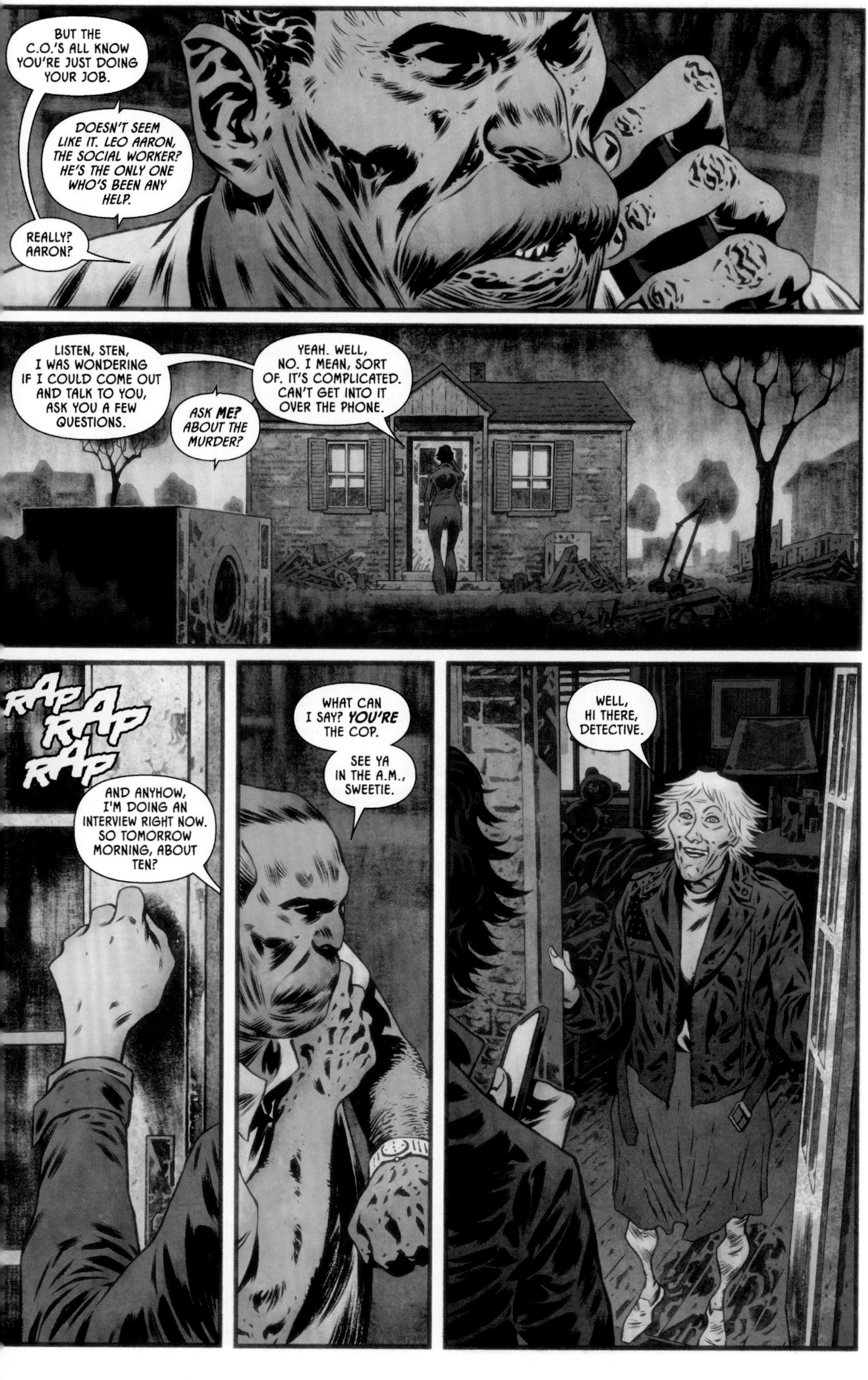

BUT THE C.O.'S ALL KNOW YOU'RE JUST DOING YOUR JOB.
DOESN'T SEEM LIKE IT. LEO AARON, THE SOCIAL WORKER? HE'S THE ONLY ONE WHO'S BEEN ANY HELP.
REALLY? AARON?
LISTEN, STEN, I WAS WONDERING IF I COULD COME OUT AND TALK TO YOU, ASK YOU A FEW QUESTIONS.
ASK ME? ABOUT THE MURDER?
YEAH. WELL, NO. I MEAN, SORT OF. IT'S COMPLICATED. CAN'T GET INTO IT OVER THE PHONE.
RAP RAP RAP
AND ANYHOW, I'M DOING AN INTERVIEW RIGHT NOW. SO TOMORROW MORNING, ABOUT TEN?
WHAT CAN I SAY? YOU'RE THE COP.
SEE YA IN THE A.M., SWEETIE.
WELL, HI THERE, DETECTIVE.

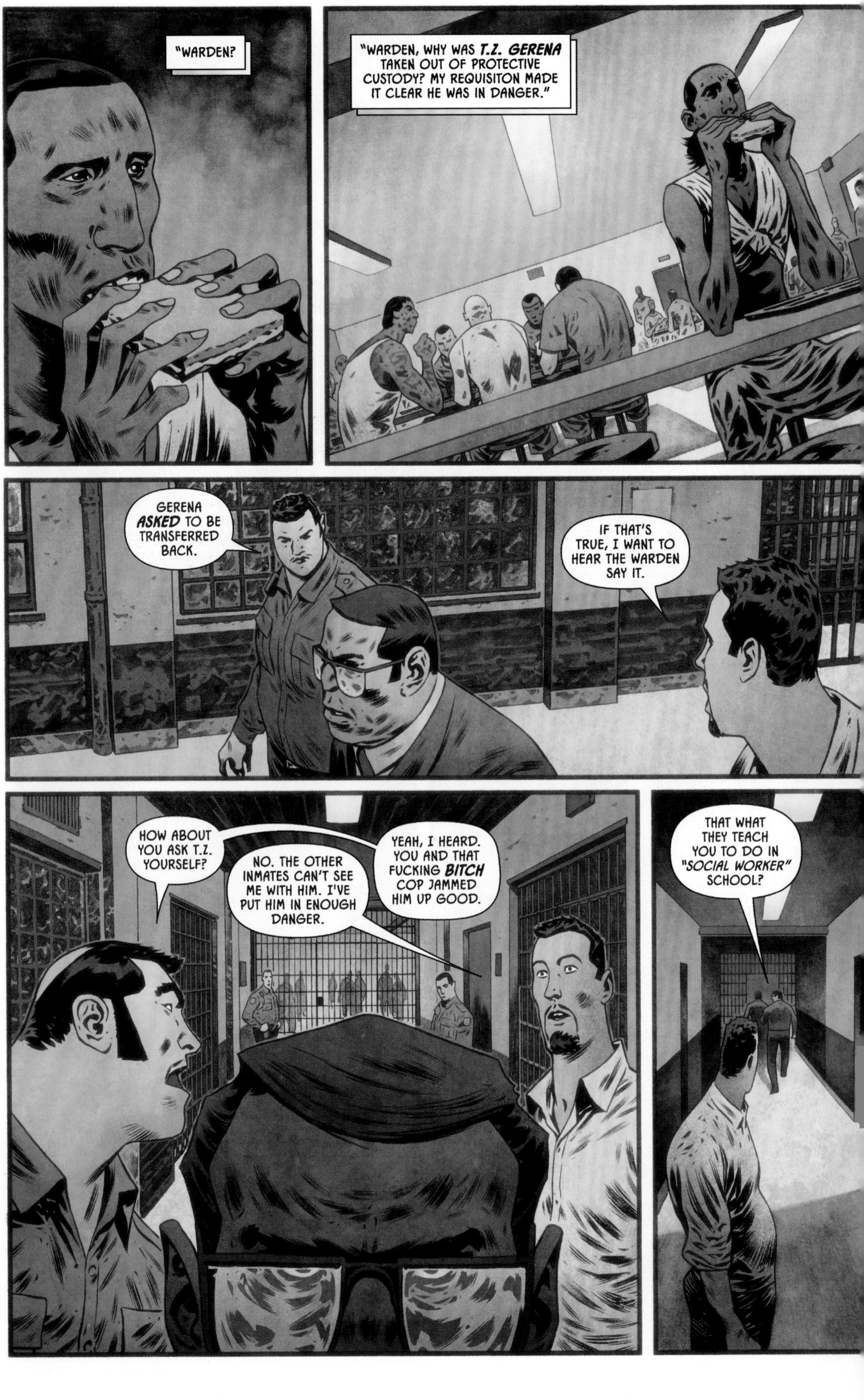
"WARDEN?
"WARDEN, WHY WAS T.Z. GERENA TAKEN OUT OF PROTECTIVE CUSTODY? MY REQUISITON MADE IT CLEAR HE WAS IN DANGER."
GERENA ASKED TO BE TRANSFERRED BACK.
IF THAT'S TRUE, I WANT TO HEAR THE WARDEN SAY IT.
HOW ABOUT YOU ASK T.Z. YOURSELF?
NO. THE OTHER INMATES CAN'T SEE ME WITH HIM. I'VE PUT HIM IN ENOUGH DANGER.
YEAH, I HEARD. YOU AND THAT FUCKING BITCH COP JAMMED HIM UP GOOD.
THAT WHAT THEY TEACH YOU TO DO IN "SOCIAL WORKER" SCHOOL?

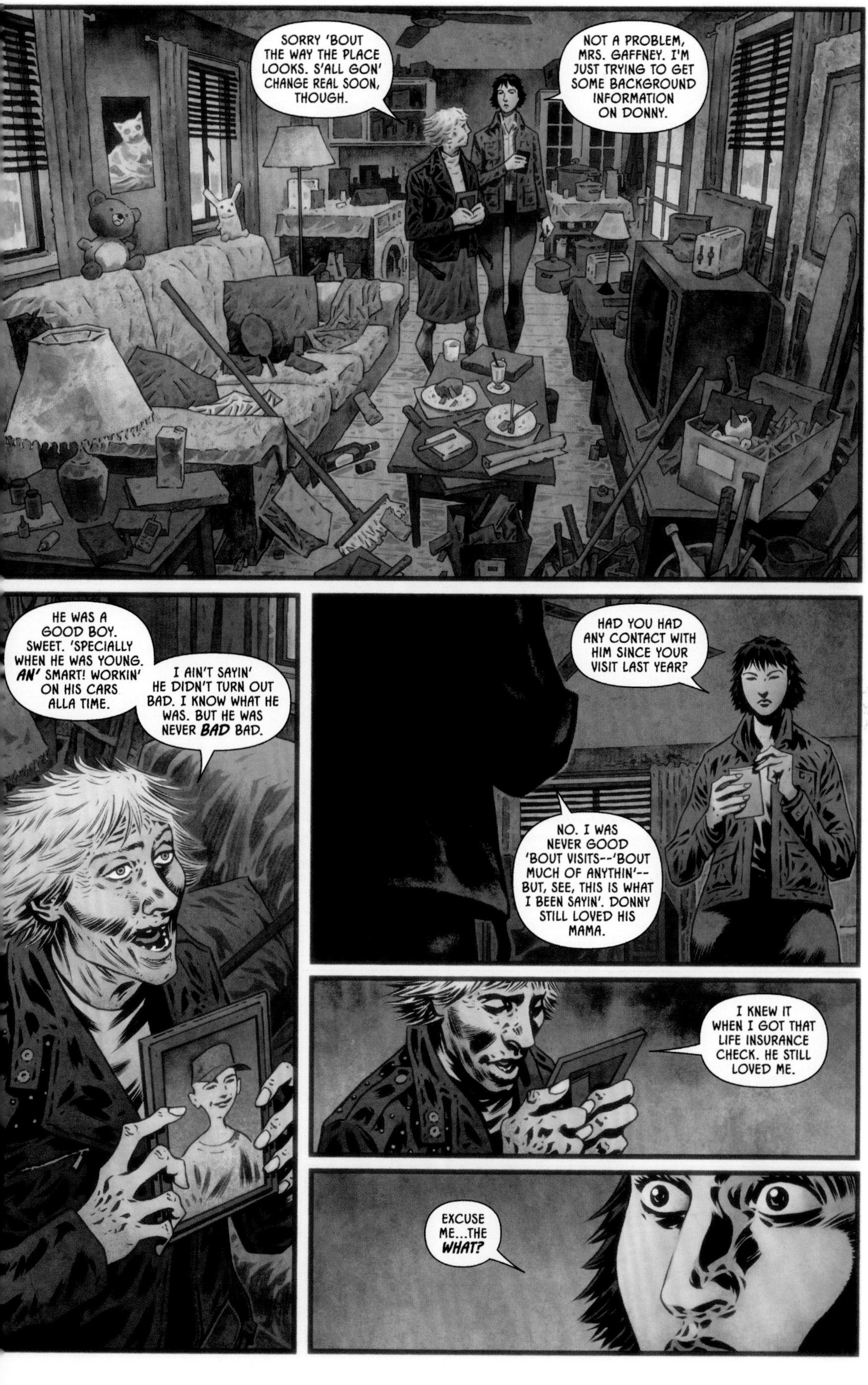
SORRY 'BOUT THE WAY THE PLACE LOOKS. S'ALL GON' CHANGE REAL SOON, THOUGH.
NOT A PROBLEM, MRS. GAFFNEY. I'M JUST TRYING TO GET SOME BACKGROUND INFORMATION ON DONNY.
HE WAS A GOOD BOY. SWEET. 'SPECIALLY WHEN HE WAS YOUNG. **AN'** SMART! WORKIN' ON HIS CARS ALLA TIME.
I AIN'T SAYIN' HE DIDN'T TURN OUT BAD. I KNOW WHAT HE WAS. BUT HE WAS NEVER **BAD** BAD.
HAD YOU HAD ANY CONTACT WITH HIM SINCE YOUR VISIT LAST YEAR?
NO. I WAS NEVER GOOD 'BOUT VISITS--'BOUT MUCH OF ANYTHIN'--BUT, SEE, THIS IS WHAT I BEEN SAYIN'. DONNY STILL LOVED HIS MAMA.
I KNEW IT WHEN I GOT THAT LIFE INSURANCE CHECK. HE STILL LOVED ME.
EXCUSE ME...THE ***WHAT?***

LIFE INSURANCE CHECK?

THAT DOESN'T MAKE ANY SENSE. HE COMMITTED SUICIDE.

AND SHE GOT THE CHECK BEFORE THE CORONER FILED HIS REPORT. IT'S *ALL* WRONG.

NOW I KNOW HOW SHE CAN AFFORD A THOUSAND-DOLLAR JACKET.

HER BANK GAVE ME AN IMAGE OF THE CHECK. DIGITALLY *"SIGNED"* AND WRITTEN FROM AN ONLINE ACCOUNT.

HUH. LOOK AT THAT. *"PAPER"* TRAIL IS A LOT EASIER NOW THAT IT'S ON THE INTERNET.

NOPE. STILL BLOWS. THE ACCOUNT'S MANAGED BY A SHELL CORPORATION OF SOME SORT. CAN'T BEGIN TO FIGURE OUT WHO'S ACTUALLY BEHIND IT.

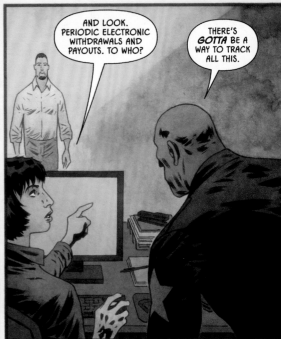

AND LOOK. PERIODIC ELECTRONIC WITHDRAWALS AND PAYOUTS. TO WHO?

THERE'S *GOTTA* BE A WAY TO TRACK ALL THIS.

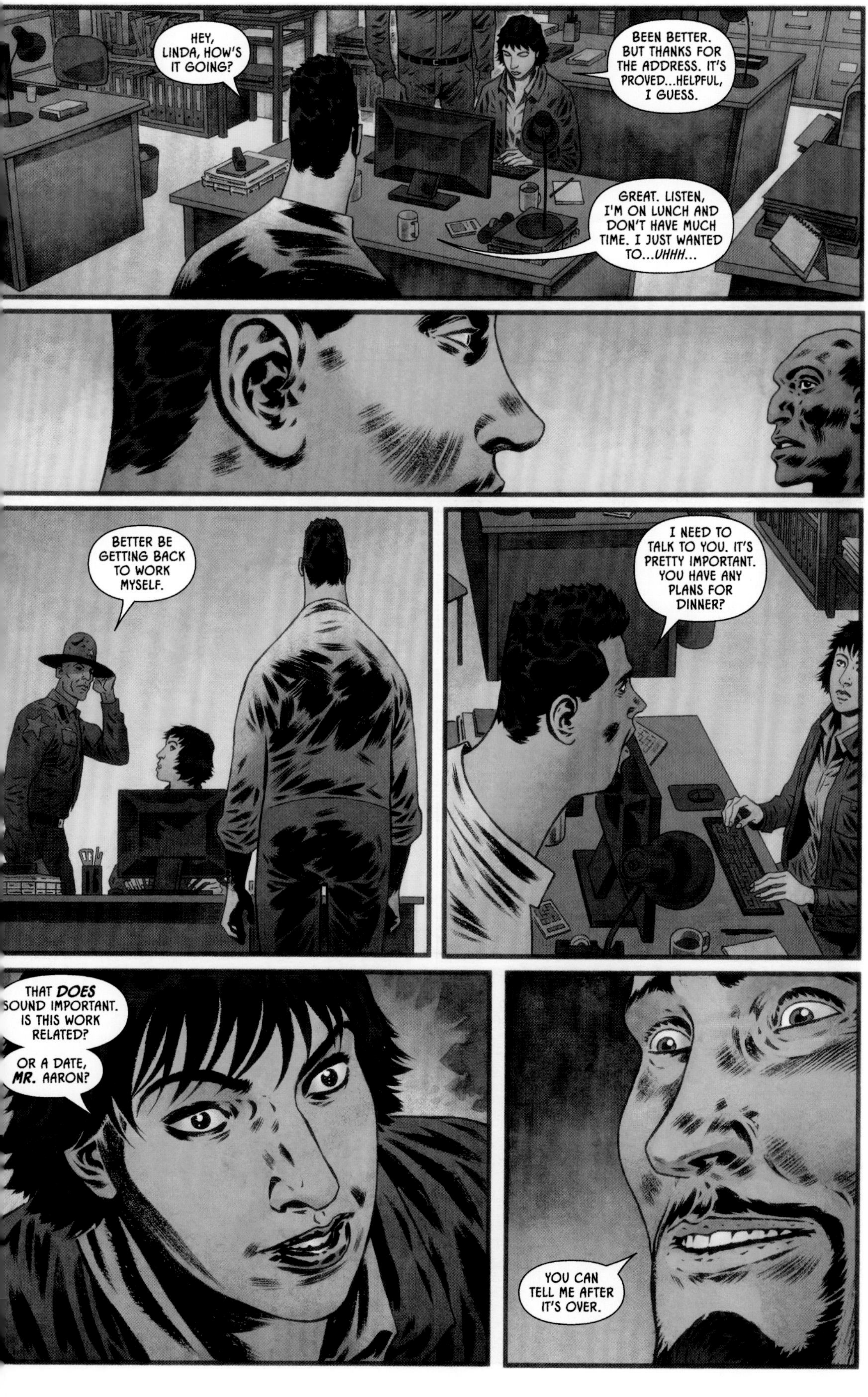
HEY, LINDA, HOW'S IT GOING?
BEEN BETTER. BUT THANKS FOR THE ADDRESS. IT'S PROVED...HELPFUL, I GUESS.
GREAT. LISTEN, I'M ON LUNCH AND DON'T HAVE MUCH TIME. I JUST WANTED TO...UHHH...
BETTER BE GETTING BACK TO WORK MYSELF.
I NEED TO TALK TO YOU. IT'S PRETTY IMPORTANT. YOU HAVE ANY PLANS FOR DINNER?
THAT DOES SOUND IMPORTANT. IS THIS WORK RELATED?
OR A DATE, MR. AARON?
YOU CAN TELL ME AFTER IT'S OVER.

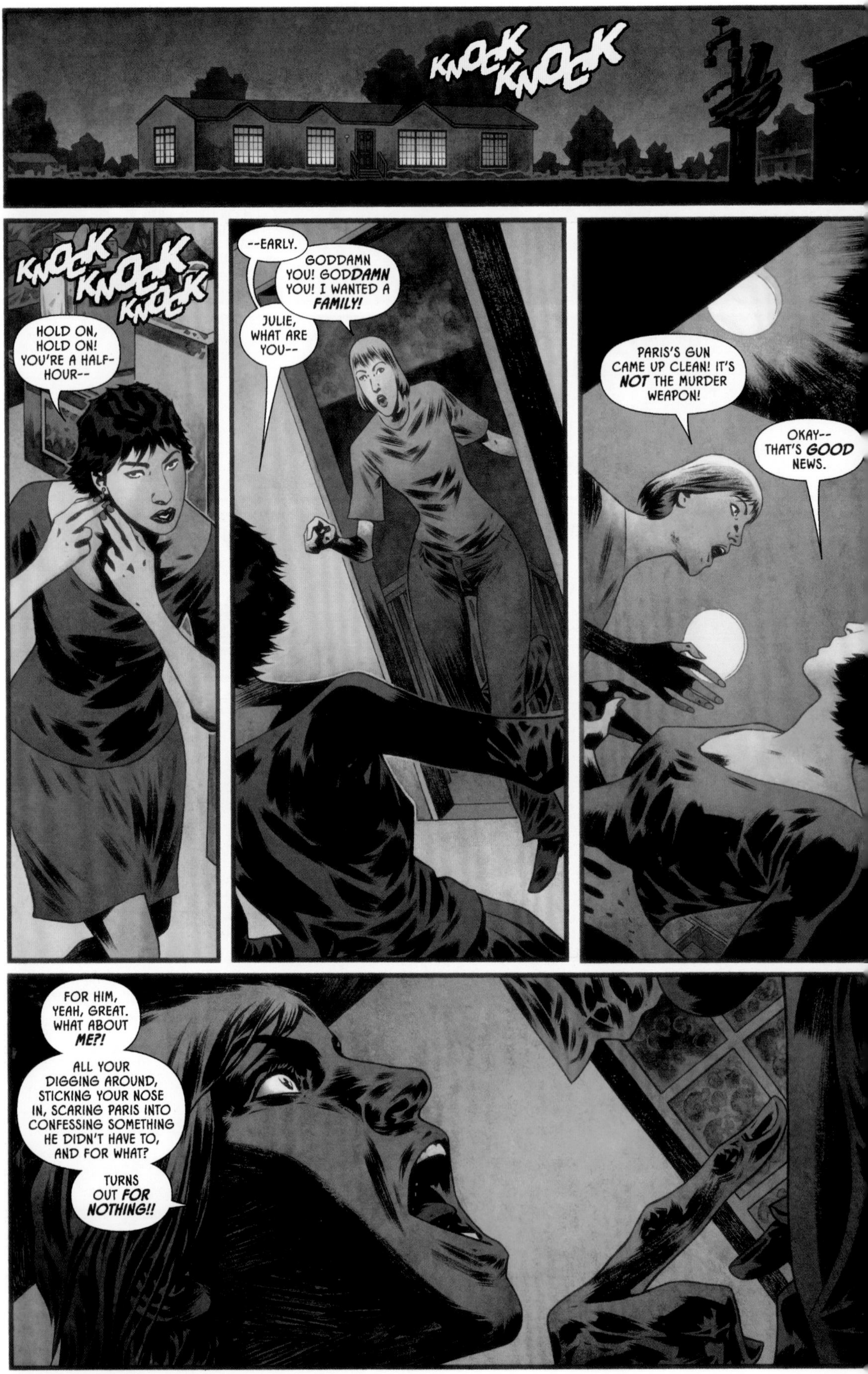
KNOCK KNOCK
KNOCK KNOCK KNOCK
HOLD ON, HOLD ON! YOU'RE A HALF-HOUR--
--EARLY.
JULIE, WHAT ARE YOU--
GODDAMN YOU! GODDAMN YOU! I WANTED A FAMILY!
PARIS'S GUN CAME UP CLEAN! IT'S NOT THE MURDER WEAPON!
OKAY-- THAT'S GOOD NEWS.
FOR HIM, YEAH, GREAT. WHAT ABOUT ME?!
ALL YOUR DIGGING AROUND, STICKING YOUR NOSE IN, SCARING PARIS INTO CONFESSING SOMETHING HE DIDN'T HAVE TO, AND FOR WHAT?
TURNS OUT FOR NOTHING!!

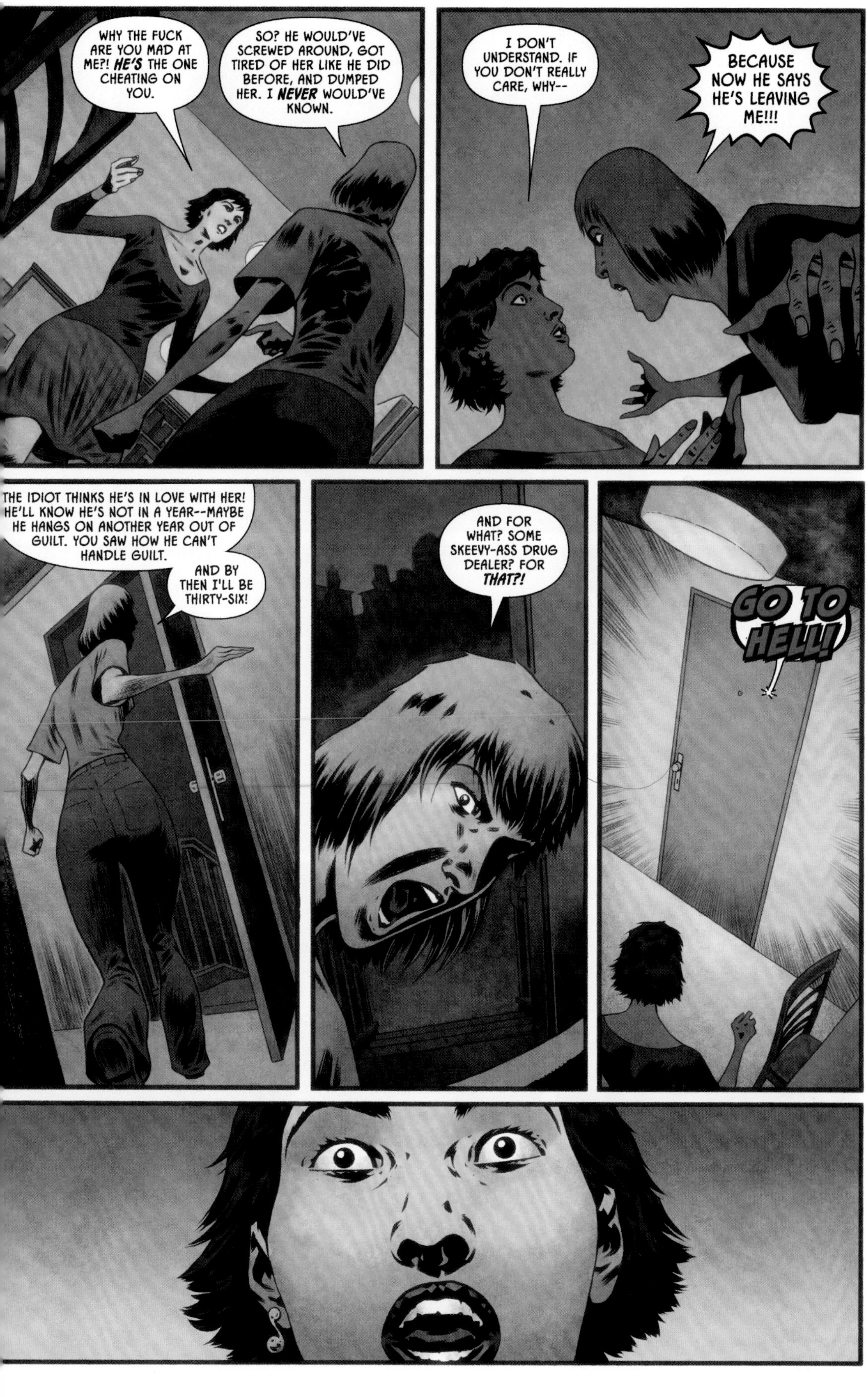

WHY THE FUCK ARE YOU MAD AT ME?! HE'S THE ONE CHEATING ON YOU.
SO? HE WOULD'VE SCREWED AROUND, GOT TIRED OF HER LIKE HE DID BEFORE, AND DUMPED HER. I NEVER WOULD'VE KNOWN.
I DON'T UNDERSTAND. IF YOU DON'T REALLY CARE, WHY--
BECAUSE NOW HE SAYS HE'S LEAVING ME!!!
THE IDIOT THINKS HE'S IN LOVE WITH HER! HE'LL KNOW HE'S NOT IN A YEAR--MAYBE HE HANGS ON ANOTHER YEAR OUT OF GUILT. YOU SAW HOW HE CAN'T HANDLE GUILT.
AND BY THEN I'LL BE THIRTY-SIX!
AND FOR WHAT? SOME SKEEVY-ASS DRUG DEALER? FOR THAT?!
GO TO HELL!

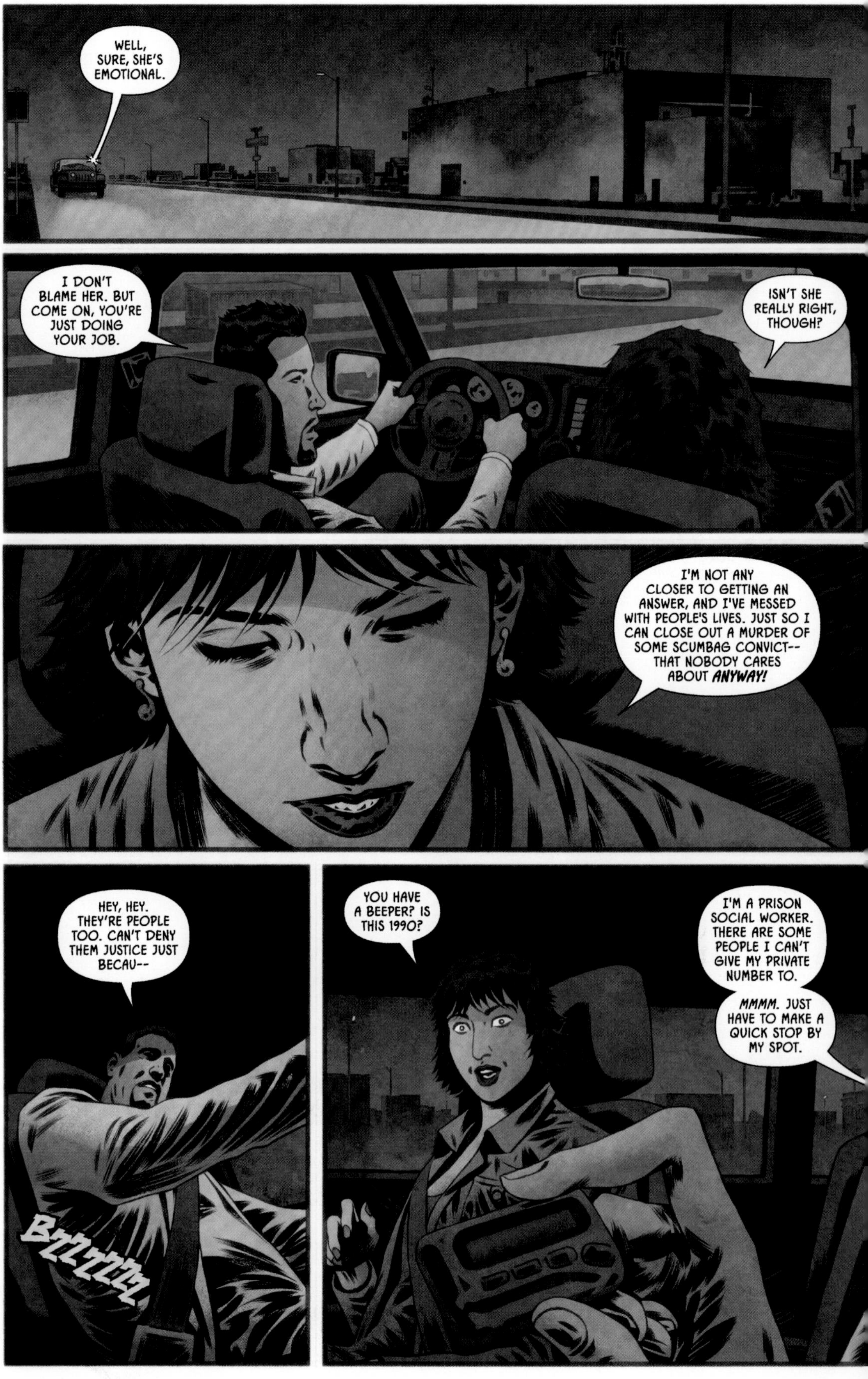
WELL, SURE, SHE'S EMOTIONAL.
I DON'T BLAME HER. BUT COME ON, YOU'RE JUST DOING YOUR JOB.
ISN'T SHE REALLY RIGHT, THOUGH?
I'M NOT ANY CLOSER TO GETTING AN ANSWER, AND I'VE MESSED WITH PEOPLE'S LIVES. JUST SO I CAN CLOSE OUT A MURDER OF SOME SCUMBAG CONVICT-- THAT NOBODY CARES ABOUT ANYWAY!
HEY, HEY. THEY'RE PEOPLE TOO. CAN'T DENY THEM JUSTICE JUST BECAU--
BZZZZZ
YOU HAVE A BEEPER? IS THIS 1990?
I'M A PRISON SOCIAL WORKER. THERE ARE SOME PEOPLE I CAN'T GIVE MY PRIVATE NUMBER TO.
MMMM. JUST HAVE TO MAKE A QUICK STOP BY MY SPOT.

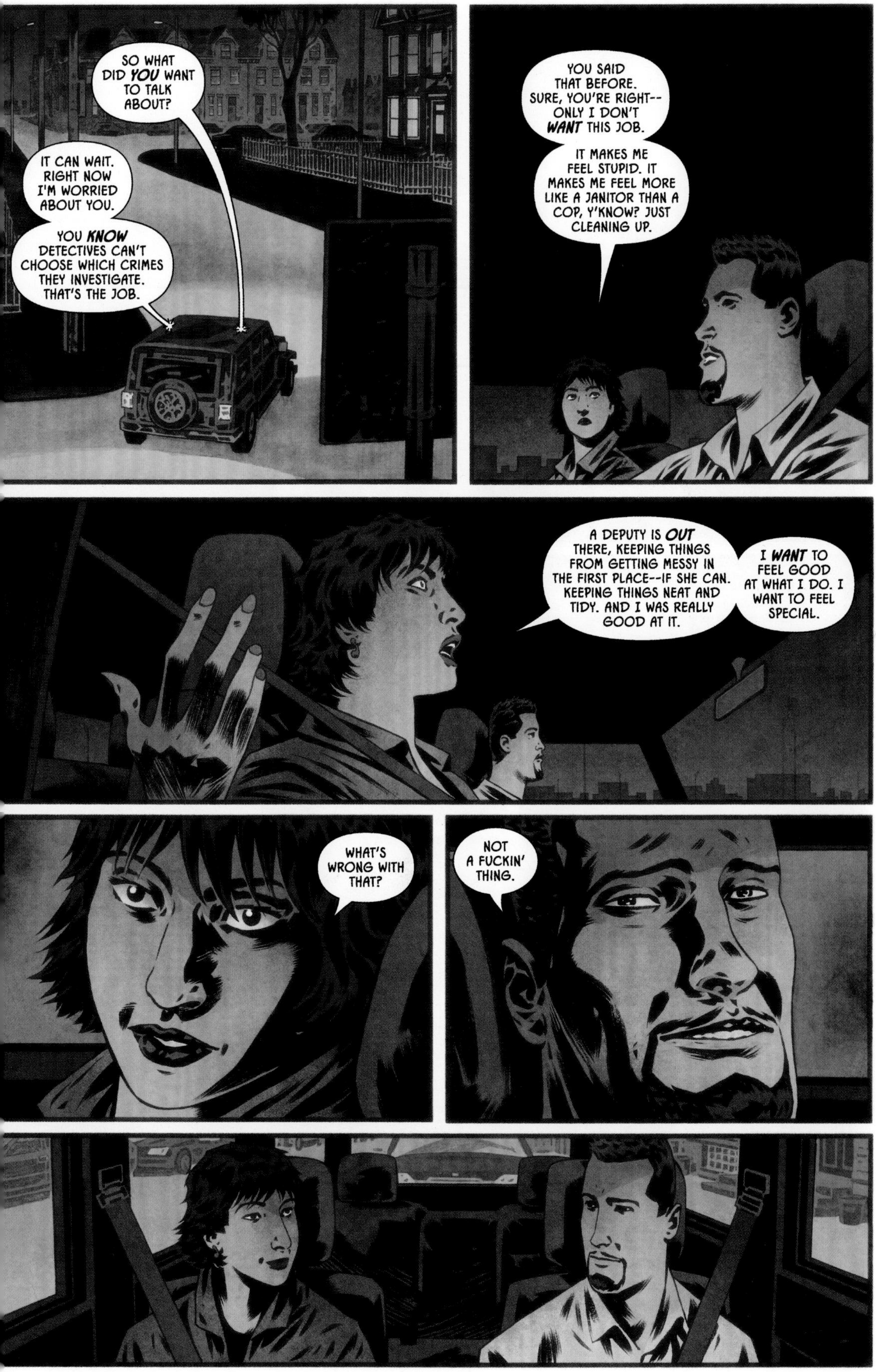
SO WHAT DID YOU WANT TO TALK ABOUT?
IT CAN WAIT. RIGHT NOW I'M WORRIED ABOUT YOU.
YOU KNOW DETECTIVES CAN'T CHOOSE WHICH CRIMES THEY INVESTIGATE. THAT'S THE JOB.
YOU SAID THAT BEFORE. SURE, YOU'RE RIGHT-- ONLY I DON'T WANT THIS JOB.
IT MAKES ME FEEL STUPID. IT MAKES ME FEEL MORE LIKE A JANITOR THAN A COP, Y'KNOW? JUST CLEANING UP.
A DEPUTY IS OUT THERE, KEEPING THINGS FROM GETTING MESSY IN THE FIRST PLACE--IF SHE CAN. KEEPING THINGS NEAT AND TIDY. AND I WAS REALLY GOOD AT IT.
I WANT TO FEEL GOOD AT WHAT I DO. I WANT TO FEEL SPECIAL.
WHAT'S WRONG WITH THAT?
NOT A FUCKIN' THING.

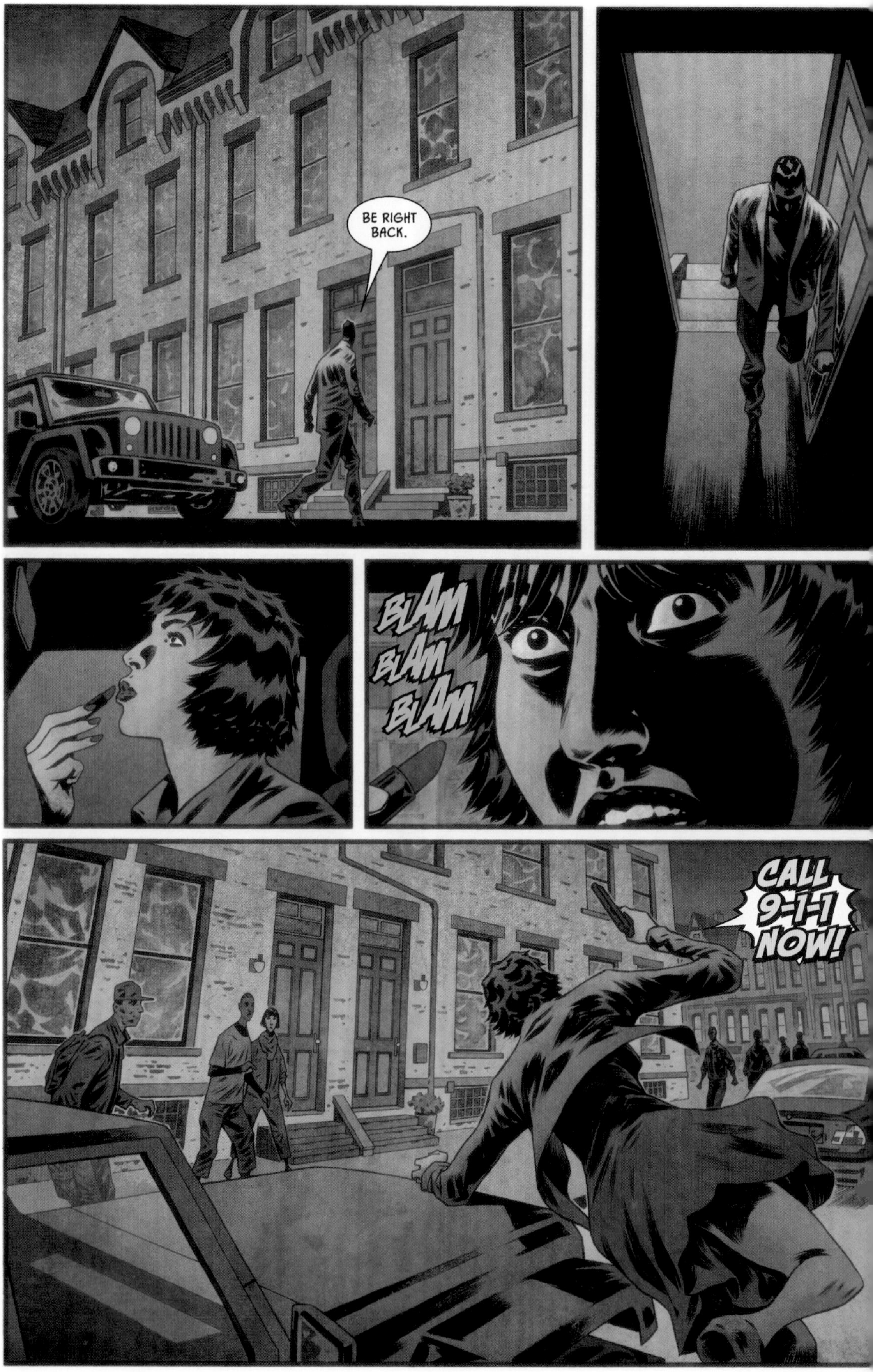
BE RIGHT BACK.
BLAM
BLAM
BLAM
CALL 9-1-1 NOW!

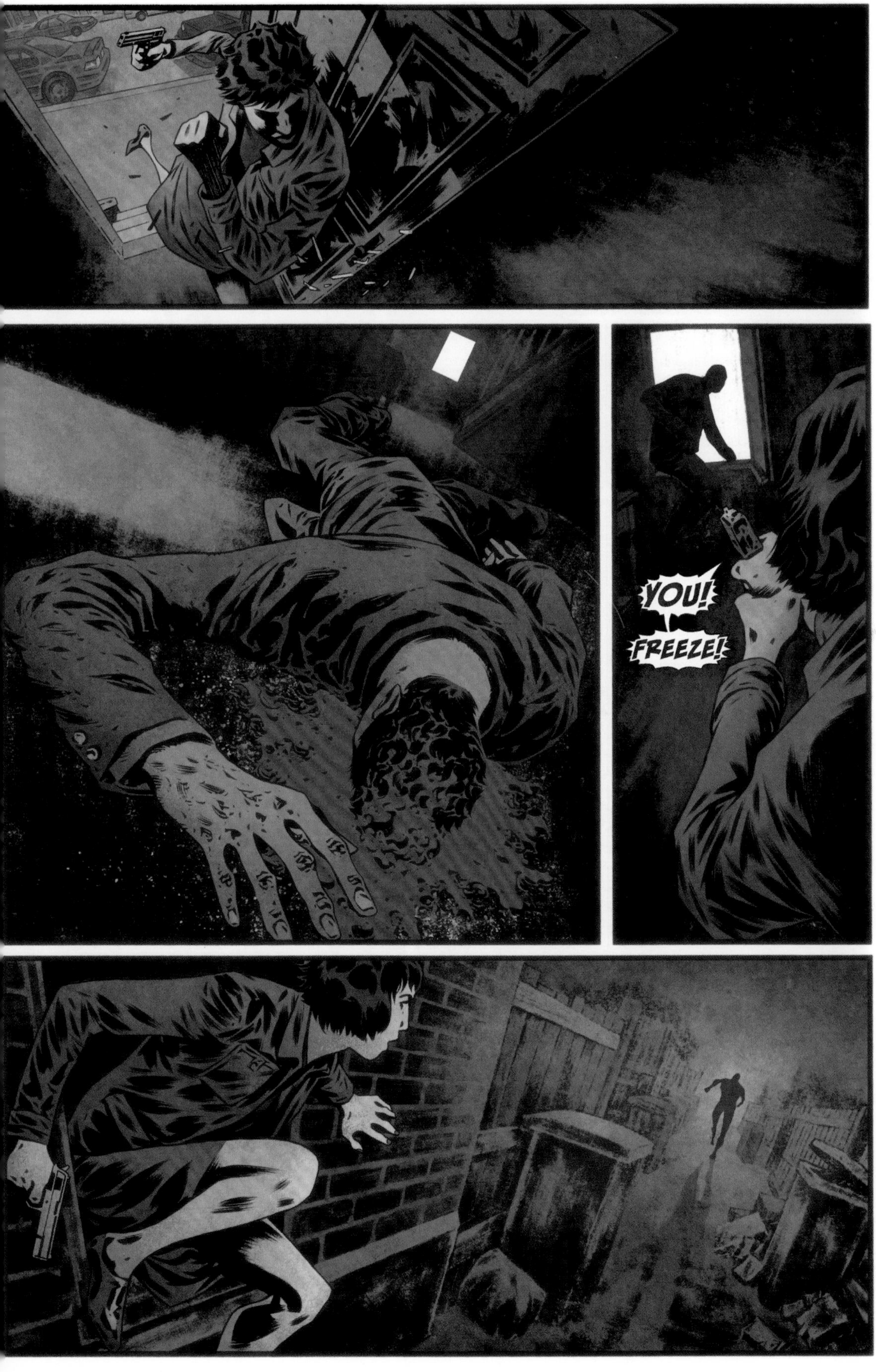
YOU!
FREEZE!

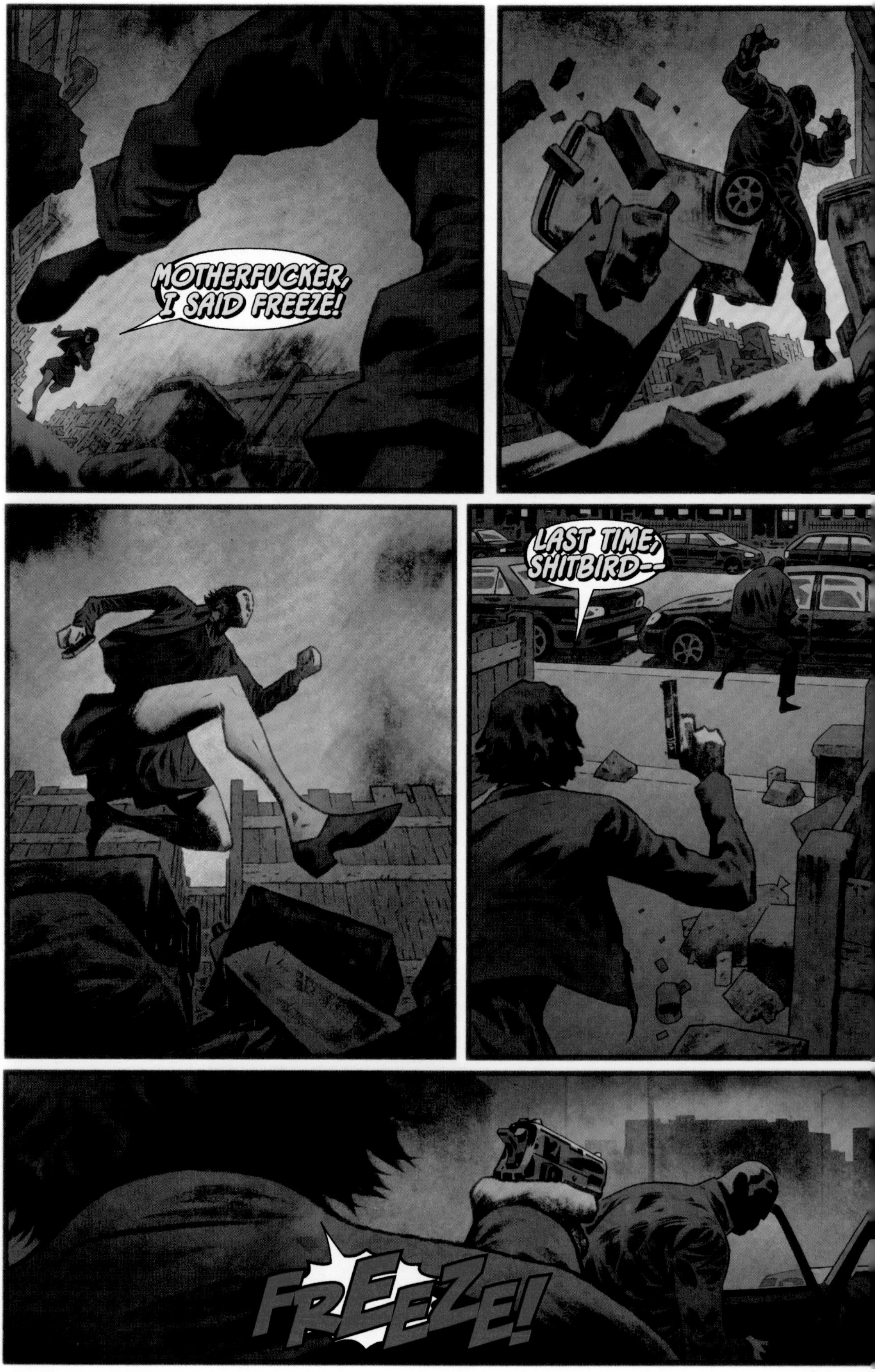
MOTHERFUCKER, I SAID FREEZE!
LAST TIME, SHITBIRD--
FREEZE!

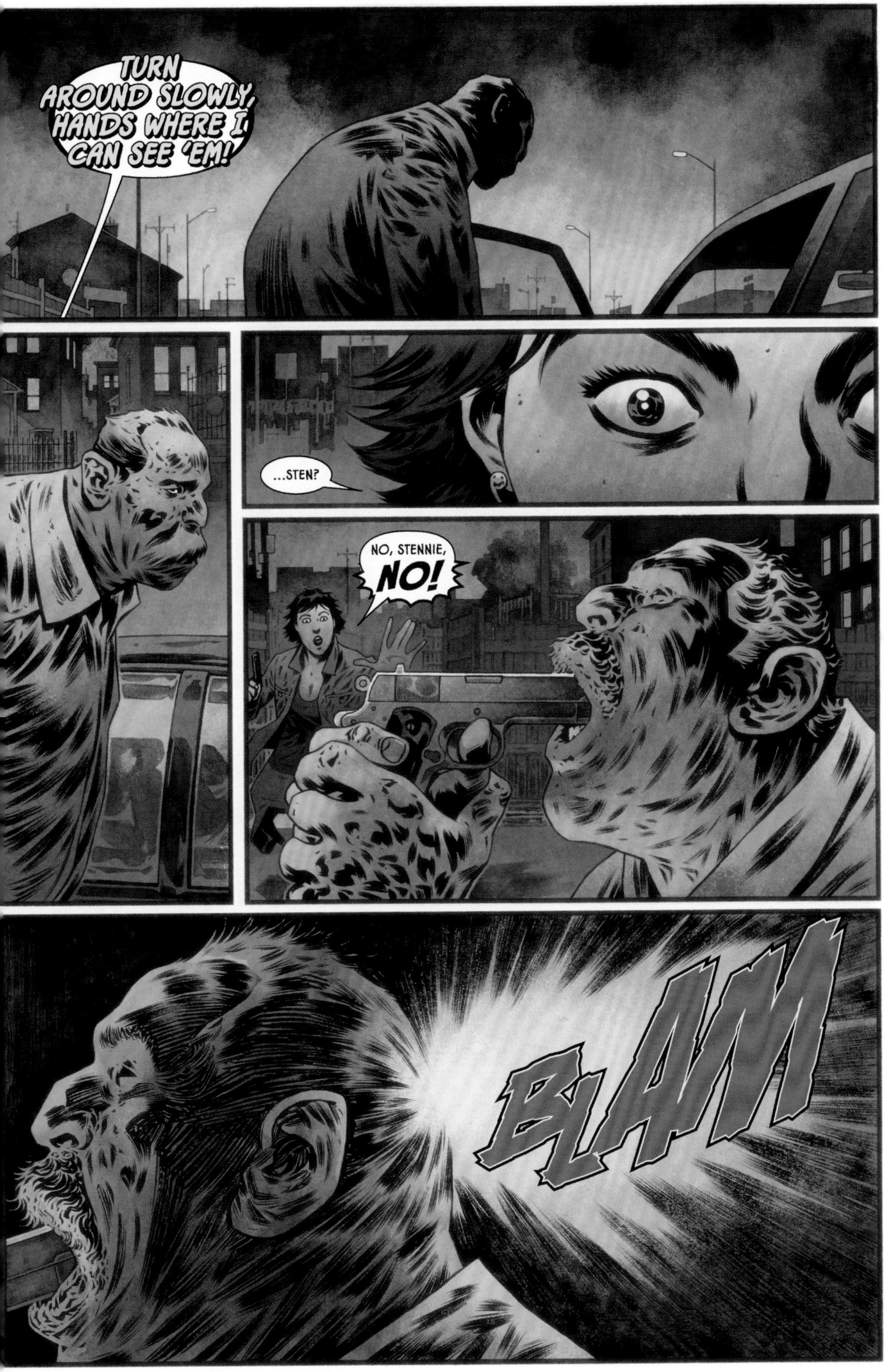
TURN AROUND SLOWLY, HANDS WHERE I CAN SEE 'EM!
...STEN?
NO, STENNIE, NO!
BLAM

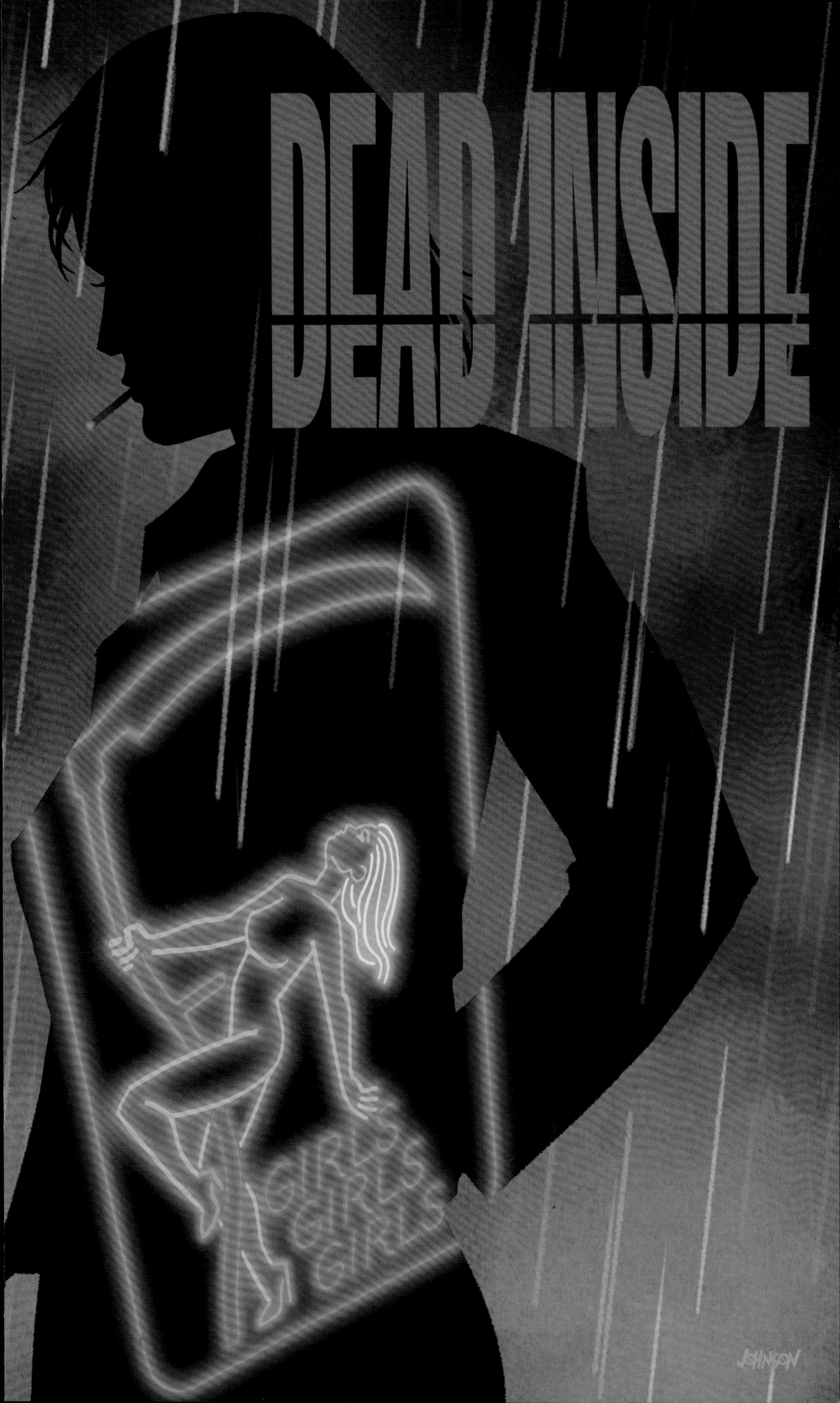
DEAD INSIDE
GIRLS
GIRLS
GIRLS
JOHNSON

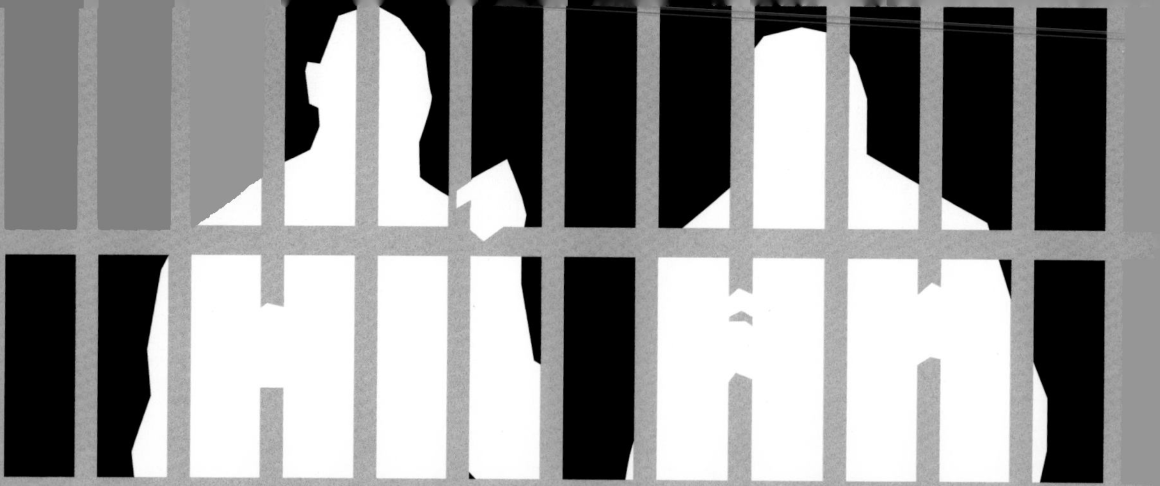

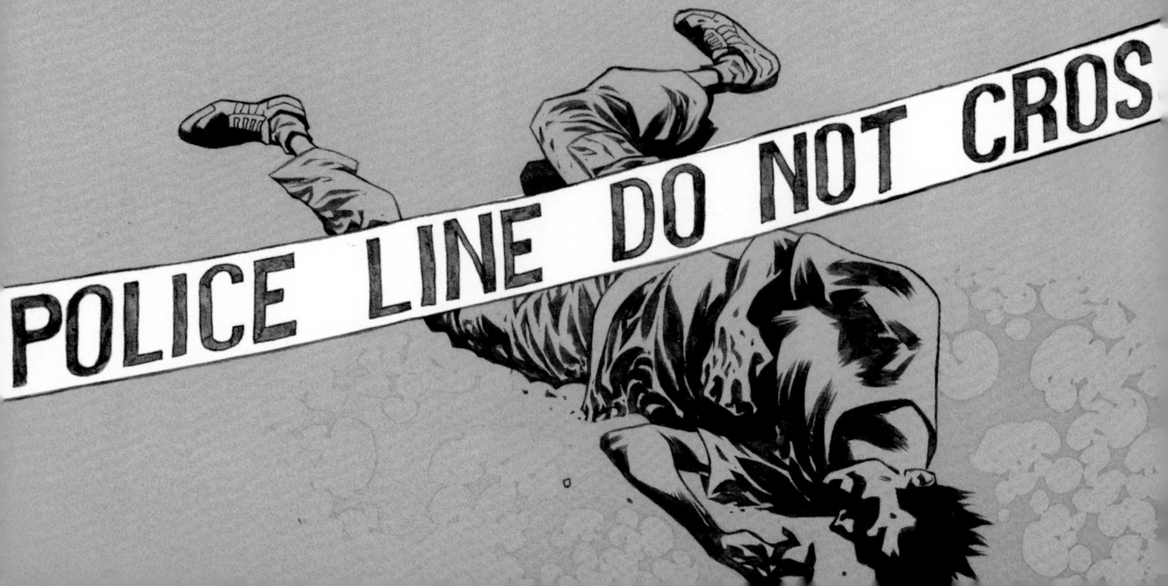
POLICE LINE DO NOT CROS

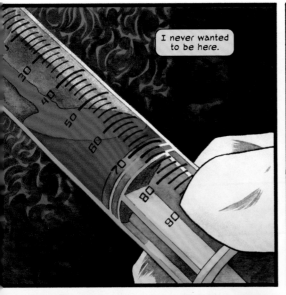

I never wanted to be here.

Not in plainclothes, not in the Detectives unit, not in Jail Crimes.

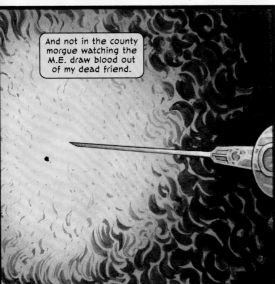

And not in the county morgue watching the M.E. draw blood out of my dead friend.

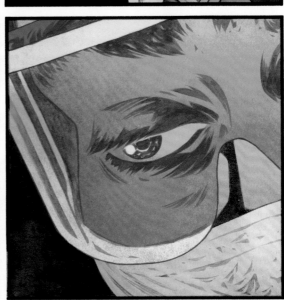

My friend. Who I didn't know at all.

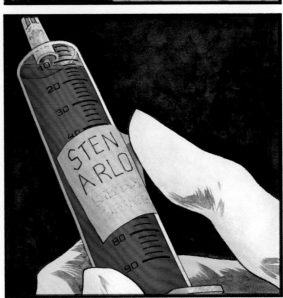

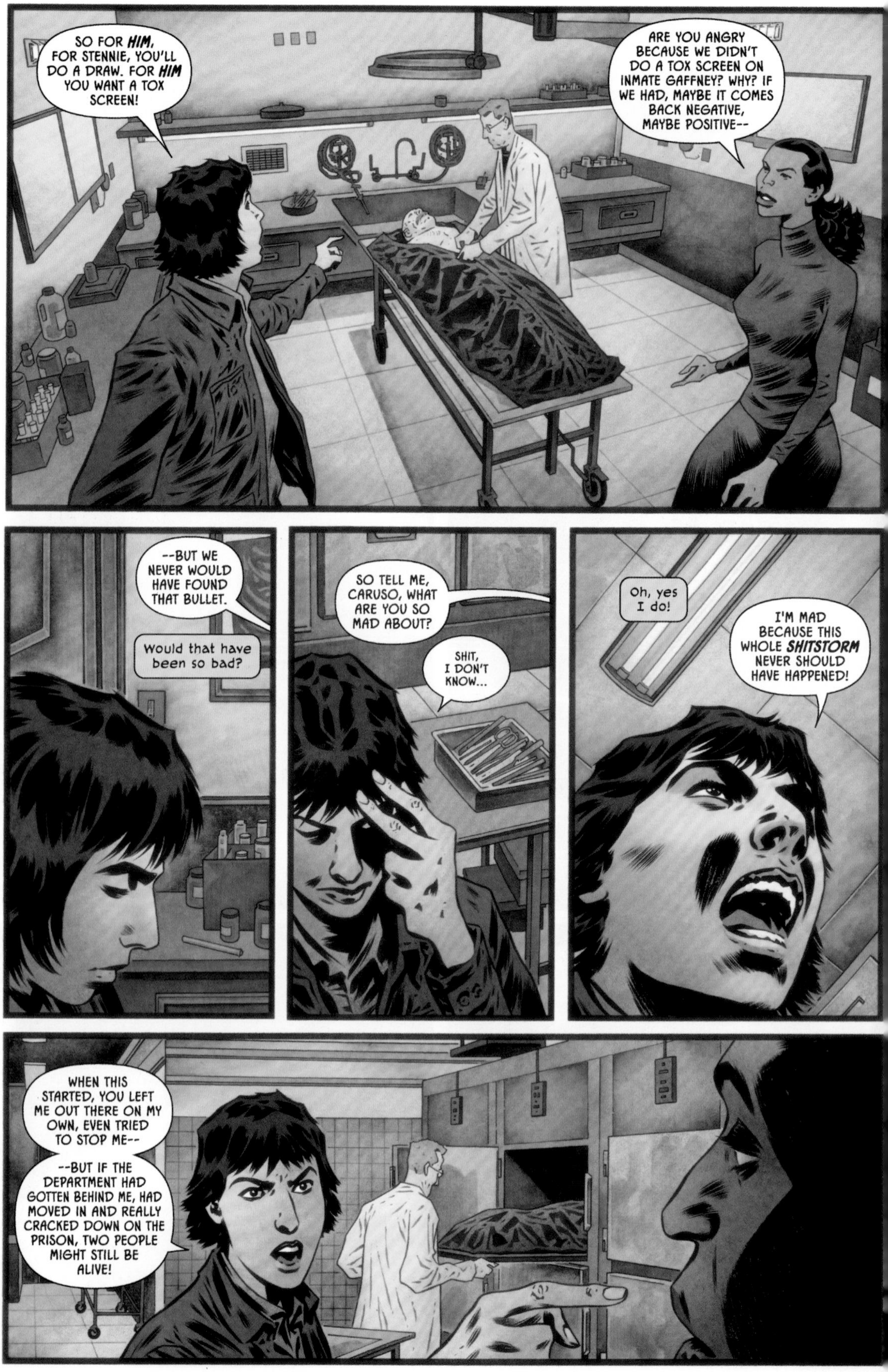

SO FOR HIM, FOR STENNIE, YOU'LL DO A DRAW. FOR HIM YOU WANT A TOX SCREEN!
ARE YOU ANGRY BECAUSE WE DIDN'T DO A TOX SCREEN ON INMATE GAFFNEY? WHY? IF WE HAD, MAYBE IT COMES BACK NEGATIVE, MAYBE POSITIVE--
--BUT WE NEVER WOULD HAVE FOUND THAT BULLET.
Would that have been so bad?
SO TELL ME, CARUSO, WHAT ARE YOU SO MAD ABOUT?
SHIT, I DON'T KNOW...
Oh, yes I do!
I'M MAD BECAUSE THIS WHOLE SHITSTORM NEVER SHOULD HAVE HAPPENED!
WHEN THIS STARTED, YOU LEFT ME OUT THERE ON MY OWN, EVEN TRIED TO STOP ME--
--BUT IF THE DEPARTMENT HAD GOTTEN BEHIND ME, HAD MOVED IN AND REALLY CRACKED DOWN ON THE PRISON, TWO PEOPLE MIGHT STILL BE ALIVE!

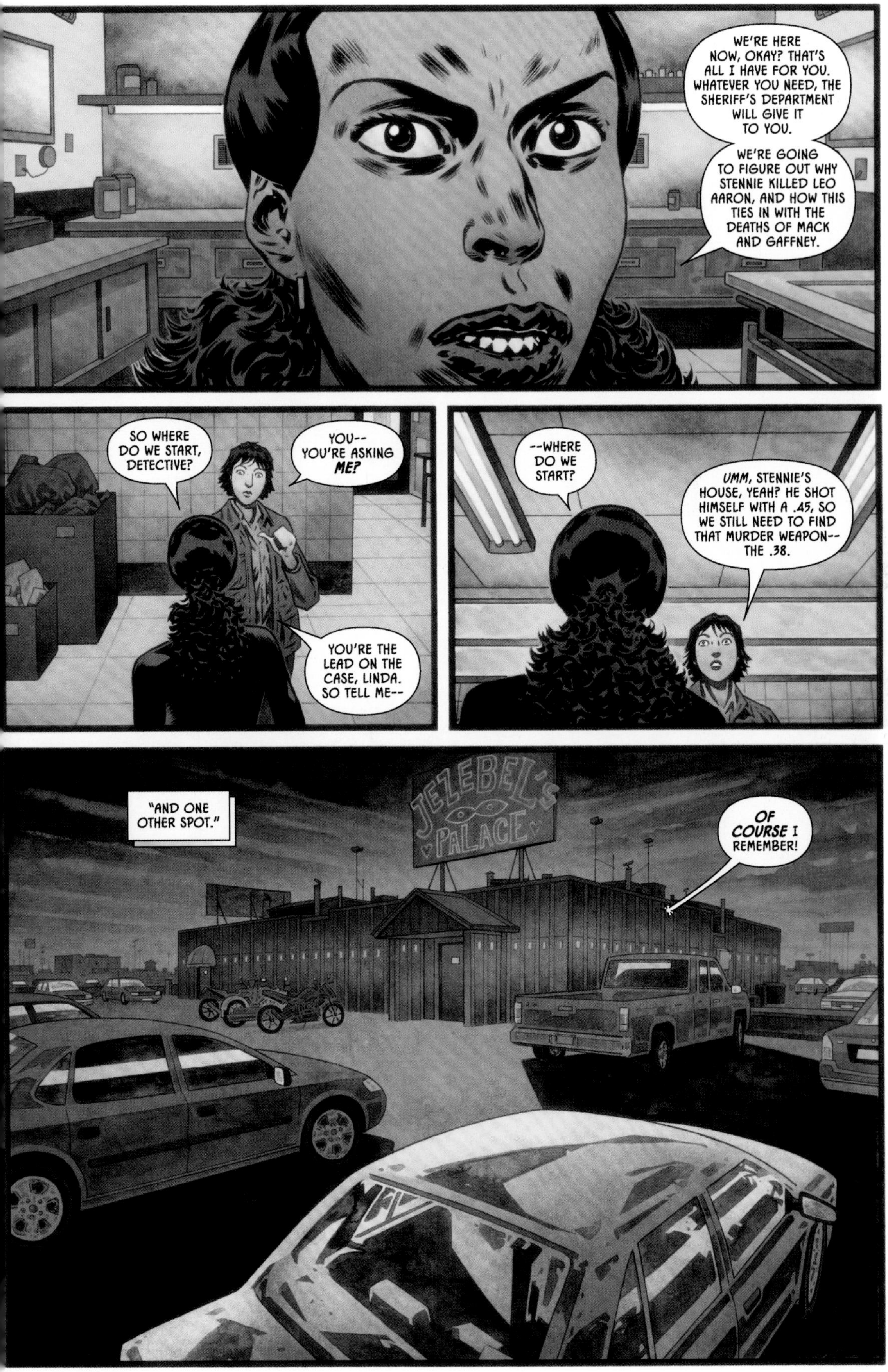
WE'RE HERE NOW, OKAY? THAT'S ALL I HAVE FOR YOU. WHATEVER YOU NEED, THE SHERIFF'S DEPARTMENT WILL GIVE IT TO YOU.
WE'RE GOING TO FIGURE OUT WHY STENNIE KILLED LEO AARON, AND HOW THIS TIES IN WITH THE DEATHS OF MACK AND GAFFNEY.
SO WHERE DO WE START, DETECTIVE?
YOU-- YOU'RE ASKING *ME?*
YOU'RE THE LEAD ON THE CASE, LINDA. SO TELL ME--
--WHERE DO WE START?
UMM, STENNIE'S HOUSE, YEAH? HE SHOT HIMSELF WITH A .45, SO WE STILL NEED TO FIND THAT MURDER WEAPON-- THE .38.
JEZEBEL'S PALACE
"AND ONE OTHER SPOT."
OF COURSE I REMEMBER!

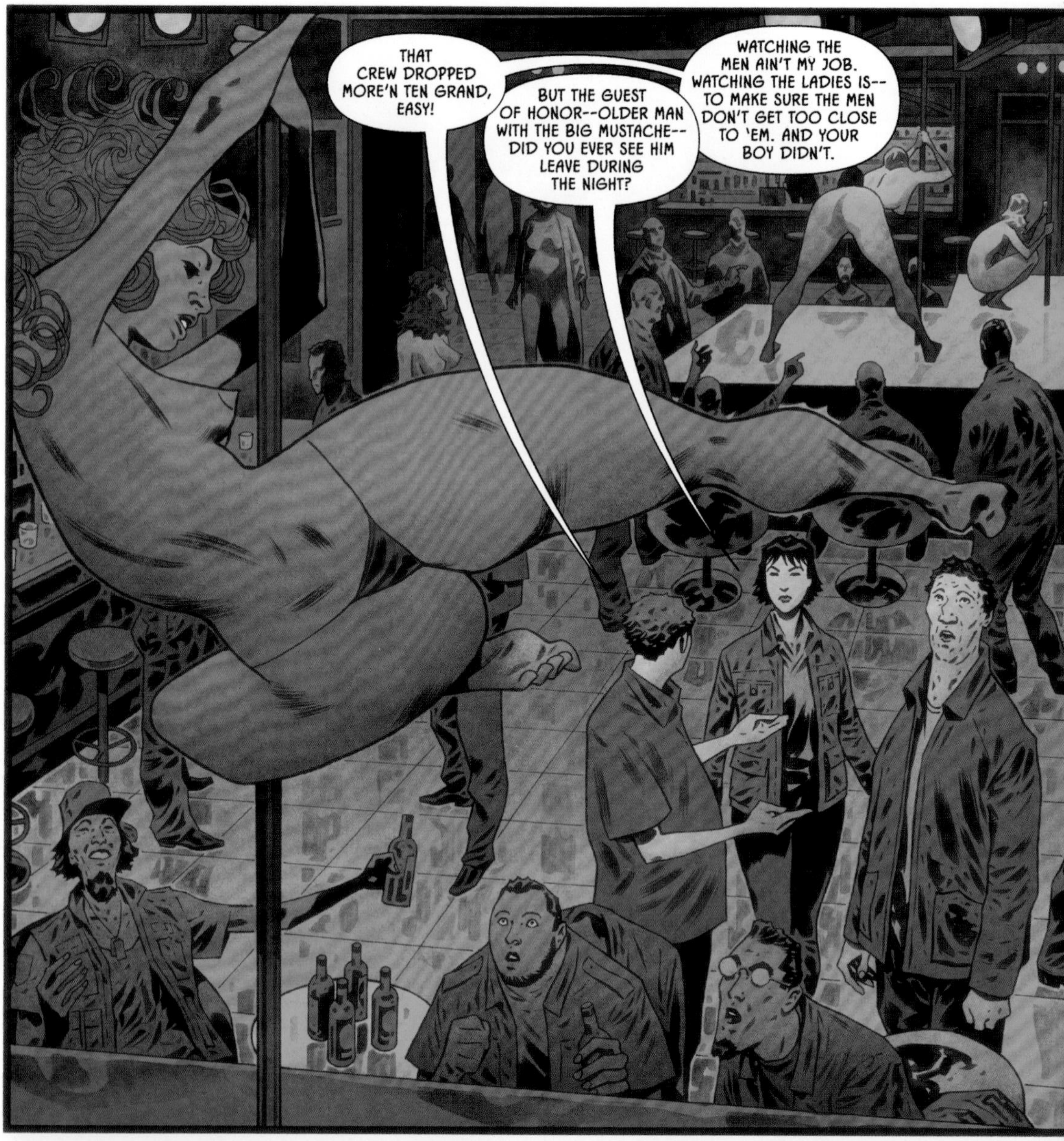
THAT CREW DROPPED MORE'N TEN GRAND, EASY!
BUT THE GUEST OF HONOR--OLDER MAN WITH THE BIG MUSTACHE--DID YOU EVER SEE HIM LEAVE DURING THE NIGHT?
WATCHING THE MEN AIN'T MY JOB. WATCHING THE LADIES IS--TO MAKE SURE THE MEN DON'T GET TOO CLOSE TO 'EM. AND YOUR BOY DIDN'T.

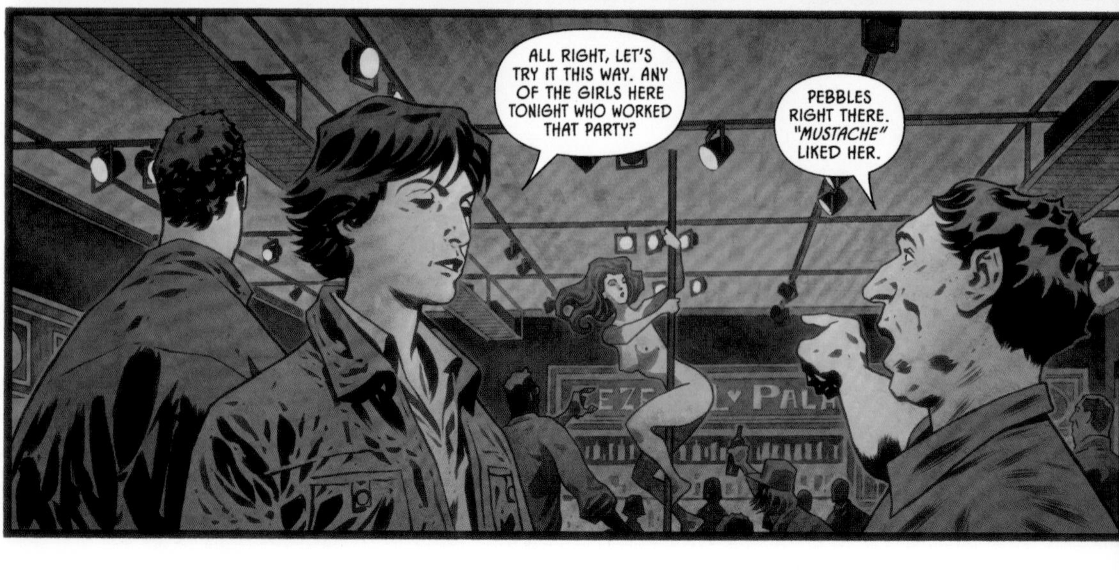
ALL RIGHT, LET'S TRY IT THIS WAY. ANY OF THE GIRLS HERE TONIGHT WHO WORKED THAT PARTY?
PEBBLES RIGHT THERE. "*MUSTACHE*" LIKED HER.

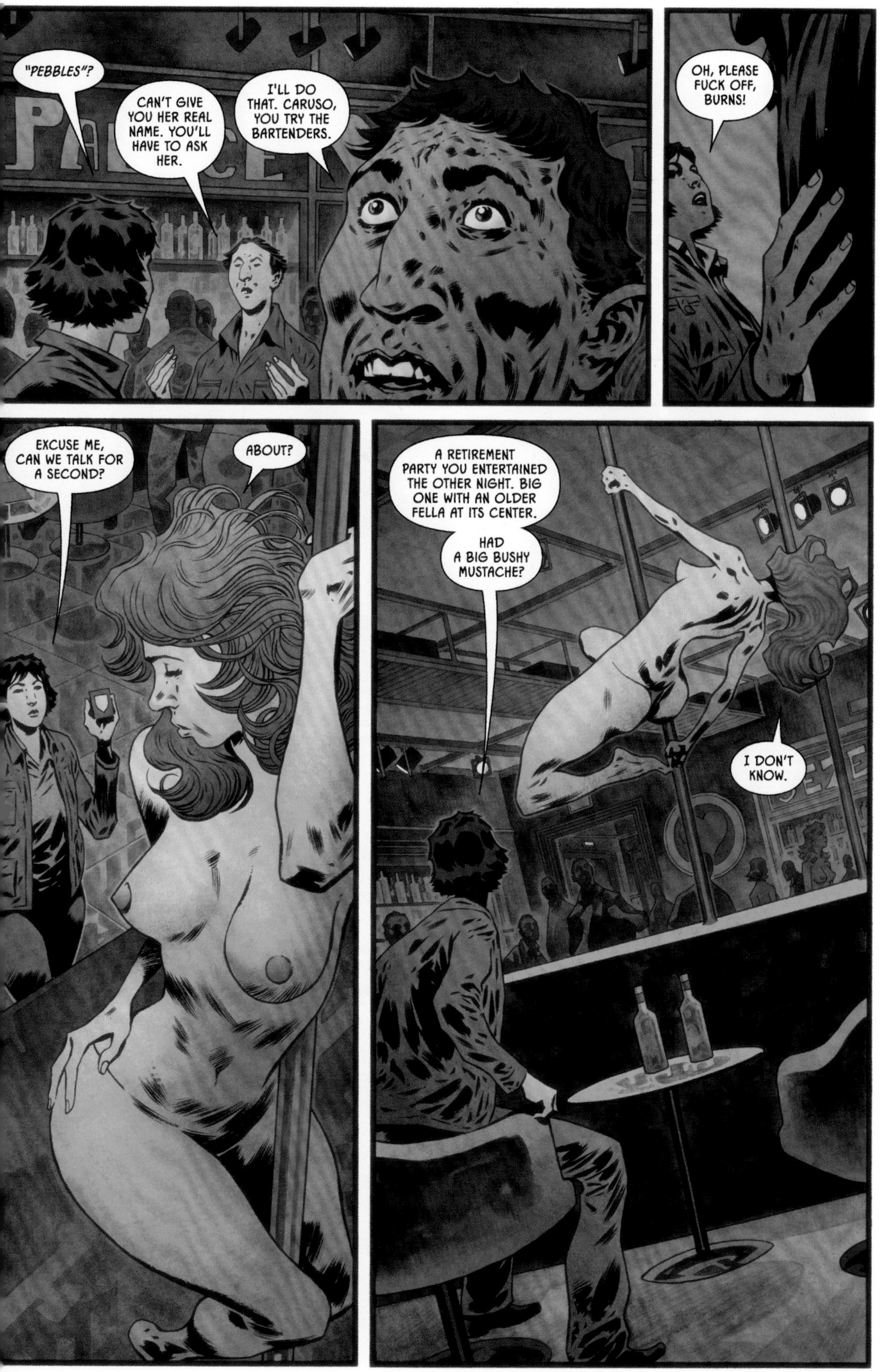
"PEBBLES"?
CAN'T GIVE YOU HER REAL NAME. YOU'LL HAVE TO ASK HER.
I'LL DO THAT. CARUSO, YOU TRY THE BARTENDERS.
OH, PLEASE FUCK OFF, BURNS!
EXCUSE ME, CAN WE TALK FOR A SECOND?
ABOUT?
A RETIREMENT PARTY YOU ENTERTAINED THE OTHER NIGHT. BIG ONE WITH AN OLDER FELLA AT ITS CENTER.
HAD A BIG BUSHY MUSTACHE?
I DON'T KNOW.

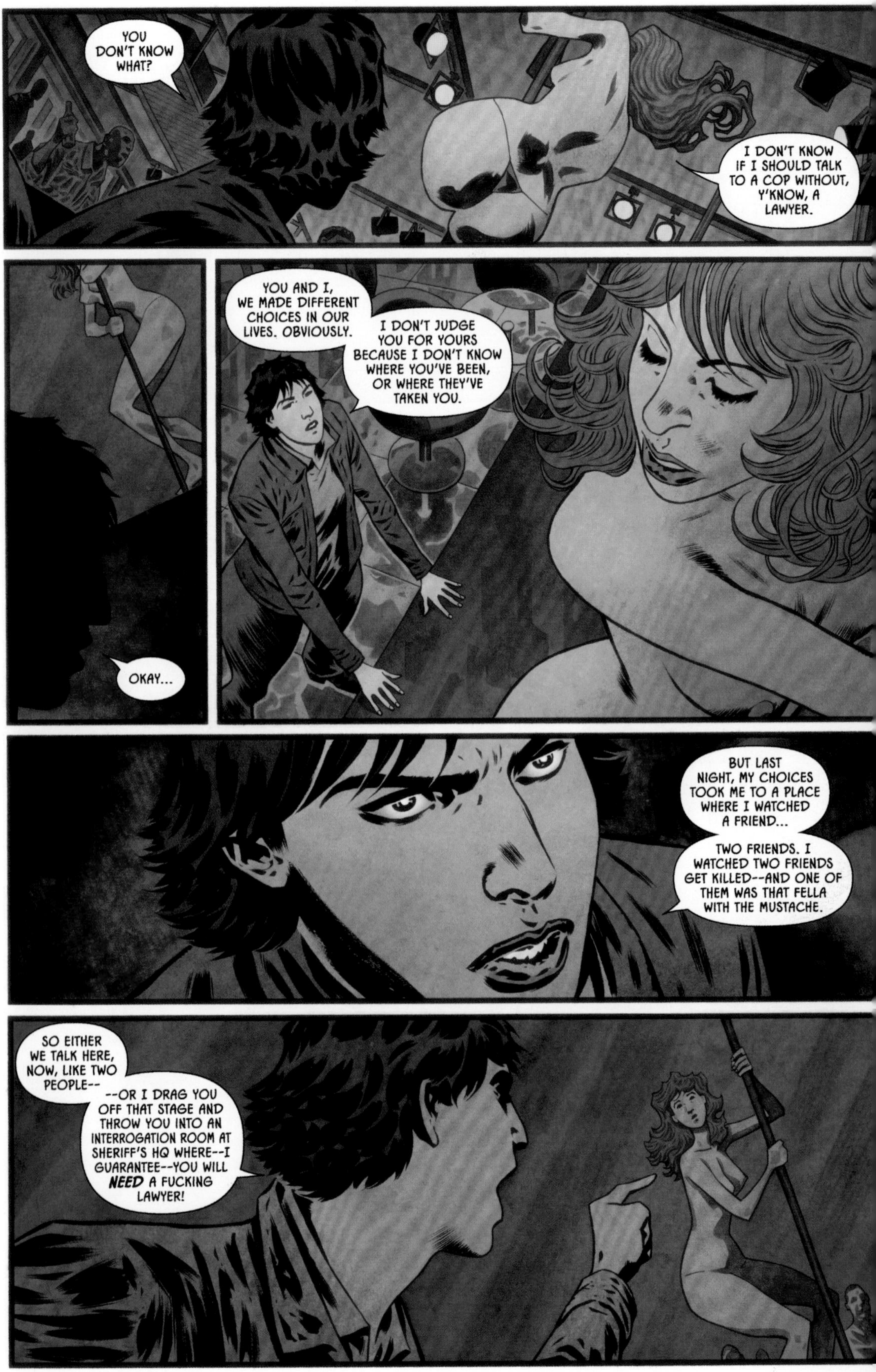
YOU DON'T KNOW WHAT?
I DON'T KNOW IF I SHOULD TALK TO A COP WITHOUT, Y'KNOW, A LAWYER.
OKAY...
YOU AND I, WE MADE DIFFERENT CHOICES IN OUR LIVES. OBVIOUSLY.
I DON'T JUDGE YOU FOR YOURS BECAUSE I DON'T KNOW WHERE YOU'VE BEEN, OR WHERE THEY'VE TAKEN YOU.
BUT LAST NIGHT, MY CHOICES TOOK ME TO A PLACE WHERE I WATCHED A FRIEND...
TWO FRIENDS. I WATCHED TWO FRIENDS GET KILLED--AND ONE OF THEM WAS THAT FELLA WITH THE MUSTACHE.
SO EITHER WE TALK HERE, NOW, LIKE TWO PEOPLE--
--OR I DRAG YOU OFF THAT STAGE AND THROW YOU INTO AN INTERROGATION ROOM AT SHERIFF'S HQ WHERE--I GUARANTEE--YOU WILL **NEED** A FUCKING LAWYER!

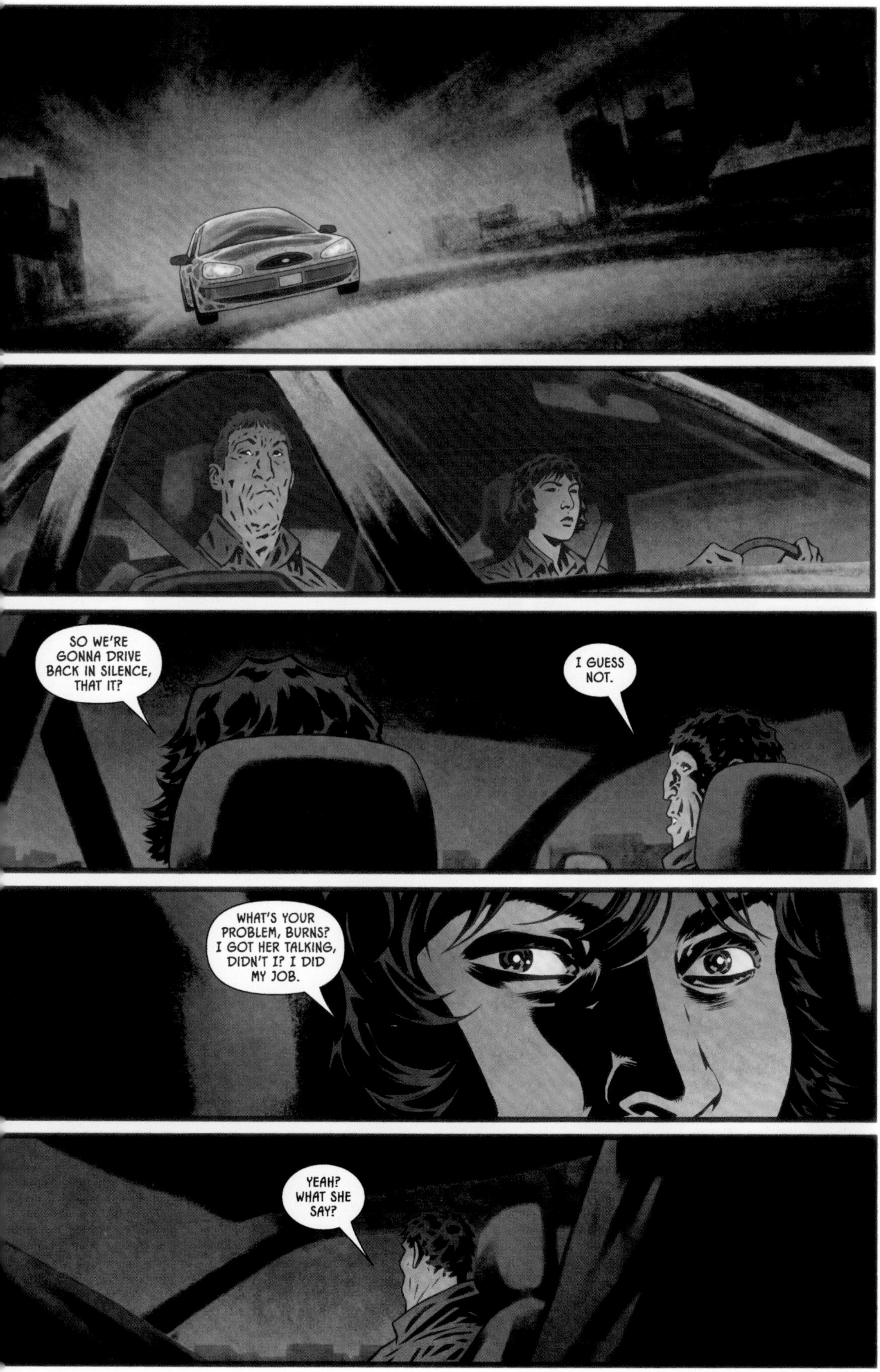
SO WE'RE GONNA DRIVE BACK IN SILENCE, THAT IT?
I GUESS NOT.
WHAT'S YOUR PROBLEM, BURNS? I GOT HER TALKING, DIDN'T I? I DID MY JOB.
YEAH? WHAT SHE SAY?

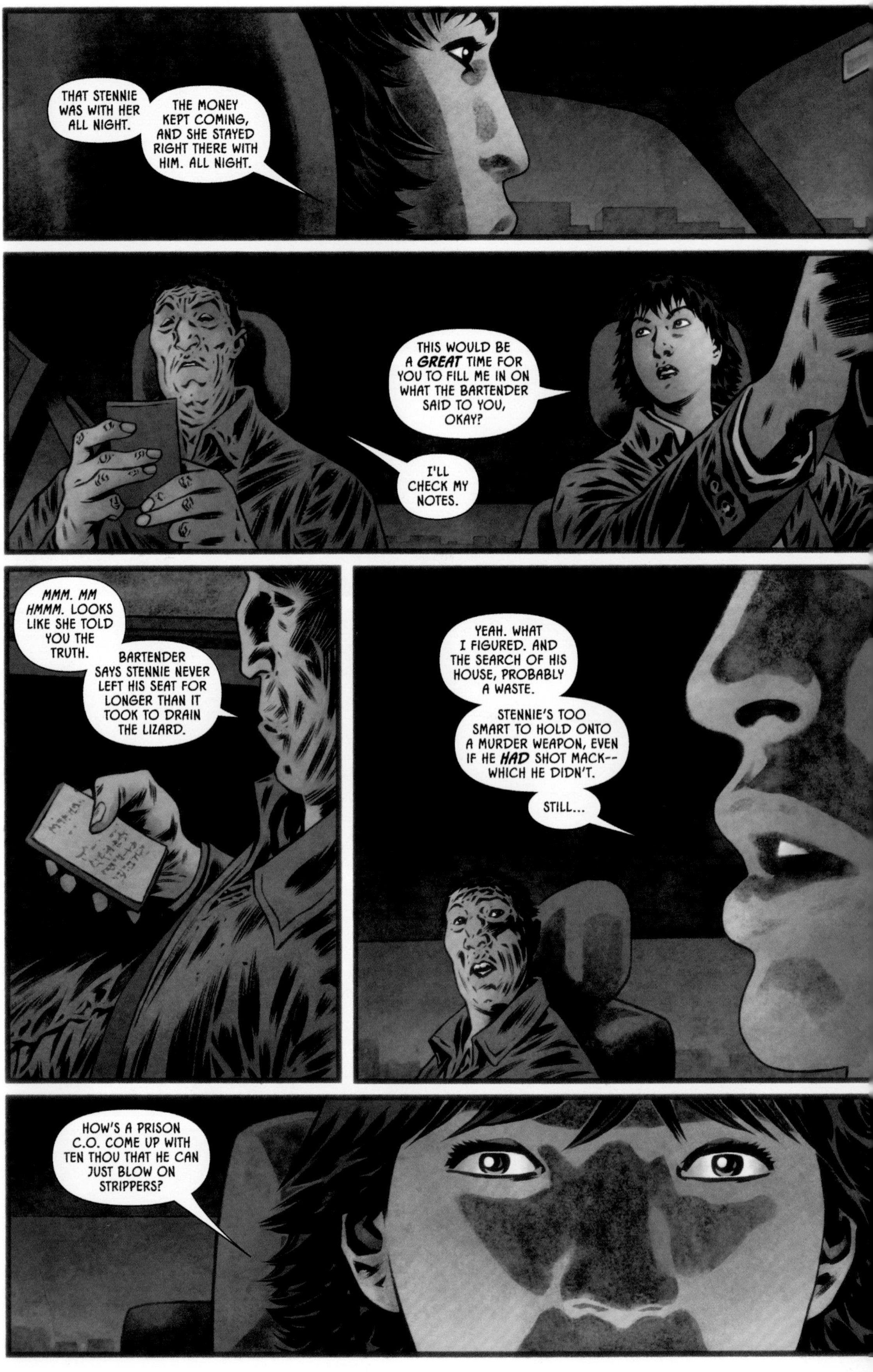

THAT STENNIE WAS WITH HER ALL NIGHT.
THE MONEY KEPT COMING, AND SHE STAYED RIGHT THERE WITH HIM. ALL NIGHT.
THIS WOULD BE A *GREAT* TIME FOR YOU TO FILL ME IN ON WHAT THE BARTENDER SAID TO YOU, OKAY?
I'LL CHECK MY NOTES.
MMM. MM HMMM. LOOKS LIKE SHE TOLD YOU THE TRUTH.
BARTENDER SAYS STENNIE NEVER LEFT HIS SEAT FOR LONGER THAN IT TOOK TO DRAIN THE LIZARD.
YEAH. WHAT I FIGURED. AND THE SEARCH OF HIS HOUSE, PROBABLY A WASTE.
STENNIE'S TOO SMART TO HOLD ONTO A MURDER WEAPON, EVEN IF HE *HAD* SHOT MACK-- WHICH HE DIDN'T.
STILL...
HOW'S A PRISON C.O. COME UP WITH TEN THOU THAT HE CAN JUST BLOW ON STRIPPERS?

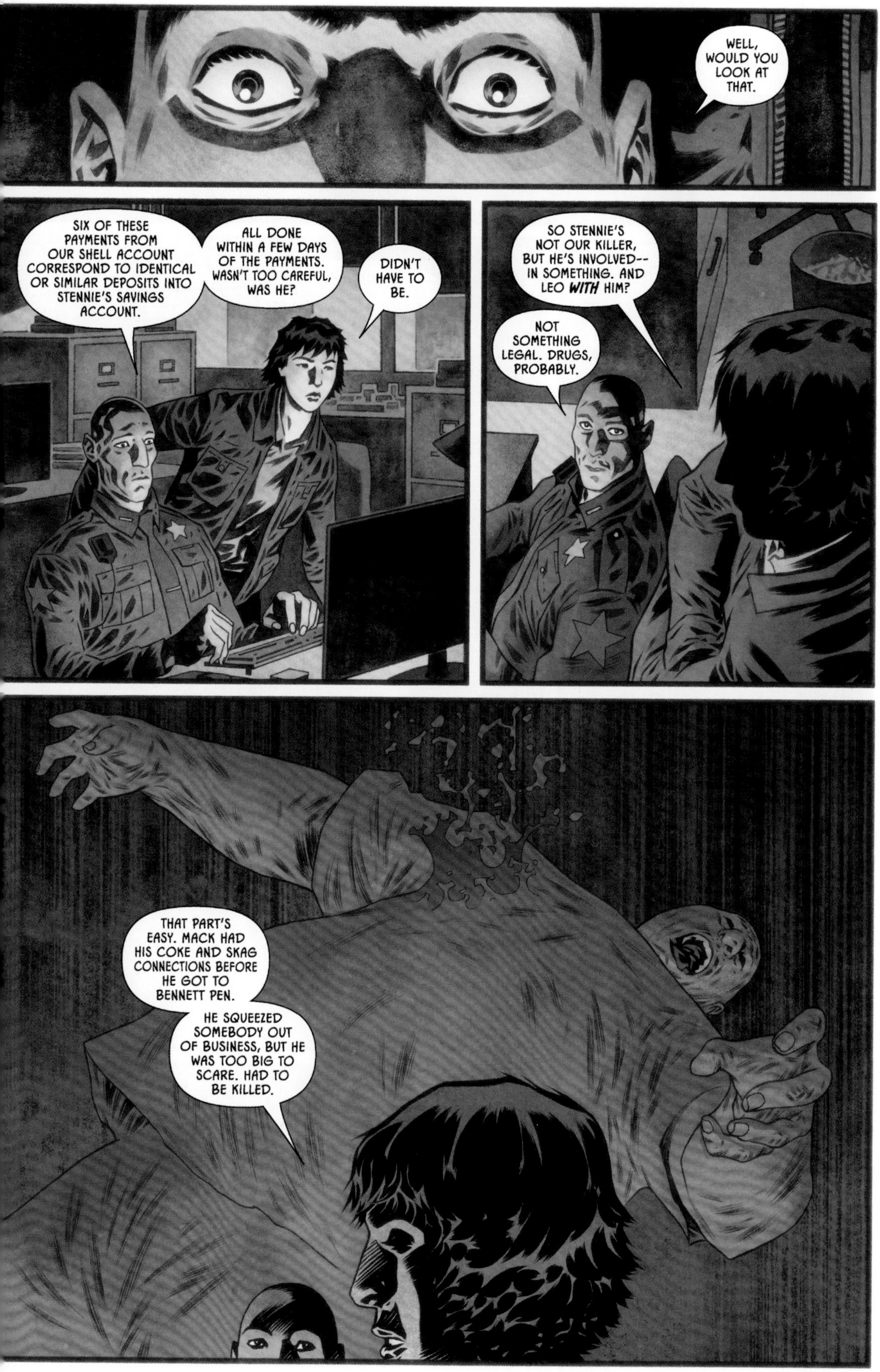

WELL, WOULD YOU LOOK AT THAT.
SIX OF THESE PAYMENTS FROM OUR SHELL ACCOUNT CORRESPOND TO IDENTICAL OR SIMILAR DEPOSITS INTO STENNIE'S SAVINGS ACCOUNT.
ALL DONE WITHIN A FEW DAYS OF THE PAYMENTS. WASN'T TOO CAREFUL, WAS HE?
DIDN'T HAVE TO BE.
SO STENNIE'S NOT OUR KILLER, BUT HE'S INVOLVED-- IN SOMETHING. AND LEO *WITH* HIM?
NOT SOMETHING LEGAL. DRUGS, PROBABLY.
THAT PART'S EASY. MACK HAD HIS COKE AND SKAG CONNECTIONS BEFORE HE GOT TO BENNETT PEN.
HE SQUEEZED SOMEBODY OUT OF BUSINESS, BUT HE WAS TOO BIG TO SCARE. HAD TO BE KILLED.

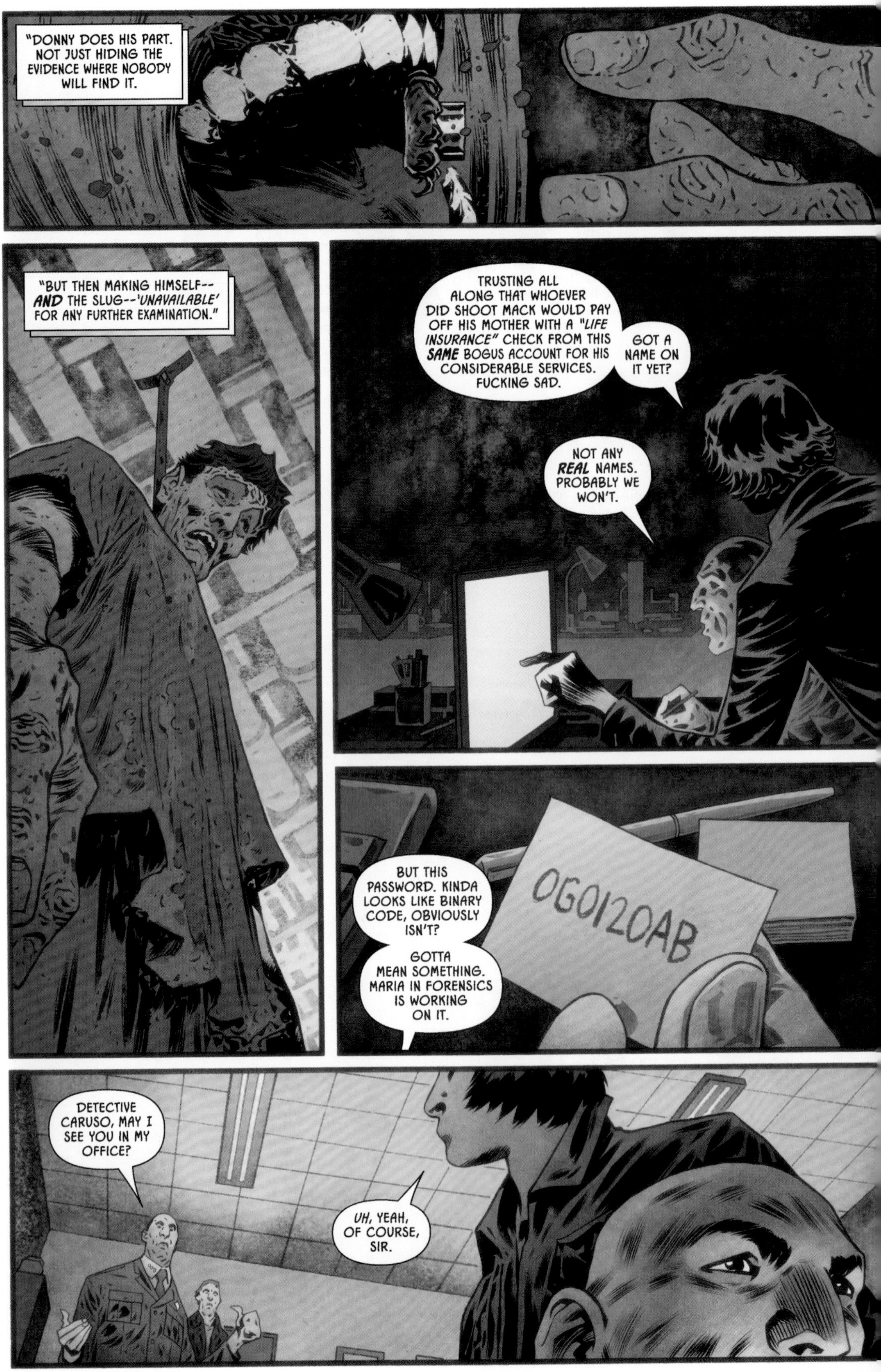
"DONNY DOES HIS PART. NOT JUST HIDING THE EVIDENCE WHERE NOBODY WILL FIND IT.
"BUT THEN MAKING HIMSELF-- *AND* THE SLUG--*'UNAVAILABLE'* FOR ANY FURTHER EXAMINATION."
TRUSTING ALL ALONG THAT WHOEVER DID SHOOT MACK WOULD PAY OFF HIS MOTHER WITH A *"LIFE INSURANCE"* CHECK FROM THIS *SAME* BOGUS ACCOUNT FOR HIS CONSIDERABLE SERVICES. FUCKING SAD.
GOT A NAME ON IT YET?
NOT ANY *REAL* NAMES. PROBABLY WE WON'T.
OG0120AB
BUT THIS PASSWORD. KINDA LOOKS LIKE BINARY CODE, OBVIOUSLY ISN'T?
GOTTA MEAN SOMETHING. MARIA IN FORENSICS IS WORKING ON IT.
DETECTIVE CARUSO, MAY I SEE YOU IN MY OFFICE?
UH, YEAH, OF COURSE, SIR.

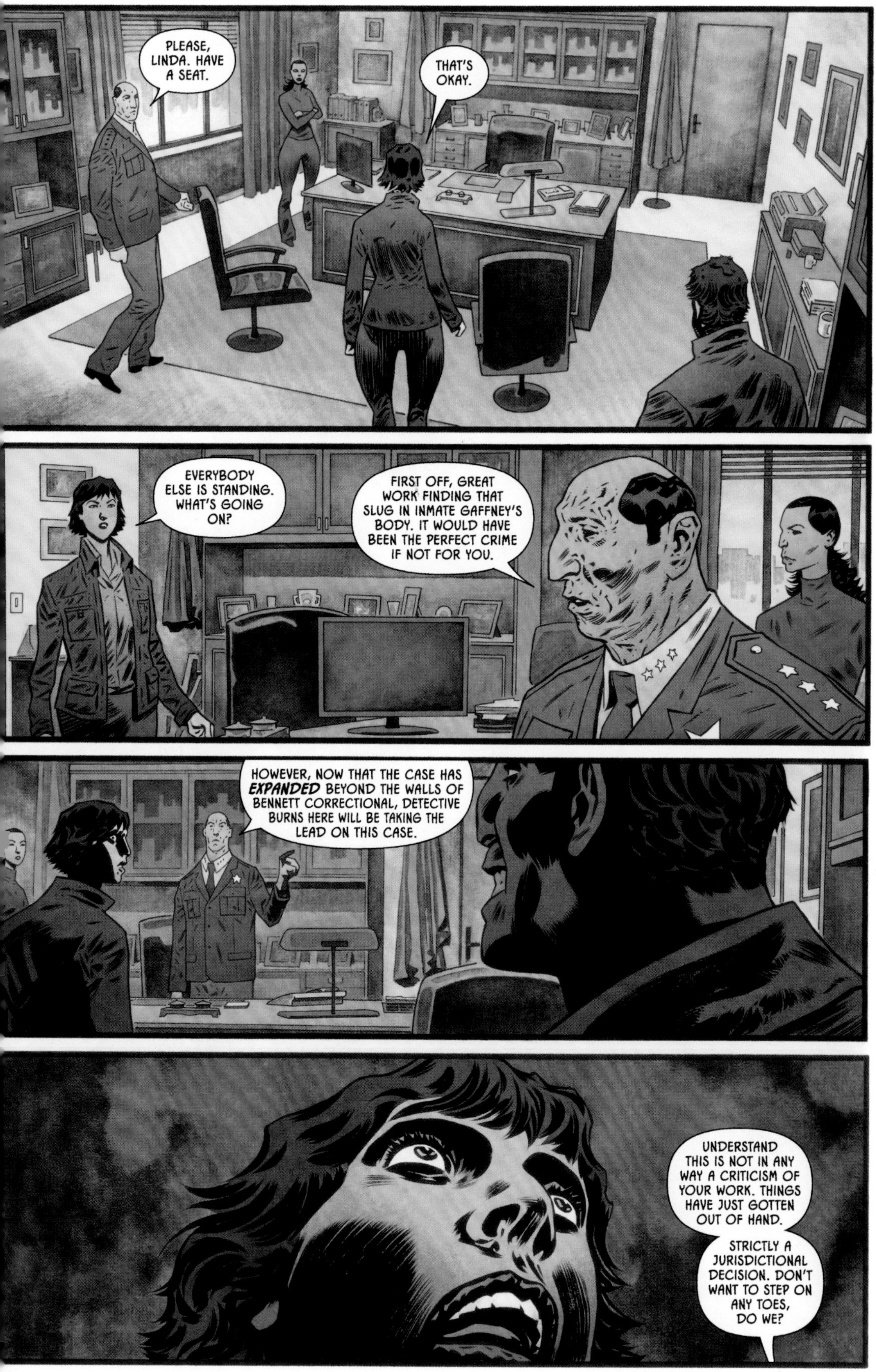
PLEASE, LINDA. HAVE A SEAT.
THAT'S OKAY.
EVERYBODY ELSE IS STANDING. WHAT'S GOING ON?
FIRST OFF, GREAT WORK FINDING THAT SLUG IN INMATE GAFFNEY'S BODY. IT WOULD HAVE BEEN THE PERFECT CRIME IF NOT FOR YOU.
HOWEVER, NOW THAT THE CASE HAS ***EXPANDED*** BEYOND THE WALLS OF BENNETT CORRECTIONAL, DETECTIVE BURNS HERE WILL BE TAKING THE LEAD ON THIS CASE.
UNDERSTAND THIS IS NOT IN ANY WAY A CRITICISM OF YOUR WORK. THINGS HAVE JUST GOTTEN OUT OF HAND.
STRICTLY A JURISDICTIONAL DECISION. DON'T WANT TO STEP ON ANY TOES, DO WE?

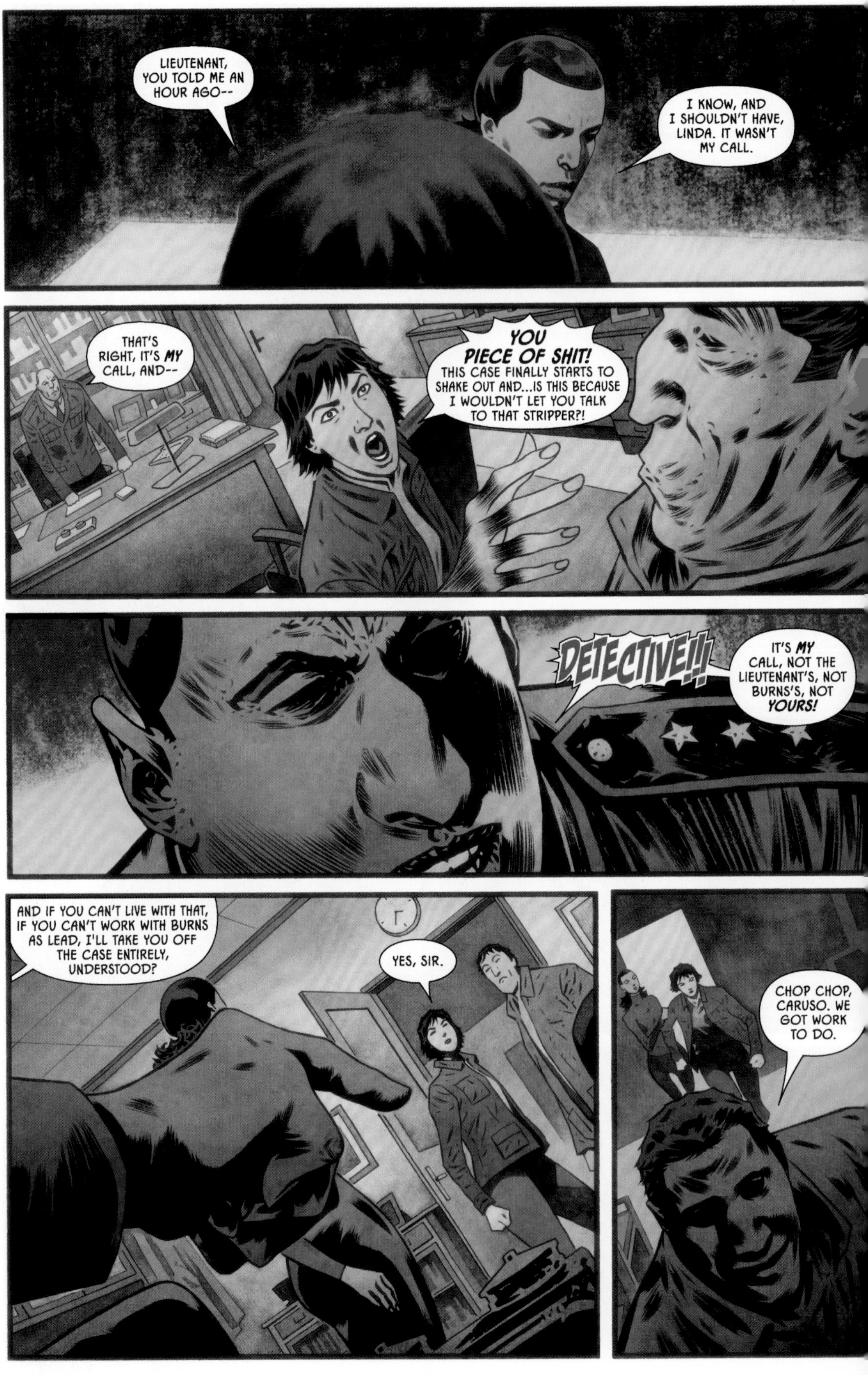
LIEUTENANT, YOU TOLD ME AN HOUR AGO--
I KNOW, AND I SHOULDN'T HAVE, LINDA. IT WASN'T MY CALL.
THAT'S RIGHT, IT'S MY CALL, AND--
YOU PIECE OF SHIT! THIS CASE FINALLY STARTS TO SHAKE OUT AND...IS THIS BECAUSE I WOULDN'T LET YOU TALK TO THAT STRIPPER?!
DETECTIVE!!!
IT'S MY CALL, NOT THE LIEUTENANT'S, NOT BURNS'S, NOT YOURS!
AND IF YOU CAN'T LIVE WITH THAT, IF YOU CAN'T WORK WITH BURNS AS LEAD, I'LL TAKE YOU OFF THE CASE ENTIRELY, UNDERSTOOD?
YES, SIR.
CHOP CHOP, CARUSO. WE GOT WORK TO DO.

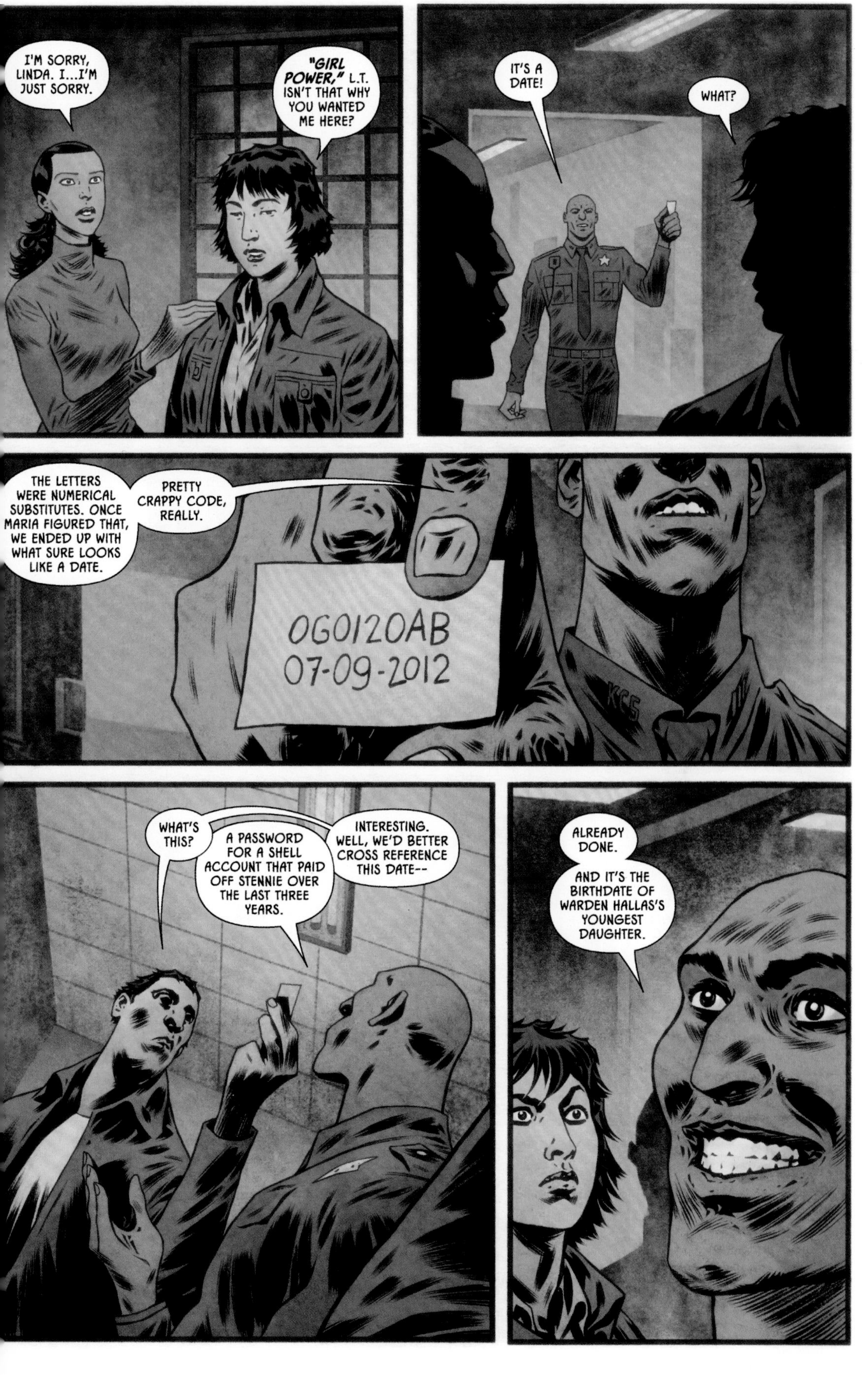
I'M SORRY, LINDA. I...I'M JUST SORRY.
"GIRL POWER," L.T. ISN'T THAT WHY YOU WANTED ME HERE?
IT'S A DATE!
WHAT?
THE LETTERS WERE NUMERICAL SUBSTITUTES. ONCE MARIA FIGURED THAT, WE ENDED UP WITH WHAT SURE LOOKS LIKE A DATE.
PRETTY CRAPPY CODE, REALLY.
OGO120AB
07-09-2012
KCS
WHAT'S THIS?
A PASSWORD FOR A SHELL ACCOUNT THAT PAID OFF STENNIE OVER THE LAST THREE YEARS.
INTERESTING. WELL, WE'D BETTER CROSS REFERENCE THIS DATE--
ALREADY DONE.
AND IT'S THE BIRTHDATE OF WARDEN HALLAS'S YOUNGEST DAUGHTER.

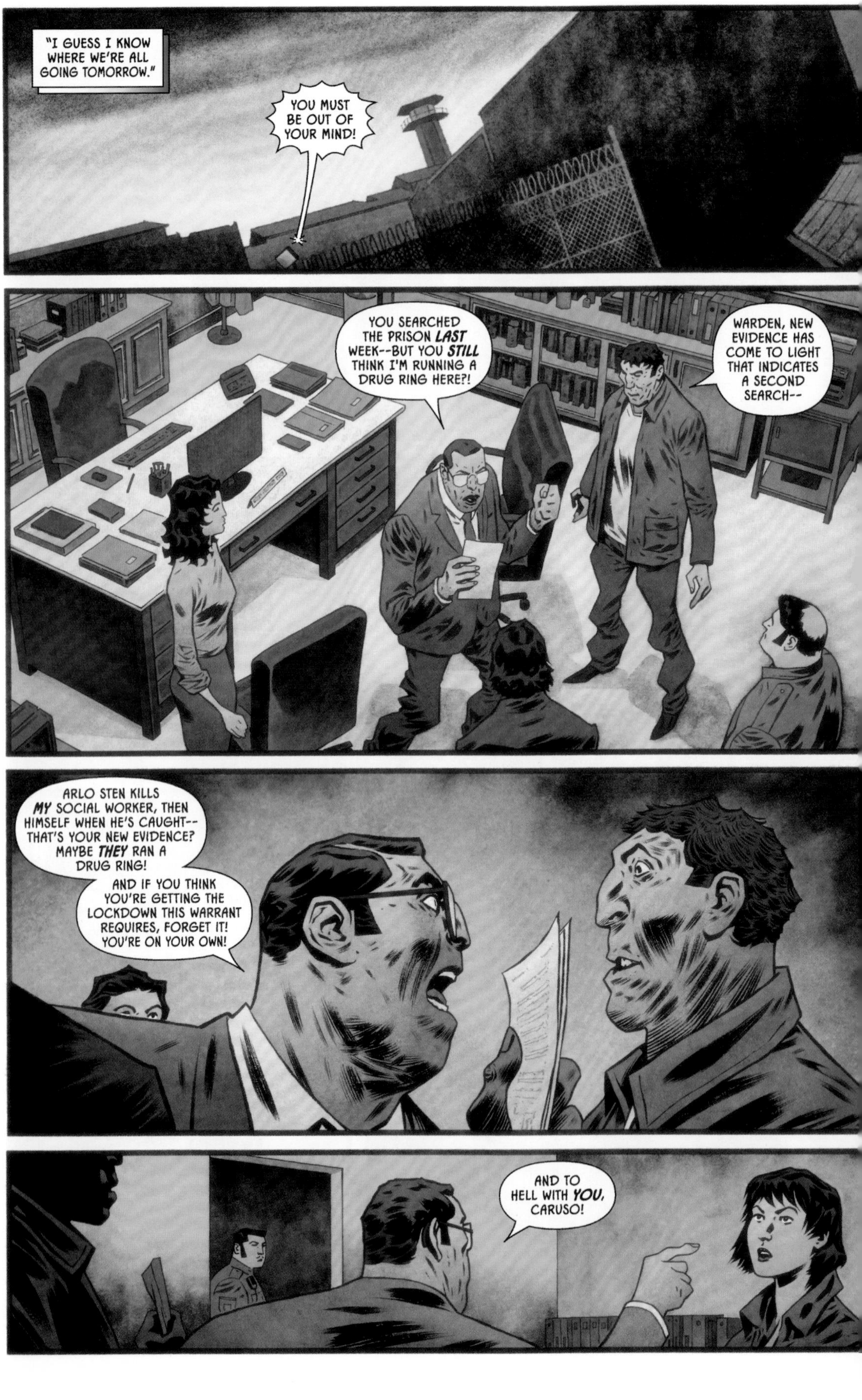
"I GUESS I KNOW WHERE WE'RE ALL GOING TOMORROW."
YOU MUST BE OUT OF YOUR MIND!
YOU SEARCHED THE PRISON LAST WEEK--BUT YOU STILL THINK I'M RUNNING A DRUG RING HERE?!
WARDEN, NEW EVIDENCE HAS COME TO LIGHT THAT INDICATES A SECOND SEARCH--
ARLO STEN KILLS MY SOCIAL WORKER, THEN HIMSELF WHEN HE'S CAUGHT-- THAT'S YOUR NEW EVIDENCE? MAYBE THEY RAN A DRUG RING!
AND IF YOU THINK YOU'RE GETTING THE LOCKDOWN THIS WARRANT REQUIRES, FORGET IT! YOU'RE ON YOUR OWN!
AND TO HELL WITH YOU, CARUSO!

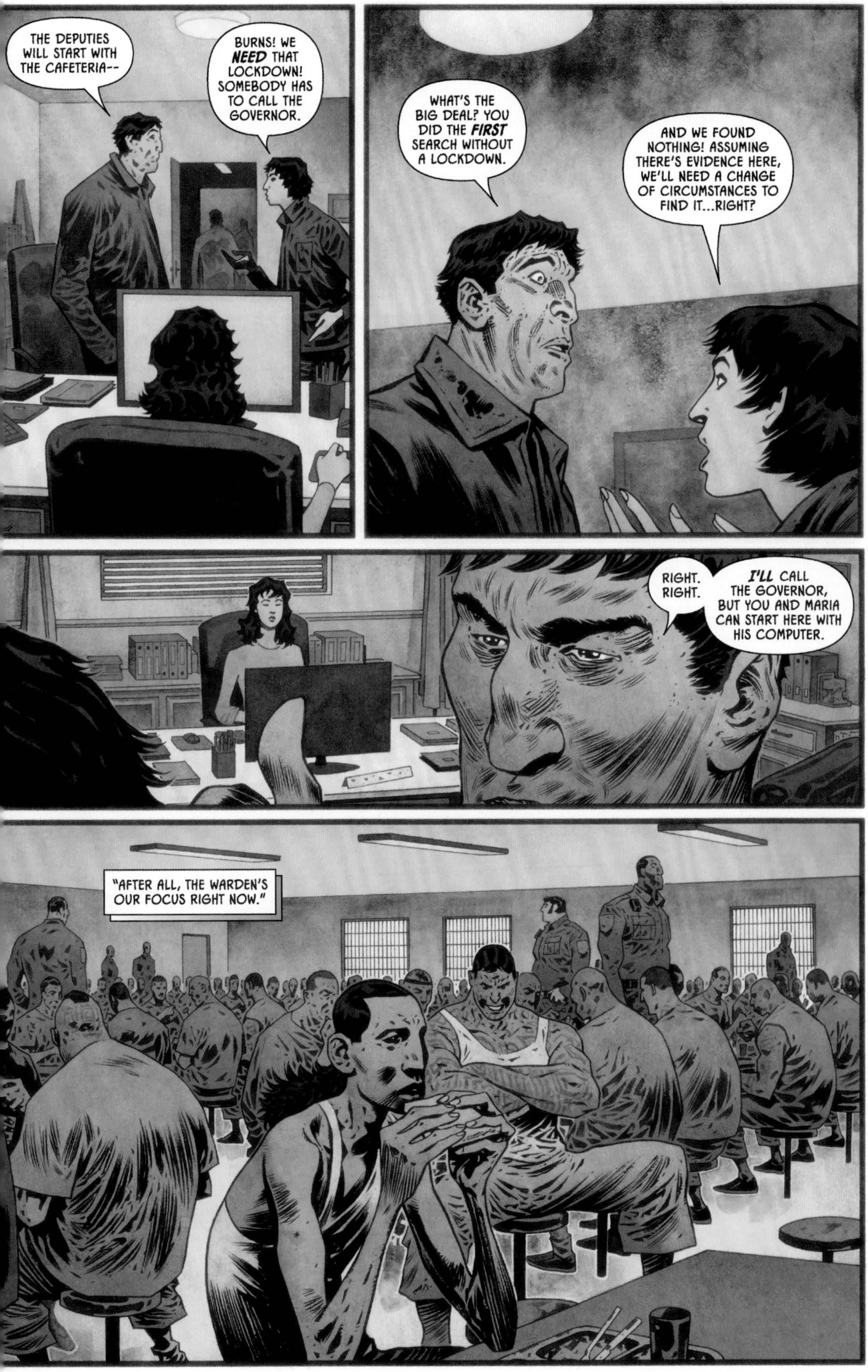
THE DEPUTIES WILL START WITH THE CAFETERIA--
BURNS! WE NEED THAT LOCKDOWN! SOMEBODY HAS TO CALL THE GOVERNOR.
WHAT'S THE BIG DEAL? YOU DID THE FIRST SEARCH WITHOUT A LOCKDOWN.
AND WE FOUND NOTHING! ASSUMING THERE'S EVIDENCE HERE, WE'LL NEED A CHANGE OF CIRCUMSTANCES TO FIND IT...RIGHT?
RIGHT. RIGHT.
I'LL CALL THE GOVERNOR, BUT YOU AND MARIA CAN START HERE WITH HIS COMPUTER.
"AFTER ALL, THE WARDEN'S OUR FOCUS RIGHT NOW."

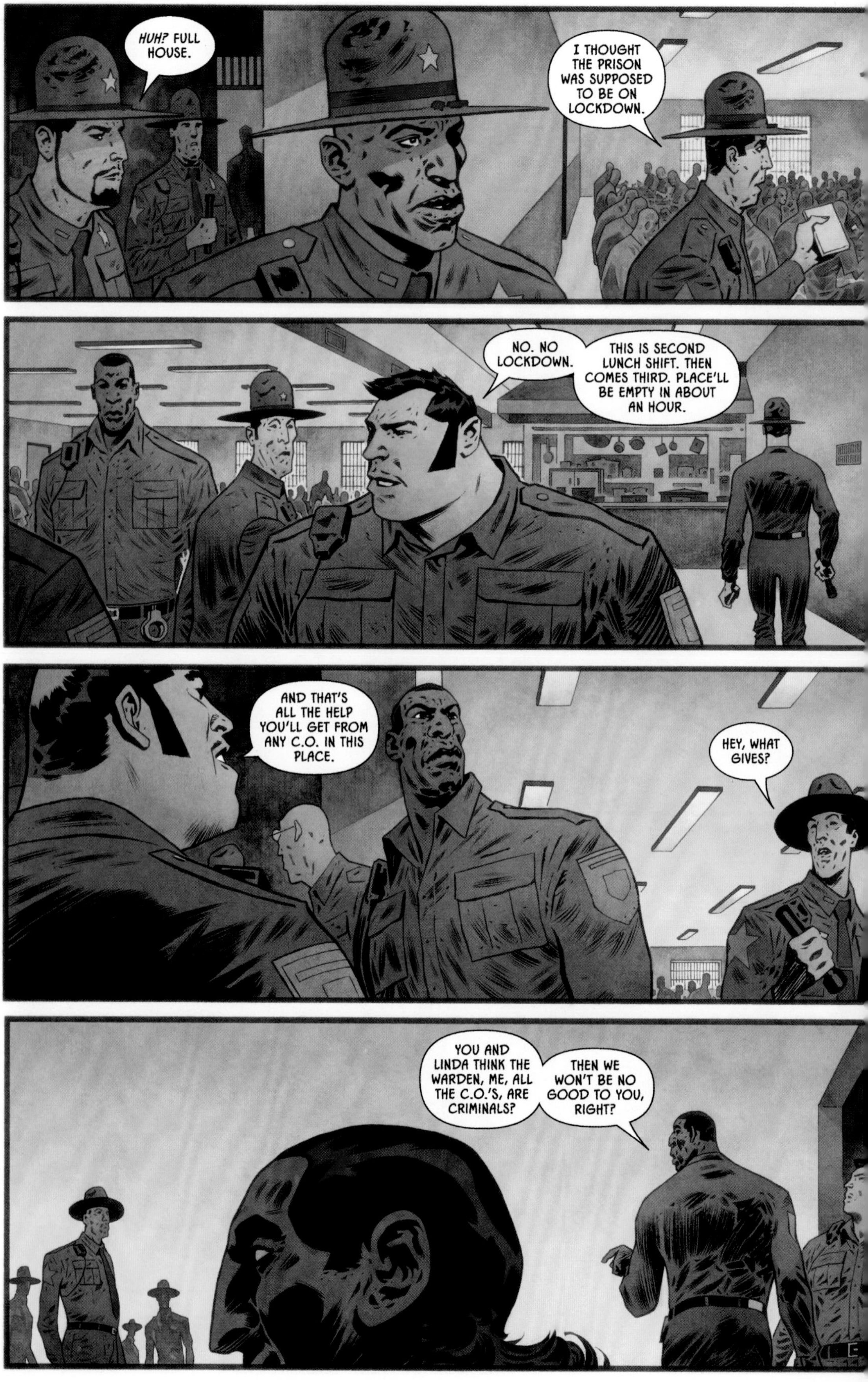
HUH? FULL HOUSE.
I THOUGHT THE PRISON WAS SUPPOSED TO BE ON LOCKDOWN.
NO. NO LOCKDOWN.
THIS IS SECOND LUNCH SHIFT. THEN COMES THIRD. PLACE'LL BE EMPTY IN ABOUT AN HOUR.
AND THAT'S ALL THE HELP YOU'LL GET FROM ANY C.O. IN THIS PLACE.
HEY, WHAT GIVES?
YOU AND LINDA THINK THE WARDEN, ME, ALL THE C.O.'S, ARE CRIMINALS?
THEN WE WON'T BE NO GOOD TO YOU, RIGHT?

JESUS, THE SHERIFF AND THE L.T. HATE CARUSO, AND NOW *THESE* GOONS!

I'M HERE ALONE *WITH* A FEW DOZEN INMATES AND *WITHOUT* MY SIDEARM. ADD ME TO THAT LIST.

C'MON, DIAZ. WE'LL COME BACK WHEN THE CAFETERIA'S EMPTY.

YEAH, THAT'S PROBABLY BEST. BE RIGHT--

--THERE?

WHAT THE HECK...?

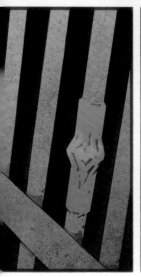

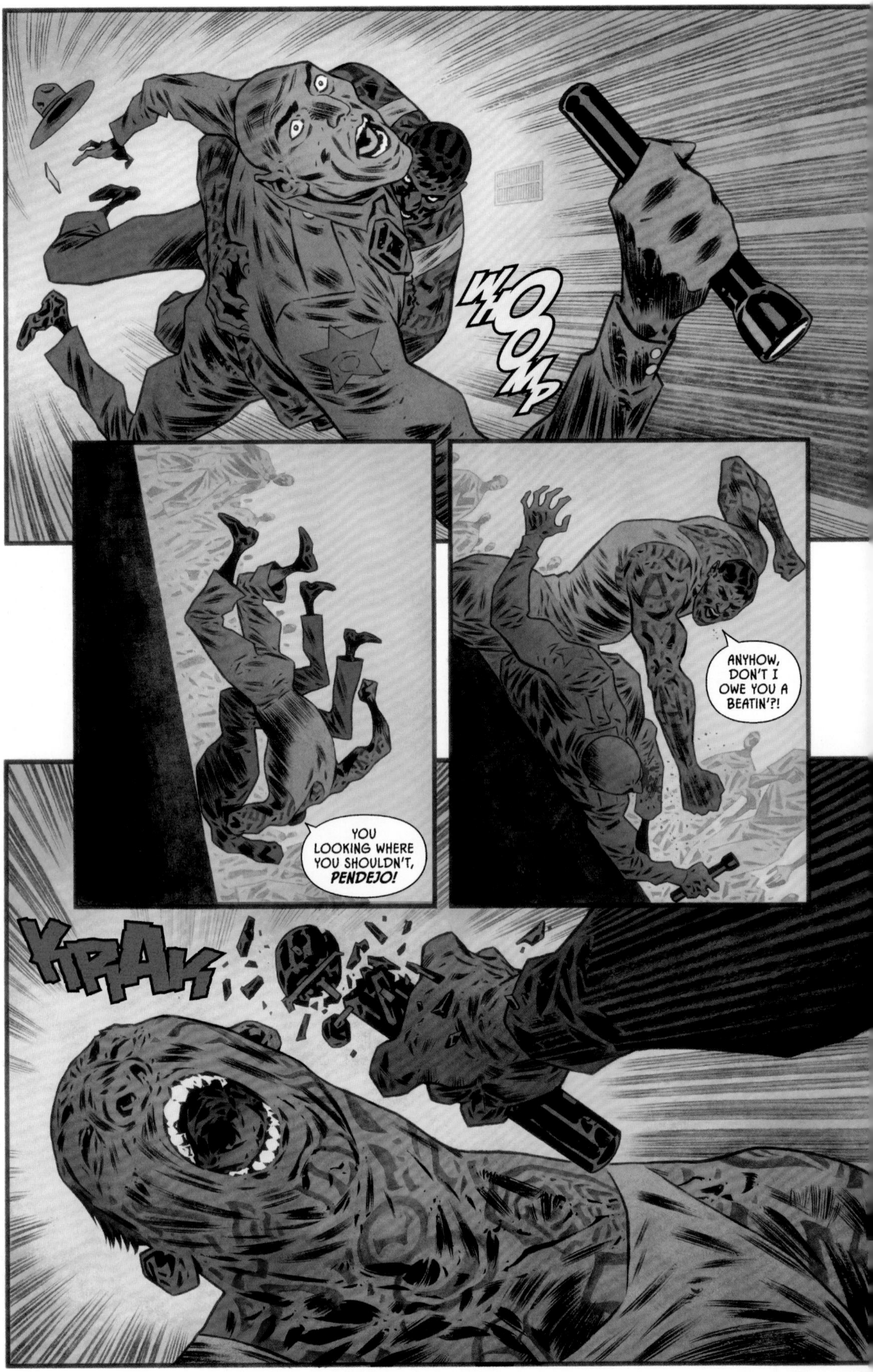
WHOOMP
YOU LOOKING WHERE YOU SHOULDN'T, *PENDEJO!*
ANYHOW, DON'T I OWE YOU A BEATIN'?!
KRAK

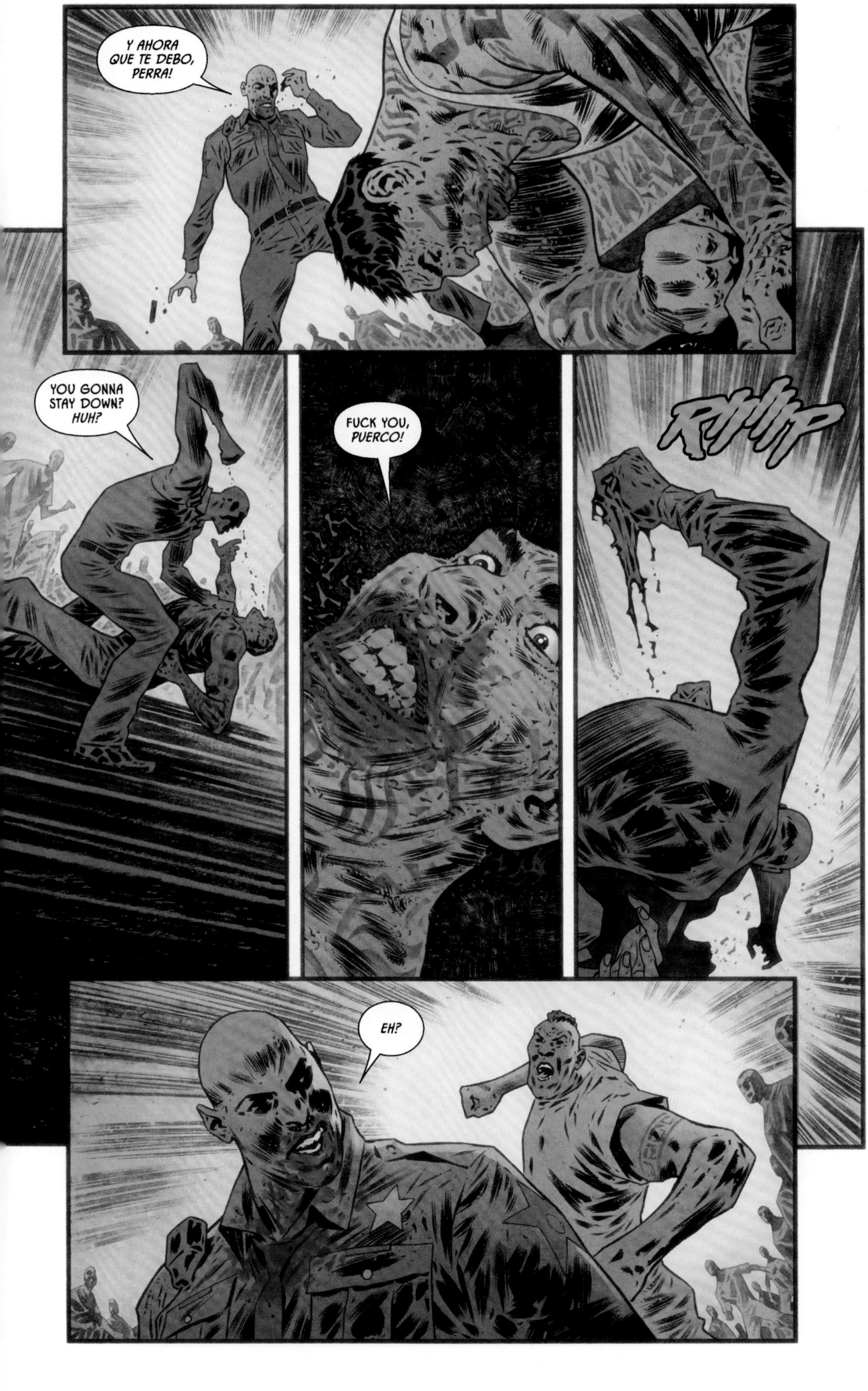

Y AHORA QUE TE DEBO, PERRA!
YOU GONNA STAY DOWN? HUH?
FUCK YOU, PUERCO!
EH?

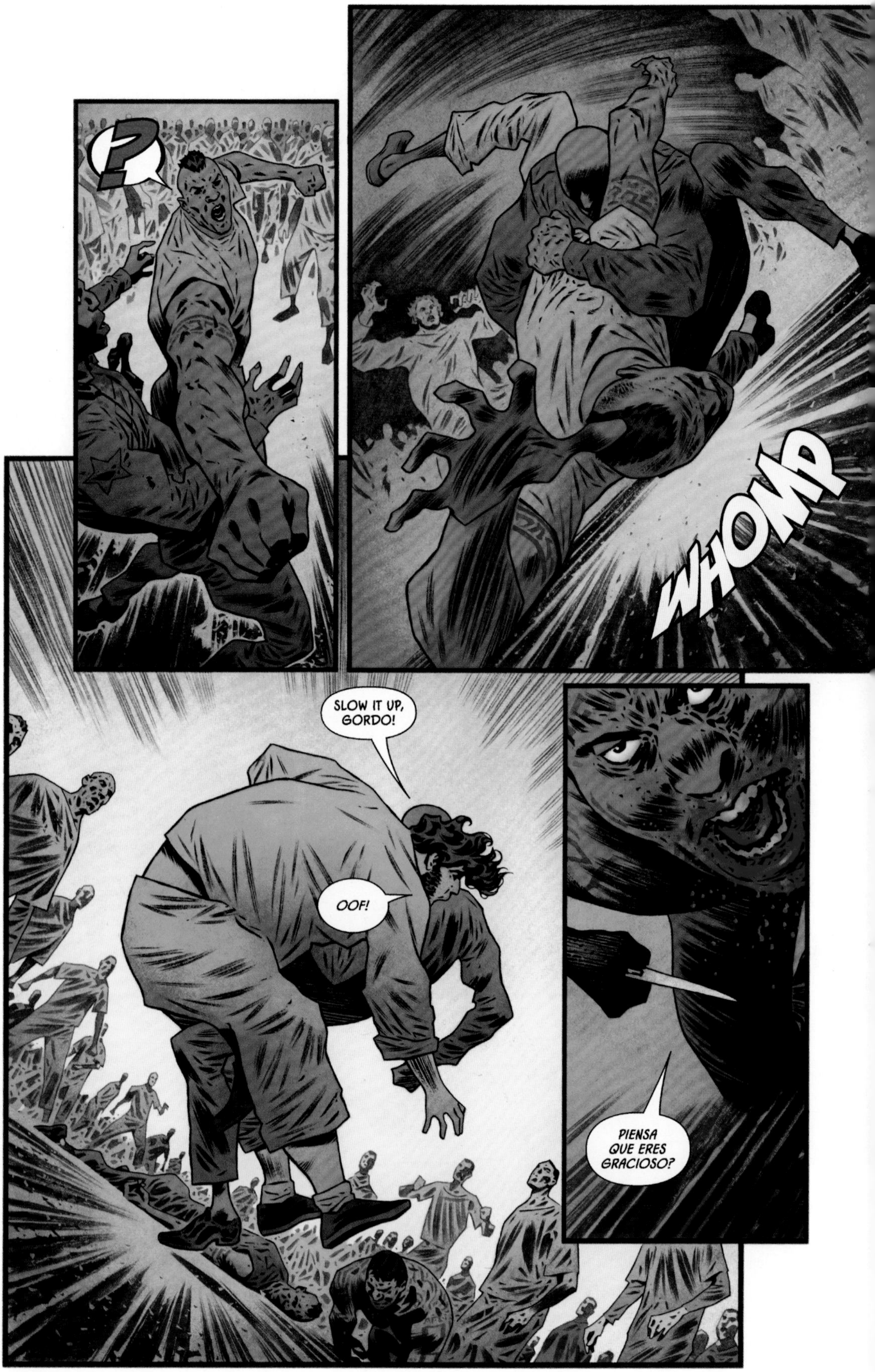
?
WHOMP
SLOW IT UP, GORDO!
OOF!
PIENSA QUE ERES GRACIOSO?

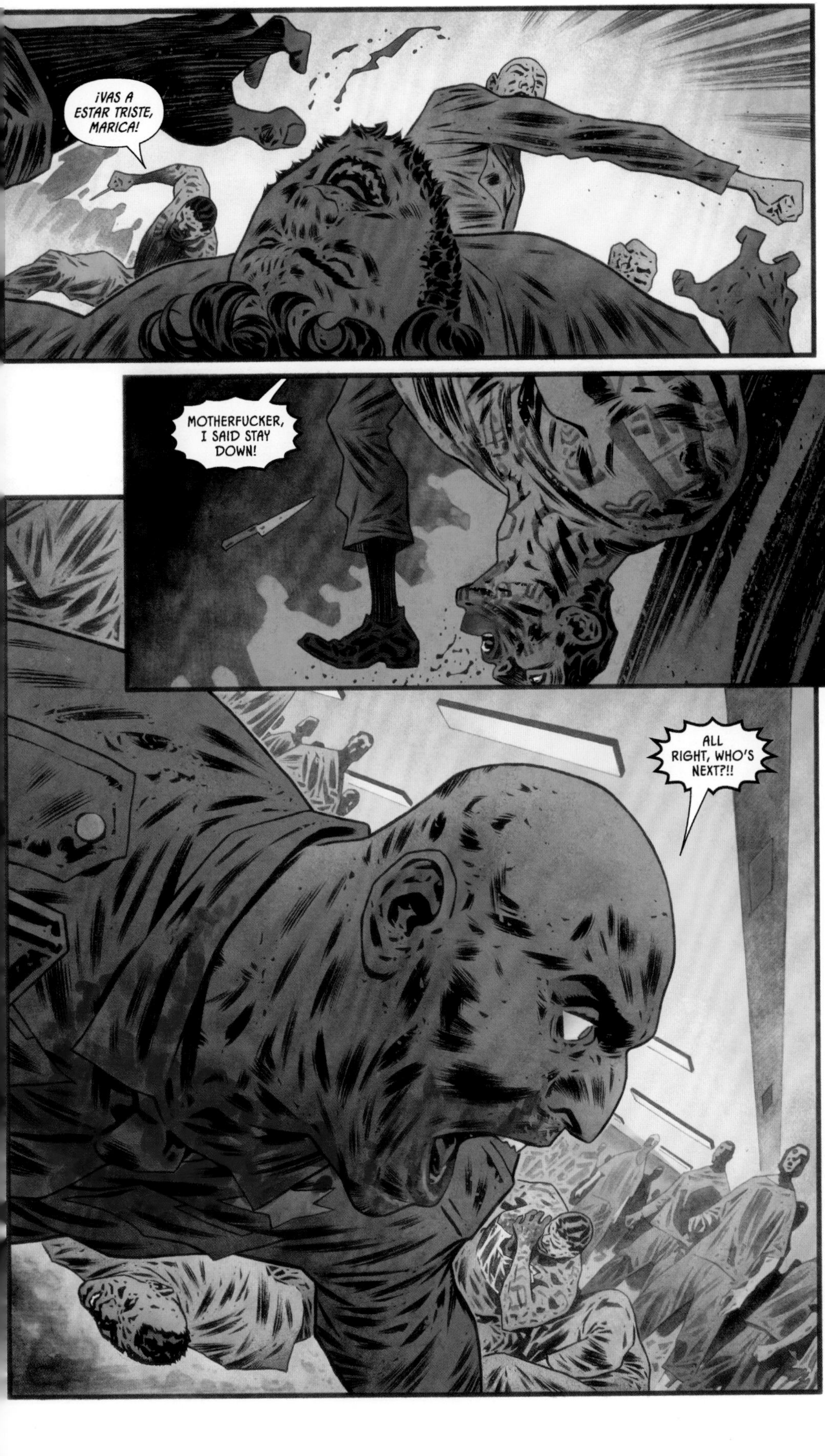
¡VAS A ESTAR TRISTE, MARICA!
MOTHERFUCKER, I SAID STAY DOWN!
ALL RIGHT, WHO'S NEXT?!!

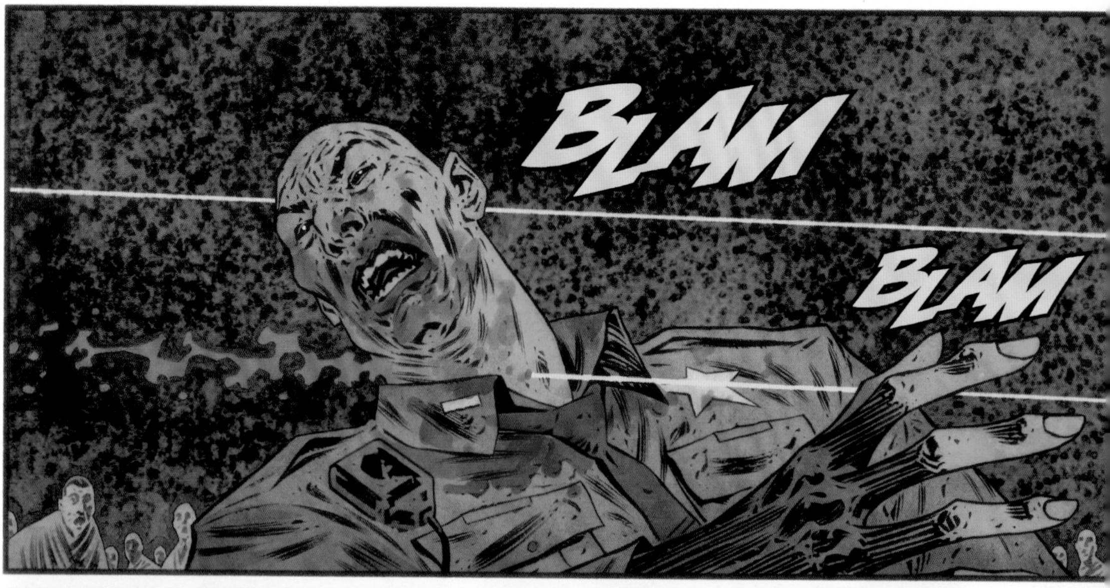
BLAM
BLAM

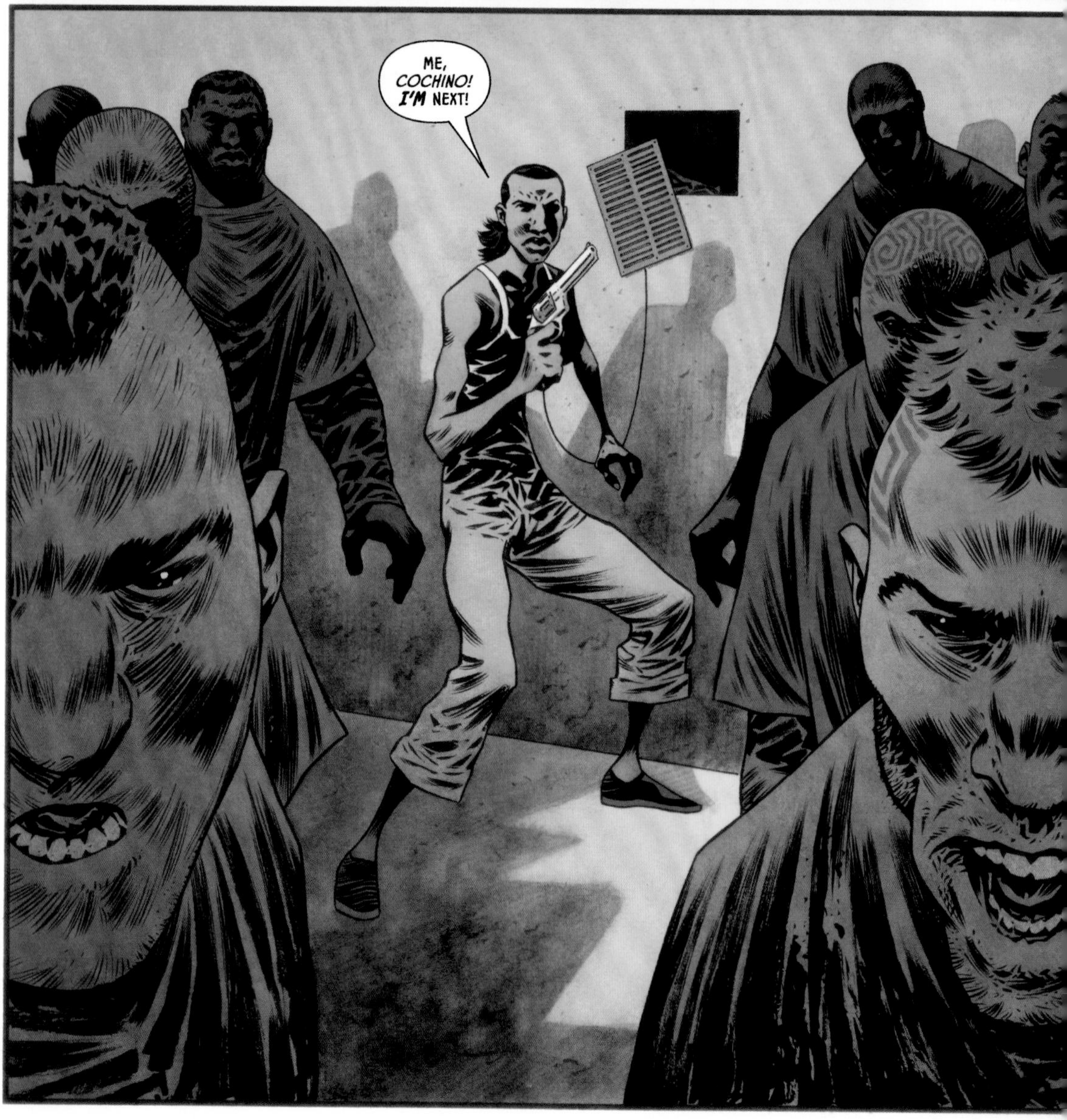
ME, COCHINO! I'M NEXT!

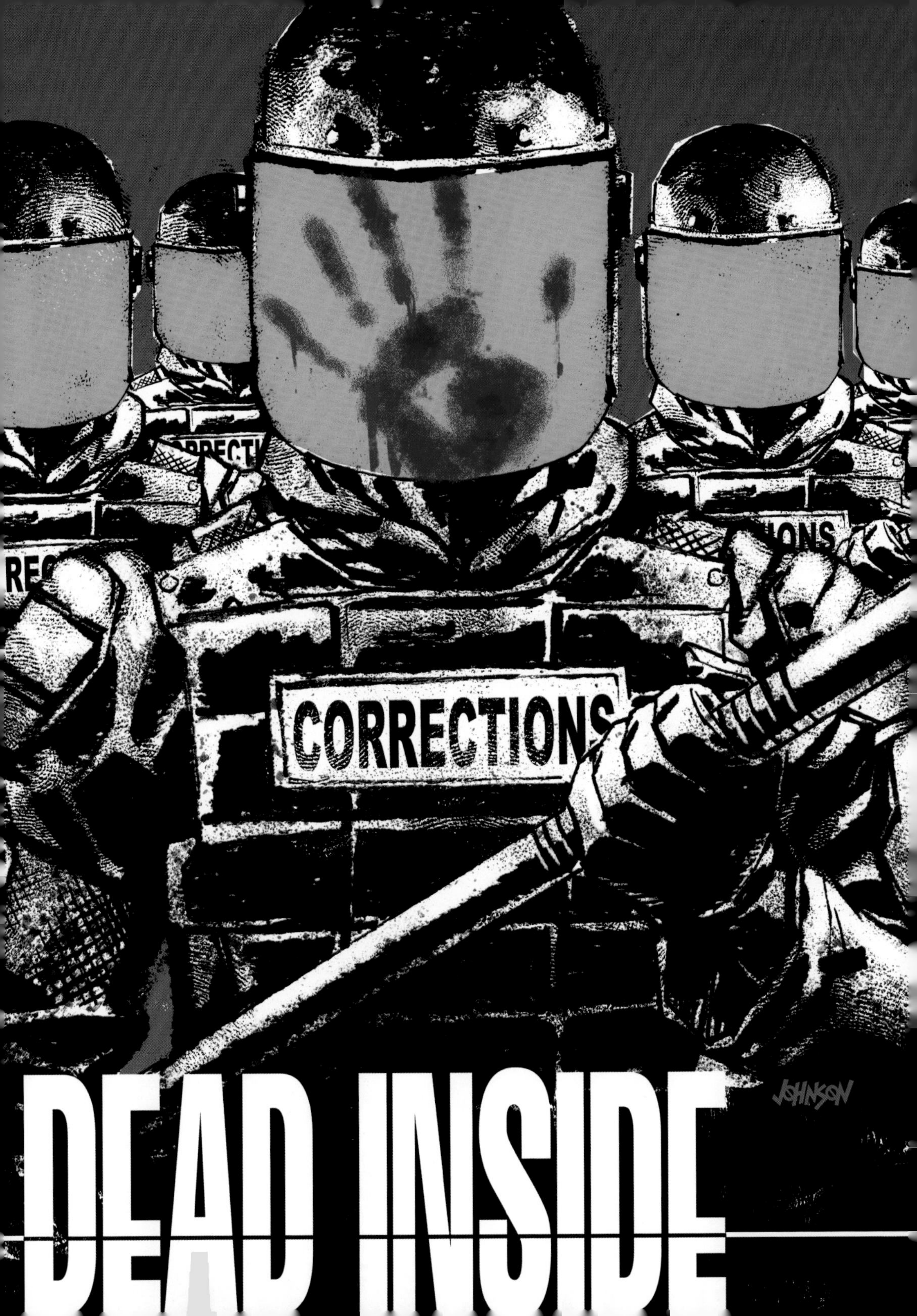
CORRECTIONS
JOHNSON
DEAD INSIDE

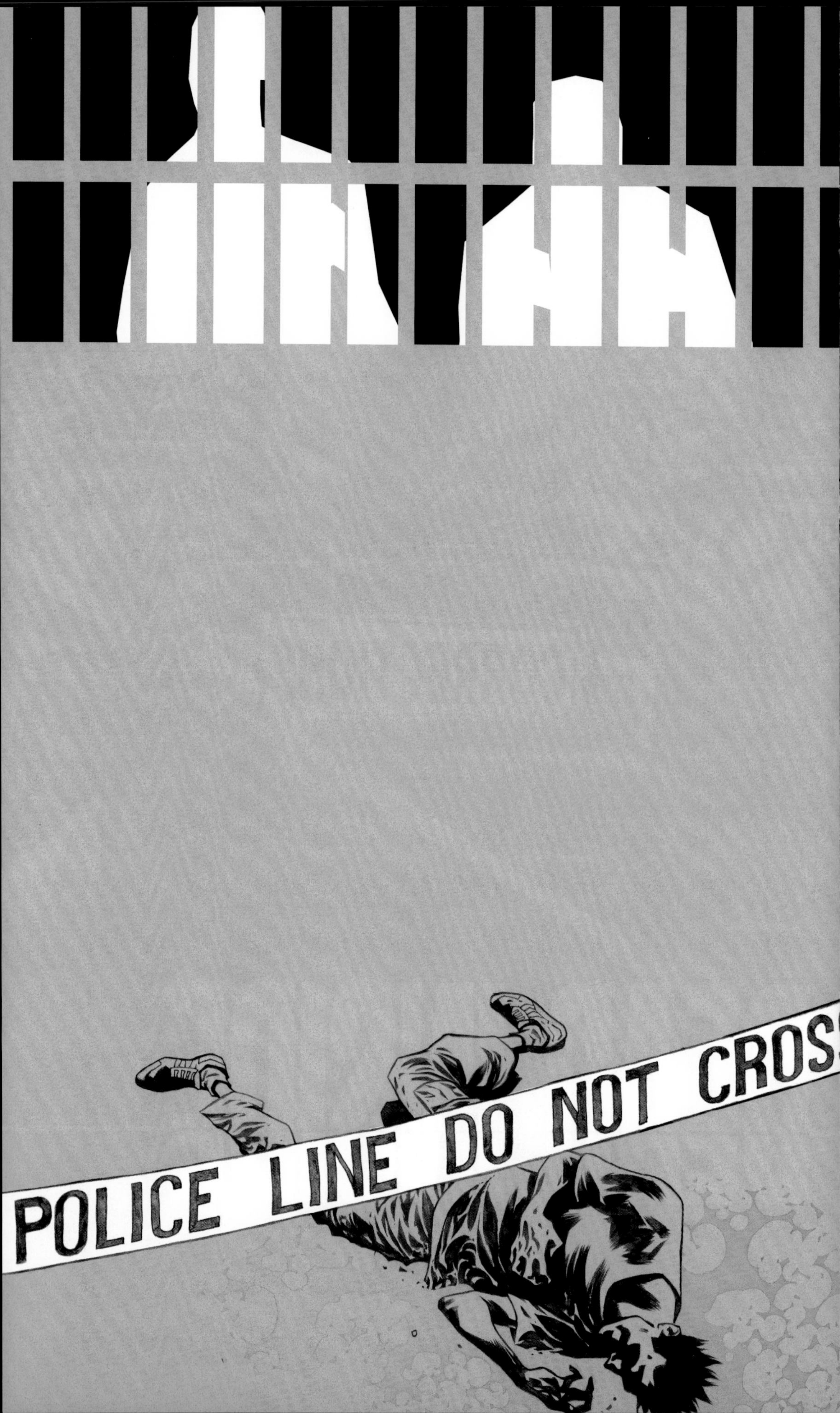
POLICE LINE DO NOT CROS

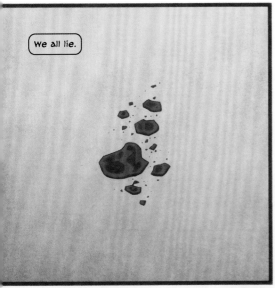

We all lie.

Every day. Every single day.

But the problem is, we need each other. We need help, we need love. We need each other. So we wait around.

We wait to see what the other person will do.

And then we know. Finally, we know the truth.

But nine times out of ten, you don't want to.

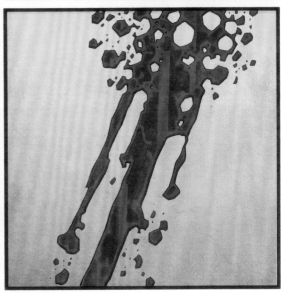

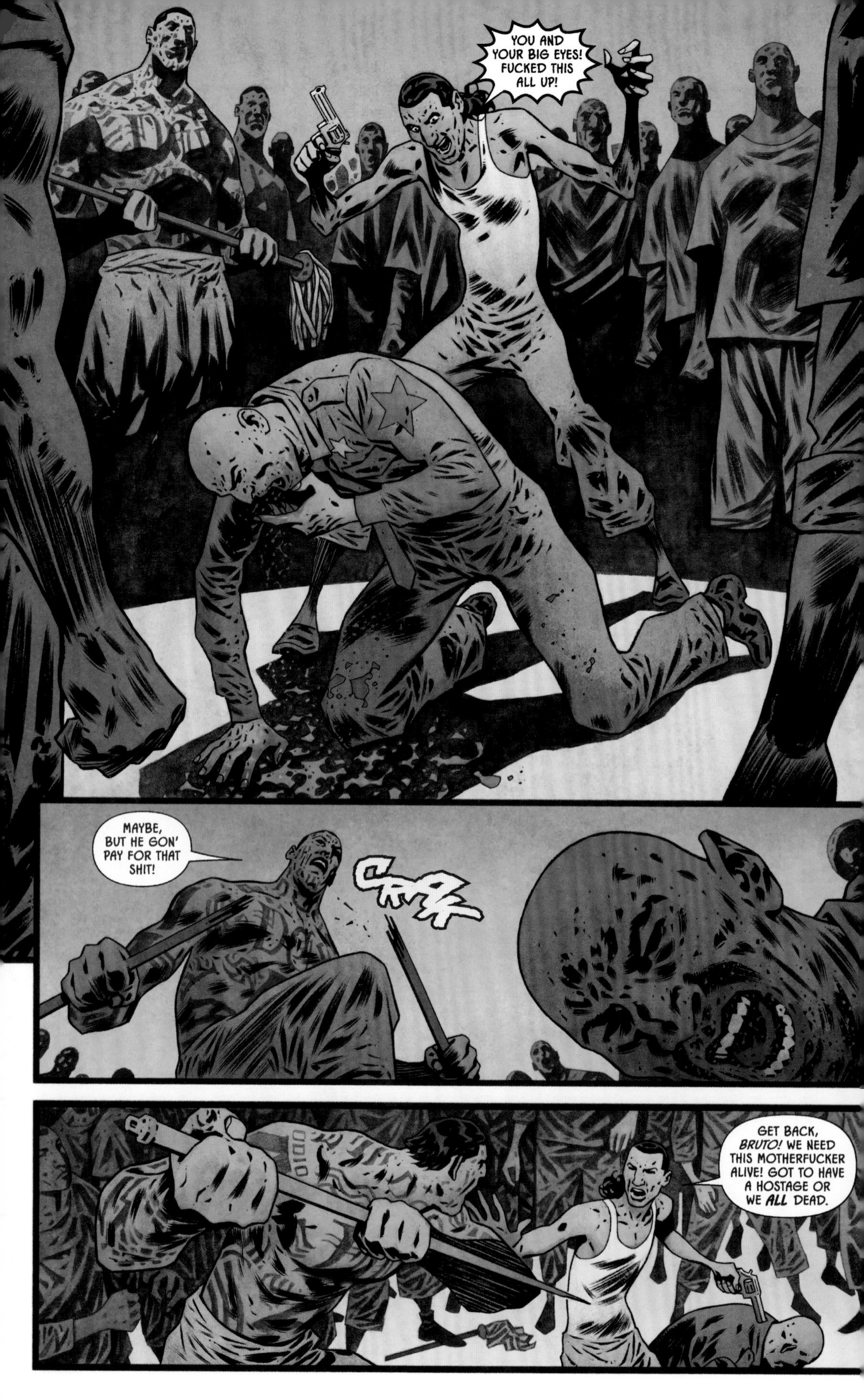
YOU AND YOUR BIG EYES! FUCKED THIS ALL UP!
MAYBE, BUT HE GON' PAY FOR THAT SHIT!
CRAK
GET BACK, *BRUTO!* WE NEED THIS MOTHERFUCKER ALIVE! GOT TO HAVE A HOSTAGE OR WE ***ALL*** DEAD.

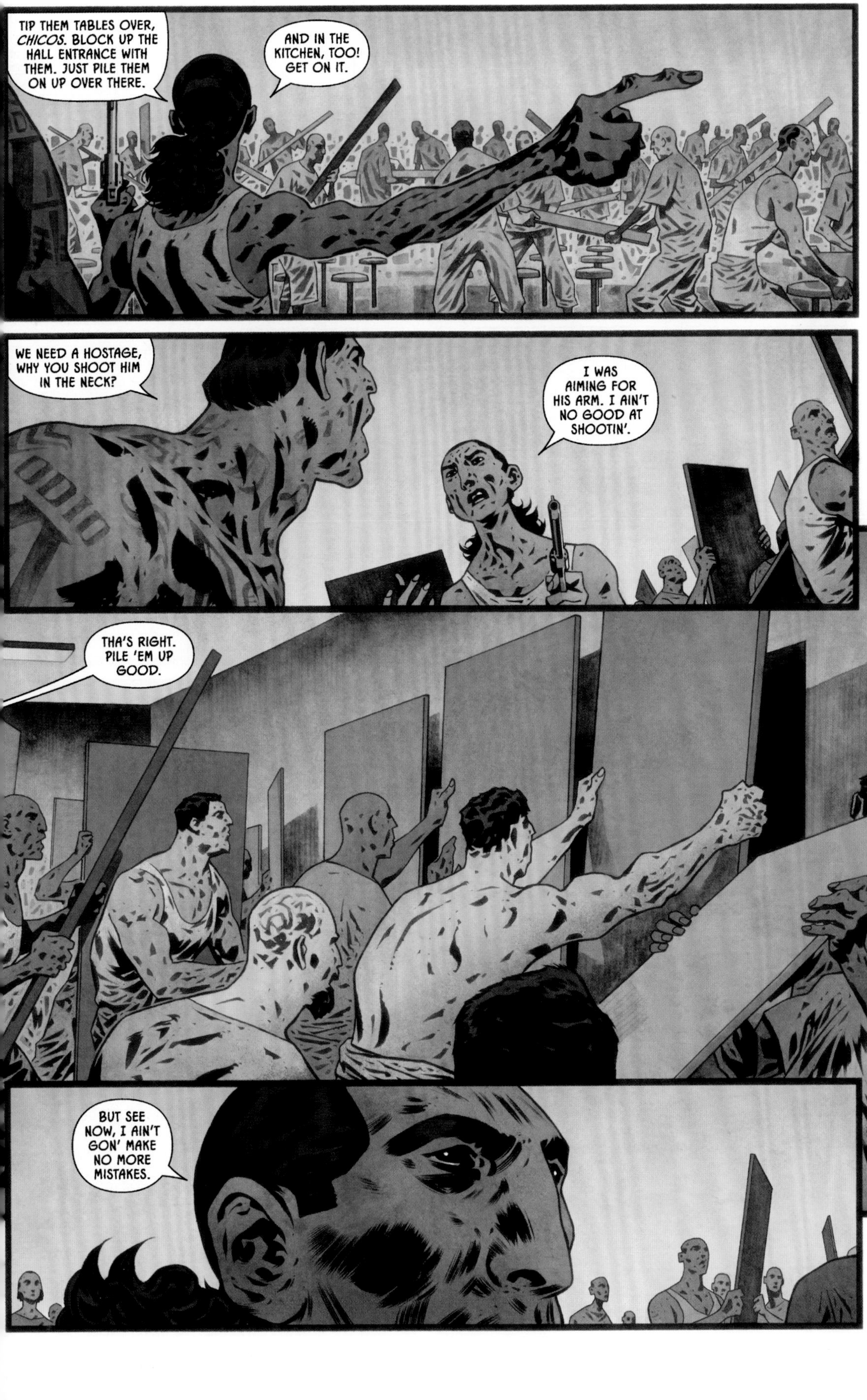
TIP THEM TABLES OVER, *CHICOS*. BLOCK UP THE HALL ENTRANCE WITH THEM. JUST PILE THEM ON UP OVER THERE.
AND IN THE KITCHEN, TOO! GET ON IT.
WE NEED A HOSTAGE, WHY YOU SHOOT HIM IN THE NECK?
I WAS AIMING FOR HIS ARM. I AIN'T NO GOOD AT SHOOTIN'.
THA'S RIGHT. PILE 'EM UP GOOD.
BUT SEE NOW, I AIN'T GON' MAKE NO MORE MISTAKES.

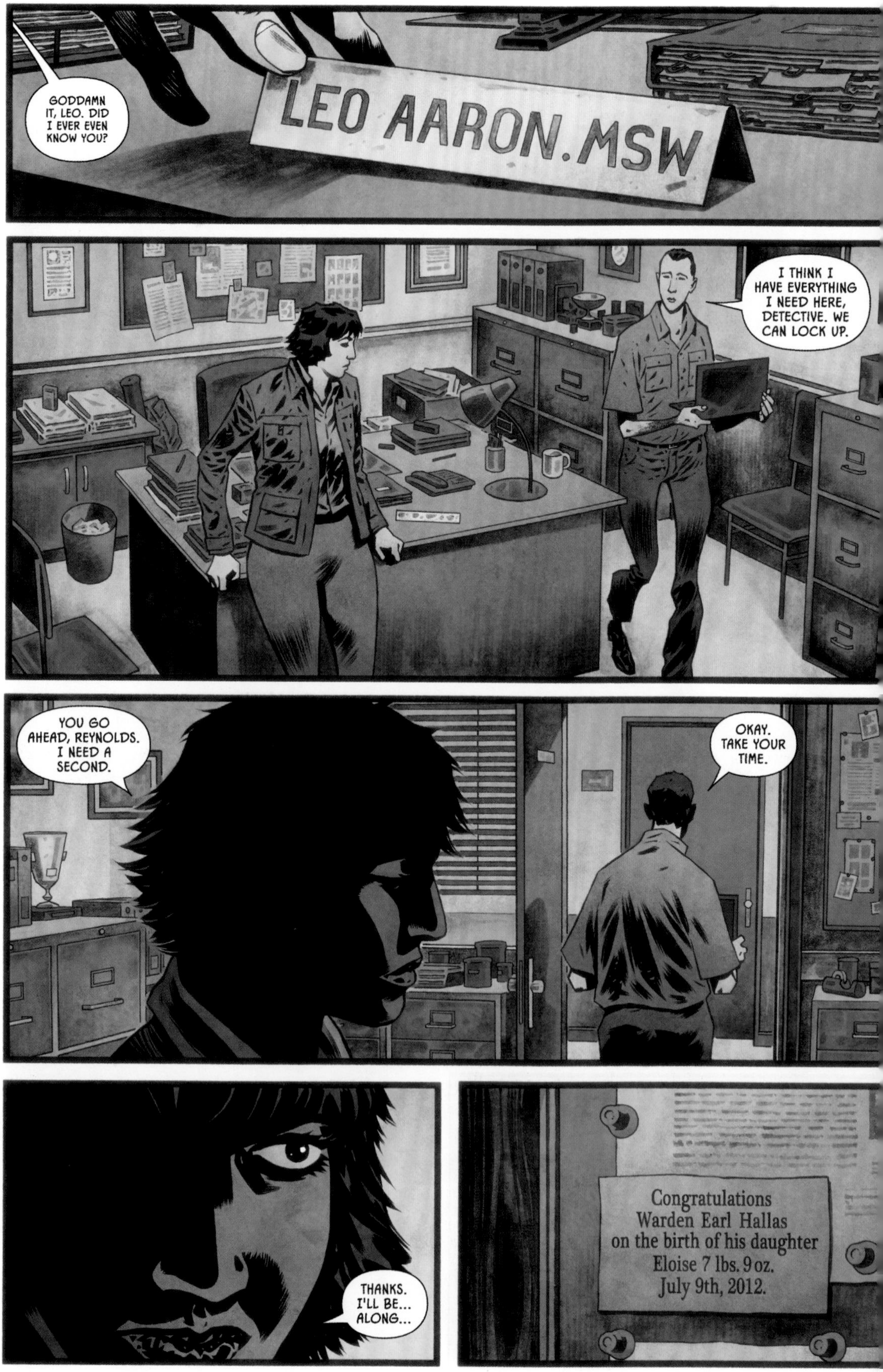
GODDAMN IT, LEO. DID I EVER EVEN KNOW YOU?
LEO AARON.MSW
I THINK I HAVE EVERYTHING I NEED HERE, DETECTIVE. WE CAN LOCK UP.
YOU GO AHEAD, REYNOLDS. I NEED A SECOND.
OKAY. TAKE YOUR TIME.
THANKS. I'LL BE... ALONG...
Congratulations
Warden Earl Hallas
on the birth of his daughter
Eloise 7 lbs. 9 oz.
July 9th, 2012.

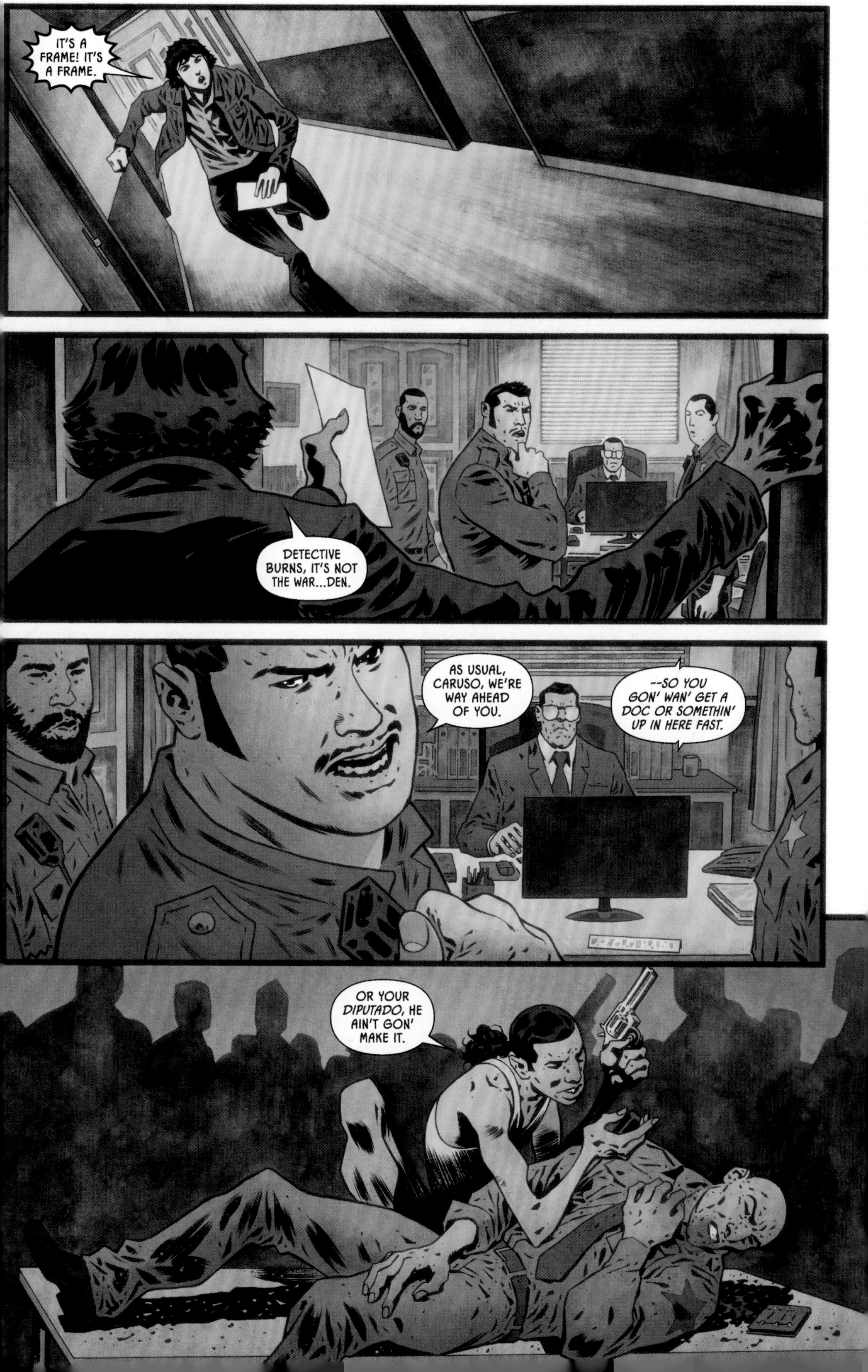
IT'S A FRAME! IT'S A FRAME.
DETECTIVE BURNS, IT'S NOT THE WAR...DEN.
AS USUAL, CARUSO, WE'RE WAY AHEAD OF YOU.
--SO YOU GON' WAN' GET A DOC OR SOMETHIN' UP IN HERE FAST.
OR YOUR *DIPUTADO*, HE AIN'T GON' MAKE IT.

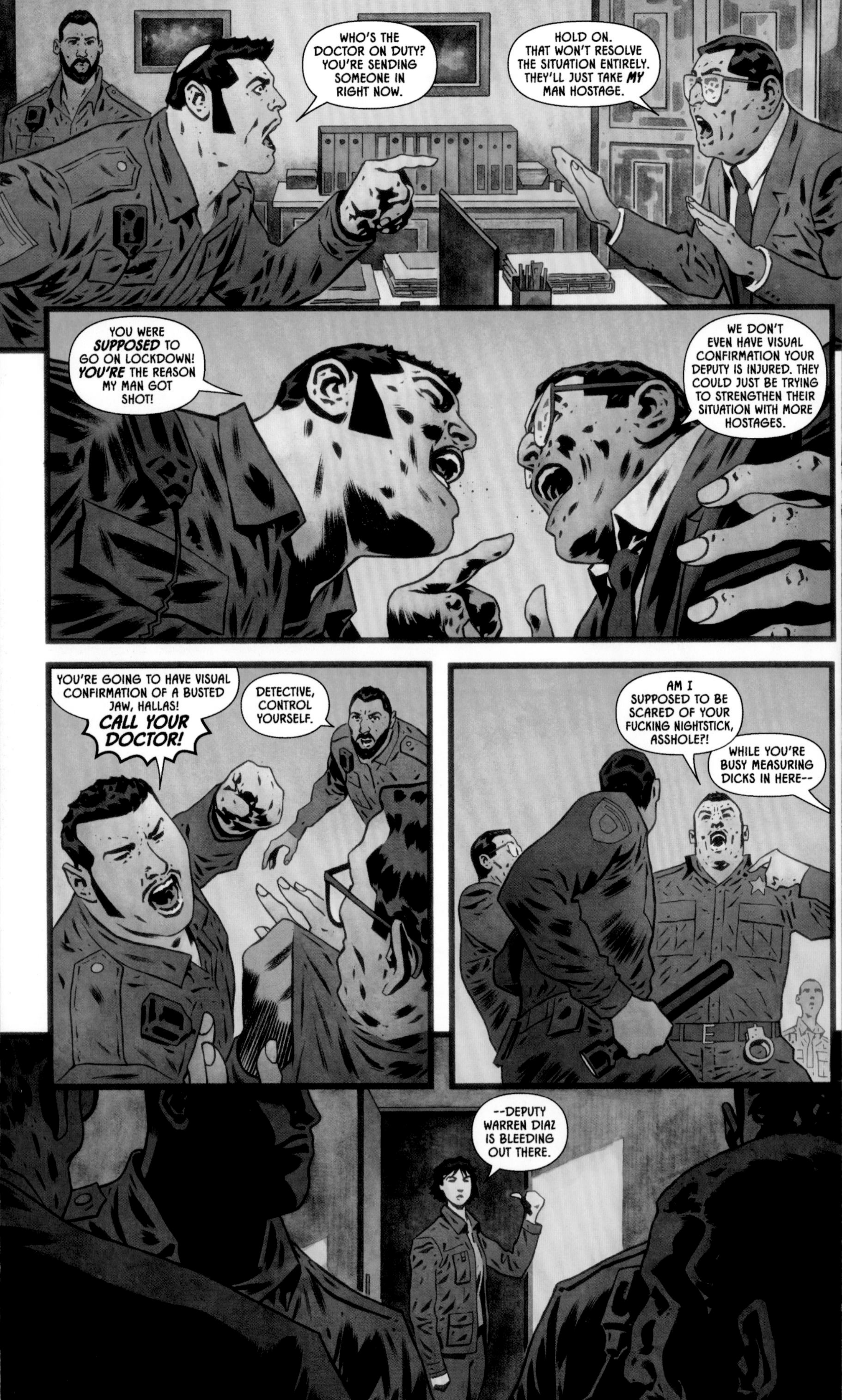

WHO'S THE DOCTOR ON DUTY? YOU'RE SENDING SOMEONE IN RIGHT NOW.
HOLD ON. THAT WON'T RESOLVE THE SITUATION ENTIRELY. THEY'LL JUST TAKE MY MAN HOSTAGE.
YOU WERE SUPPOSED TO GO ON LOCKDOWN! YOU'RE THE REASON MY MAN GOT SHOT!
WE DON'T EVEN HAVE VISUAL CONFIRMATION YOUR DEPUTY IS INJURED. THEY COULD JUST BE TRYING TO STRENGTHEN THEIR SITUATION WITH MORE HOSTAGES.
YOU'RE GOING TO HAVE VISUAL CONFIRMATION OF A BUSTED JAW, HALLAS! CALL YOUR DOCTOR!
DETECTIVE, CONTROL YOURSELF.
AM I SUPPOSED TO BE SCARED OF YOUR FUCKING NIGHTSTICK, ASSHOLE?!
WHILE YOU'RE BUSY MEASURING DICKS IN HERE--
--DEPUTY WARREN DIAZ IS BLEEDING OUT THERE.

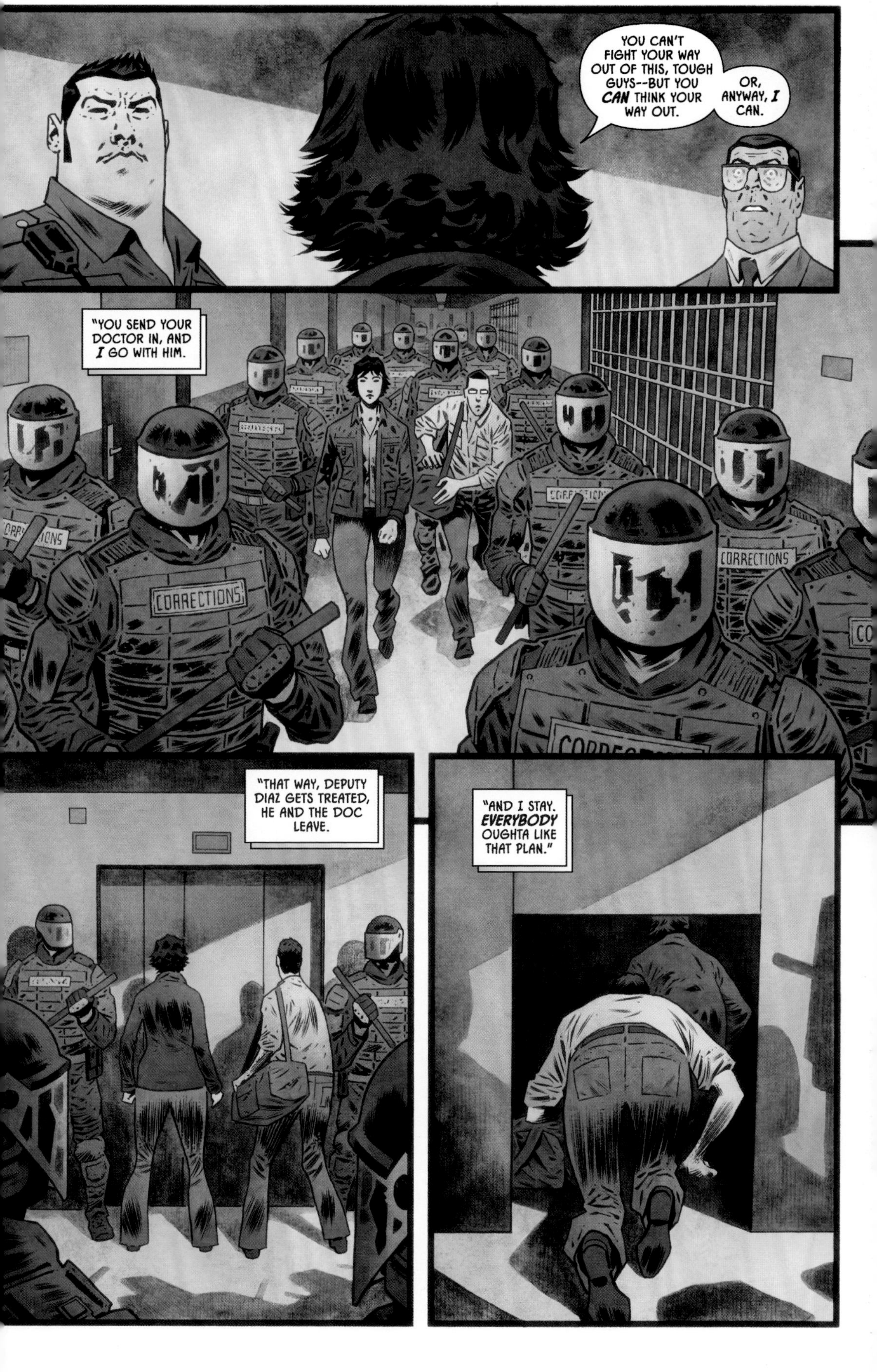
YOU CAN'T FIGHT YOUR WAY OUT OF THIS, TOUGH GUYS--BUT YOU CAN THINK YOUR WAY OUT.
OR, ANYWAY, I CAN.
"YOU SEND YOUR DOCTOR IN, AND I GO WITH HIM.
CORRECTIONS
CORRECTIONS
CORRECTIONS
"THAT WAY, DEPUTY DIAZ GETS TREATED, HE AND THE DOC LEAVE.
"AND I STAY. EVERYBODY OUGHTA LIKE THAT PLAN."

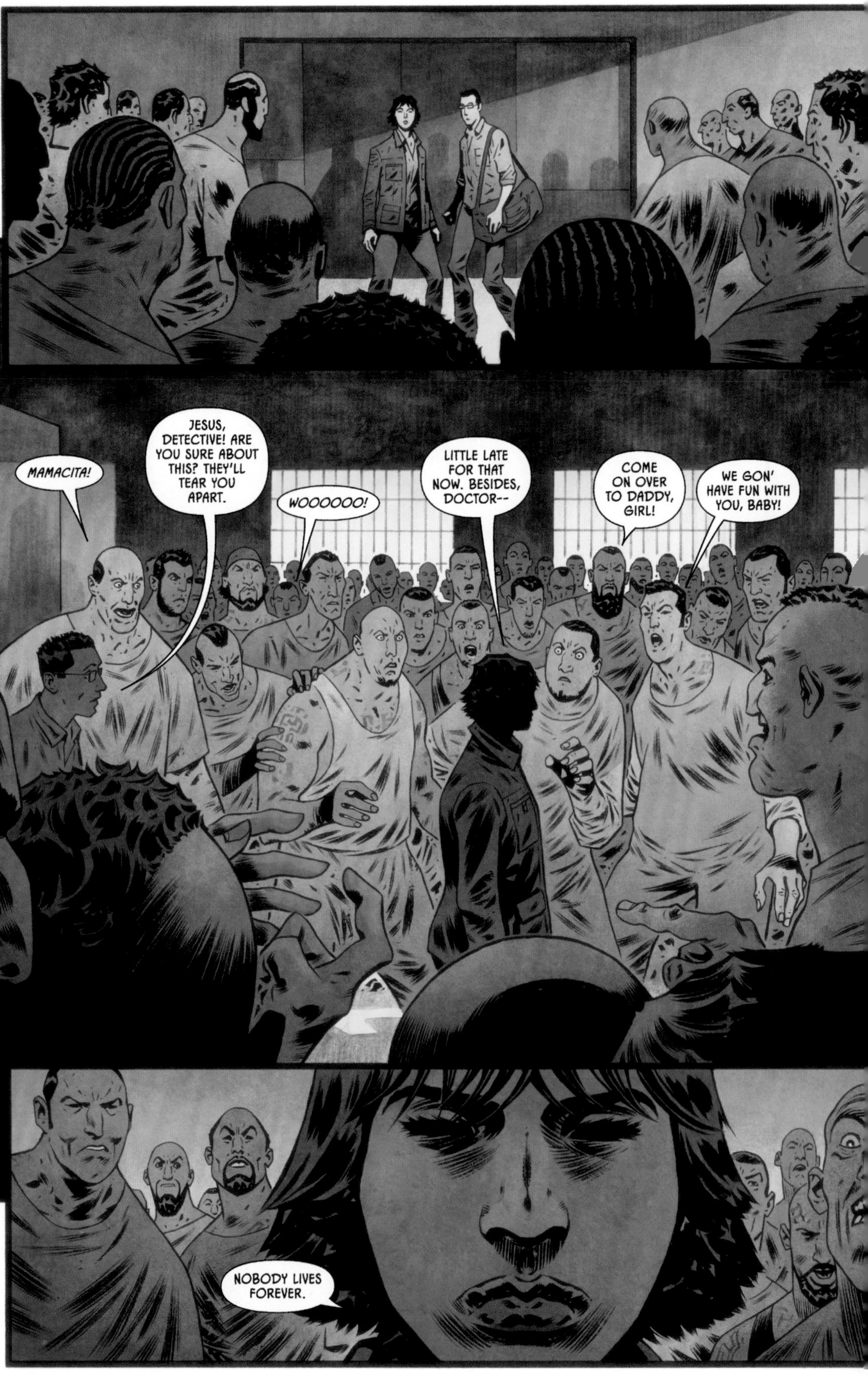
MAMACITA!
JESUS, DETECTIVE! ARE YOU SURE ABOUT THIS? THEY'LL TEAR YOU APART.
WOOOOOO!
LITTLE LATE FOR THAT NOW. BESIDES, DOCTOR--
COME ON OVER TO DADDY, GIRL!
WE GON' HAVE FUN WITH YOU, BABY!
NOBODY LIVES FOREVER.

SNIIIFFFF

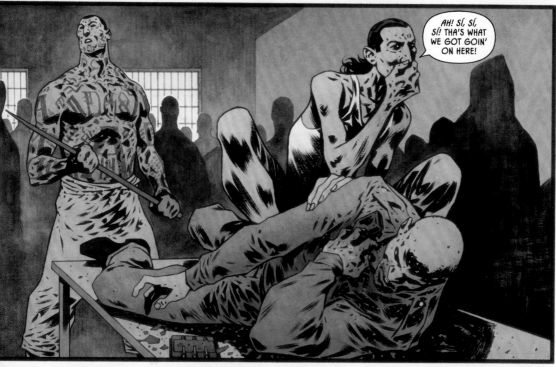

AH! SÍ, SÍ, SÍ! THA'S WHAT WE GOT GOIN' ON HERE!

'EY! GOOD TO SEE YOU AGAIN, POLICÍA LADY. I WAS REAL GLAD WHEN THEY SAID YOU'S COMIN' IN!

BUT YOU BE NICE TO MY BOY ALESSANDRO. I STILL GOT THREE BULLETS IN THIS GAT, SO BE NICE.

HEAR THAT, CHICA? THINGS BE DIFFERENT *THIS* TIME.

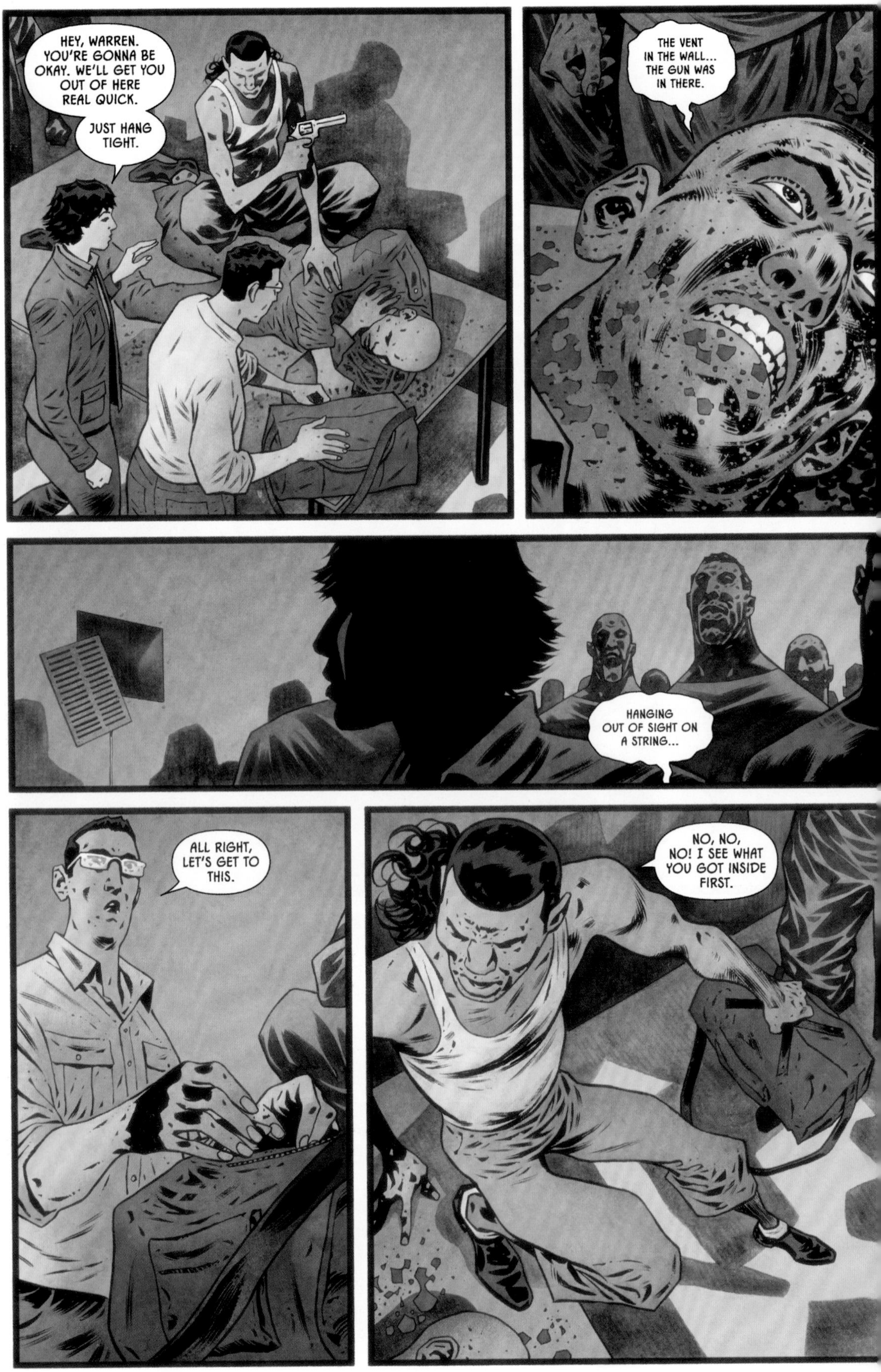
HEY, WARREN. YOU'RE GONNA BE OKAY. WE'LL GET YOU OUT OF HERE REAL QUICK.
JUST HANG TIGHT.
THE VENT IN THE WALL... THE GUN WAS IN THERE.
HANGING OUT OF SIGHT ON A STRING...
ALL RIGHT, LET'S GET TO THIS.
NO, NO, NO! I SEE WHAT YOU GOT INSIDE FIRST.

OH, *MÉDICO!* ALL **KINDS** OF KNIVES IN HERE!
LOOK, GERENA, YOU WIN, OKAY? YOU TRICKED ME GOOD, YOU'VE GOT THE GUN. JUST GIVE US THE BAG.
I TRICKED YOU? HOW I DO THAT?
COME OFF IT, GERENA. THE FIRST TIME WE TALKED YOU IMPLICATED THE GUARDS IN MACK'S MURDER. YOU SAID IT WAS A POWER PLAY IN THE PRISON DRUG TRADE.
"AND THEN YOU TRIED TO FRAME WARDEN HALLAS BY USING HIS DAUGHTER'S BIRTHDAY AS A PASSWORD ON THE SHELL BANK ACCOUNT--WHERE ***ALL*** YOUR DRUG MONEY WENT.
Congratulations Warden Earl Hallas on the birth of his daughter Eloise 7 lbs. 9 oz. July 9th, 2012.
"IT WAS NEVER THE WARDEN--NEVER ANYBODY IN THE PRISON EXCEPT ARLO STEN. HE SET IT ALL UP FOR YOU, DIDN'T HE? ***AND*** COLLECTED CASH AS YOUR ENFORCER."

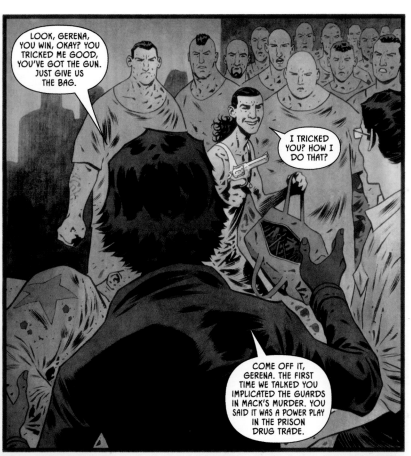

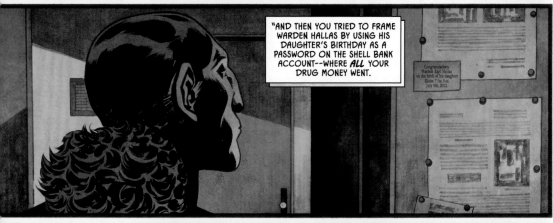

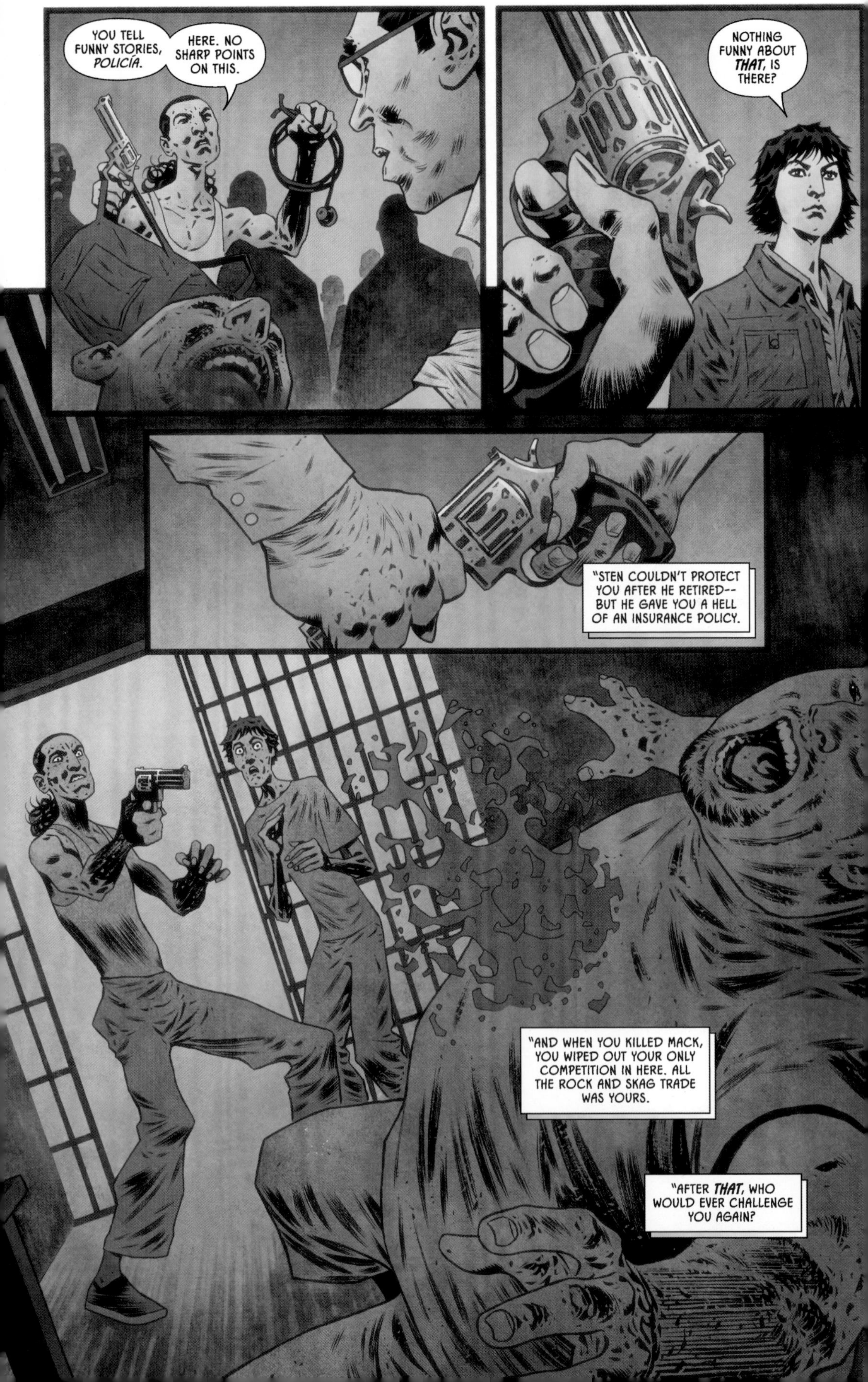
YOU TELL FUNNY STORIES, *POLICÍA*.
HERE. NO SHARP POINTS ON THIS.
NOTHING FUNNY ABOUT ***THAT***, IS THERE?
"STEN COULDN'T PROTECT YOU AFTER HE RETIRED-- BUT HE GAVE YOU A HELL OF AN INSURANCE POLICY.
"AND WHEN YOU KILLED MACK, YOU WIPED OUT YOUR ONLY COMPETITION IN HERE. ALL THE ROCK AND SKAG TRADE WAS YOURS.
"AFTER ***THAT***, WHO WOULD EVER CHALLENGE YOU AGAIN?

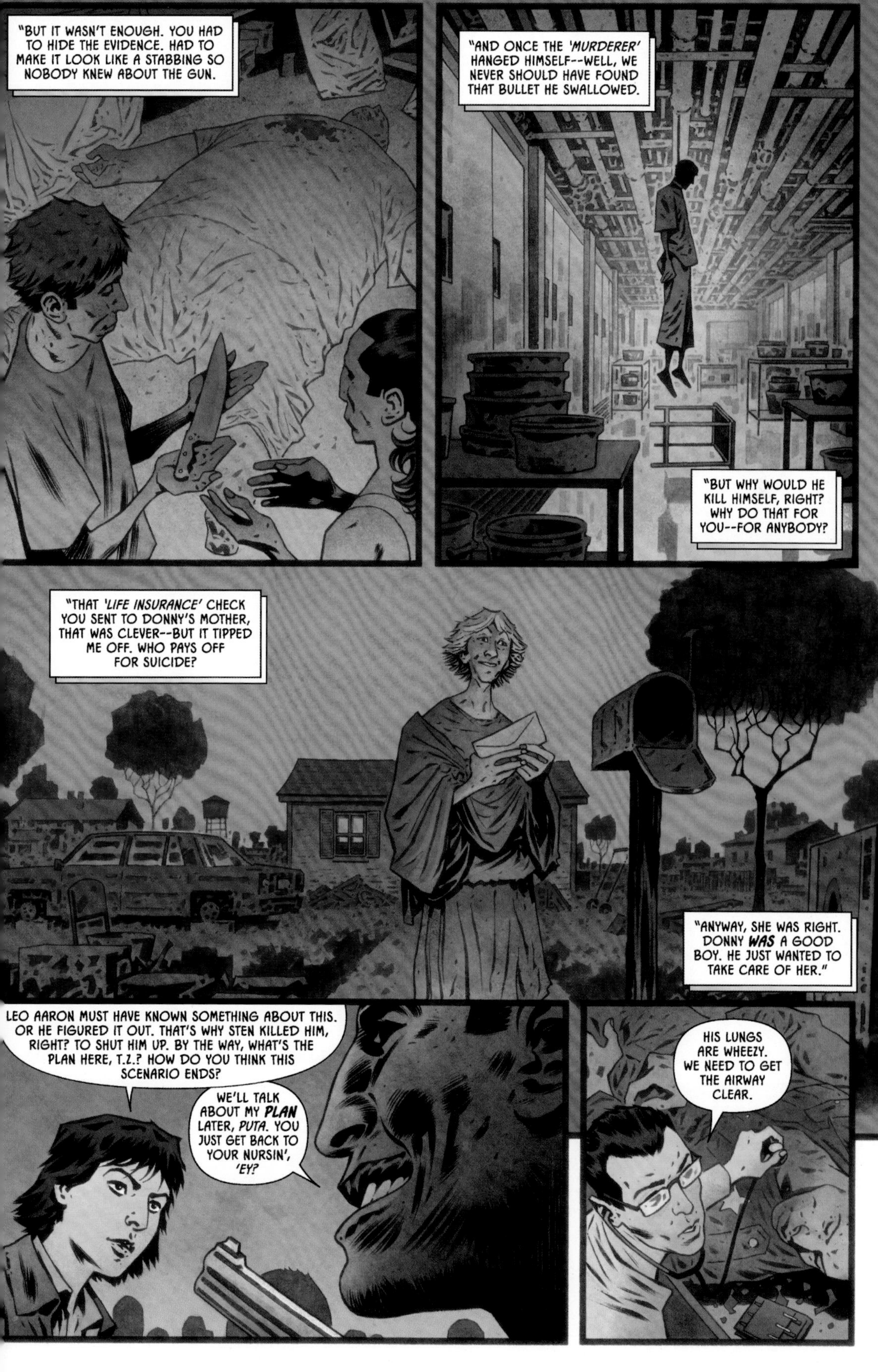
"BUT IT WASN'T ENOUGH. YOU HAD TO HIDE THE EVIDENCE. HAD TO MAKE IT LOOK LIKE A STABBING SO NOBODY KNEW ABOUT THE GUN.
"AND ONCE THE 'MURDERER' HANGED HIMSELF--WELL, WE NEVER SHOULD HAVE FOUND THAT BULLET HE SWALLOWED.
"BUT WHY WOULD HE KILL HIMSELF, RIGHT? WHY DO THAT FOR YOU--FOR ANYBODY?
"THAT 'LIFE INSURANCE' CHECK YOU SENT TO DONNY'S MOTHER, THAT WAS CLEVER--BUT IT TIPPED ME OFF. WHO PAYS OFF FOR SUICIDE?
"ANYWAY, SHE WAS RIGHT. DONNY WAS A GOOD BOY. HE JUST WANTED TO TAKE CARE OF HER."
LEO AARON MUST HAVE KNOWN SOMETHING ABOUT THIS. OR HE FIGURED IT OUT. THAT'S WHY STEN KILLED HIM, RIGHT? TO SHUT HIM UP. BY THE WAY, WHAT'S THE PLAN HERE, T.Z.? HOW DO YOU THINK THIS SCENARIO ENDS?
WE'LL TALK ABOUT MY PLAN LATER, PUTA. YOU JUST GET BACK TO YOUR NURSIN', 'EY?
HIS LUNGS ARE WHEEZY. WE NEED TO GET THE AIRWAY CLEAR.

I NEED MY BAG. JUST ONE KNIFE--

BITCH, YOU THINK *YOU* IN CHARGE?! BANDAGE HIM UP AND PUSH THE TABLE OUTTA HERE *NOW!*

A BANDAGE WILL SUFFOCATE HIM. HE NEEDS A TRACHEOTOMY.

DON'T WASTE TIME WITH HIM.

MY PARENTS TAUGHT ME A TRICK WHEN I WAS A KID.

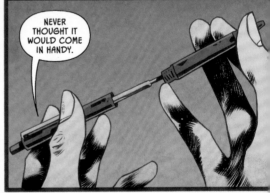

NEVER THOUGHT IT WOULD COME IN HANDY.

WHAT YOU DOIN'! WHAT'S THESE WHISPERS ABOUT?!

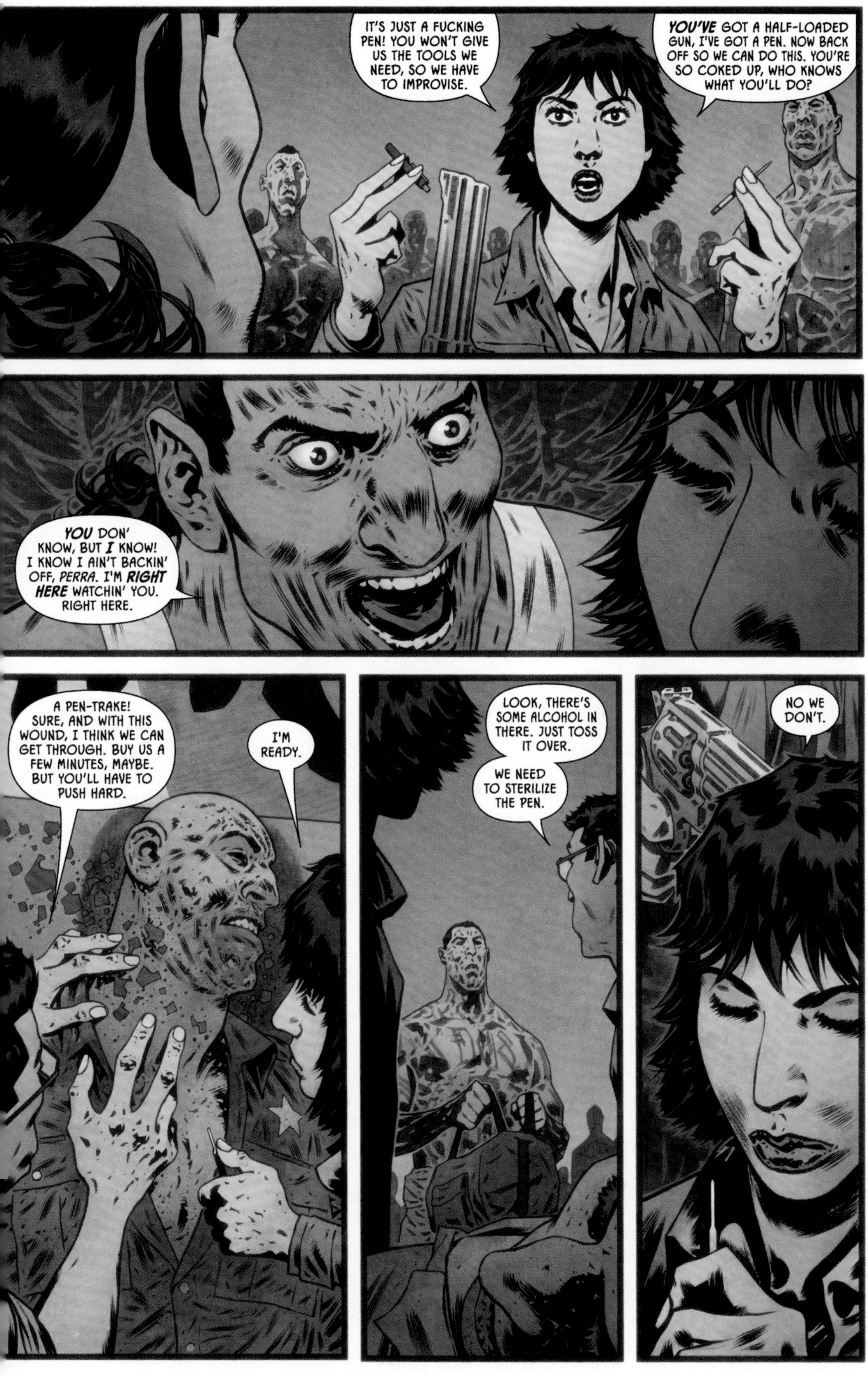
IT'S JUST A FUCKING PEN! YOU WON'T GIVE US THE TOOLS WE NEED, SO WE HAVE TO IMPROVISE.
YOU'VE GOT A HALF-LOADED GUN, I'VE GOT A PEN. NOW BACK OFF SO WE CAN DO THIS. YOU'RE SO COKED UP, WHO KNOWS WHAT YOU'LL DO?
YOU DON' KNOW, BUT I KNOW! I KNOW I AIN'T BACKIN' OFF, PERRA. I'M RIGHT HERE WATCHIN' YOU. RIGHT HERE.
A PEN-TRAKE! SURE, AND WITH THIS WOUND, I THINK WE CAN GET THROUGH. BUY US A FEW MINUTES, MAYBE. BUT YOU'LL HAVE TO PUSH HARD.
I'M READY.
LOOK, THERE'S SOME ALCOHOL IN THERE. JUST TOSS IT OVER.
WE NEED TO STERILIZE THE PEN.
NO WE DON'T.

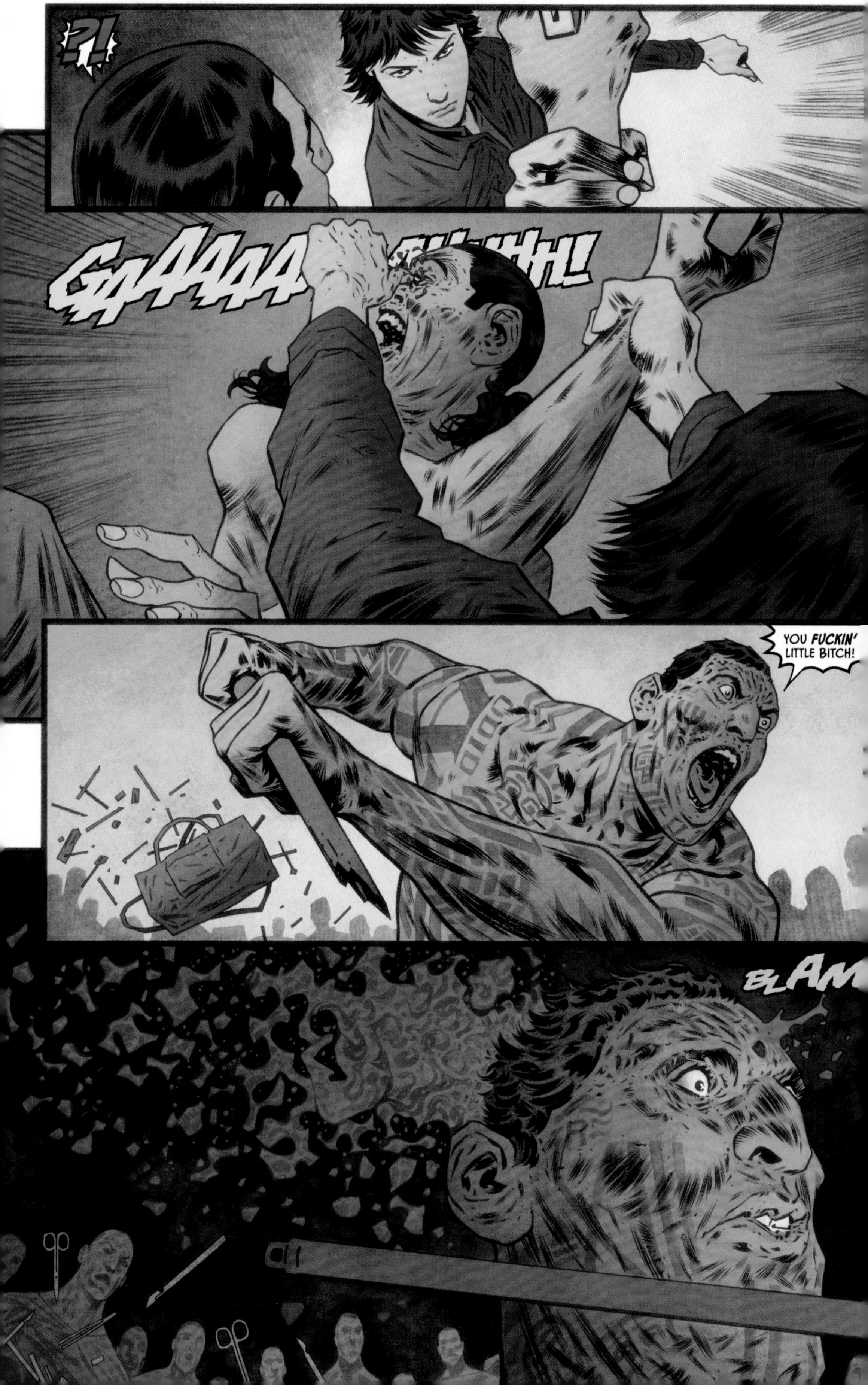
?!
YOU FUCKIN' LITTLE BITCH!
BLAM

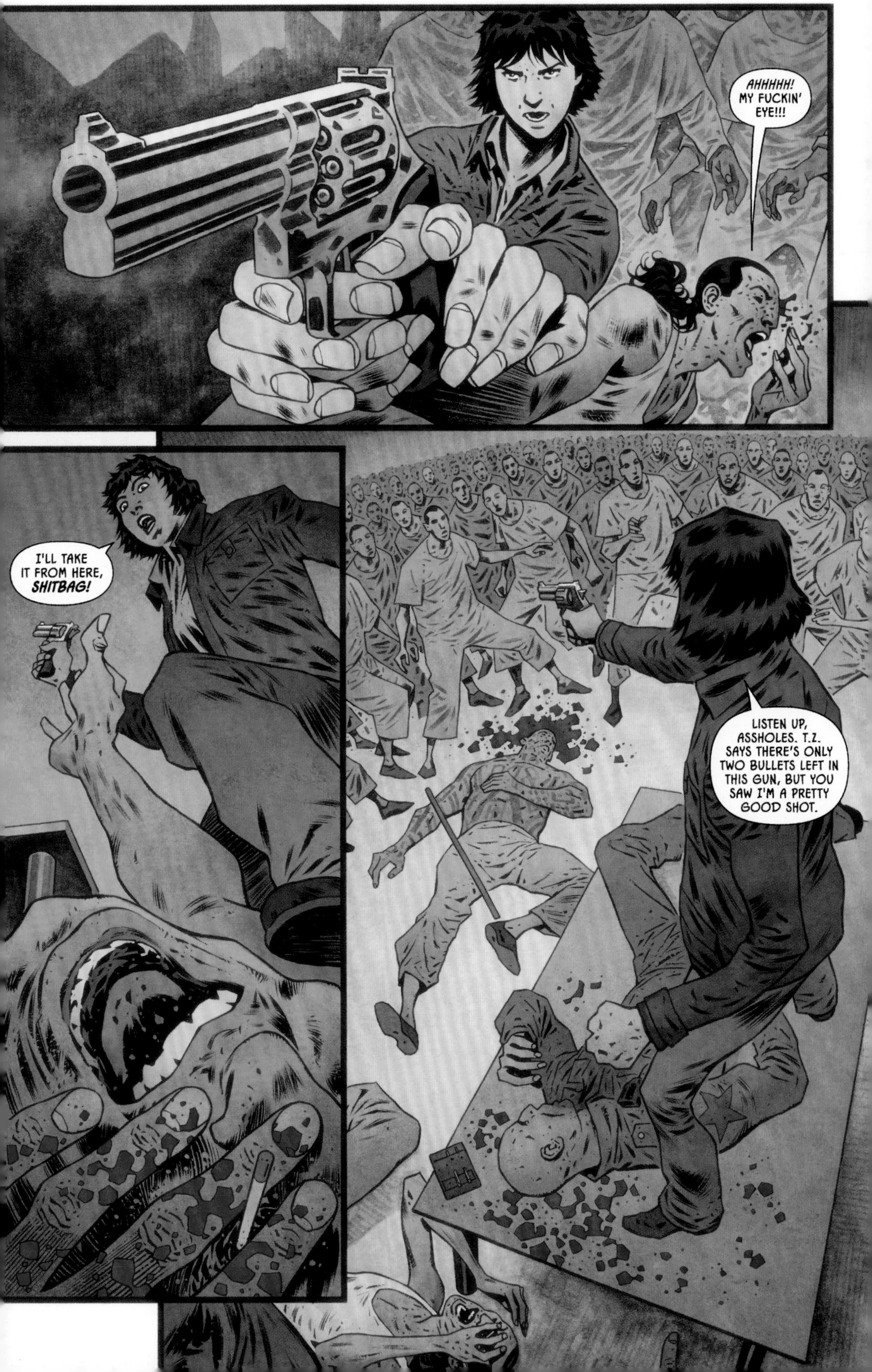
AHHHHH! MY FUCKIN' EYE!!!
I'LL TAKE IT FROM HERE, SHITBAG!
LISTEN UP, ASSHOLES. T.Z. SAYS THERE'S ONLY TWO BULLETS LEFT IN THIS GUN, BUT YOU SAW I'M A PRETTY GOOD SHOT.

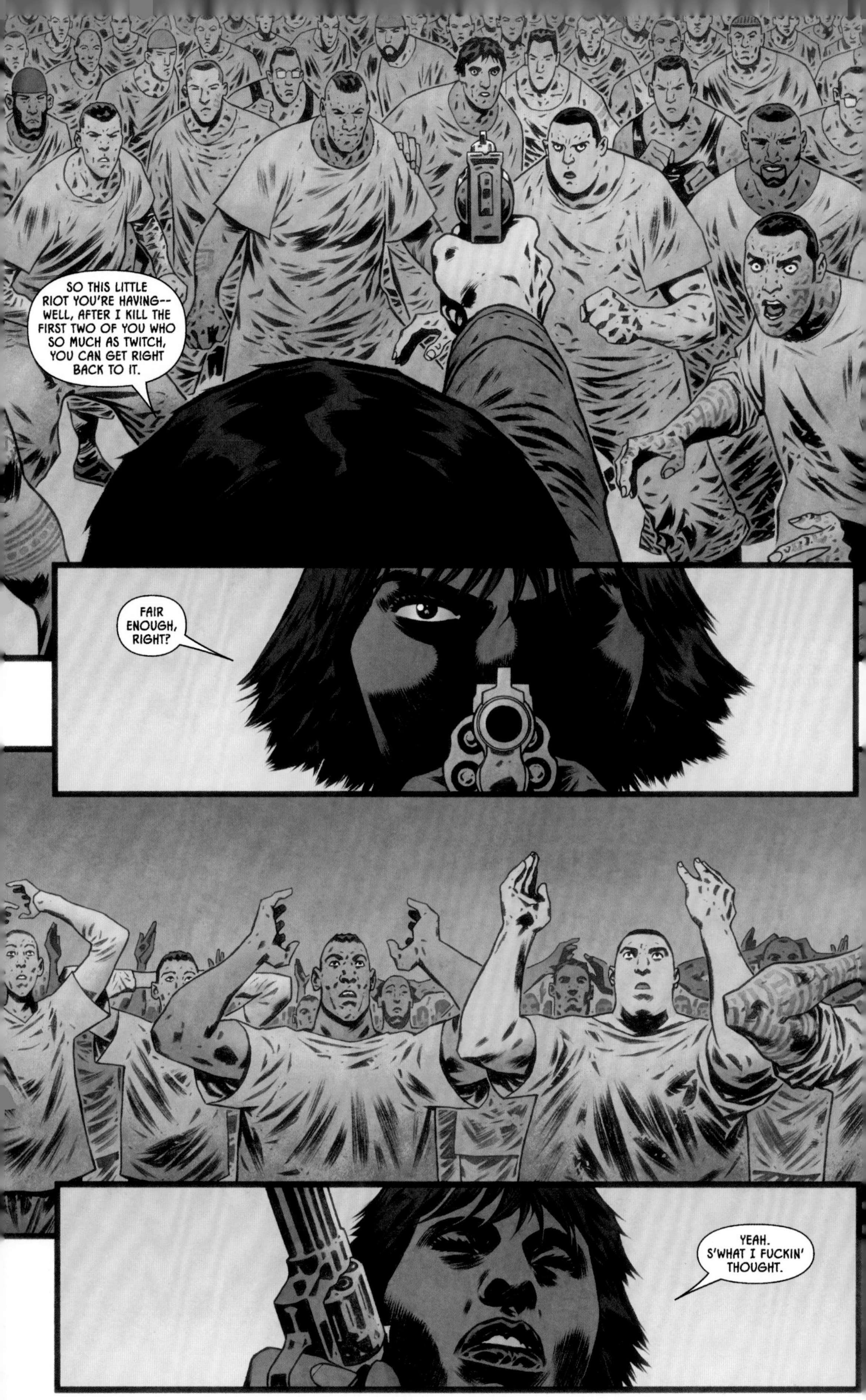
SO THIS LITTLE RIOT YOU'RE HAVING-- WELL, AFTER I KILL THE FIRST TWO OF YOU WHO SO MUCH AS TWITCH, YOU CAN GET RIGHT BACK TO IT.
FAIR ENOUGH, RIGHT?
YEAH. S'WHAT I FUCKIN' THOUGHT.

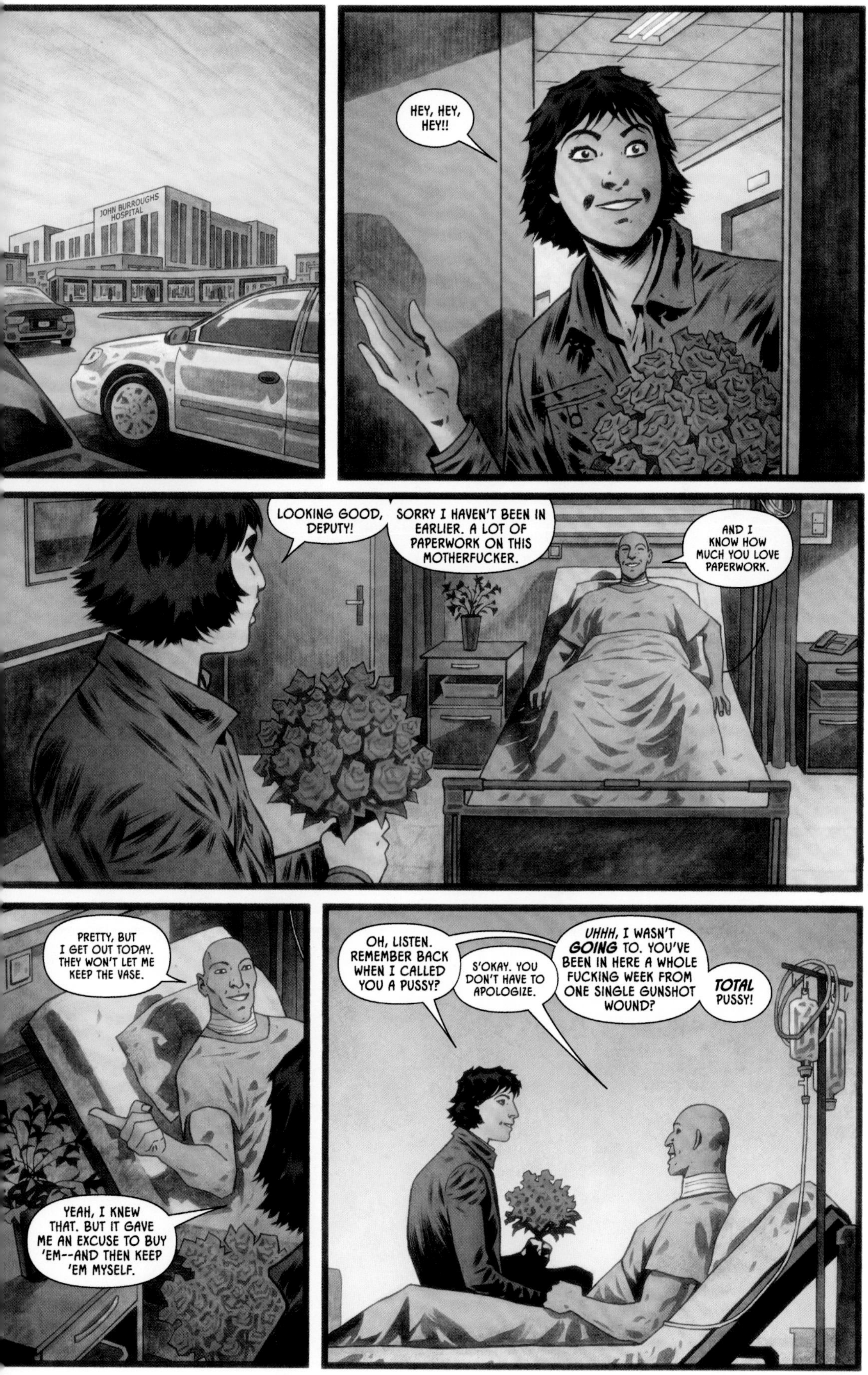
JOHN BURROUGHS HOSPITAL
HEY, HEY, HEY!!
LOOKING GOOD, DEPUTY!
SORRY I HAVEN'T BEEN IN EARLIER. A LOT OF PAPERWORK ON THIS MOTHERFUCKER.
AND I KNOW HOW MUCH YOU LOVE PAPERWORK.
PRETTY, BUT I GET OUT TODAY. THEY WON'T LET ME KEEP THE VASE.
YEAH, I KNEW THAT. BUT IT GAVE ME AN EXCUSE TO BUY 'EM--AND THEN KEEP 'EM MYSELF.
OH, LISTEN. REMEMBER BACK WHEN I CALLED YOU A PUSSY?
S'OKAY. YOU DON'T HAVE TO APOLOGIZE.
UHHH, I WASN'T GOING TO. YOU'VE BEEN IN HERE A WHOLE FUCKING WEEK FROM ONE SINGLE GUNSHOT WOUND?
TOTAL PUSSY!

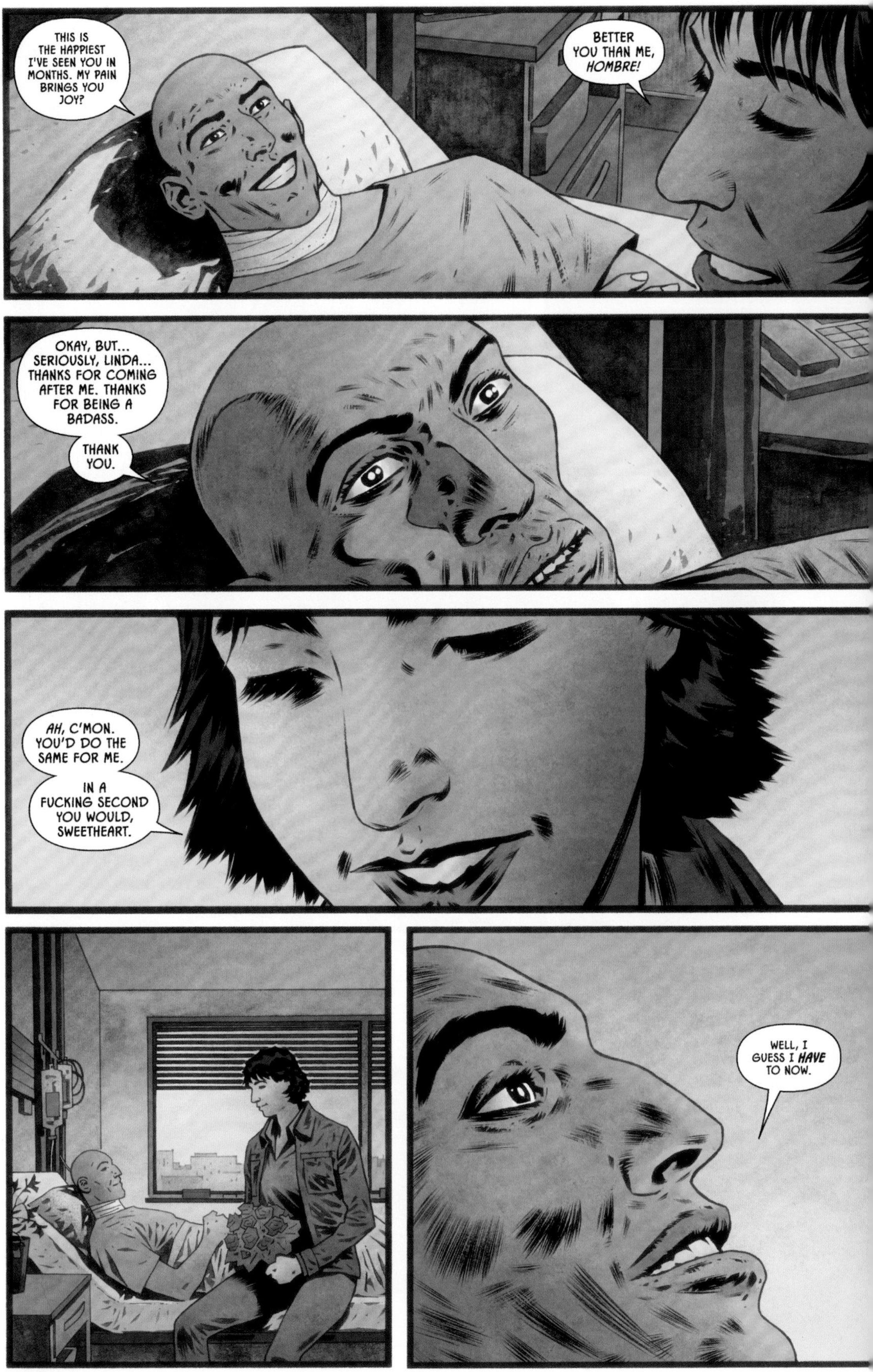
THIS IS THE HAPPIEST I'VE SEEN YOU IN MONTHS. MY PAIN BRINGS YOU JOY?
BETTER YOU THAN ME, *HOMBRE!*
OKAY, BUT... SERIOUSLY, LINDA... THANKS FOR COMING AFTER ME. THANKS FOR BEING A BADASS.
THANK YOU.
AH, C'MON. YOU'D DO THE SAME FOR ME.
IN A FUCKING SECOND YOU WOULD, SWEETHEART.
WELL, I GUESS I ***HAVE*** TO NOW.

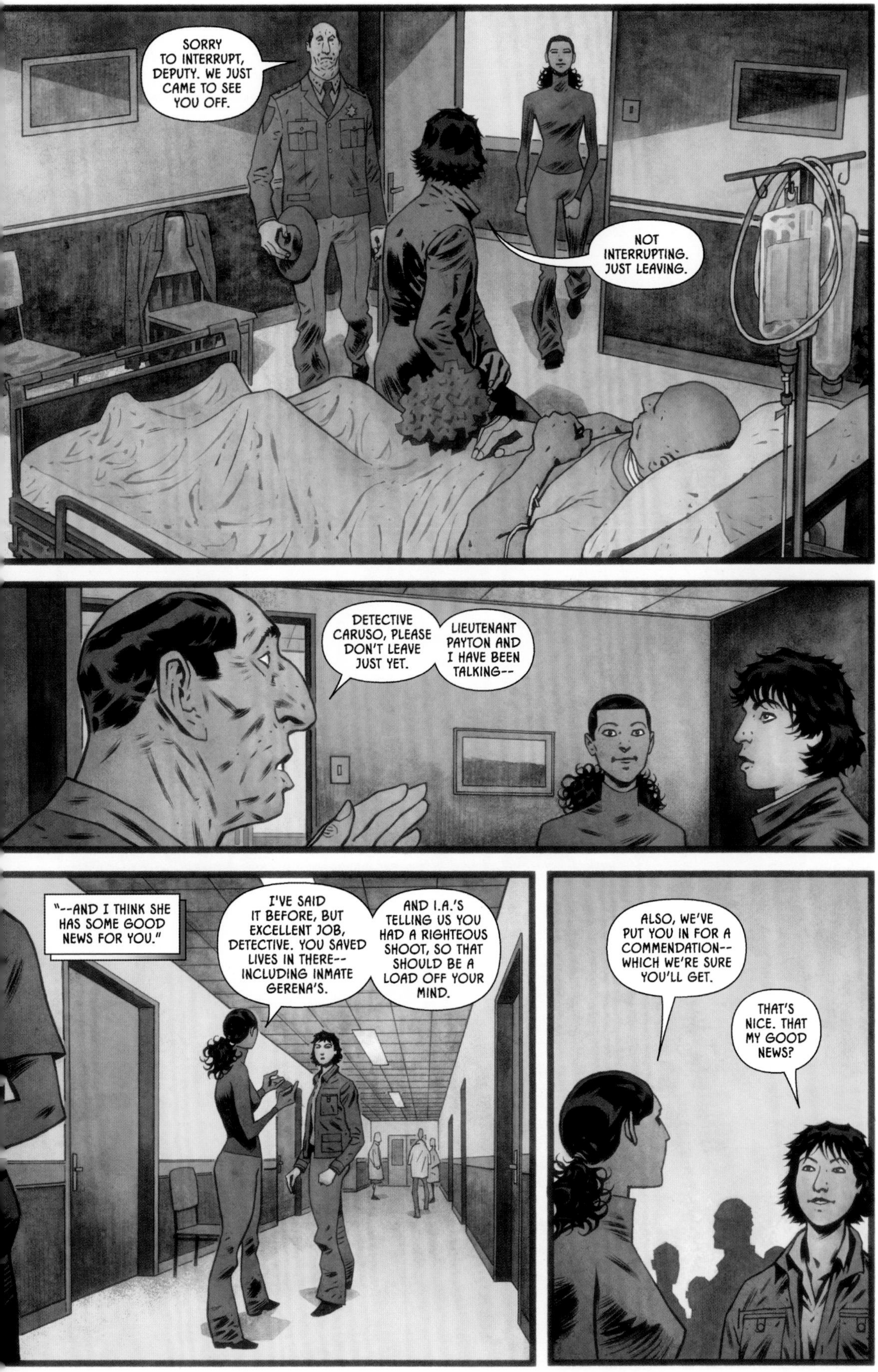
SORRY TO INTERRUPT, DEPUTY. WE JUST CAME TO SEE YOU OFF.
NOT INTERRUPTING. JUST LEAVING.
DETECTIVE CARUSO, PLEASE DON'T LEAVE JUST YET.
LIEUTENANT PAYTON AND I HAVE BEEN TALKING--
"--AND I THINK SHE HAS SOME GOOD NEWS FOR YOU."
I'VE SAID IT BEFORE, BUT EXCELLENT JOB, DETECTIVE. YOU SAVED LIVES IN THERE--INCLUDING INMATE GERENA'S.
AND I.A.'S TELLING US YOU HAD A RIGHTEOUS SHOOT, SO THAT SHOULD BE A LOAD OFF YOUR MIND.
ALSO, WE'VE PUT YOU IN FOR A COMMENDATION--WHICH WE'RE SURE YOU'LL GET.
THAT'S NICE. THAT MY GOOD NEWS?

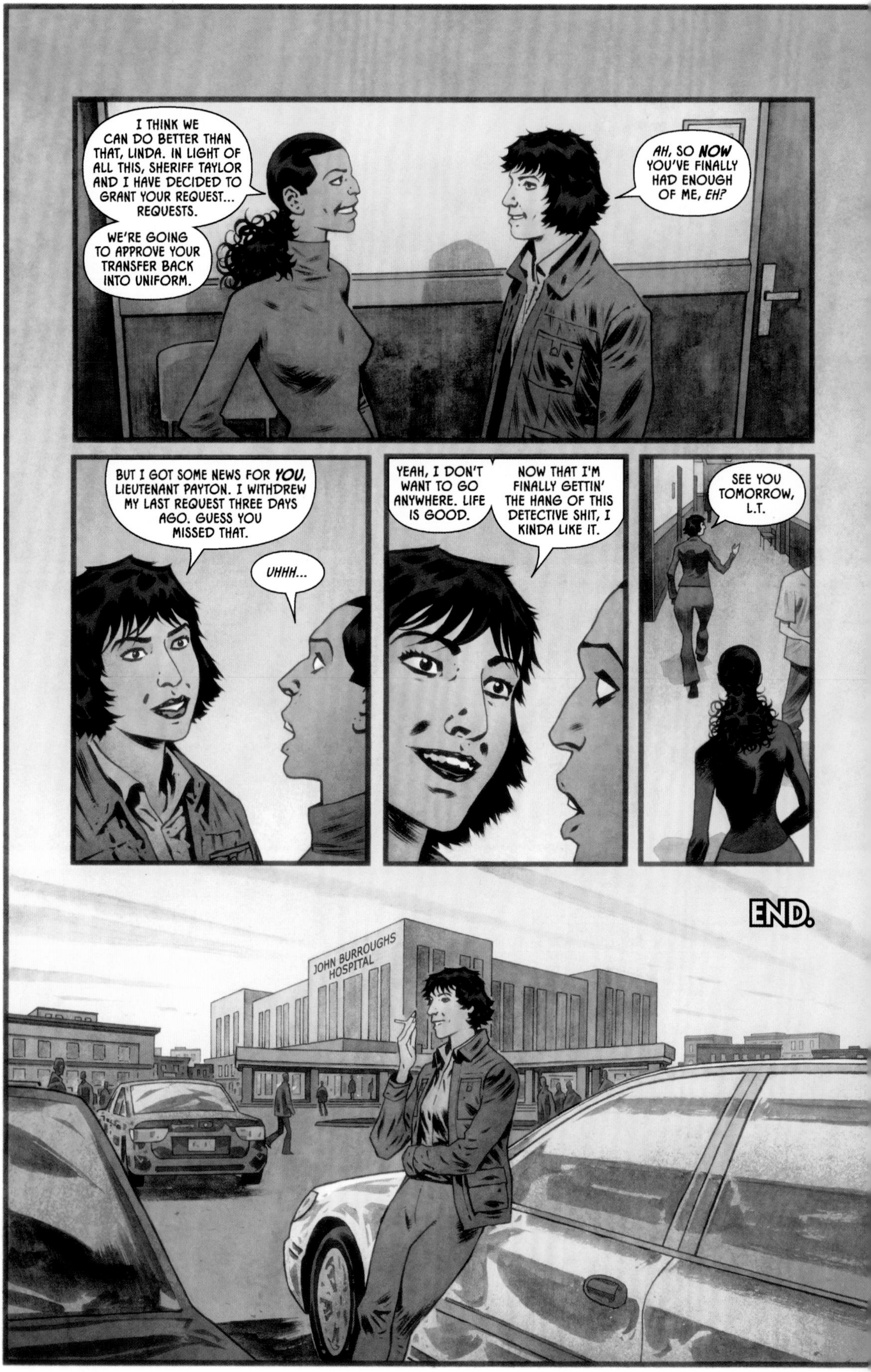
I THINK WE CAN DO BETTER THAN THAT, LINDA. IN LIGHT OF ALL THIS, SHERIFF TAYLOR AND I HAVE DECIDED TO GRANT YOUR REQUEST... REQUESTS.
WE'RE GOING TO APPROVE YOUR TRANSFER BACK INTO UNIFORM.
AH, SO **NOW** YOU'VE FINALLY HAD ENOUGH OF ME, *EH?*
BUT I GOT SOME NEWS FOR ***YOU***, LIEUTENANT PAYTON. I WITHDREW MY LAST REQUEST THREE DAYS AGO. GUESS YOU MISSED THAT.
UHHH...
YEAH, I DON'T WANT TO GO ANYWHERE. LIFE IS GOOD.
NOW THAT I'M FINALLY GETTIN' THE HANG OF THIS DETECTIVE SHIT, I KINDA LIKE IT.
SEE YOU TOMORROW, L.T.
END.
JOHN BURROUGHS HOSPITAL

NOTES BY **TONI FEJZULA**

DEAD INSIDE

SKETCHBOOK

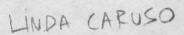

LINDA CARUSO

For Linda, John asked for a woman in her thirties, with wider hips and thighs and a healthy appearance in spite of her unhealthy way of life.

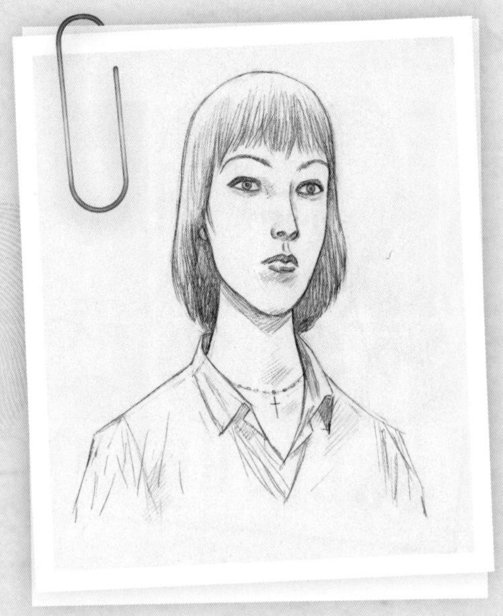

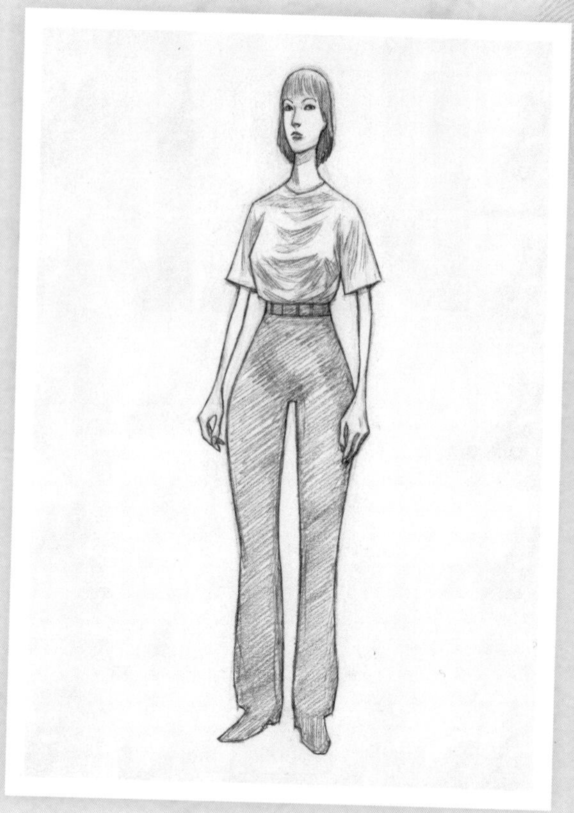

JULIA TAYLOR

I usually draw characters by opposition. That means if Linda has a round face, Julia's will be long. Her straight hair is the opposite of Linda's short, curly brunette hair.

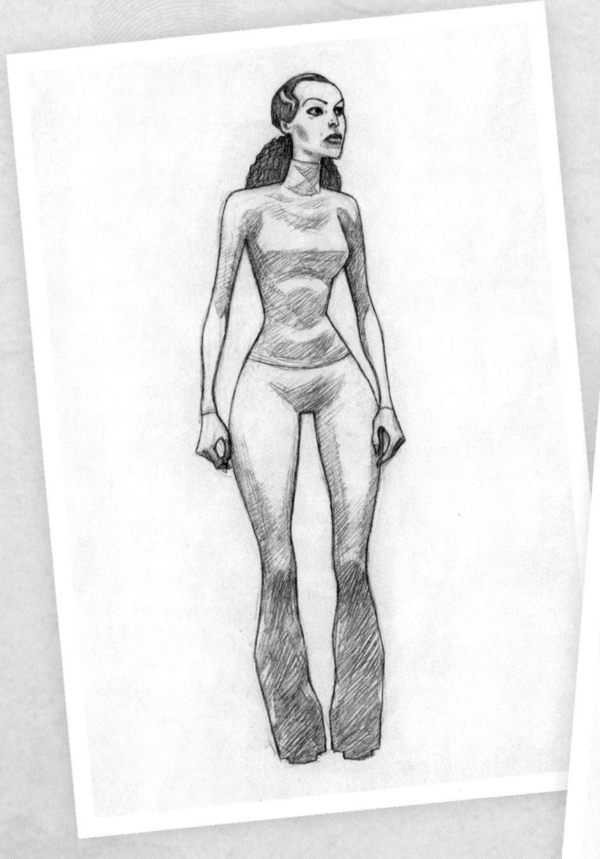

Here's the design for Ellie. A strong, ambitious woman who loves to have control.

ELLIE PAYTON

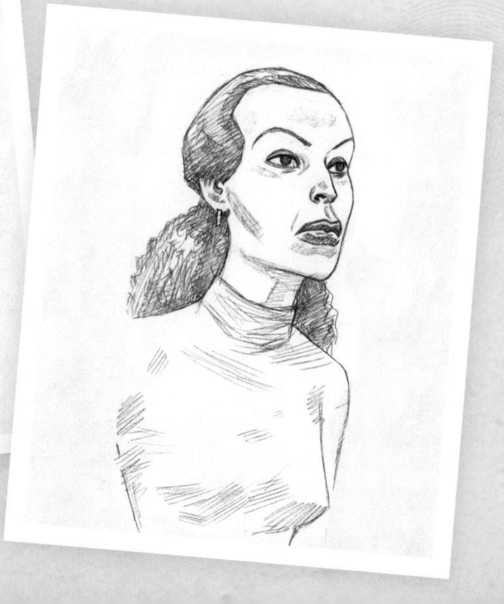

LEO AARON

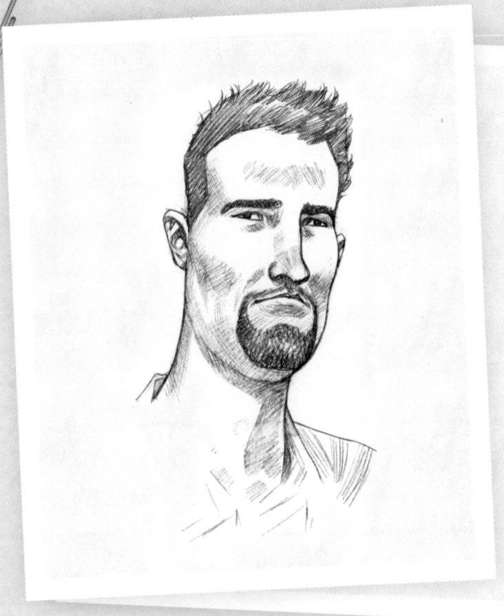

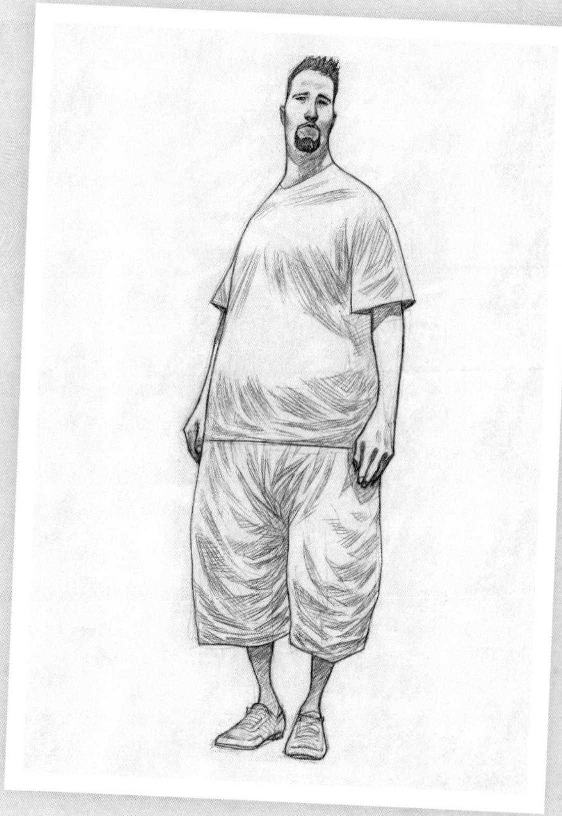

There are a lot of big, muscular guys in this book. Leo had to be tall, but not athletic. A well-mannered guy who seems to have good intentions toward people. Not very handsome but nice enough for Linda to feel a certain interest in him.

PARIS TAYLOR

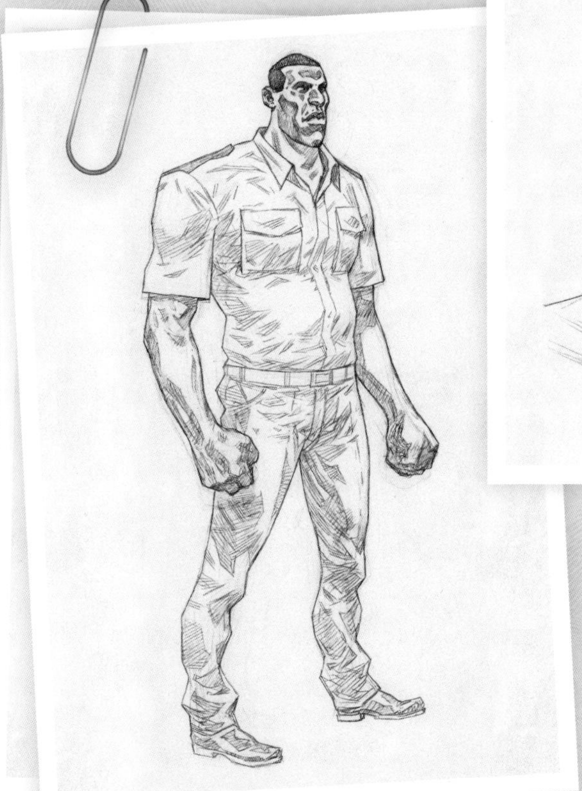

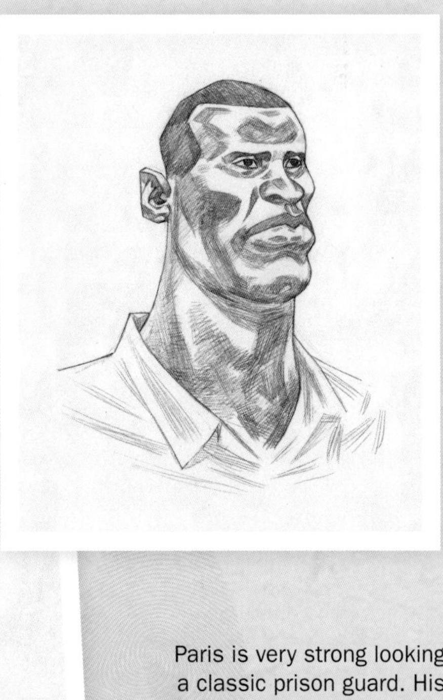

Paris is very strong looking, like a classic prison guard. His face gained some seriousness as I kept developing it.

WARREN DIAZ

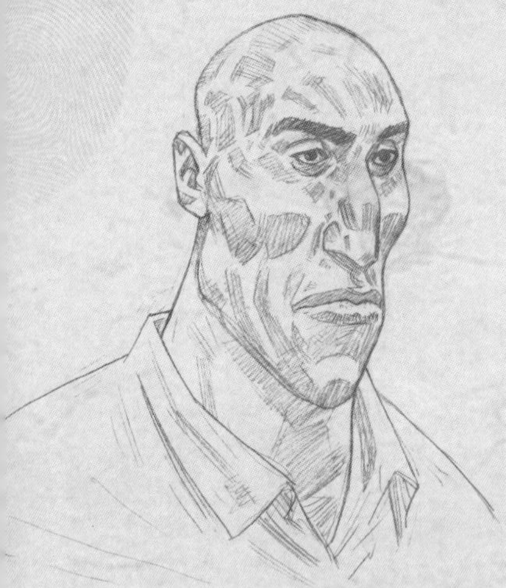

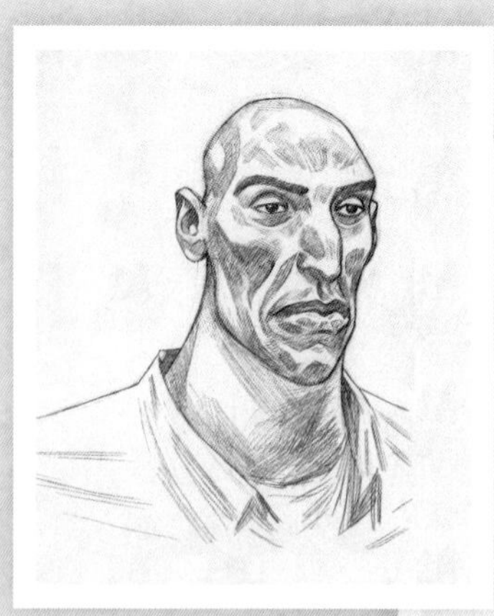

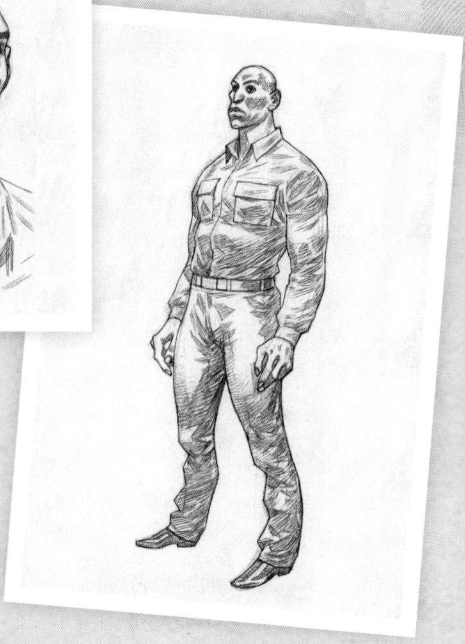

John made me change Diaz's first designs because he seemed less intelligent with that prominent jaw. He's about forty, a very strong and athletic man, but I tried to make his face look older, carved with life experience.

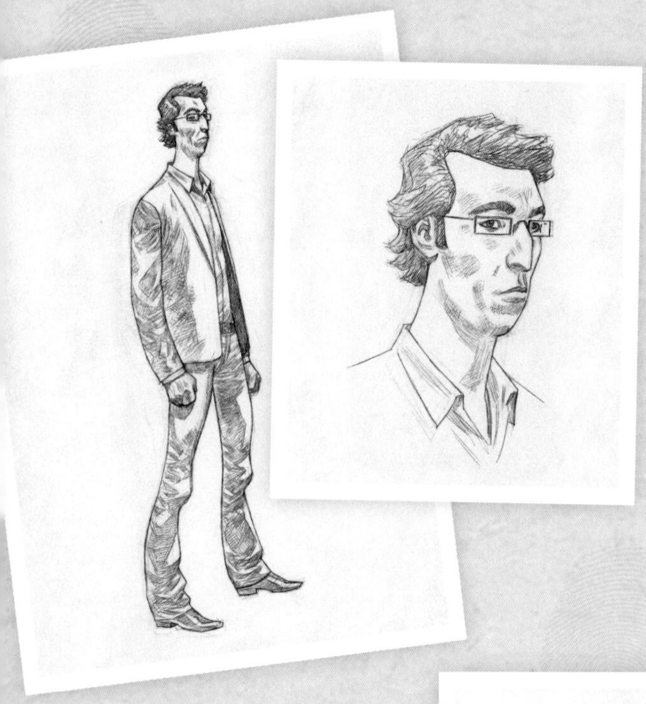

KYLE ROMERO

Kyle Romero appears very briefly in this series, and that's a pity because I love this character. I imagined how someone capable of working with Linda over many years would look, so I designed a calm, softhearted, slim, healthy man, the same age as Linda.

WARDEN HALLAS

Perhaps my favorite character. I saw him as a not-so-successful political type, someone difficult to deal with if he feels his position is threatened. Maybe because of some stereotypes and misguided beliefs he has, I always felt he's the most dangerous guy in this story.

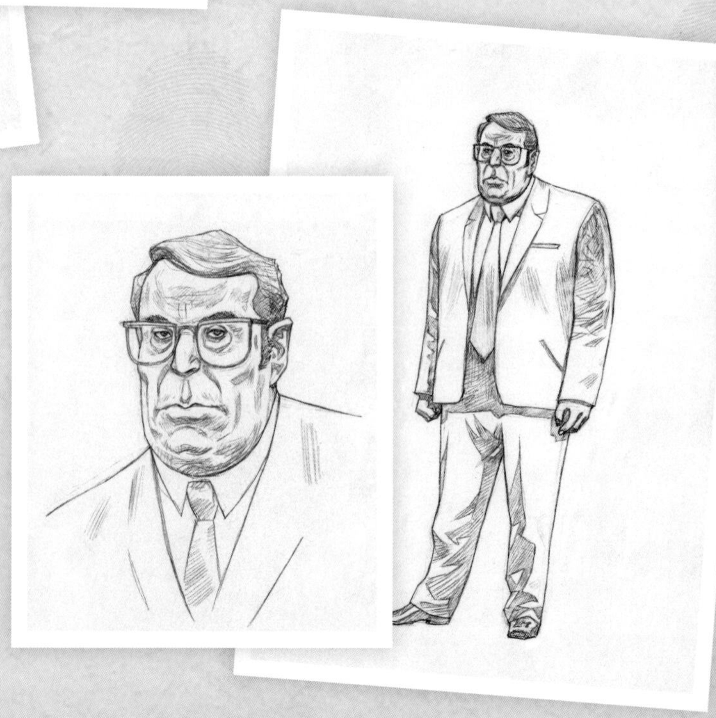

Sten appeared younger in the first roughs, so John had me add wrinkles and bleach his hair. I saw him as a former rugby and baseball player. I placed some objects in his flat that indicate he was a trophy-winning athlete in his youth whose life went downhill at some point.

STEN

This wasn't in the script, but it seemed logical to me that Sten could have been an alcoholic when this story happened.

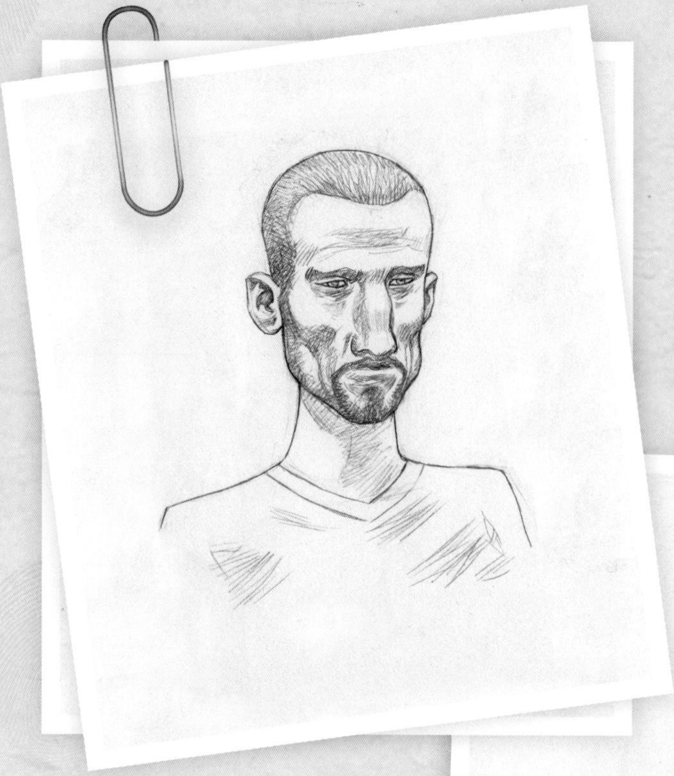

TZ GERENA

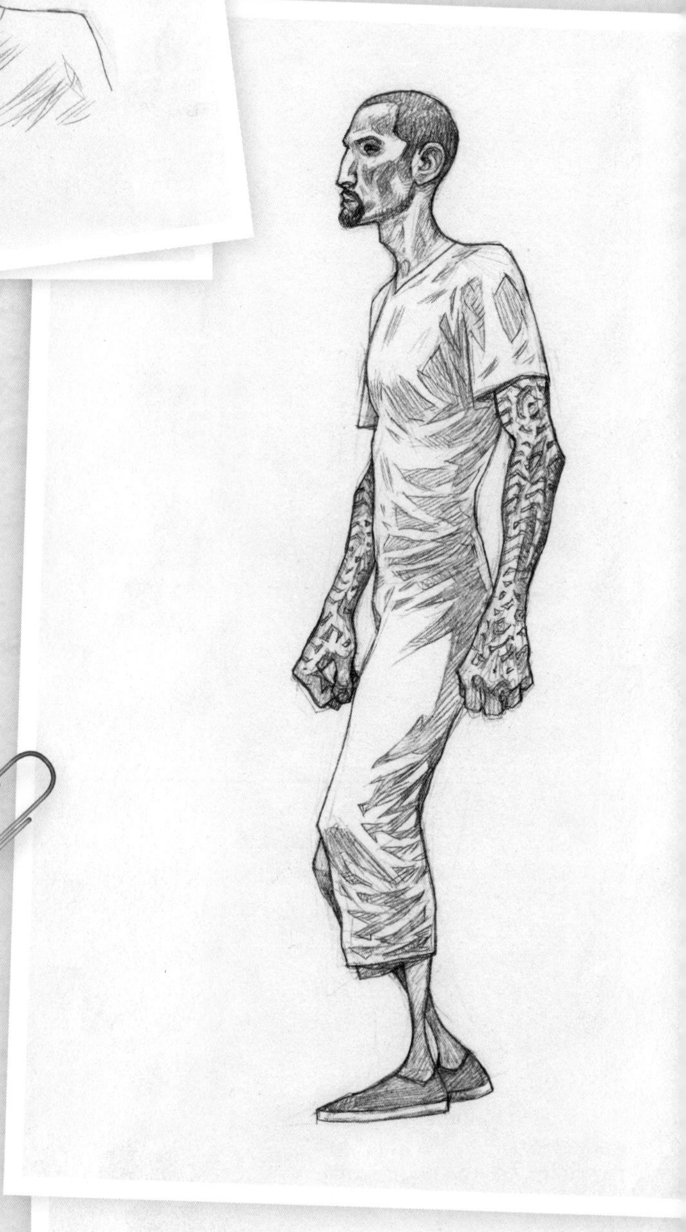

TZ's face and body complexity didn't change much from these first roughs. I decided to remove all those tattoos over his hands because Alessandro, his prison mate, had to have some very prominent ones as a specific part of his characterization. TZ is the hidden predator or alpha male. However, he's probably the only character in this book as small as Donny.

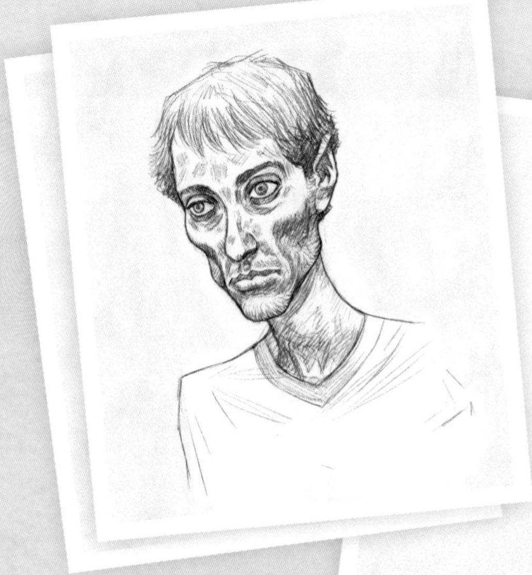

DONNY

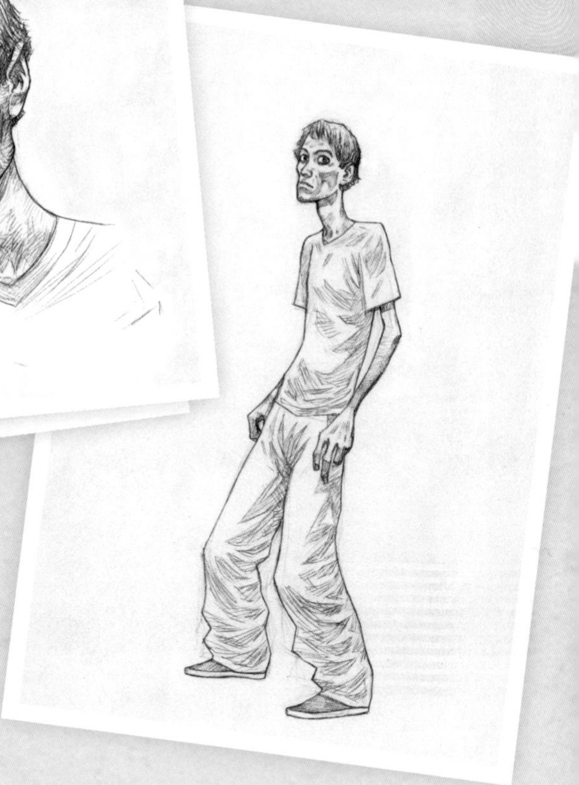

Yes, the smallest and the most tragic guy. John gave me some very specific direction for him. He might be the character with the biggest and saddest eyes (besides his mother). The main differences between TZ and Donny are the way he walks, his neck position, and his shoulders and arms.

MACK

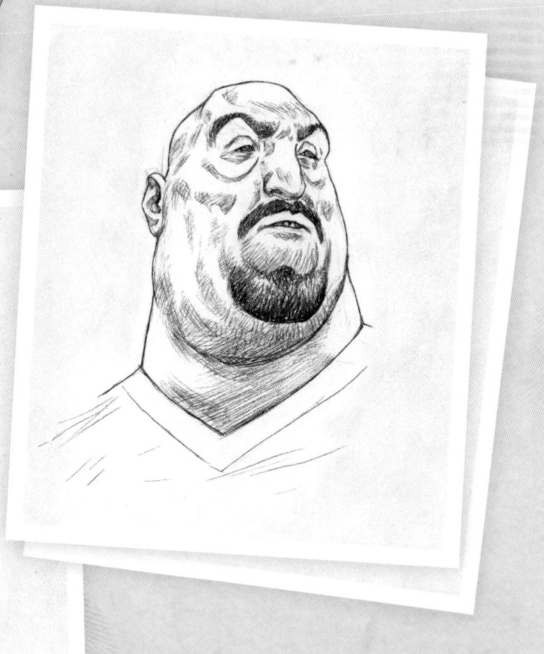

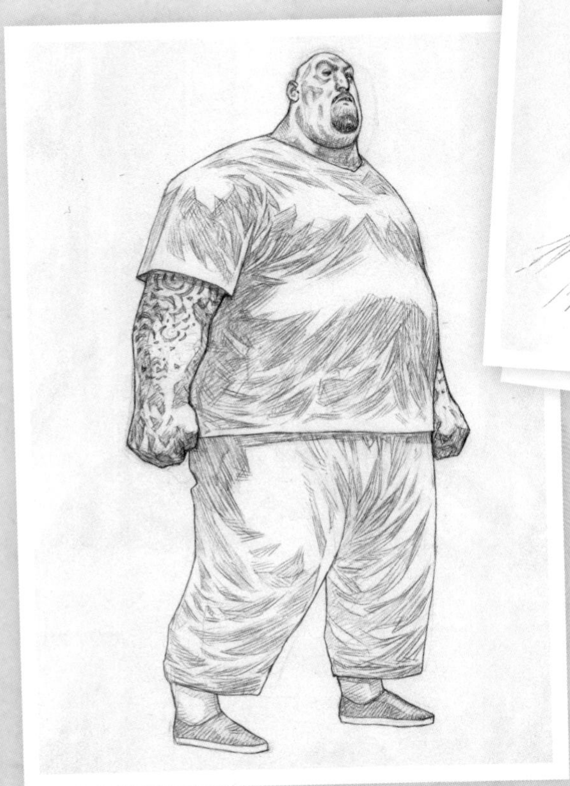

The contrast between the exaggerated slimness of Donny and Mack's weight is something I played with intentionally.

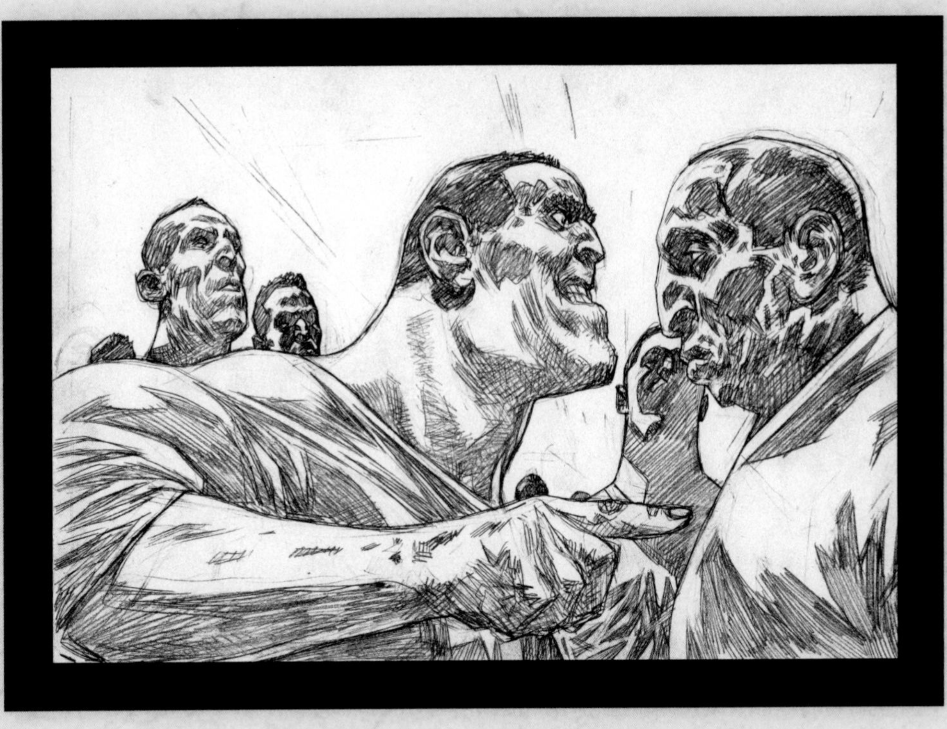

The illustrations from these two pages were done to promote the series.

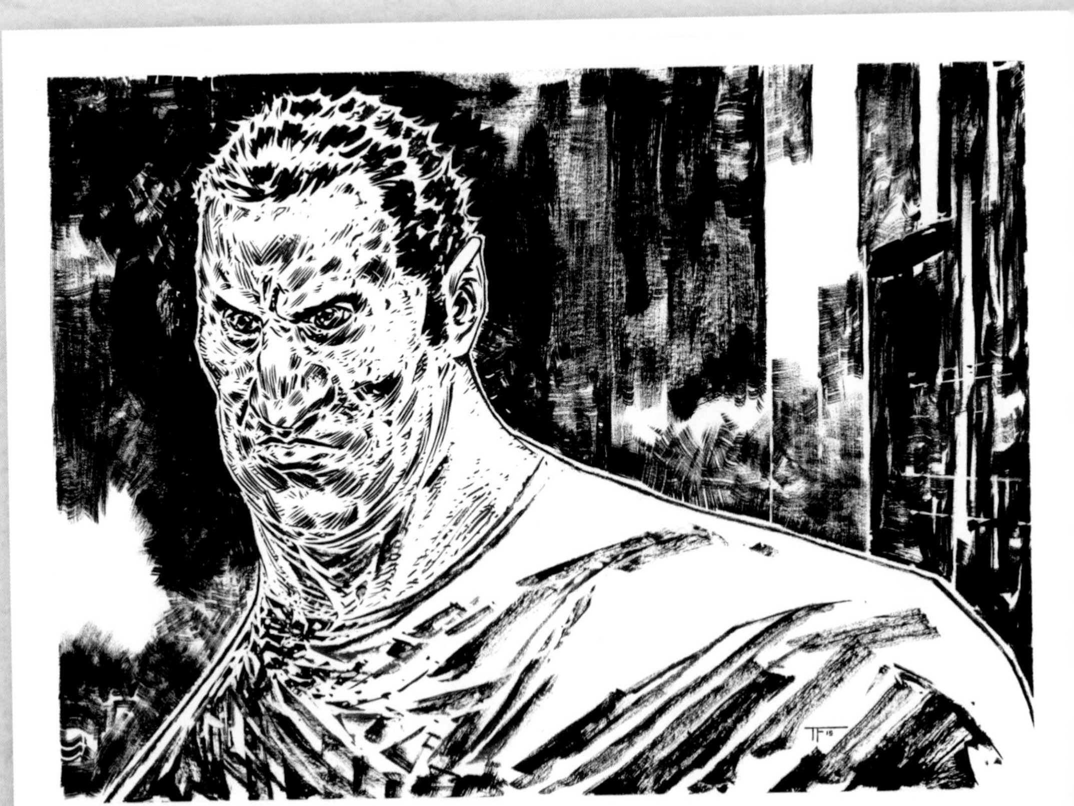

These are the very first images I did for *Dead Inside*. John asked me to use a specific drawing style that I used for many years before I drew my comic series *Veil*, with very dirty brush inks which are pretty far from the stained glass look I used in *Veil* and in the comic *Lobster Johnson*.

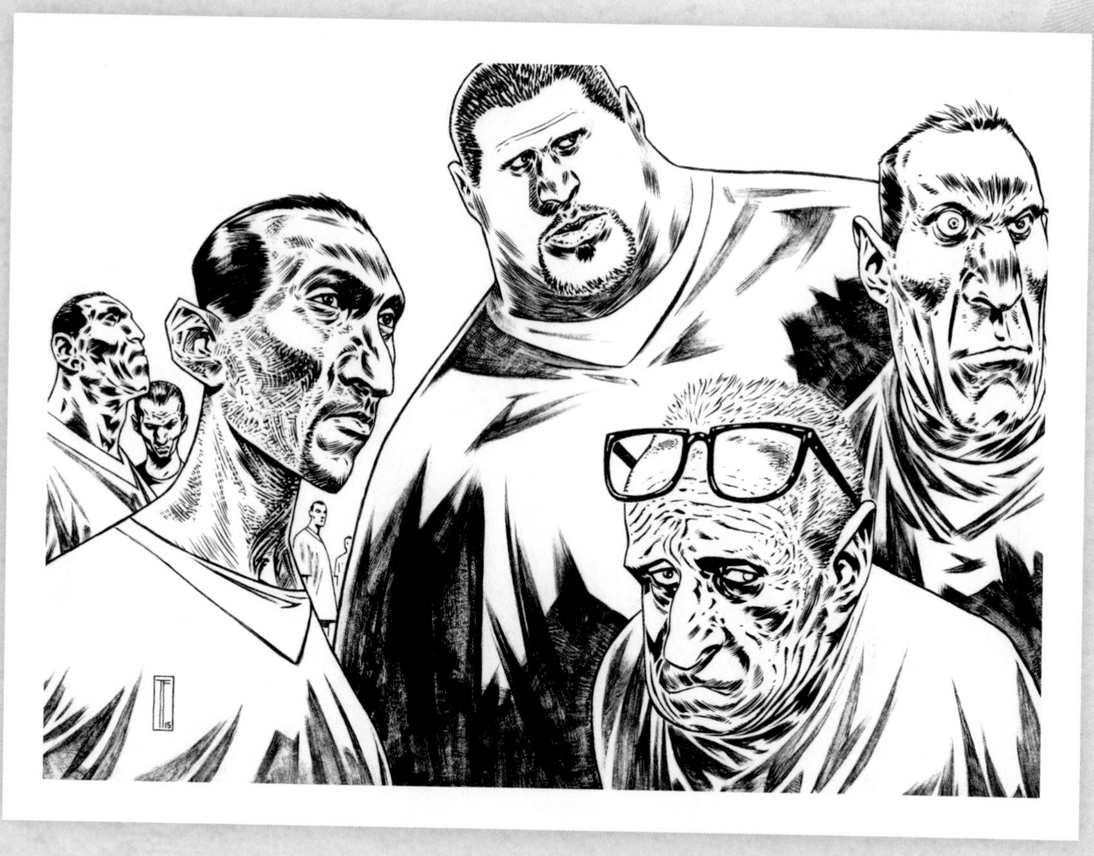

When I drew these, I only had a few words from John saying it was a crime story set in a prison. Linda hadn't been mentioned yet. She definitely changed my approach for the book, and also gave some sense to the exaggeration of some of these physiognomies.

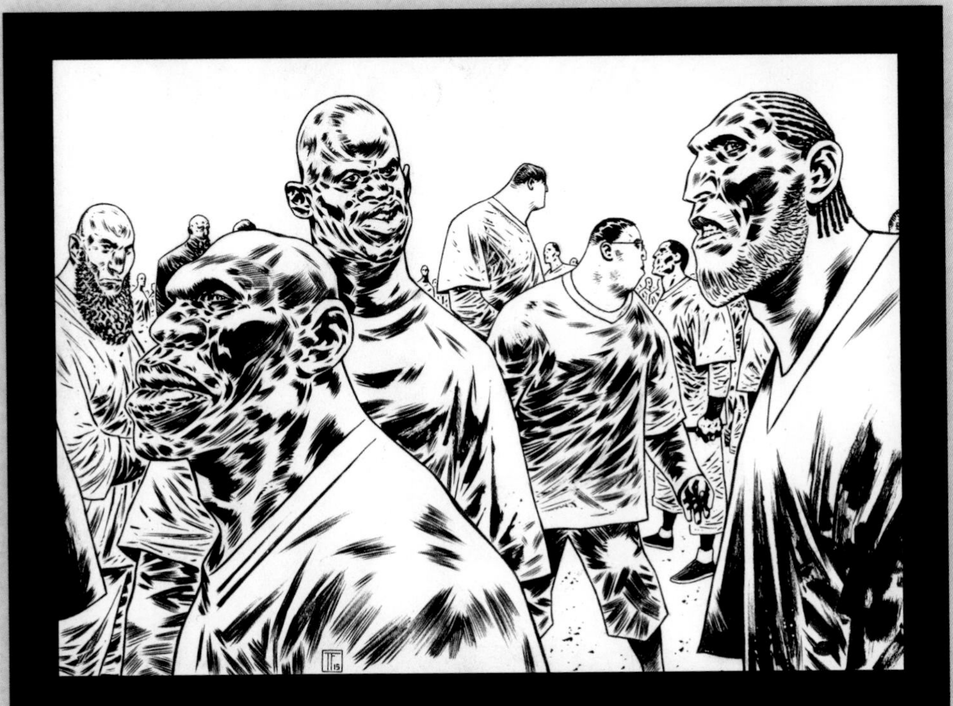

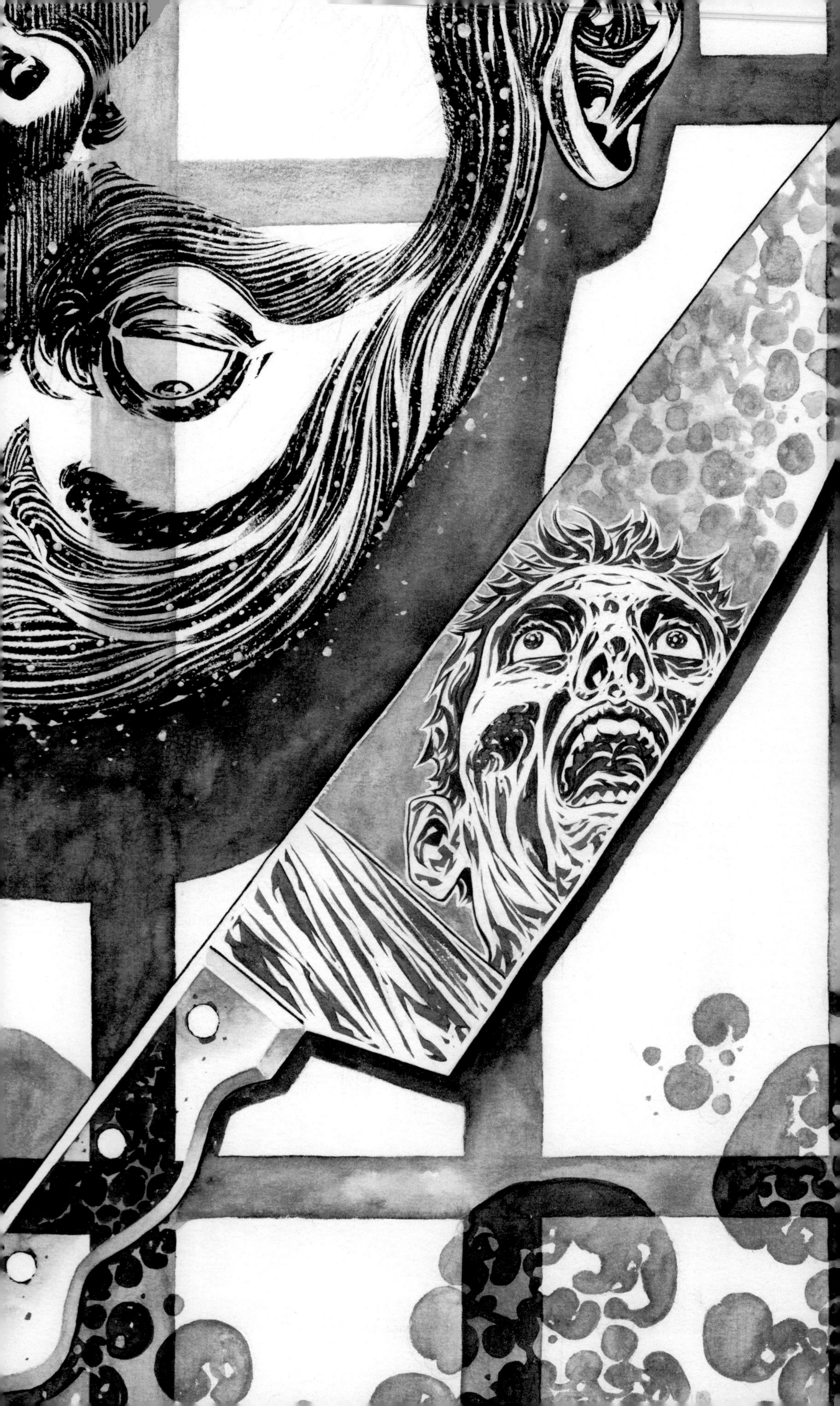

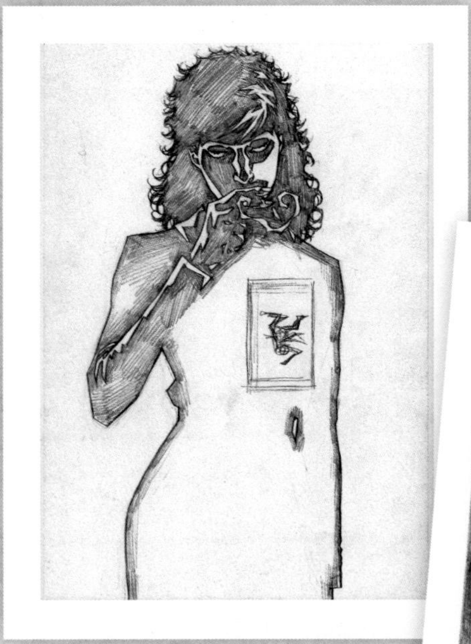

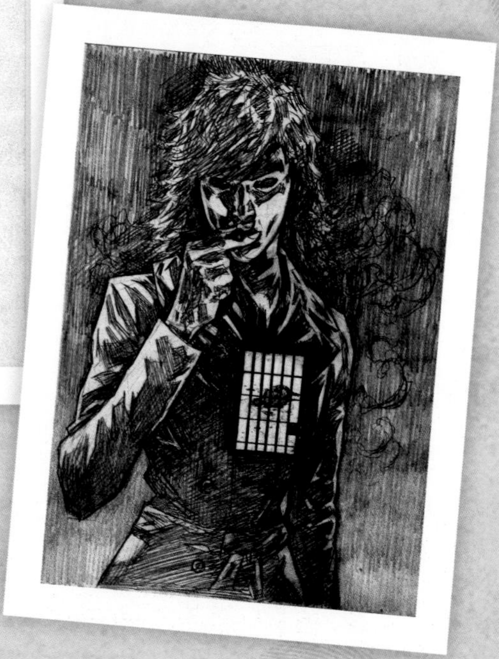

John was always very sure of what he wanted for the cover for issue #1: a dead body behind bars in a cell over Linda's silhouette (over her heart). I did some sketches to provide Dave Johnson with inspiration.

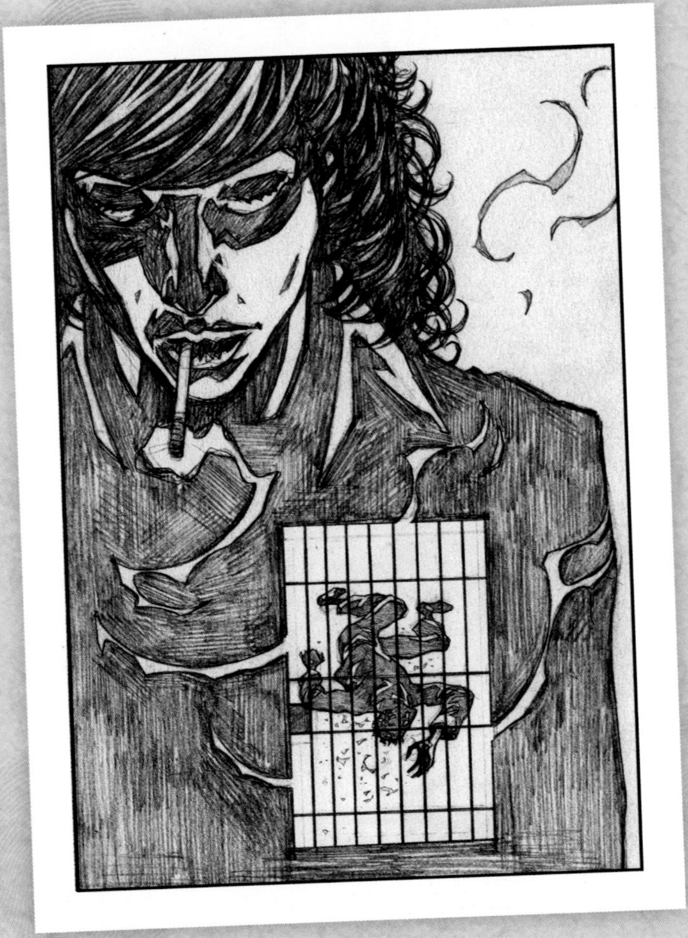

All these versions were done before I knew how Linda would really look. She's still by far the most realistic character in the book. I never felt I really nailed her face. Unlike in *Veil*, Linda is a very real person to me, so I identified with her.

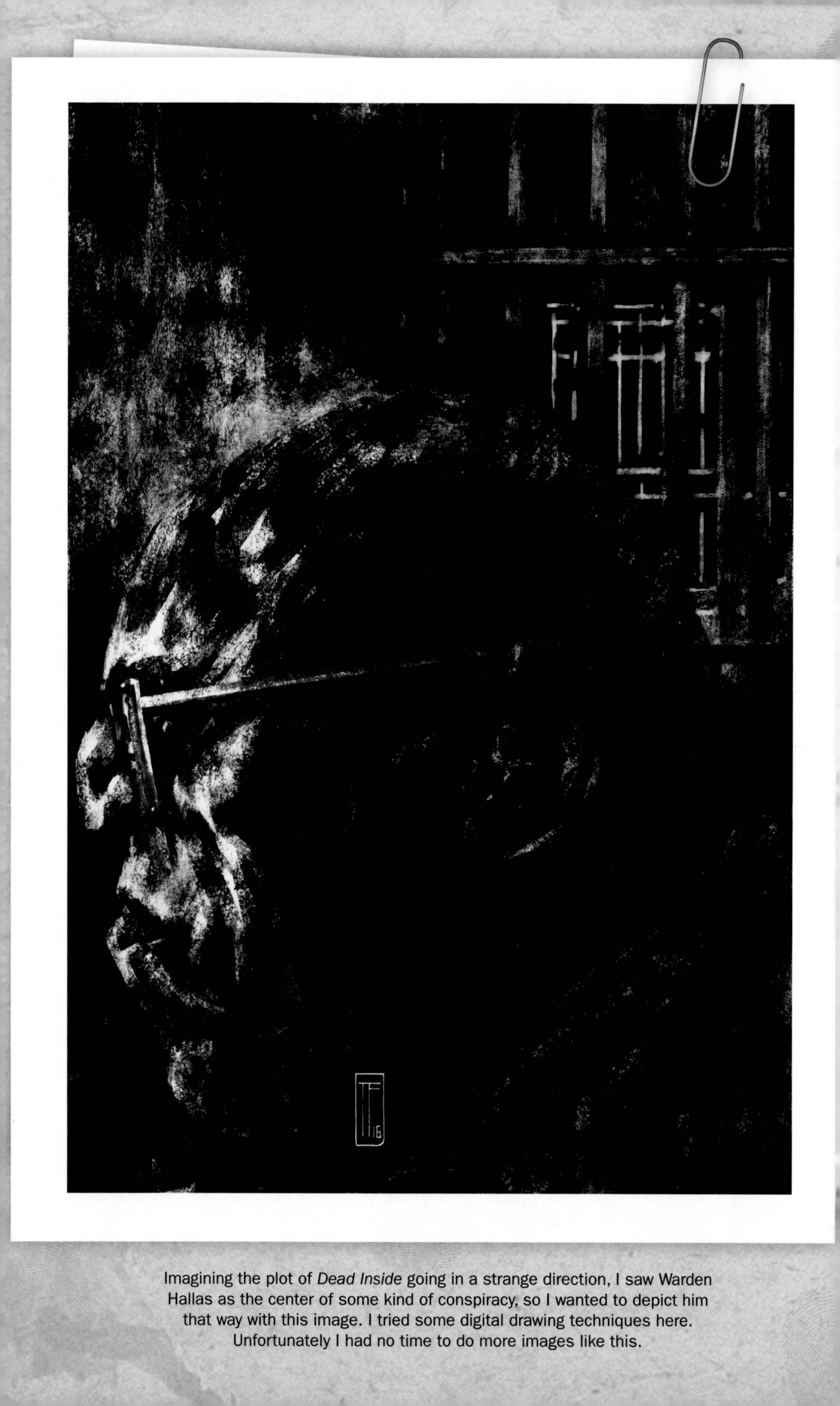

Imagining the plot of *Dead Inside* going in a strange direction, I saw Warden Hallas as the center of some kind of conspiracy, so I wanted to depict him that way with this image. I tried some digital drawing techniques here. Unfortunately I had no time to do more images like this.

DEAD INSIDE

PINUP GALLERY

FRANCIS PORTELA

DANIJEL ZEZELJ

R. M. GUÉRA

FERNANDO BLANCO

MANU RIPOLL

MARCIAL TOLEDANO

PATRICIO DELPECHE

ELENA GUIDOLIN

ORIOL HERNÁNDEZ

ROGER VIDAL

JAVIER HERNANDEZ

DIEGO OLMOS

JOSE ROBLEDO

DANI PARIENTE

ALEKSA GAJIĆ

MARTÍN PARDO

ROGER IBÁÑEZ

JORDI PASTOR

MAX FIUMARA

SANTI ARCAS

ENRIQUE FERNÁNDEZ

ALBA CARDONA

NICO BARRIOS

JUAN DÍAZ CANALES

RAQUEL RÓDENAS

JUAN SANTACRUZ

FRAN MARISCAL

DANIDE

SAGAR FORNIÉS

JUAN SANMIGUEL

CARLOS MORENO

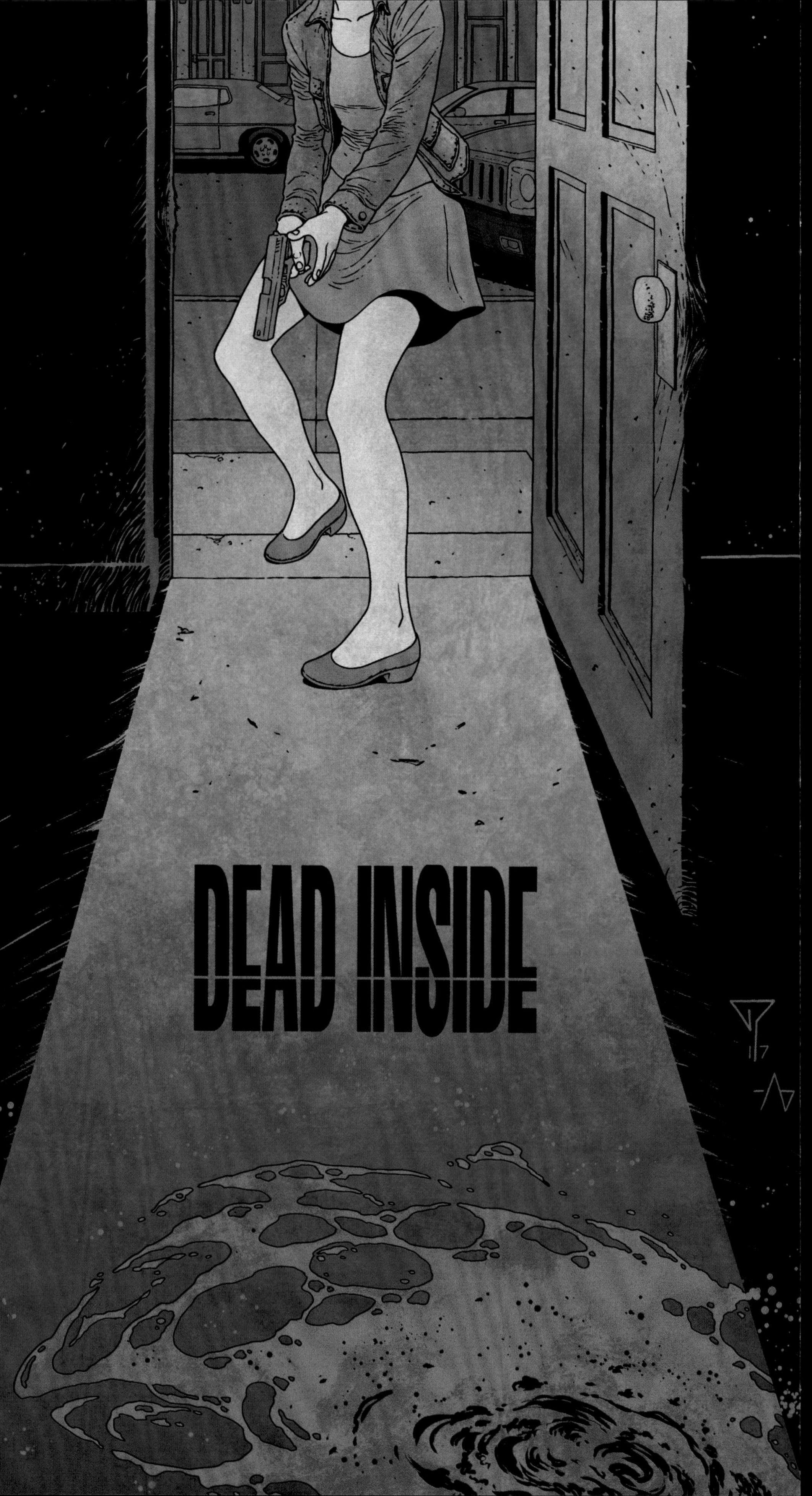
DEAD INSIDE

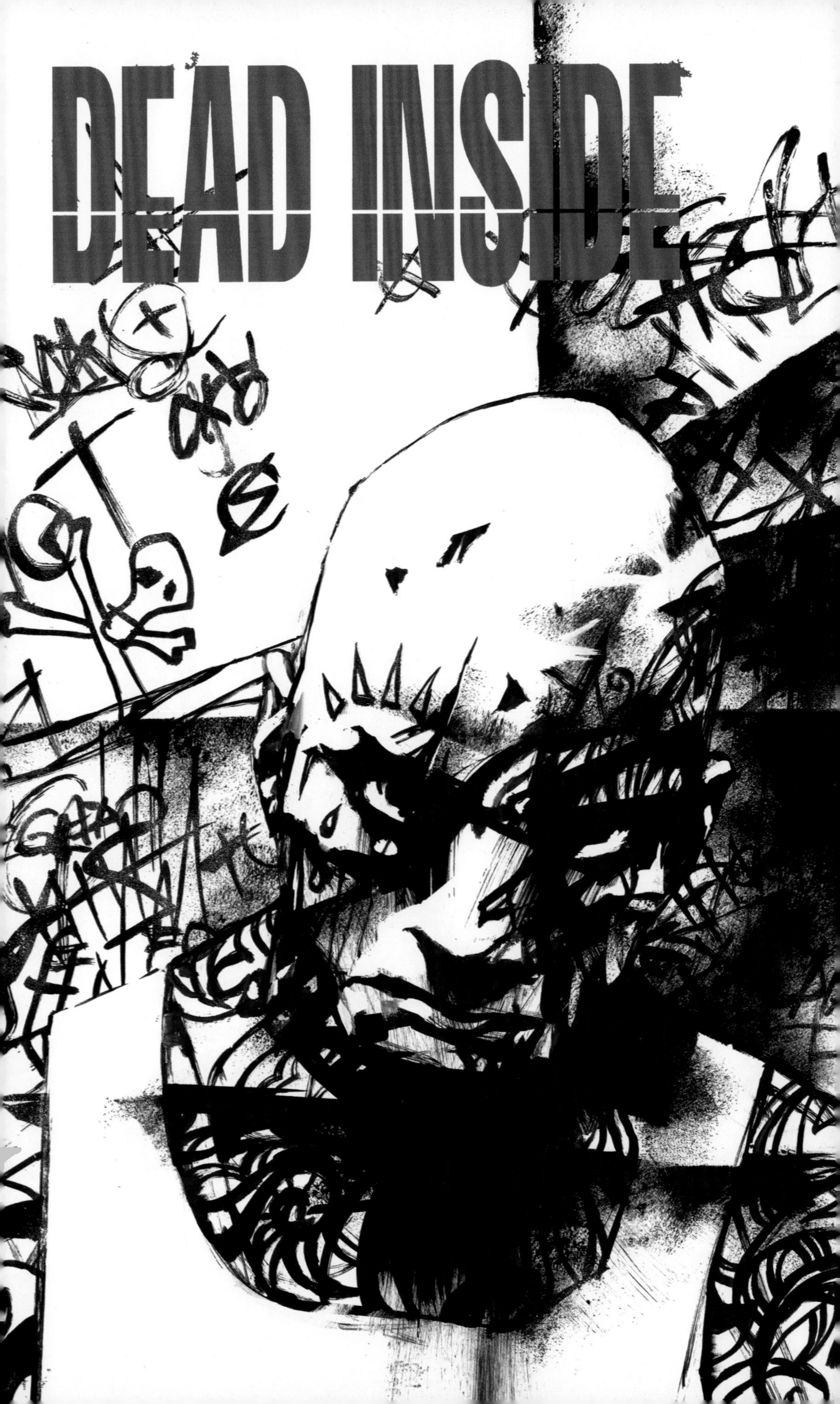
DEAD INSIDE

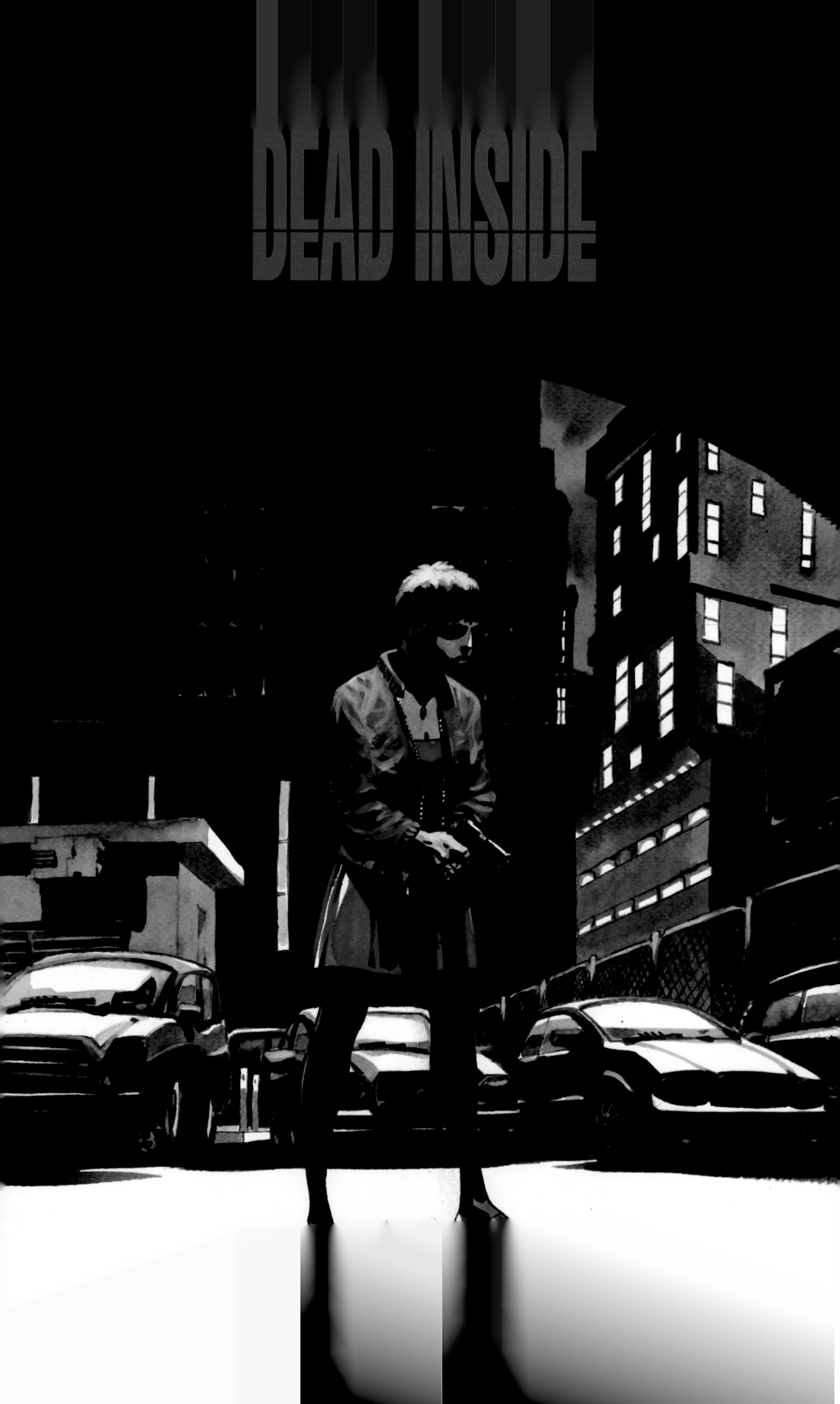
DEAD INSIDE

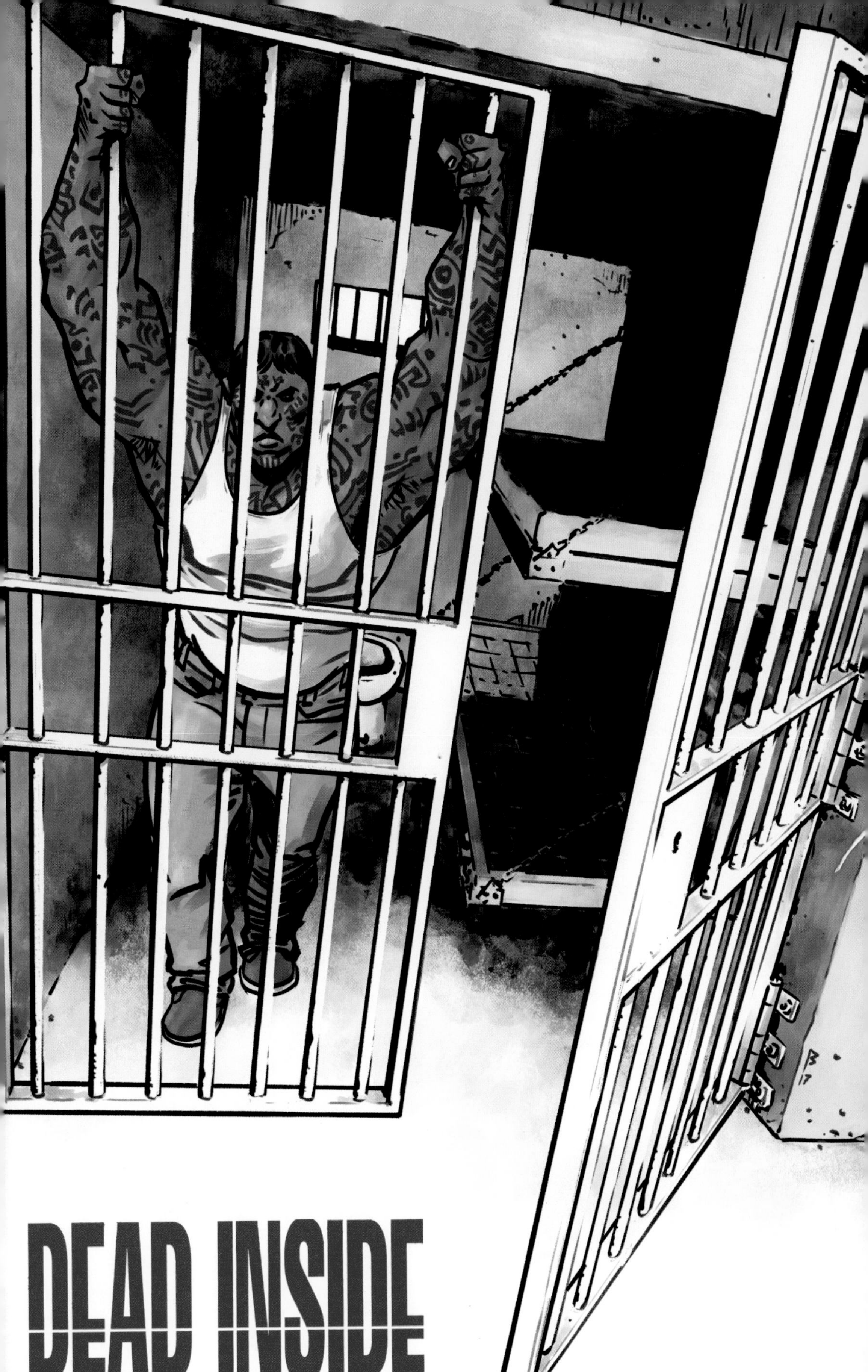

DEAD INSIDE

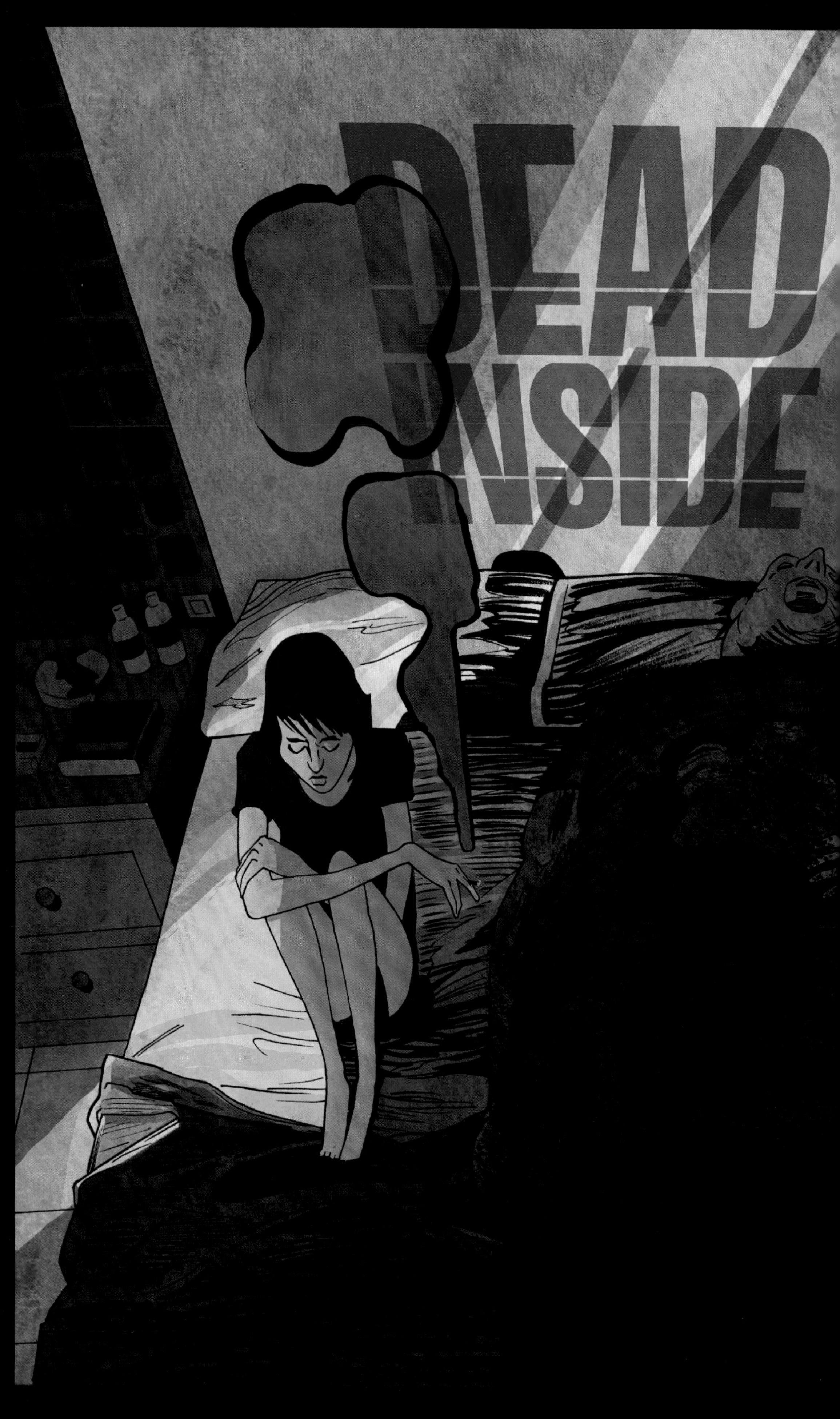
DEAD
INSIDE

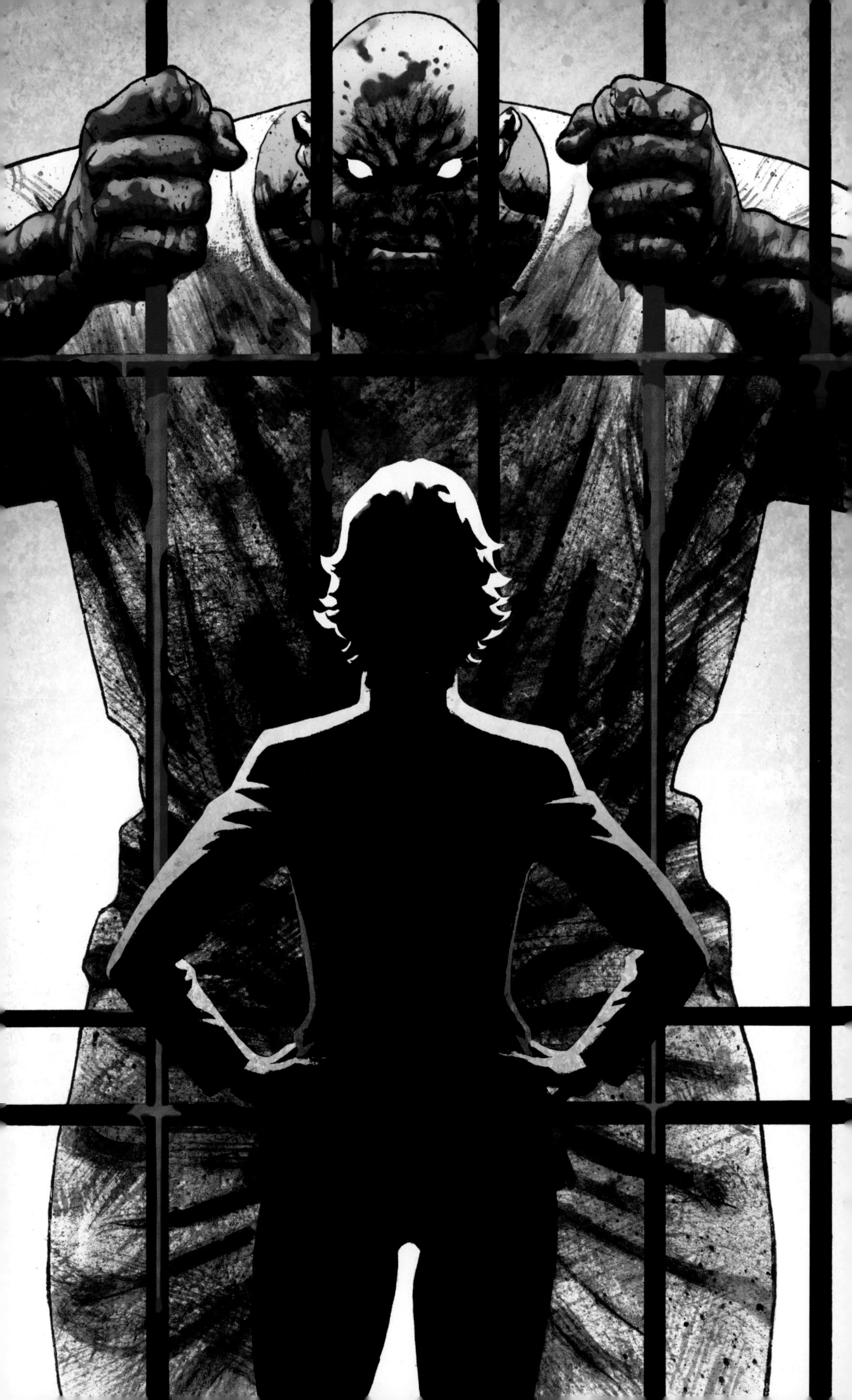

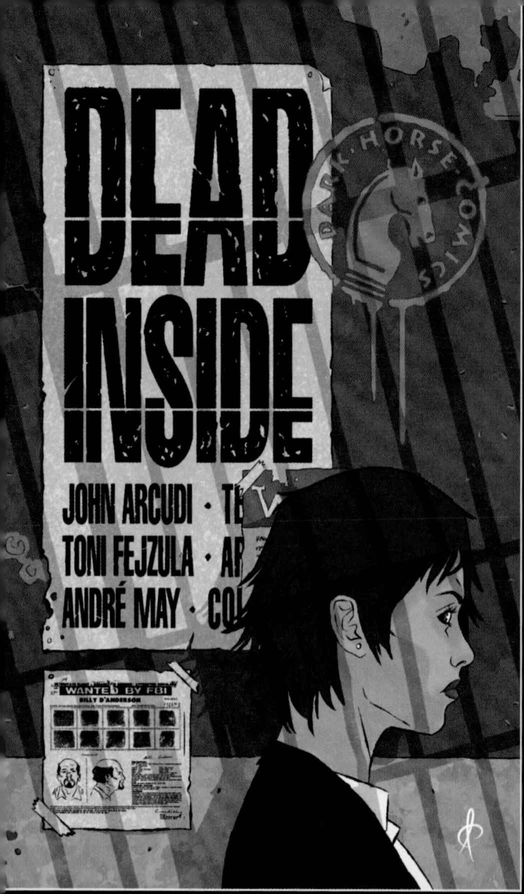
DEAD INSIDE
DARK HORSE COMICS
JOHN ARCUDI · TE
TONI FEJZULA · AR
ANDRÉ MAY · CO
WANTED BY FBI
BILLY D'ANDERSON

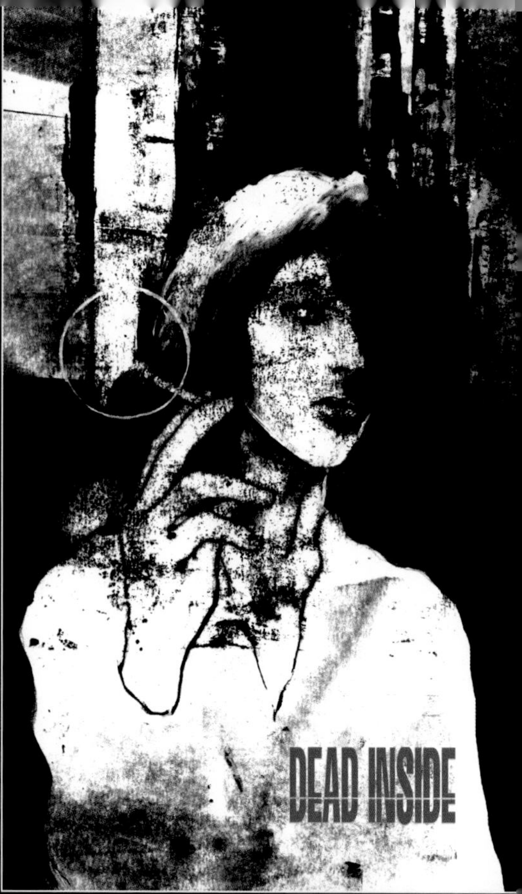
DEAD INSIDE

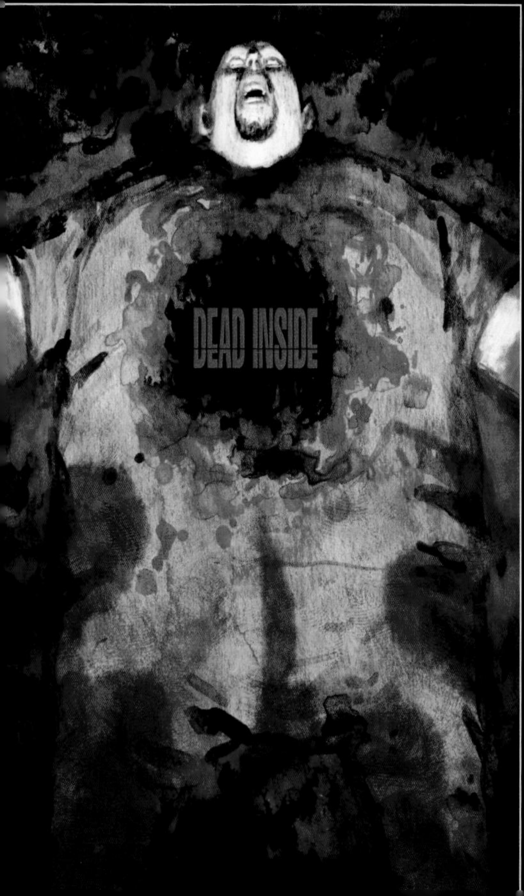
DEAD INSIDE

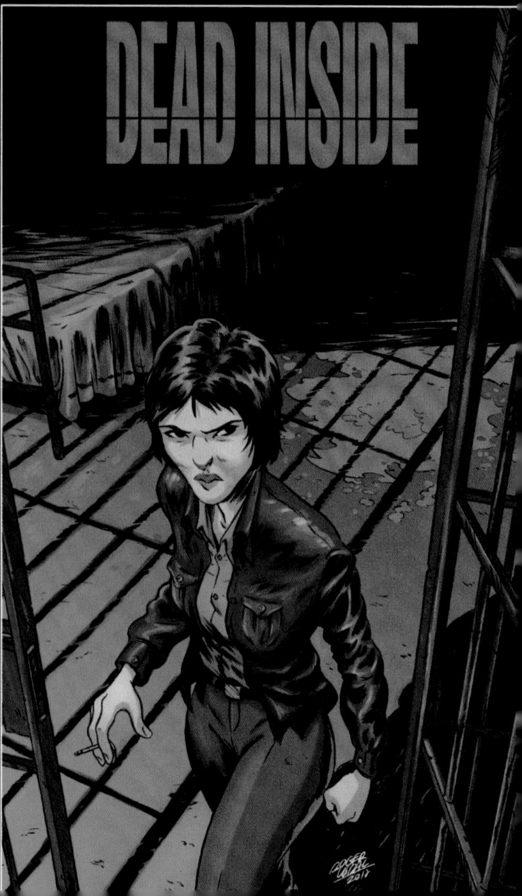
DEAD INSIDE

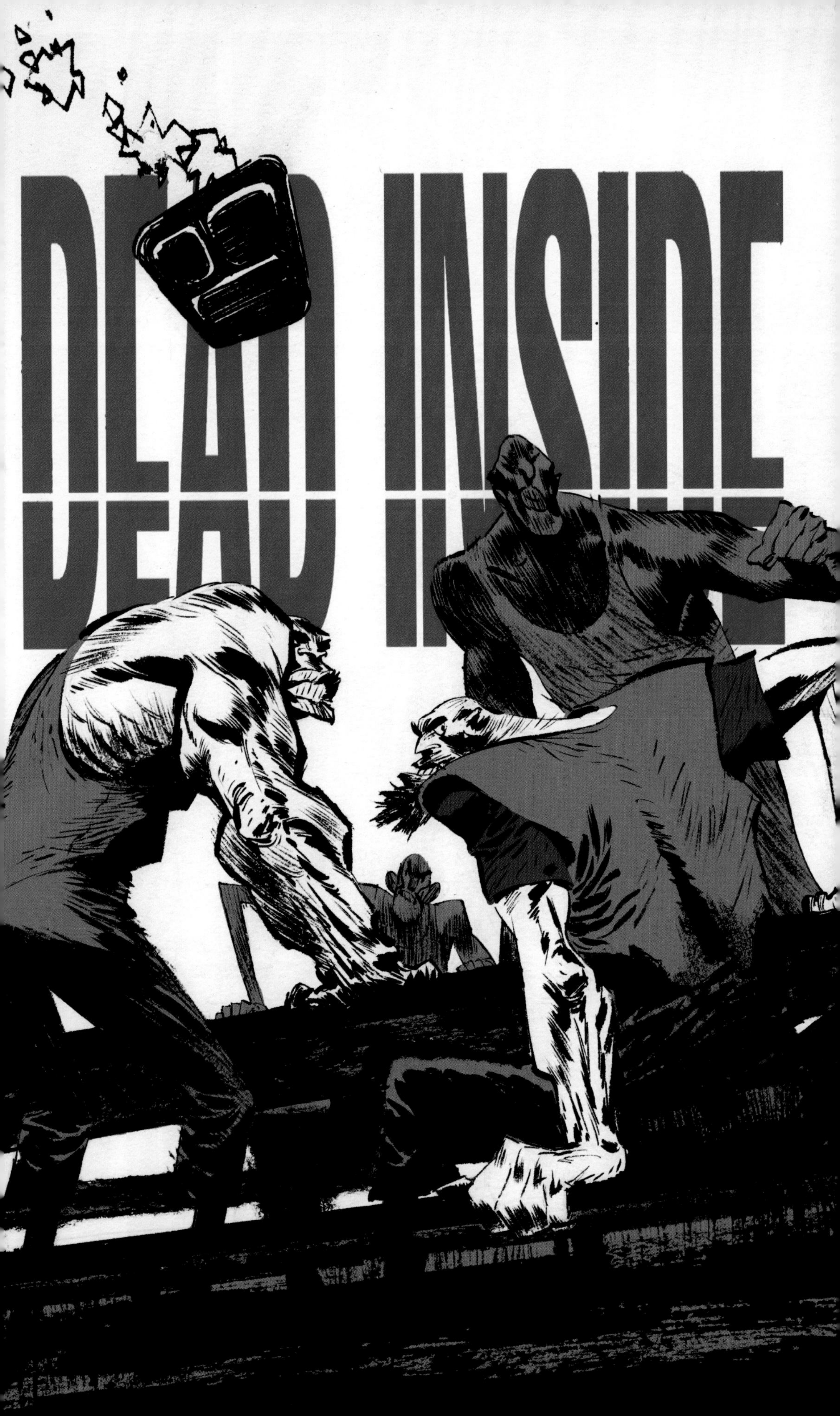
DEAD INSIDE

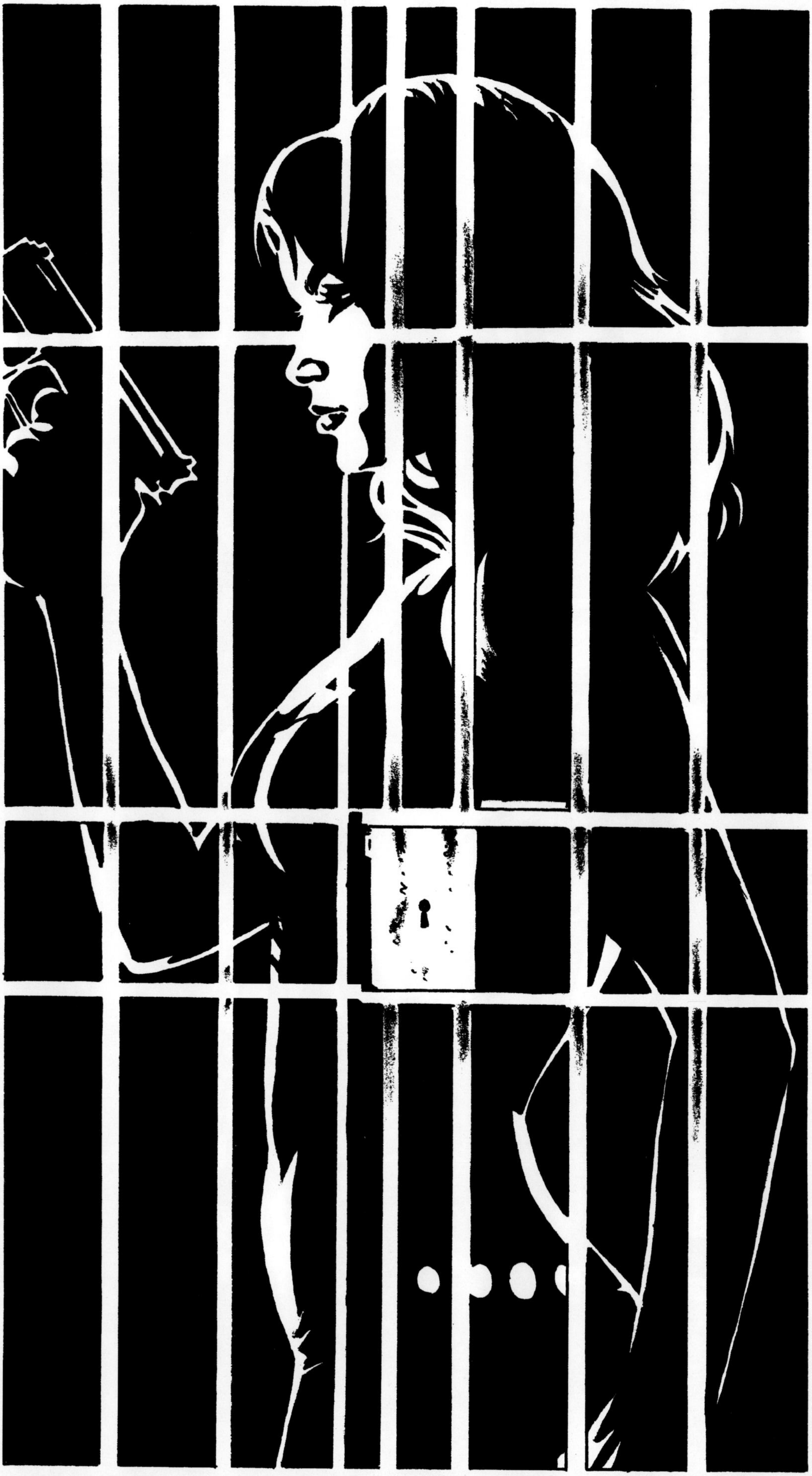

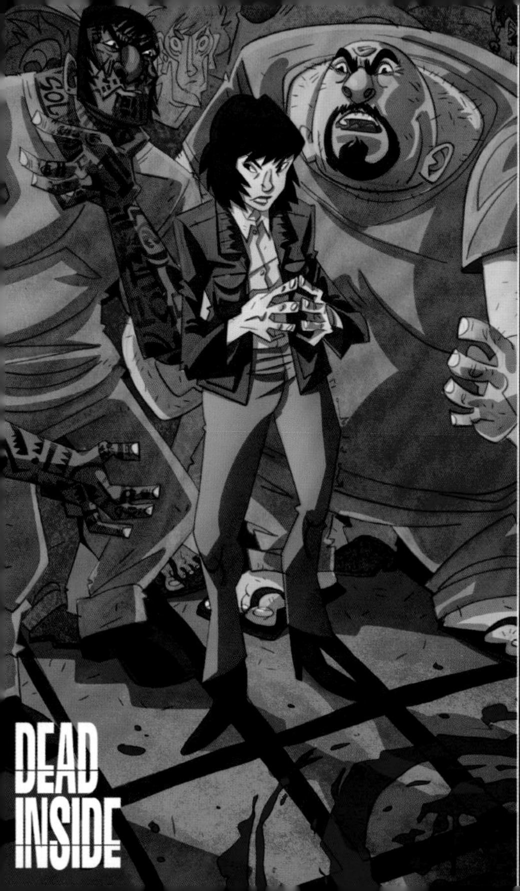
DEAD
INSIDE

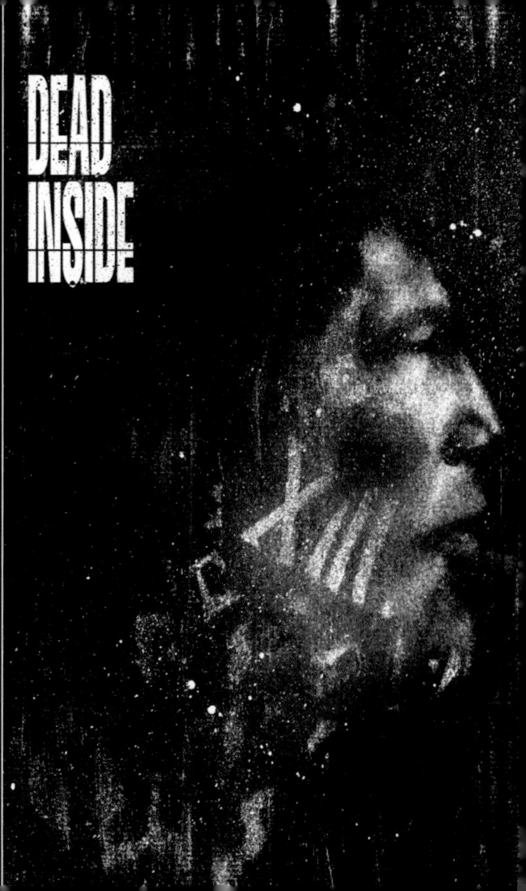
DEAD
INSIDE

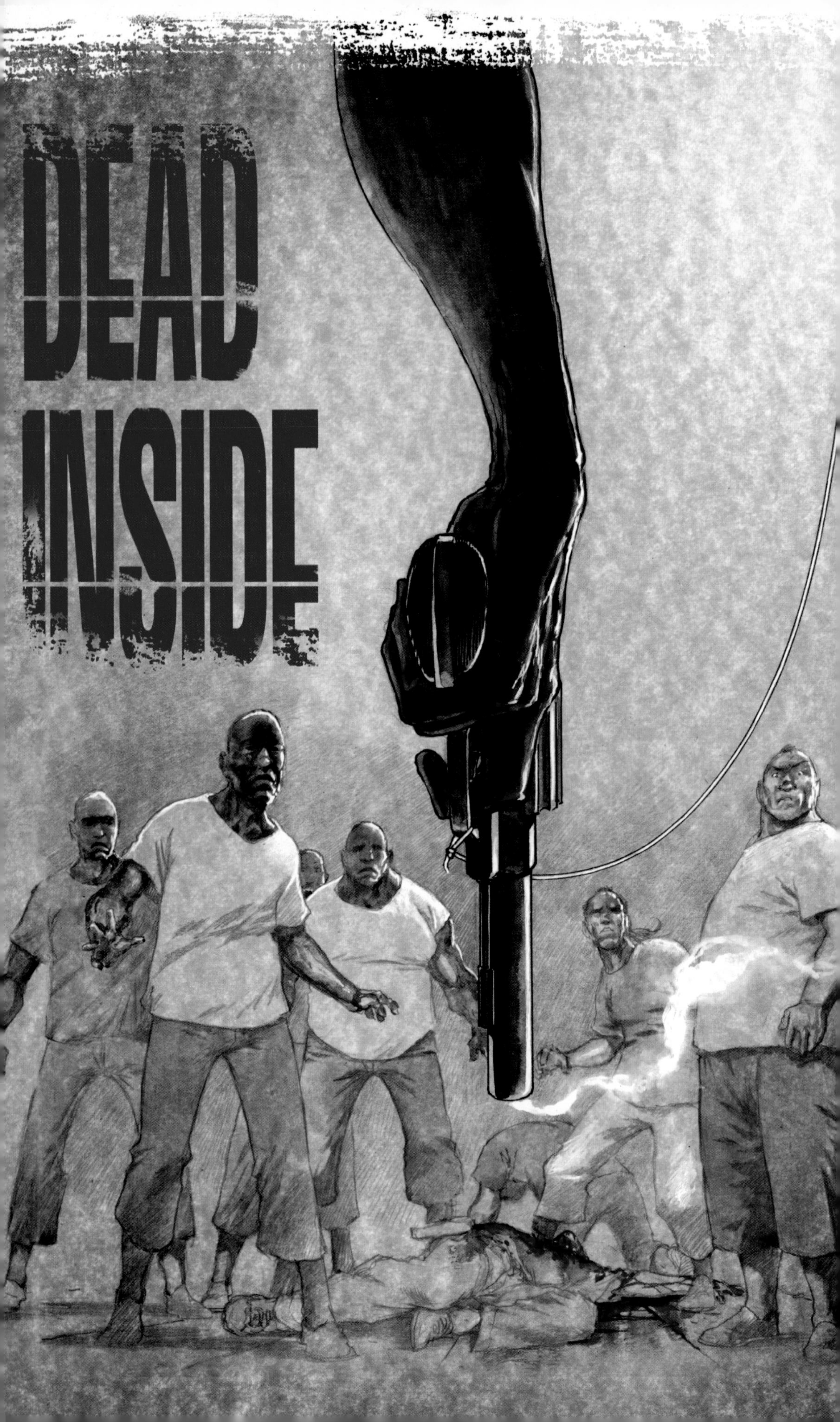
DEAD
INSIDE

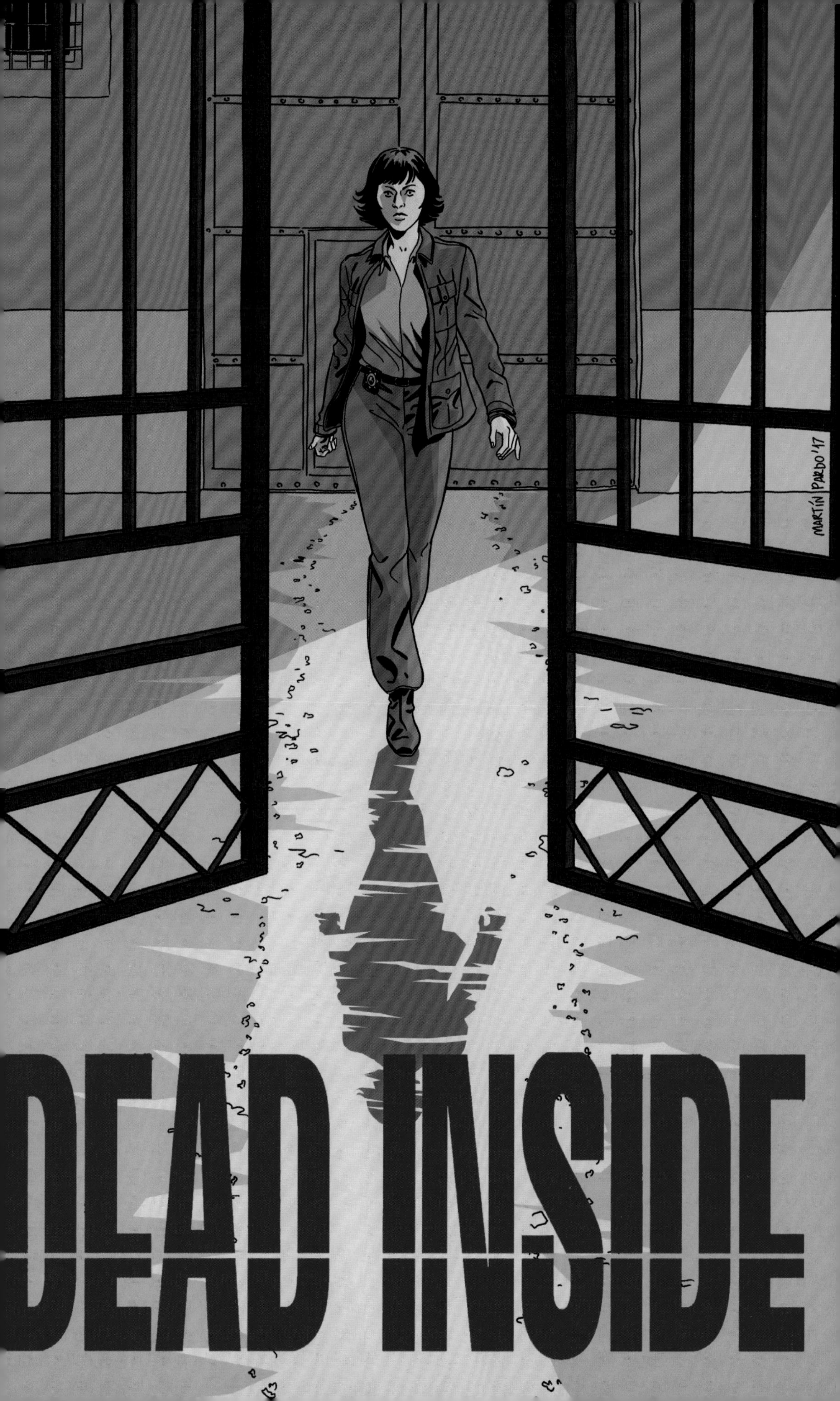
MARTÍN PARDO '17
DEAD INSIDE

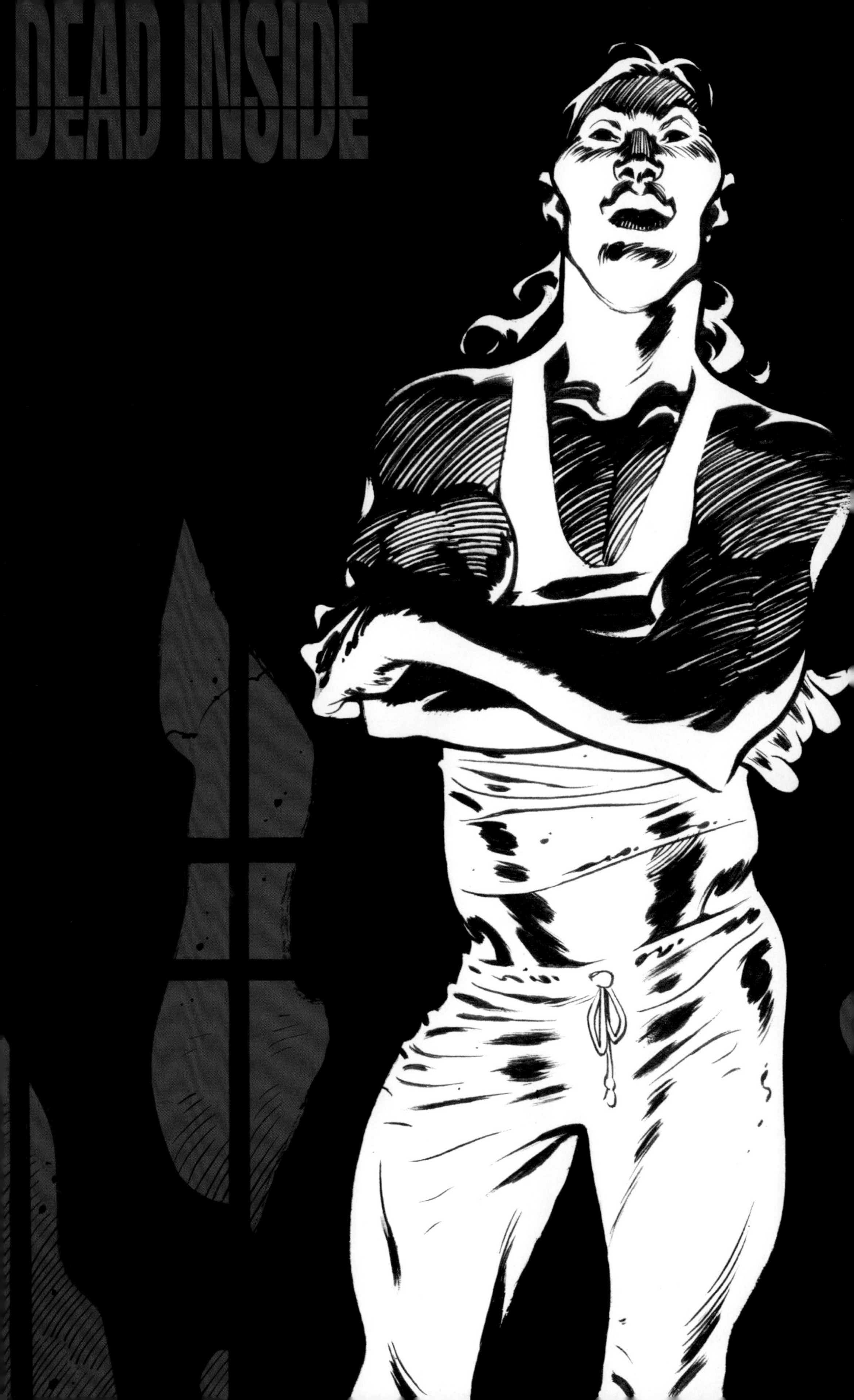
DEAD INSIDE

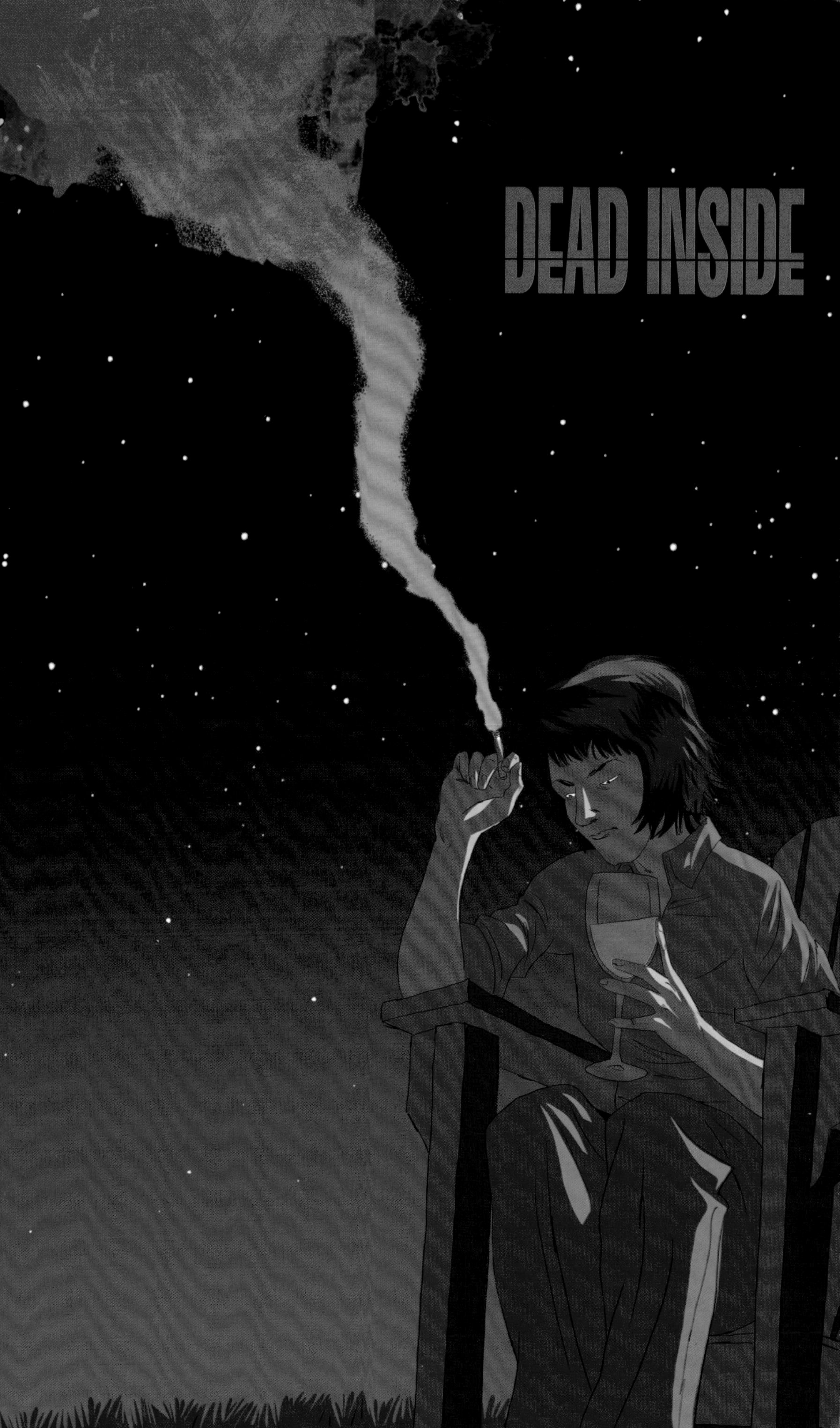
DEAD INSIDE

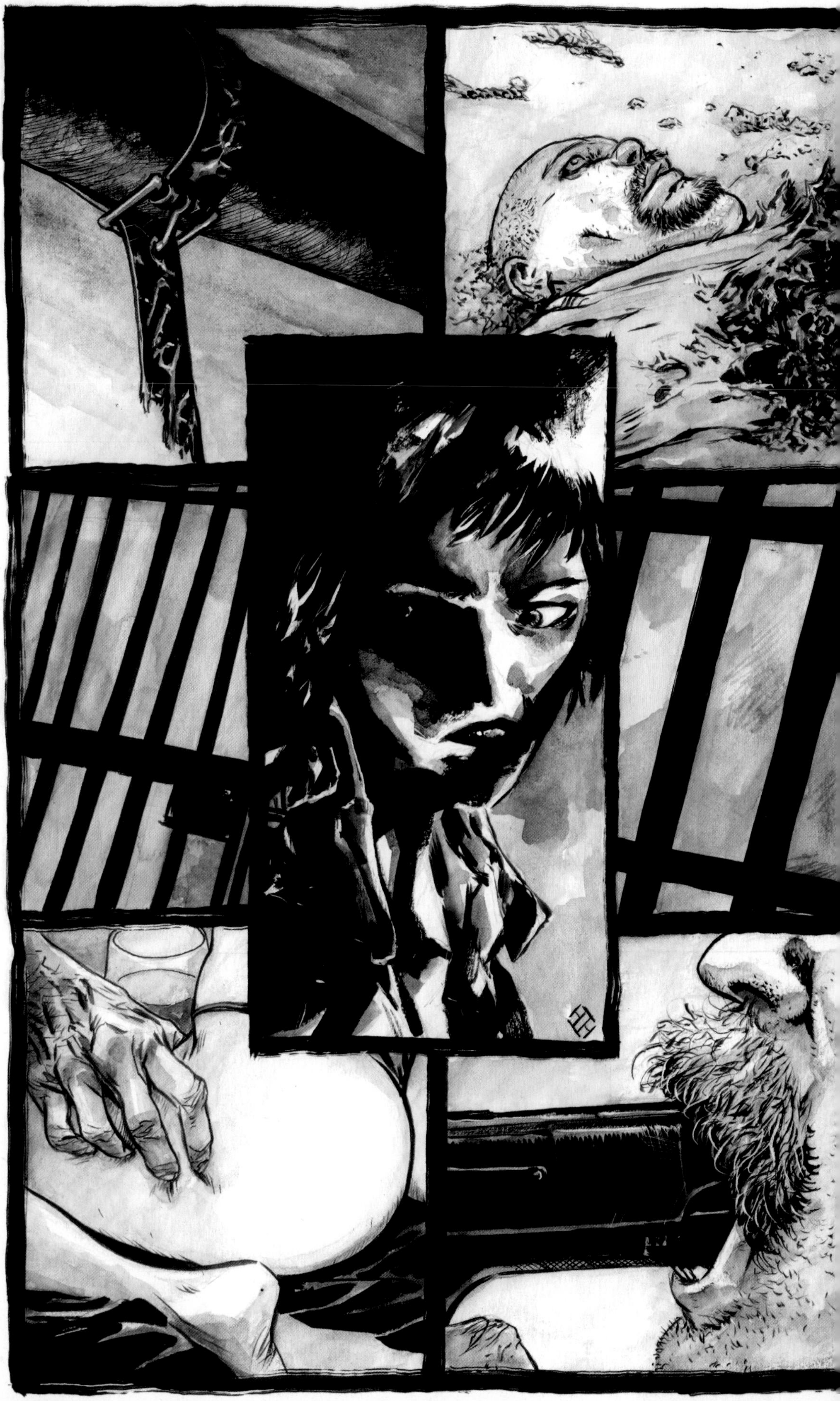

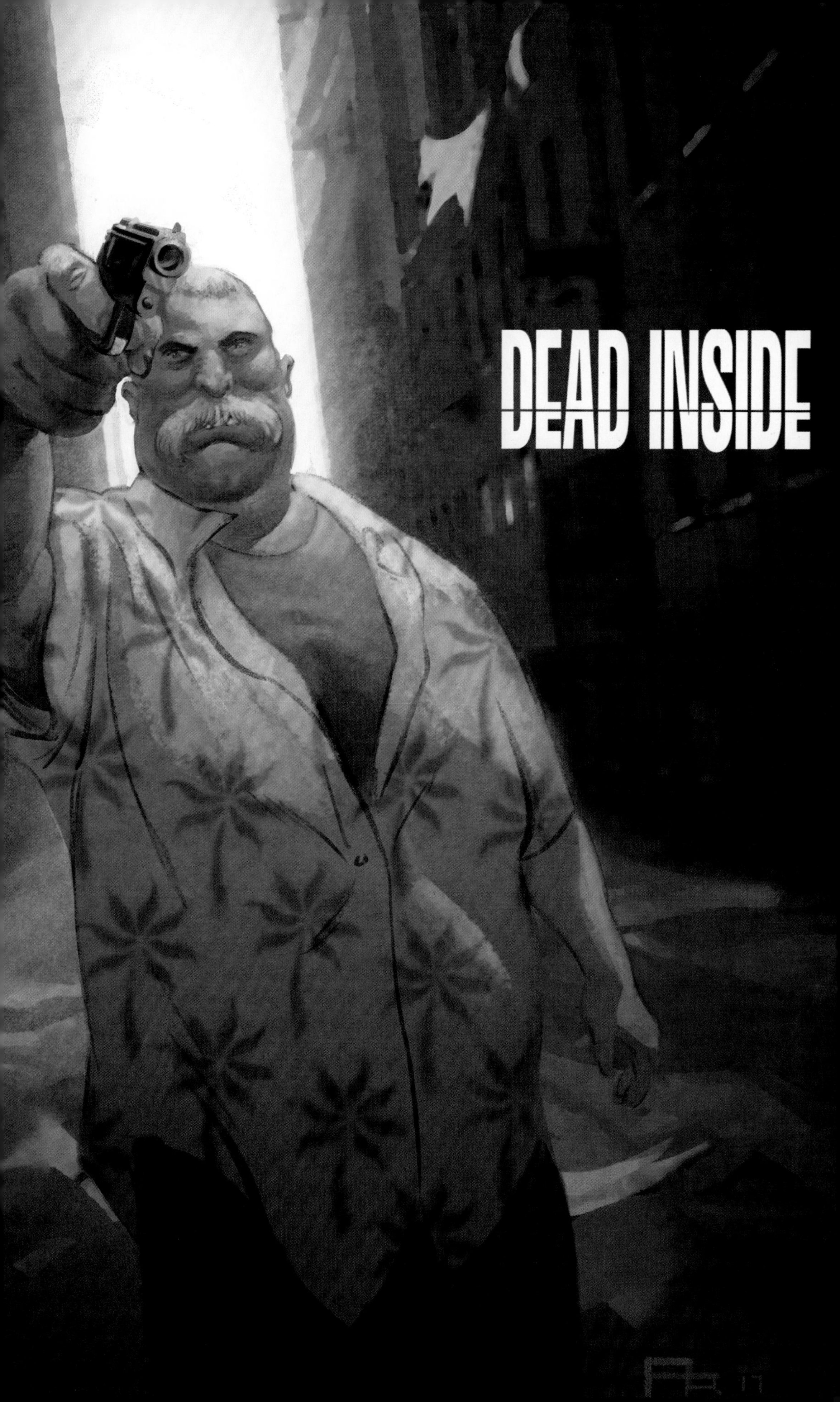
DEAD INSIDE

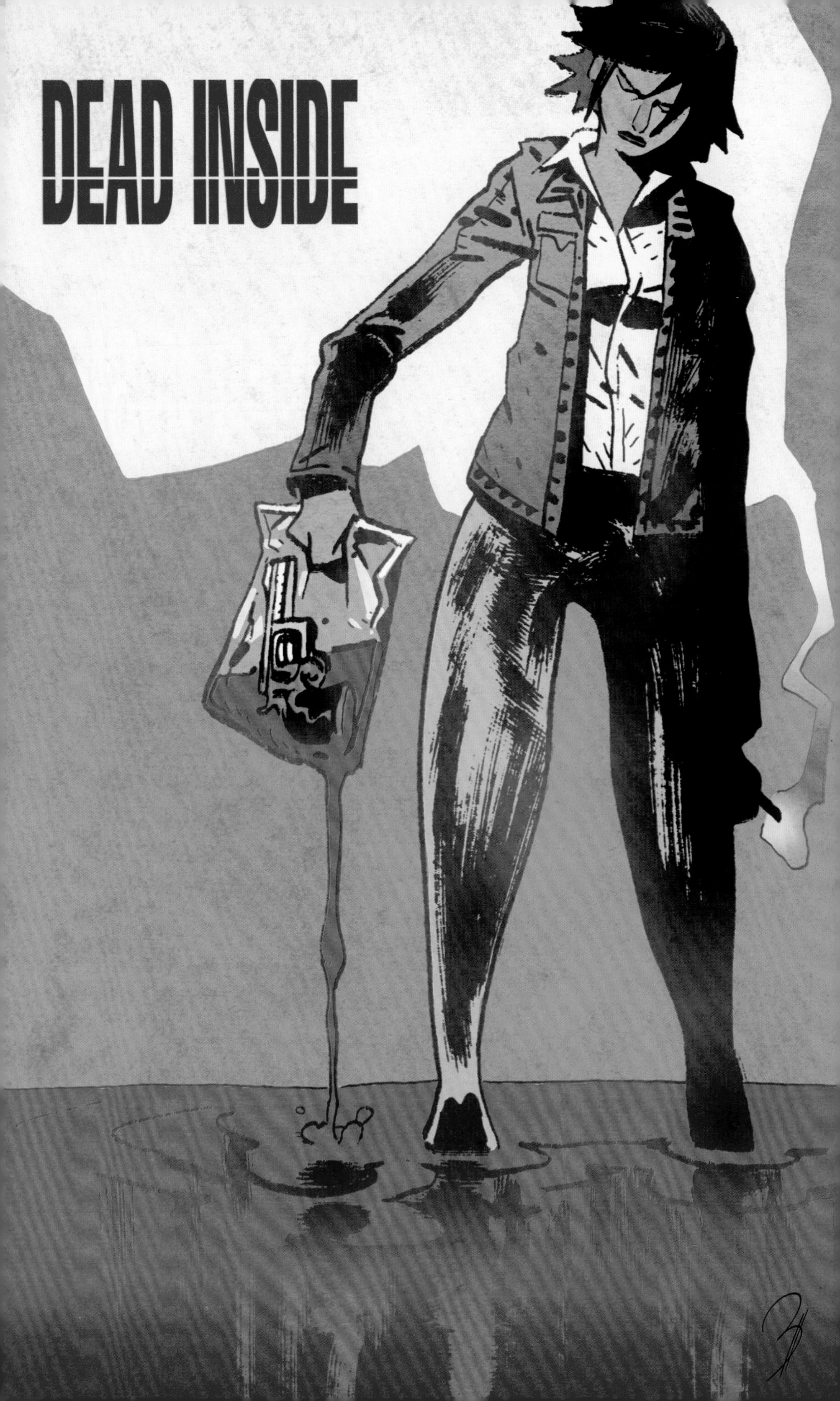
DEAD INSIDE

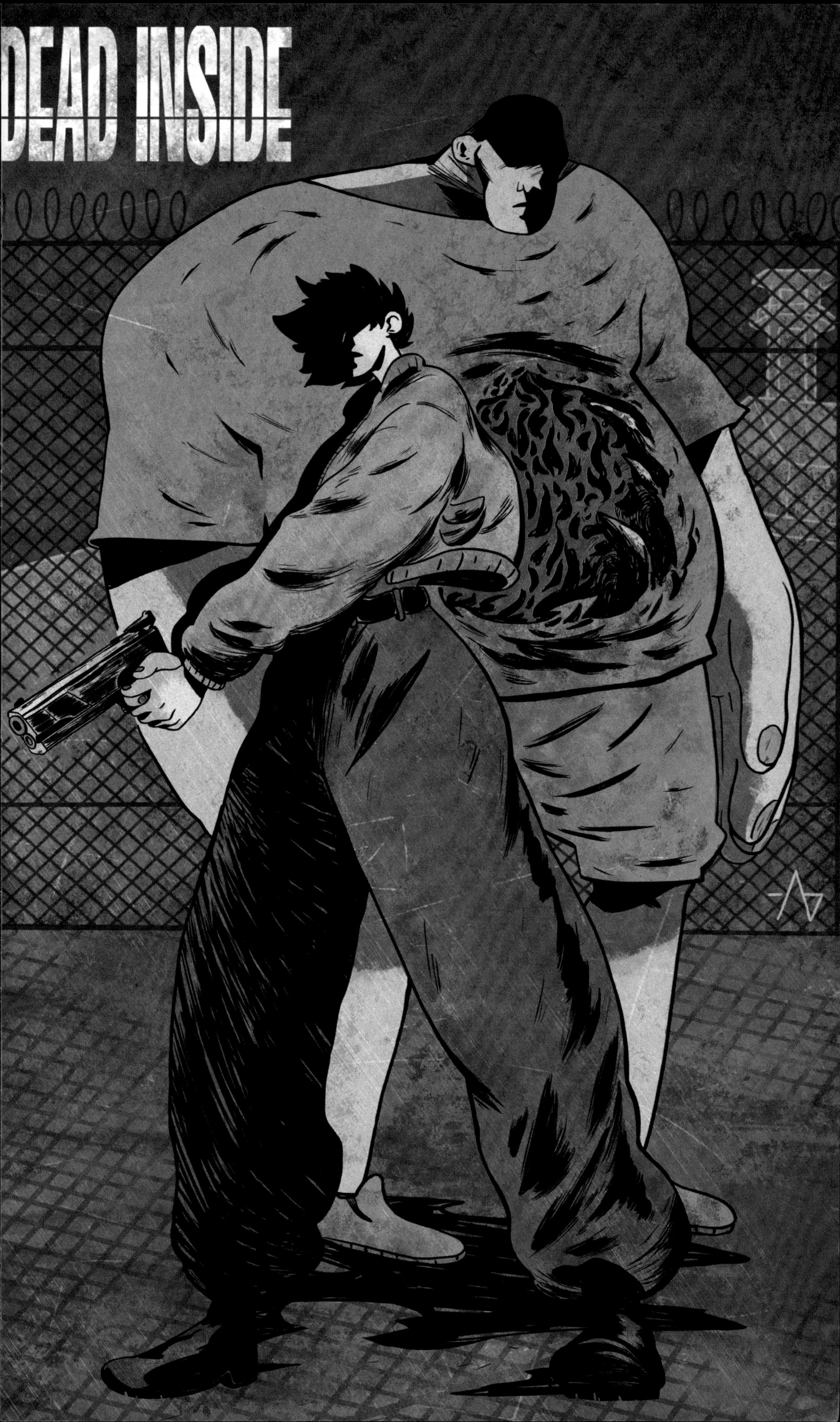
DEAD INSIDE

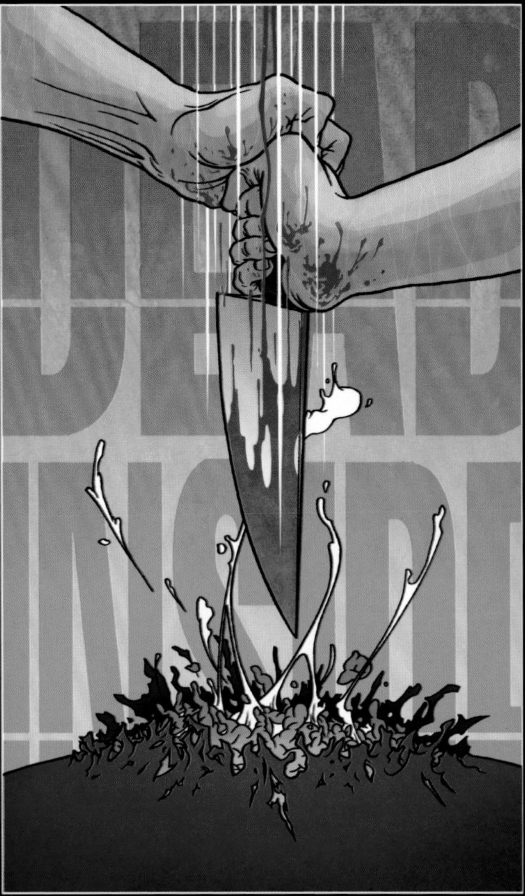

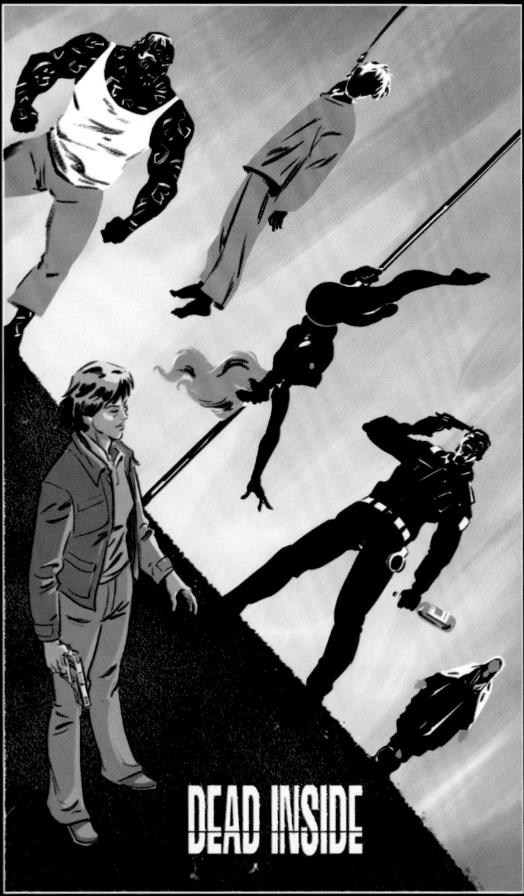
DEAD INSIDE

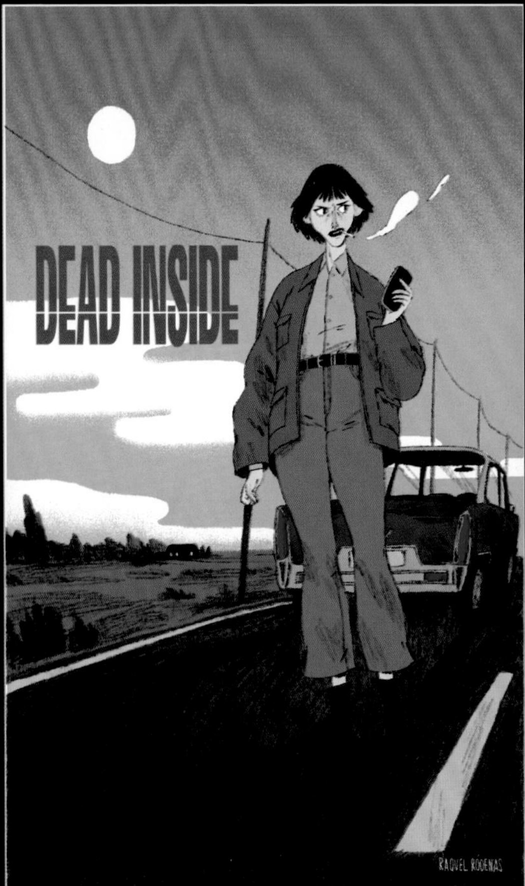
DEAD INSIDE
RAQUEL RODENAS

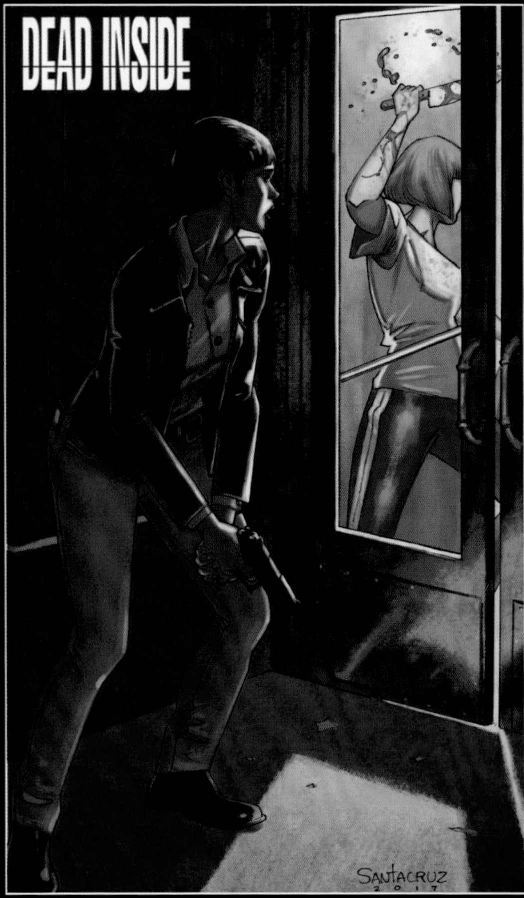
DEAD INSIDE
SANTACRUZ

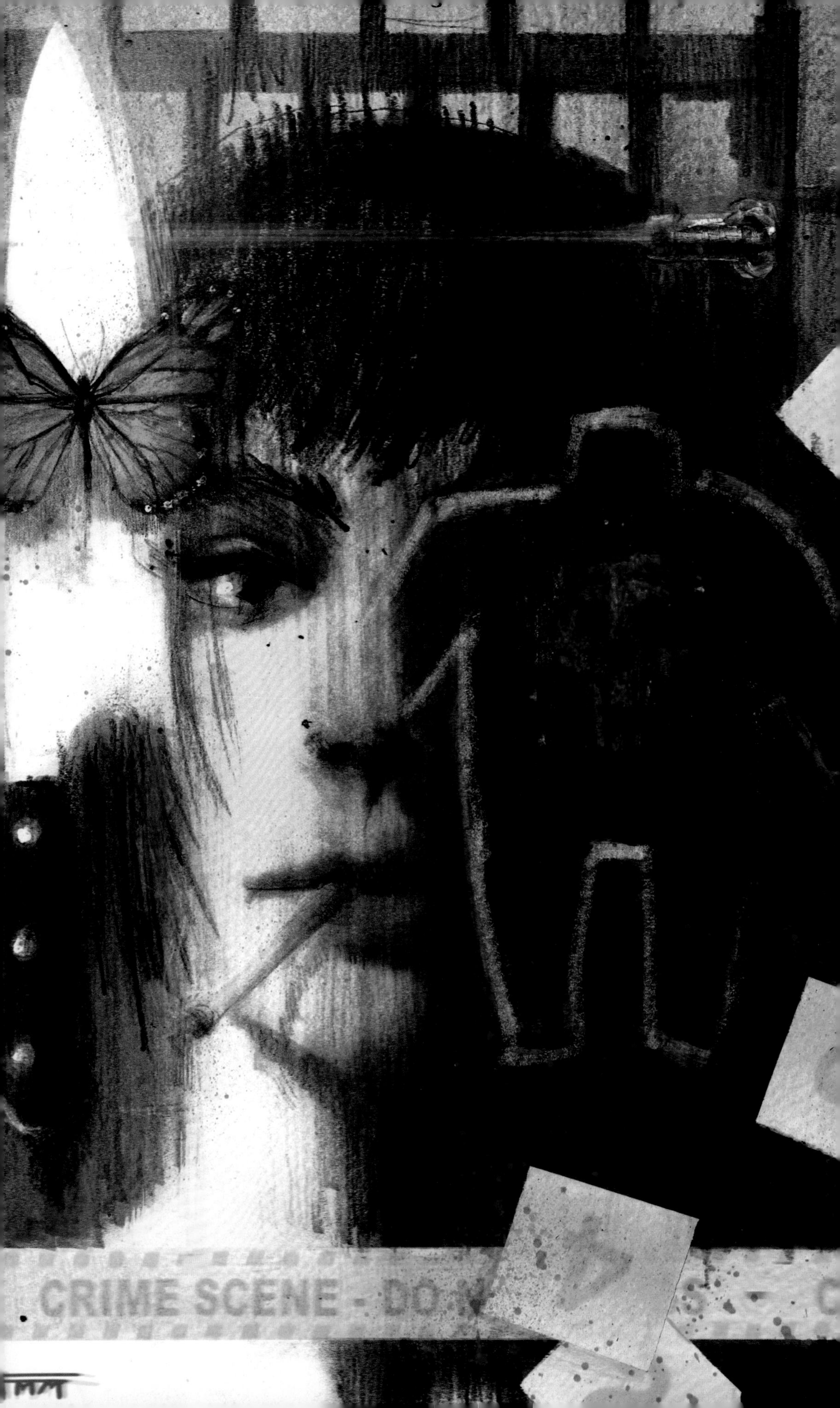
CRIME SCENE - DO

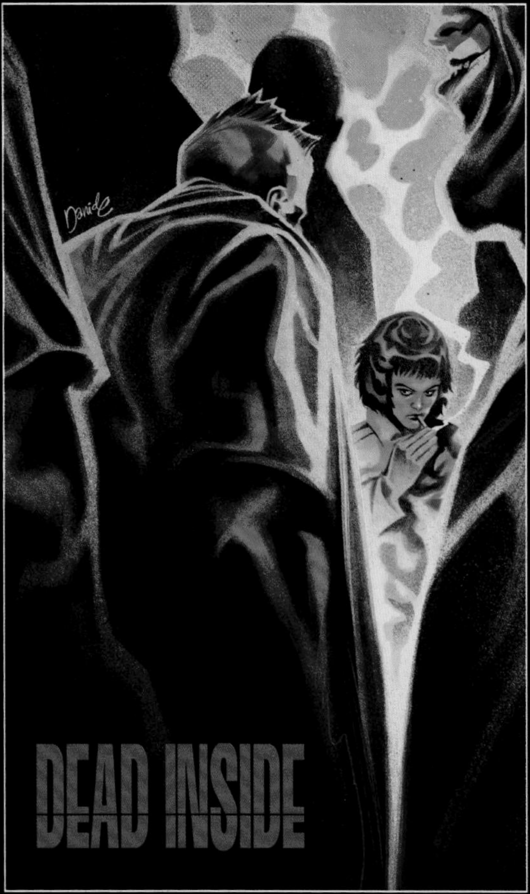
DEAD INSIDE

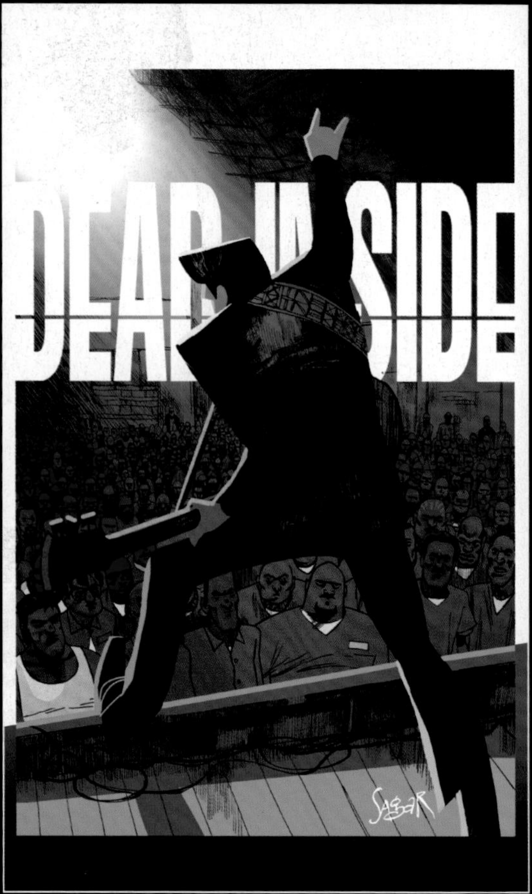
DEAD INSIDE
Sagar

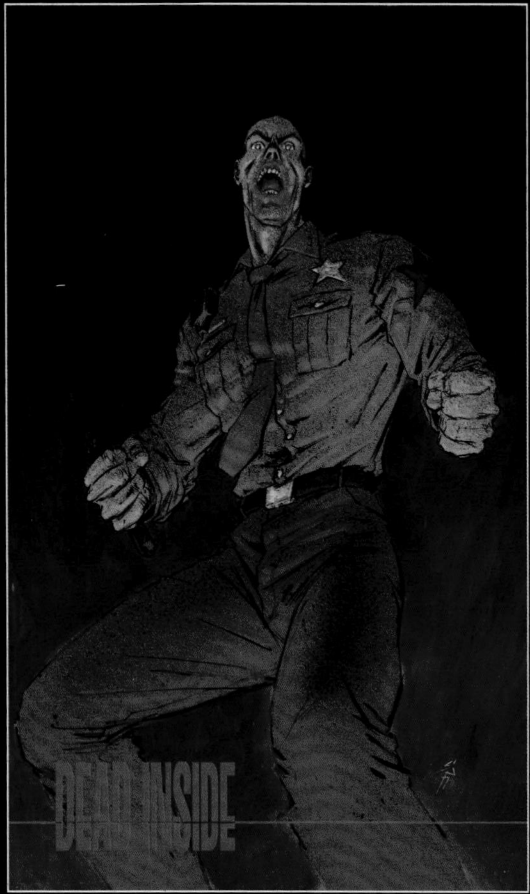
DEAD INSIDE

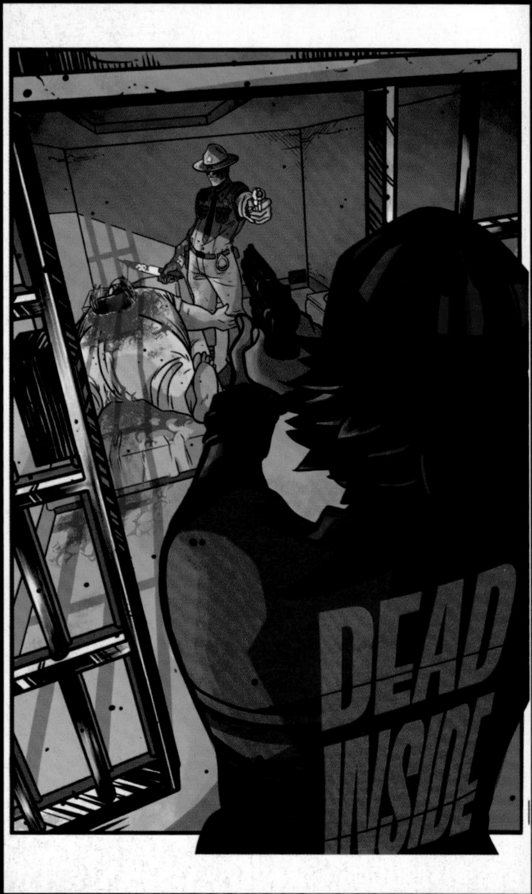
DEAD INSIDE